Library of
Davidson College

To
Promote
Prosperity

To Promote Prosperity

U.S. Domestic Policy in the Mid-1980s

John H. Moore, editor

Foreword by W. Glenn Campbell

Hoover Institution Press
Stanford University, Stanford, California

The Hoover Institution on War, Revolution and Peace, founded at Stanford University in 1919 by the late President Herbert Hoover, is an interdisciplinary research center for advanced study on domestic and international affairs in the twentieth century. The views expressed in its publications are entirely those of the authors and do not necessarily reflect the views of the staff, officers, or Board of Overseers of the Hoover Institution.

Hoover Press Publication 295
Copyright 1984 by the Board of Trustees of the
  Leland Stanford Junior University
All rights reserved. No part of this publication may be reproduced, stored in a retrieval system, or transmitted in any form or by any means, electronic, mechanical, photocopying, recording, or otherwise, without written permission of the publisher.
First printing, 1984
Manufactured in the United States of America
88 87 86 85 84   9 8 7 6 5 4 3 2 1

Library of Congress Cataloging in Publication Data
Main entry under title:

To promote prosperity.

  (Hoover Press publication ; 295)
  1. United States—Economic policy—1981–
2. United States—Social policy—1980–   . 3. United States—Politics and government—1981–   . I. Moore, John Hampton, 1935–   .
HC106.8.T6 1984   338.973   83-26372
ISBN 0-8179-7951-4

Design by P. Kelley Baker

Contents

Foreword by W. Glenn Campbell ——— ix
Acknowledgments ——— xiii
Contributors ——— xv
Introduction by John H. Moore ——— xxi

1   **An Economic Bill of Rights** ——— 1
Martin Anderson

2   **Monetary Policy for the 1980s** ——— 23
Milton Friedman

3   **Monetary Policy for Noninflationary Growth** ——— 61
Robert E. Hall

4   **Supply-Side Economics, Growth, and Liberty** ——— 73
Paul Craig Roberts

5   **Social Security Reform: A Mature System in an Aging Society** ——— 91
Rita Ricardo-Campbell

Contents

6 Health Policy in 1984: The Crisis in Costs ___ 125
Patricia Munch Danzon

7 Poverty and Welfare ___ 137
John C. Goodman

8 Insurance in the Workplace: Experience Is the Best Guide ___ 153
Daniel K. Benjamin

9 Farm Policy at a Crossroads: Critical Choices Facing U.S. Agriculture ___ 169
Stuart B. Hardy

10 The Federal Budget: Problems and Prospects ___ 183
Annelise Graebner Anderson

11 Controlling the Federal Budget ___ 199
Alvin Rabushka

12 Congress and the President ___ 217
Richard T. Burress

13 Reagan's Regulatory Record ___ 239
Thomas Gale Moore

14 The Future of Bank Regulation ___ 259
Kenneth Scott

15 Transportation: Policy, Goals, Accomplishments ___ 275
Darrell M. Trent

16 The Agenda for Corporate Reform ___ 287
Robert Hessen

17 Corporate Income Tax: Restoration, Integration, or Elimination? ___ 303
Charles E. McLure, Jr.

18 Pursuit of Excellence? The Income and the Outcome of Education ___ 319
Roger A. Freeman

Contents

19   **The Politicization of the University** —— 343
Sidney Hook

20   **Civil Rights: The Reagan Record** —— 355
John H. Bunzel

21   **Demographic Dilemmas in the Mid-1980s** —— 369
Kingsley Davis

22   **The Economy, Elections, and Public Opinion** —— 393
Seymour Martin Lipset

Foreword

Four years ago, as a contribution to public understanding during the national elections of 1980, the Hoover Institution published a collection of essays entitled *The United States in the 1980s*. In the foreword written for that volume, I noted that the spirit of optimism that had characterized America from the end of the Korean War until we became heavily involved in the Vietnam conflict had disappeared in the 1970s and was muted at the beginning of this decade. Domestically, Americans faced high taxes, rapid inflation, burgeoning government regulation, fuel shortages, and huge governmental bureaucracies. In foreign affairs, the United States appeared to have lost its vision of how to act as a great power and its knowledge of how to project power and influence through the rest of the world.

Today, it can be said that we have made great progress against the grave economic problems that beset the nation at the beginning of the decade, and we are beginning to re-establish international credibility as the world's principal defender of freedom. But the tasks that confronted us four years ago are by no means completed. We face problems in both domestic and foreign affairs that are of the gravest concern not only to our own citizens but also to our friends throughout the world. At the same time, we must not overlook the fact that the resurgent American economy and the reassertion of American world leadership provide unique opportunities in both domestic and foreign policy. How we meet and resolve these problems and take advantage of the opportunities that are opening up to us will profoundly affect the future of the United States and consequently of the rest of the world.

The idea of collecting the essays in this volume and its companion volume on foreign policy was conceived in recognition of this conjuncture of problems and opportunities. The central purpose of both volumes is the same: in this year of national elections, to contribute to public discussion and debate by publishing the views of leading experts on a wide range of key public policy issues. Four years ago, in the similar undertaking that resulted in *The United States in the 1980s*, essays were prepared by experts from the Hoover Institution and elsewhere for publication in a single volume dealing with the entire range of policy issues.

The success of that volume played an important role in our decision to proceed with a similar project this year. After considerable discussion among the editors of the two volumes, Senior Fellows John H. Moore and Dennis L. Bark, and members of the Hoover Institution senior staff, it was decided that our purpose this year would best be served by the publication of separate volumes on domestic and foreign policy. It was further agreed that the breadth and depth of knowledge possessed by scholars and experts associated with the Hoover Institution made it unnecessary to seek others from outside the Institution as authors for the project. The 22 essays in this volume and the 17 in its companion, spanning virtually all the crucial public policy areas of concern to the nation, are the result. The two volumes are in every sense a Hoover Institution project. Therefore, I am especially pleased and gratified at the publication of these two collections.

Recently, there have been signs that the national mood is gradually shifting away from the dark pessimism of the 1970s that itself was one of the nation's most serious problems. Indeed, in my view, one of the most important achievements of the past few years has been the restoration of optimism. Americans are beginning to regain confidence in their economic future and are starting to hold their heads high once more as citizens of this great nation. This change in mood may be only temporary. If it is not based on solid achievement in both the domestic and the foreign policy arena, it certainly will not be durable. Whether it continues or whether we revert to the pessimism and lack of confidence that plagued us for so long will depend in large measure on the

Foreword

actions taken by the government we will elect this year. It is to inform the electorate of the issues and alternative approaches to them that this volume is offered, to help ensure that the choices made are well advised.

Hoover Institution
Stanford University

W. Glenn Campbell
Director

Acknowledgments

Any book of this type is the product not of one but of many individuals. Valuable advice regarding its contents was received from many members of the Hoover Institution staff, especially Rita Ricardo-Campbell and Dennis L. Bark. Phyllis M. Cairns, publications manager of the Hoover Institution Press, guided the design and production of the book with professionalism and efficiency, and David L. Fleenor, director of marketing for the Press, provided valuable advice on its creation and promotion. The editor and contributors to the volume also owe a debt of gratitude to Nancy J. Hinsen, whose work on the manuscript was accurate and efficient.

Contributors

Annelise Graebner Anderson, a Senior Research Fellow at the Hoover Institution, served as Associate Director of the Office of Management and Budget, Economics and Government, from 1981 to 1983. An economist, Anderson's scholarly interests include the budgetary process of the federal government and the economics of crime. She has written numerous articles for books and professional journals. Among her recent works is *The Business of Organized Crime: A Cosa Nostra Family*.

Senior Fellow **Martin Anderson** served as Assistant to the President for Policy Development, 1981–82. He is a member of the President's Economic Policy Advisory Board and the President's Foreign Intelligence Advisory Board. Among his many publications concerning economic and societal issues are *Welfare: The Political Economy of Welfare Reform in the United States*; *Registration and the Draft*; and *The Military Draft: Selected Readings on Conscription*.

Daniel K. Benjamin is Acting Assistant Secretary of Labor for Policy. A 1978–79 National Fellow at the Hoover Institution, Benjamin has written and published widely on labor economics and other economic topics. Before joining the Department of Labor, Benjamin taught at the University of Washington.

Senior Research Fellow **John H. Bunzel** specializes in current political and educational problems and frequently writes and lectures for the public on political and educational issues. Before joining the Hoover Institution, Bunzel was President of San Jose State University. In January 1974, the San Francisco Board of Supervisors awarded him its Certificate of Honor for "unswerving devotion to the highest ideals of brotherhood and service to mankind and dedicated efforts looking to the elimination of racial and religious bigotry and discrimination."

Richard T. Burress is Associate Director and Senior Fellow at the Hoover Institution. Burress has been Chairman of the Renegotiation Board; Deputy Counsel to the President of the United States, working with Arthur F. Burns in domestic program development; Assistant to the President for Domestic Affairs; and Deputy Assistant General Counsel of the National Labor Relations Board.

The main research interests of Senior Research Fellow **Patricia Munch Danzon** are the economics of health care and regulation. A graduate of Oxford University and the University of Chicago, she was formerly a research economist at the Rand Corporation and an instructor in regulation and public policy at the Rand Institute for Policy Studies. She has published numerous articles in professional journals on the economics of health.

Senior Research Fellow **Kingsley Davis** is Distinguished Professor of Sociology at the University of Southern California. Recipient of the 1982 Career of Distinguished Scholarship Award of the American Sociological Association, he is widely known for his studies of population problems in all parts of the world. Among other topics, he has dealt with world population growth and resources, the history and theory of international migration, world urbanization, population growth and economic development, and population policy. His books include *The Population of India and Pakistan*; *World Urbanization*; and *Cities: Their Origin, Growth and Human Impact*.

Roger A. Freeman, a Senior Fellow Emeritus at the Hoover Institution, is a two-time winner of the George Washington Honor Medal Award, Freedoms Foundation at Valley Forge (1967, 1973). He has served in numerous governmental and nongovernmental positions, including Vice President of the Institute for Social Science Research, Research Director of the Institute for Studies in Federalism at

Contributors

xvii

Claremont Men's College, and Chairman of the Advisory Council on Financial Aid to Students. Among his publications are *The Growth of American Government: A Morphology of the Welfare State*; *The Wayward Welfare State*; and *Crisis in College Finance?*

Nobel Laureate **Milton Friedman** is a Senior Research Fellow at the Hoover Institution. He is widely regarded as the leader of the Chicago School of monetary economics, which stresses the importance of the quantity of money as an instrument of governmental policy and a determinant of business cycles. In addition to writing a regular column for *Newsweek*, Friedman has published numerous journal articles and books, including *A Monetary History of the United States* (with Anna J. Schwartz); *Capitalism and Freedom*; and *Free To Choose* (with Rose Friedman).

John C. Goodman, a 1975–76 Hoover Institution National Fellow, is a Professor of Economics and Director of the Center for Health Policy Studies at the University of Dallas. The author of numerous books and articles on welfare, health care, and related issues, Goodman is also President of the National Center for Policy Analysis in Dallas. He has taught at Dartmouth College and Columbia and Southern Methodist universities.

Robert E. Hall is a Senior Fellow at the Hoover Institution and Professor of Economics at Stanford University. Hall is director of the Research Program on Economic Fluctuations of the National Bureau of Economic Research. His research interests include inflation, monetary policy, and unemployment. With his Hoover Institution colleague Alvin Rabushka, Hall is an active proponent of the flat tax. Their book, *Low Tax, Simple Tax, Flat Tax*, played a major role in stimulating interest in the flat tax.

Stuart B. Hardy is Assistant Executive Secretary of the National Association of State Departments of Agriculture. He was a Public Affairs Fellow at the Hoover Institution during the 1974–75 academic year. Prior to assuming his present post, he served on the staff of Senator Robert Dole and as a Professional Staff Member of the U.S. Senate Committee on Agriculture, Nutrition and Forestry.

Senior Research Fellow **Robert Hessen** is a specialist on American economic and business history and a lecturer at the Stanford

Graduate School of Business. He speaks frequently to business and academic audiences on government regulation of industry. Hessen's books include *Steel Titan: The Life of Charles M. Schwab* and *In Defense of the Corporation*.

Senior Research Fellow **Sidney Hook,** Emeritus Professor of Philosophy and former head of the All-University Department at New York University, is perhaps the nation's most highly regarded social philosopher. He organized the New York University Institute of Philosophy and has had a singularly successful career as a teacher in academic institutions. His most recent books are *Pragmatism and the Tragic Sense of Life*; *Revolution, Reform and Social Justice*; *Philosophy and Public Policy*; and *Marxism and Beyond*.

Senior Fellow **Seymour Martin Lipset** serves as Caroline S. G. Munro Professor of Political Science and Professor of Sociology at Stanford University. He is a former president of the American Political Science Association and is president-elect of the Sociological Research Association and the World Association for Public Opinion Research. His major work has been in the fields of political sociology, social stratification, public opinion, and the sociology of intellectual life. Among his award-winning books are *Political Man* and *The Politics of Unreason*. Lipset has authored or coauthored seventeen books and monographs, has edited twenty books, and published more than 250 articles.

The research speciality of Senior Fellow **Charles E. McLure, Jr.,** is taxation, including the exporting of state and local taxes, federal tax policy, state and local taxation and fiscal federalism, and taxation in developing countries. He was named Deputy Assistant Secretary of the Treasury for Tax Analysis in October 1983. McLure has authored or edited several books and has published numerous journal articles. He has been a member of the editorial advisory board of the *National Tax Journal* since 1972.

John H. Moore is Acting Deputy Director and Senior Fellow of the Hoover Institution. His scholarly interests include the workings of the market economic system and the Soviet and Yugoslav economic systems. He is the author of *Growth with Self-Management: Yugoslav Industrialization, 1952–1975* and has published numerous articles on economic theory and comparative economic systems. He is a member of the National Science Board.

Contributors

Senior Fellow **Thomas Gale Moore** is Coordinator of the Domestic Studies Program at the Hoover Institution. He is an expert on the economics of regulation and deregulation, with particular interests in energy, transportation, and the environment. Among his recent publications are *Public Claims on U.S. Output*; *Trucking Regulation: Lessons from Europe*; and *Uranium Enrichment and Public Policy*.

Senior Fellow **Alvin Rabushka** specializes in the domestic public policy areas of taxation, aging, and housing. He is the author or coauthor of ten books covering topics that include race and ethnic politics, aging and housing policies, and the political economy of Hong Kong's free enterprise economic system. His most recent books are *The Tax Revolt* (with Pauline Ryan) and *Low Tax, Simple Tax, Flat Tax* (with Robert E. Hall).

Rita Ricardo-Campbell, a Senior Fellow at the Hoover Institution, is an expert on the economics of health care, Social Security, and drug industry regulation. She is a member of the President's Economic Policy Advisory Board and the National Council on the Humanities. In addition to many articles written for scholarly books and professional journals, she has authored several books, including *Social Security: Promises and Reality*; *The Economics and Politics of Health*; and *Economics of Health and Public Policy*.

Senior Research Fellow **Paul Craig Roberts** was Assistant Secretary of the Treasury for Economic Policy from 1981 to 1982. He was a National Fellow at the Hoover Institution in 1971–72 and served on the staff of the House of Representatives Appropriations Committee in 1975. He is also a fellow at the Georgetown Center for Strategic and International Studies and holds the William E. Simon Chair for Political Economy at Georgetown University. His publications include *Alienation and the Soviet Economy* and *Marx's Theory of Exchange, Alienation and Crisis* (with Matthew A. Stephenson).

Kenneth Scott, a Senior Research Fellow at the Hoover Institution, is an expert on the law and economics of corporate regulation, securities, and banking. He holds the Ralph E. Parsons Professorship in Law and Business at the Stanford University Law School. Professor Scott served as General Counsel of the Federal Home Loan Bank Board in Washington, D.C., before joining the Stanford faculty in 1968. He is the coauthor of two books: *Retail Banking in the Electronic Age* and *Economics of Corporation Law and Securities Regulation*.

Senior Research Fellow **Darrell M. Trent** is Chairman, with rank of Ambassador, of the U.S. Civil Aviation Delegation to the continuing Atlantic airline pricing negotiations with member-countries of the European Civil Aviation Convention. Trent served as Deputy Secretary of Transportation from January 1981 until his appointment as Ambassador in May 1983. He is coauthor, with Robert Kupperman, of *Terrorism: Threat, Reality and Response*.

Introduction

Human prosperity, according to Adam Smith, the founder of modern economics, rarely lasts longer than two hundred years. At the time he wrote his most famous work, Adam Smith regarded North America as the land of opportunity and the place on earth best suited for the rapid development of prosperity. And he was correct. In the two hundred years that followed publication of *The Wealth of Nations*, America recorded the most rapid sustained economic progress the world has ever seen. Yet at the end of those two centuries, doubts about the continuation of America's prosperity were commonplace. The economy seemed gripped in the new malaise of our time, stagflation, and Adam Smith's aphorism appeared only too apt.

Indeed, by the beginning of the 1980s, pessimism about the nation's economic prospects was rife. Inflation was at a record peacetime high; so were interest rates. Unemployment was high and confidence low, and the problems posed for economic policy were exceedingly difficult and complex. Much progress has been made toward resolving these problems. But the agenda for domestic policy remains crowded with issues. In the chapters that follow, 22 authors discuss the problems, both past and present, as they see them and propose directions in which domestic public policy could effectively move in the years to come.

Martin Anderson describes how the comprehensive economic policy proposals of the 1980 Reagan presidential campaign and the program President Reagan sought to have enacted after his inauguration addressed economic problems at the beginning of the decade. Much of the program was adopted, and by late 1983 dramatic improvements were visible—the virtual elimination of inflation, interest rates cut in half, surging economic growth, rising real incomes. The picture was not all bright: unemployment, although falling, remained high; the economy was still burdened by extensive regulation; and a large federal deficit was a cause for concern.

More important, Anderson points out, the achievements may prove ephemeral; a future Congress or administration less committed to the objectives of reduced government control over the economy and greater reliance on individual incentive and responsibility can easily reverse them. Attaining these objectives requires a reduction in the government's role in the economy, both in its share of total spending and in the interference caused by regulation, but a retention, on the other hand, of the traditional governmental function of providing a stable framework for economic activity.

Anderson argues that these objectives cannot be attained by ordinary legislative processes. In his view, constitutional change is the only reliable way to achieve long-term economic stability and sustained economic growth. He therefore proposes an economic bill of rights—a constitutional amendment—that would restrict governmental powers in the economic sphere just as the Bill of Rights restricts governmental powers in the area of personal freedoms. Anderson realizes that such an amendment would not guarantee prosperity, but argues that it would do much to ensure responsible economic policy.

Despite great progress in reducing inflation by fall 1983, worries about monetary policy remained. Milton Friedman describes the roller coaster of monetary policy since the mid-1960s, a roller coaster that has intensified in the past few years. Long-run stability in the money supply, essential for a resumption of sustained economic growth, will remain uncertain as long as the Federal Reserve continues to use its present methods and, more fundamentally, to operate within the present institutional framework.

Changes in the Fed's tactics might stave off a monetary crisis, but Friedman is pessimistic about avoiding such a crisis. Should one occur, a thoroughgoing reform of our monetary institutions might be required. The only reliable reform under such a circumstance, according to Friedman, is ending the power of the Federal Reserve to issue money. History shows that monetary stability in either the short- or the

Introduction

long-run will not be achieved as long as the Federal Reserve possesses that power because it allows even the best-intentioned officials to engage in destabilizing acts.

Robert Hall is also concerned about the long-range outlook for monetary policy. However, his recommendation for reform differs sharply from Friedman's. Hall recommends that the Federal Reserve adopt a rule of keeping nominal GNP on a steady growth path. Monetary policy should be adjusted in accordance with this objective: if growth of nominal GNP falls below the path, money growth should be increased; if it rises above the target path, the growth of the money supply should be reduced. This "fail-soft" policy, according to Hall, would prevent both severe recession and rapid, sustained inflation. Hall considers a number of alternatives, but finds that none has this fail-soft property.

Focusing on economic growth, Paul Craig Roberts emphasizes that policies based on Keynesian economic doctrine for managing aggregate demand ignore the impact of relative price changes on economic behavior. In particular, taxation affects the prices of goods and services that determine changes in productivity and the rate of economic growth. Roberts shows how high tax rates reduce both of these measures of economic health.

He goes beyond economic theory to emphasize the fact, confirmed by American history and the experience of communist societies, that economic and political independence are prerequisites to sustained and continued economic prosperity. High taxes reflect the large and growing role of government in American society and represent a concomitant erosion of both forms of freedom.

Economists often point out that the best measure of the cost of government to a society is total government spending, rather than total taxes. By that measure, Social Security is the most costly of all federal programs. Legislation in 1983 to overcome the Social Security system's financial crisis was intended to erase a projected immediate deficit, but left for future legislative action the handling of a projected deficit beginning in the second decade of the next century.

Based on a painstaking analysis of the assumptions on which the Social Security Administration's projections are founded, Rita Ricardo-Campbell's essay challenges these forecasts, arguing that a deficit may recur by the late 1980s. She also examines the treatment of women under the Social Security system, pointing out that the existing benefit structure provides significantly lower benefits to two-worker families than it does to one-worker families with the same earnings and taxes and at the same ages, an inequity representing discrimination against women. She also notes that previously accepted intergenerational inequities in the system are progressively less acceptable, given changing demographics and improvement in the economic position of the aged relative to younger generations.

Spending on health care has grown far more rapidly than GNP in the past twenty years, with the result that health care expenditures amounted to nearly 10 percent of GNP in 1980. The figure is even higher today. Patricia Danzon notes that controlling health care costs requires modification of the incentives facing patients and providers. She surveys a variety of proposed reforms, including changes in tax, regulatory, and antitrust policies, and discusses public sector expenditures, including Medicare and Medicaid, the two largest federal spending programs, and the increasingly important problem of long-term care.

Social Security and health insurance have been major components in the efforts to alleviate poverty that have consumed huge amounts of money and public attention since the declaration of the War on Poverty in the mid-1960s. Yet, according to the U.S. Bureau of the Census, more people were living in poverty in 1982 than in 1954. John C. Goodman examines this seeming paradox, seeking reasons why such an extensive effort should have had such small apparent impact. He shows that official definitions of poverty, by omitting welfare payments received in kind rather than in cash, significantly overstate the extent of poverty. Second, he argues that the welfare system encourages individuals to seek to be designated as living below the poverty line because they then become eligible for a wide variety of benefits. The disincentives to work built into the system are reflected in extremely high effective marginal income tax rates faced by persons who "cross over" the poverty line. Moreover, the system discourages savings and stimulates the breakup of families. Goodman concludes by proposing a set of criteria for reform of the welfare system.

Until mid-1983, unemployment was the principal labor issue. By midyear, however, the best possible solution to that critical issue—rapid economic recovery—was well under way. Daniel Benjamin reminds readers that unemployment is not the only labor issue in the 1980s and identifies another category of problems that looms large on the public policy horizon: the rapidly rising costs of public insurance programs for the workplace. Pointing to unemployment insurance, workers' compensation, and pension plan termination insurance, Benjamin argues that the failure of existing programs to establish a clear connection between the experience of firms with these risks and the

Introduction

insurance premiums they pay is a major factor in rising costs. Not only that, the failure to apply risk and experience rating discourages insured firms from working to avoid these risks.

U.S. farm policy, in the eyes of many, has been a costly failure. Despite inauguration of the payment-in-kind program, farm support programs in fiscal year 1983 cost taxpayers a record $22 billion. Yet, as Stuart B. Hardy points out, American agriculture is suffering severe financial problems, with farm income and purchasing power low and indebtedness high. Hardy shows how the existing system of nonrecourse commodity loans and target prices for major commodities has failed to stabilize farm incomes. Especially in the past few years, the system has provided incentives for farmers that ran counter to emerging market forces and thus were doomed to failure. He summarizes current proposals for changing this situation and advocates increased reliance on market forces in a program that would include the phased reduction or elimination of most price supports and supply management programs and a strong emphasis on the expansion of export markets.

The importance of achieving effective control over spending is emphasized by Annelise Anderson. In mid-1983, federal expenditures for the year were expected to exceed 25 percent of GNP. In only four years since 1945 have budget receipts exceeded 20 percent of GNP, and for 1983 they were expected to drop below 19 percent. Anderson calculates that increasing revenues to 23 percent of GNP—which would still leave a deficit of more than $60 billion—would require a surcharge on corporate and individual income taxes of over 40 percent. She argues that sustained economic growth is the best tonic for the deficit problem. Five years of steady growth might, according to Anderson, reduce expenditures to about 22 percent of GNP—still substantially greater than revenues. Any increase in spending, of course, would create even larger deficits.

Federal spending has risen dramatically in recent years, and deficits have risen along with spending, as Congress has been unable or unwilling to impose the taxes required to finance the huge expenditures it has approved. Alvin Rabushka identifies sources of bias toward large deficits. First, benefits of spending programs tend to be concentrated among relatively few individuals, with correspondingly strong vested interests, while costs are spread across all citizens, whose incentives to resist any single program are weak. Second, the separation of the expenditure and revenue sides of the budget process makes Congress less sensitive to deficits than it would otherwise be.

Legislative efforts to control spending or to require a balanced budget have been notable for their failure. Rabushka therefore advocates a constitutional amendment, a view that has found expression in pressure from the states to convene a constitutional convention and the introduction in Congress of such an amendment, Senate Joint Resolution 5, now awaiting congressional action.

The problem of continuing large federal deficits may be exacerbated by the ongoing struggle between the executive and legislative branches for dominance in domestic as well as foreign policy. Richard Burress traces the recent history of this struggle, showing how congressional reaction to President Johnson's early domination and the opportunity presented by the Watergate episode led to a resurgence of congressional control of the budget process.

However, as Burress notes, there is evidence that the process established by the resulting Congressional Budget and Impoundment Control Act of 1974 is failing, foundering on intra-congressional jurisdictional wrangling and the production of unrealistic budget documents that, if adopted at all, are subsequently so modified by legislative committees and presidential vetoes that they bear little resemblance to the original. As a control on spending, the process appears to be ineffectual.

The economic problems caused by high federal spending and large deficits are exacerbated by the complex web of regulations affecting both businesses and individuals. The complexities and difficulties are well illustrated by Thomas Moore's evaluation of the Reagan administration's record in deregulation. Moore finds the record of executive and independent agency actions disappointing. The deregulatory reforms that have been adopted were in some cases proposed by the previous administration. They usually have been merely administrative, rather than legislative, and thus can easily be reversed by a succeeding administration. The courts have made matters worse by extensive second-guessing of deregulatory actions. The administration has achieved some notable successes—including the acceleration in deregulation of crude oil prices and allocation, the adoption of the "bubble" concept in applying the Clean Air Act, and the settlement of the AT&T antitrust case. But, especially in view of the increasingly important role of the courts in administrative reform, legislative action may be the only reliable approach to successful, durable deregulation.

Economic regulation always represents an effort by the government to modify or constrain market forces that would otherwise shape economic outcomes. There is thus a perpetual conflict between market forces and the effectiveness of regulation, and the outcome of that con-

Introduction

flict is a key determinant of the structure and nature of the regulated industry.

The banking industry presents a prime example in which economic and technological developments have led public policy, causing changes that are radically altering the structure and relationships of financial institutions in the United States. Kenneth Scott argues that the impact of these changes is more likely to be felt in the patterns of business done by banks and savings and loans than in fundamental regulatory changes because of vested interests in the existing system. He believes that regulatory change will take place in a piecemeal fashion, more as an accommodation to powerful market and technological forces than as the result of regulatory initiatives.

Transportation policy, according to Darrell M. Trent, exemplifies the principles of the Reagan administration's approach to economic policy: reliance on the private marketplace for the provision of goods and services; emphasis on state and local governments where government intervention is deemed necessary; or, where there is an overriding national concern, federal involvement with minimum burdens on private citizens or other government units. Trent shows how these principles were translated into specific budgetary and legislative initiatives of the Department of Transportation, such as the application of user fees to finance federal transportation outlays, deregulation of the transportation industry to the greatest extent feasible, and reform of existing regulations to reduce compliance costs and burdens on the regulated industries.

Robert Hessen examines another aspect of regulation, the possibility of fundamental change in the nature of the corporation. Critics assert that corporations are controlled by their top executive officers, rather than by the shareholders or the shareholders' presumed agents, corporate boards of directors. Executives, according to the critics, are accountable to no one. Their power in society, however, dictates the opposite: they should be accountable not merely to the owners of the corporation but also to the public at large. At a minimum, corporate boards should be reconstituted so that they are dominated by "outsiders"—persons with no economic interest in the firm's affairs. Hessen examines these arguments and finds them either illogical or inconsistent. The proposed changes would seriously damage corporate efficiency and would penalize the most successful firms.

Besides regulatory reform, the 1980 campaign promised tax relief for individuals and corporations. Both were achieved, although Congress enacted a smaller personal income tax reduction than that proposed by the administration. Reductions in corporate income taxes due to the Economic Recovery Tax Act (ERTA) of 1981 were partially offset by the Tax Equity and Fiscal Responsibility Act (TEFRA) of 1982, but some relief nevertheless remained.

In a discussion focused on structural reform and its impact on resource allocation and equity, Charles McLure steps back from the details of specific tax bills to consider the fundamental issue: whether the corporate income tax should be eliminated, integrated with the individual income tax, or, as some critics suggest, restored to the form and level it had prior to ERTA.

McLure sets forth the traditional arguments favoring integration of the corporate income tax with the personal income tax and shows how recent analyses and the reduction of corporate income taxes in ERTA, even as modified by TEFRA, have reduced the case for integration. He concludes that it is more important to restore neutrality to the taxation of income retained by corporations than to integrate the present corporate tax with the personal income tax.

Prosperity, in the long run, depends significantly on the educational system of the nation. Education, of course, has a much broader role than job training. But no matter how its function is conceived, there is broad agreement that the public education system in the United States is suffering from many problems.

Roger Freeman points out that the major educational problem has changed in recent years from one of quantity—that of dealing with growing numbers of students—to one of quality—that of providing a stable or declining student population with a level of education appropriate to the last part of the twentieth century. Freeman shows that the problem is not inadequate funding; per-student expenditures, in inflation-adjusted dollars, have nearly tripled in the past three decades. Nor is it true that the deterioration is the fault of increasing class sizes. Standards have declined, but it is futile to hope that this will be corrected by state and local school boards since they in effect condoned the decline. At the same time, little can be expected from the federal government. Freeman notes that raising standards for all students would mean that more would be held back each year. He advocates instead wide adoption of tracking for students, observing that the United States is virtually the only industrialized nation that does not have such a system. He also argues for improved discipline in the schools and for merit pay for outstanding teachers.

Sidney Hook examines changes in higher education that threaten its very essence. To him, universities and colleges have become increasingly politicized; in so doing, they have departed from their central academic value—objective impartiality. Hook examines the three principal arguments used to justify the taking of political stands by universities—that political neutrality is impossible; that universities have taken political stands in the past and it is hypocritical to expect them to refrain from doing so now; and that universities commonly take political positions on one issue (academic freedom) and are therefore justified in taking them on others—and finds them all wanting. He argues that those seeking help in avoiding politicization will not find it in government. Somehow, faculties themselves must take this responsibility.

Education has been, of course, one of the principal arenas of civil rights activity in the past twenty years. John H. Bunzel argues that a Reagan administration misstep in educational policy—the effort to revoke the long-standing policy of withholding tax exemptions from schools that may discriminate against blacks—had serious consequences for its efforts in other civil rights areas. Bunzel lists a number of administration achievements in civil rights, but says that President Reagan's view that race, sex, and color are inappropriate tests of an individual's worth and his belief in the color-blind concept of nondiscrimination have not satisfied his critics. In part, according to Bunzel, what some see as a neglect of civil rights issues results from a preoccupation with economic and national security affairs. But the administration has also been reluctant to become involved in such politically volatile issues when the political equation did not appear favorable. The resulting inaction, according to Bunzel, is likely to result in an implicit ratification of affirmative action, including preferential treatment and quotas, as administration policy in the field of civil rights.

Demographic change is a fundamental factor in social, economic, and political change, but it seldom enters public policy discussions. Kingsley Davis points out that the United States has never had an explicit population policy and discusses a number of major demographic problems that challenge national policy. He notes that the present low birthrate is likely to persist because of social changes accompanying industrialization and urbanization. Population growth, therefore, would naturally decline, were it not for immigration. The aging of the population that is the inevitable result of a low birthrate also implies an aging of the labor force. An aging population and forced retirement at an early age may produce heavy financial burdens on the working population. The problem is exacerbated by the fact that improvements in longevity have not been matched by decreases in morbidity, a fact that underscores the importance of allowing healthy older workers to remain working. Davis also shows that many of the international problems of concern to the United States have their origins in demographic change, particularly in rapid population growth in Third World countries, and urges a stronger American policy regarding world population growth.

Did the 1980 election of Ronald Reagan signal a shift to conservatism in the United States? Seymour Martin Lipset argues that it did not. Even though a larger proportion of voters identified themselves as conservatives in 1980 than in 1974, they nevertheless continue to support liberal programs. Ideologically more conservative, they remain pragmatically liberal. This is shown not only in attitudes toward programs that might directly benefit the individual concerned, but also in attitudes toward programs that affect others, such as aid to the poor.

In Lipset's view, the 1980 election represents a good example of an international phenomenon in democratic elections—the overwhelming importance of economic conditions. Poor economic performance, particularly high inflation and unemployment rates, has been associated with changes of government in many countries. However, no ideological pattern is evident in these changes. To Lipset, economic instability has played a key role in producing cynicism about government in the electorate. The same cynicism may be producing instability in government by causing electoral shifts from one party to another as the economic winds blow.

There is much more to domestic policy than economics, and prosperity is only one among many national policy objectives. But as the experience of history and the evidence of public attitudes show, the effort to promote prosperity through sound economic policy has an importance more profound than the material well-being of a citizenry. In fact, it is central to a nation's political future. The essays presented in this volume are intended as a contribution to the study of prosperity and the political and social benefits that may accompany it as the nation approaches the midpoint of the 1980s.

Stanford
December 1983

John H. Moore
Senior Fellow

1
An Economic Bill of Rights

Martin Anderson

The key issue in the 1980 presidential campaign was economic policy. After more than a decade of irresponsible spending, increasing tax rates, large and continuing deficits, layer after layer of new government regulations, and an uncertain, unpredictable monetary policy, our economy was reeling.

Inflation had climbed into the double-digit range and was close to the previously unthinkable level of 20 percent. The prime interest rate charged by banks was over 20 percent. Unemployment was high. Taxes on individuals and businesses were at record levels, and laws then on the books would soon push them to even higher levels. Economic growth and productivity were at a virtual standstill, and waves of new regulations were washing over the economy with little consideration for their potential economic damage.

People were frightened, perhaps even wondering whether the U.S. economy could be going the way of some of the more volatile Latin American economies. The public was deeply pessimistic, doubting that anyone, including the president and the Congress, could do anything about it.

One of the great advantages of presidential campaigns is that they wonderfully focus the attention of elected officials (especially potential elected officials) on the critical problems facing the country. The 1980 campaign put enormous pressure on the major candidates to come up with a viable economic program that would restore the health of the economy. That pressure was greatest for Ronald Reagan, who was the leading challenger to the incumbent, Jimmy Carter.

As Reagan's chief domestic and economic policy adviser during the campaign, I was deeply involved in the formulation of that economic policy. Reagan had decided early that the complicated problems of our national economy could not be solved by any single proposal, that any hope for economic recovery lay in a comprehensive program that would attack the root causes of our economic ills, not the symptoms.

To all sophisticated observers, it was clear that many things were wrong. The rapidly escalating cost of living, soaring interest rates, and the high rate of unemployment were caused by many factors—by high tax rates, by spending that far exceeded government revenues, by counterproductive government regulations, and by an unsteady monetary policy.

In the summer of 1979, Reagan's approach to resolving these economic difficulties was spelled out in an internal memorandum that became the basis for the economic policies of his 1980 campaign and the economic recovery program he began to implement after his election.

There were five basic parts to the program.

The first was to control the rate of increase of government spending to reasonable, prudent levels.

The second was to reduce personal income tax rates and to accelerate and simplify business depreciation schedules in an orderly, systematic way to remove the increasing disincentives to work, to save, to invest, and to produce.

The third was to reform, reduce, and eliminate economic regulations so as to encourage economic growth.

The fourth was to establish a stable and sound monetary policy.

The fifth was to follow a consistent economic policy strategy that did not change from month to month.

During 1979 and 1980, Reagan assembled a group of some of the most distinguished economists in the country to advise him. Eventually headed by George Shultz, the group included Arthur F. Burns, Milton Friedman, Alan Greenspan, William Simon, Paul McCracken, Murray Weidenbaum, and about half a dozen others. They totally endorsed Reagan's basic economic strategy and helped him refine it to meet the rapidly deteriorating economic conditions the country was experiencing in 1980.

A large part of that program was enacted into law in late 1981, and by the middle of 1983 it had produced substantial results. Inflation was dramatically lower, falling close to zero. Interest rates had been cut in half. Real economic growth was spurting, exceeding 9 percent during the second quarter of 1983. People's real wages were beginning to increase for the first time in many years. But it was by no means an across-the-board success. Unemployment, while going down somewhat, was still unacceptably high. Regulatory reform was slow. The deficit had sharply increased to about $200 billion a year. We were moving in the right direction, but the economic goal of steady, balanced economic prosperity was still a goal.

In sum, our economic problems, caused by decades of following irresponsible economic policies, were serious and dangerous by 1980. Some important, basic corrective actions were taken in 1981 and 1982 that produced striking results in inflation and interest rates. But by no means had we completely cured our problems, nor had we guaranteed that they could not quickly return.

The task of economic recovery in this country was only begun with the passage of the Economic Recovery Act in 1981. Much more needs to be done. And what remains to be done probably cannot be accomplished by normal political means.

The federal government plays a crucial role in the functioning of our economy. The amount of money it spends, the revenue it raises by taxes and the way it taxes, the loans it makes and the private loans it guarantees, the regulations it imposes on business, the monetary policy it follows, and the degree to which it restricts or promotes free trade in the international arena all have a powerful effect on the economic well-being of Americans.

Ideally, we should try to do something about all these things immediately. But the ideal world does not usually take into account political reality, and if we are ever going to get anything done, we will have to focus on what is politically possible, or what could be politically possible, within a few years.

By early 1981, our economic problems had become so serious that the political climate changed enough to make it possible to slow the growth of federal spending somewhat, to stop the increase in tax rates, to curb the regulatory excesses that were helping throttle the economy, and to steady monetary policy. But those changes were fragile and can all too easily be changed by a shift of a handful of votes in the Congress. Fortunately, the political climate is continuing to change in favor of more stable, more responsible economic policies, and we are entering a time when it is at least possible to contemplate the possibility of accomplishing some more enduring changes in certain critical economic policy areas.

Three basic economic policy areas are especially critical: (1) fiscal policy, (2) monetary policy, and (3) government regulation. In the years ahead, these are the areas we must concentrate on. If we can establish an economic framework that will make it possible for people to count on just three things: (1) a responsible fiscal policy that, by controlling spending and keeping tax rates low, eliminates the deficit, (2) a predictable monetary policy that produces sound money, and (3) sensible regulations that do not interfere unduly with the economy, then we can ensure steady economic growth and undreamed-of prosperity in the years ahead.

Today it is widely believed that the federal budget is out of control. That, like some other pieces of conventional wisdom, is wrong.

It is true that we are running unprecedented deficits, on the order of $200 billion a year, as far into the future as we can reasonably see. It is true that the combined spending for national defense, social programs, and interest that is deemed absolutely necessary far exceeds the taxing capacity of our country. And it is true that there is much anguished wringing of hands over the fact that apparently nothing can be done about it. It looks like the budget is out of control.

But it really isn't.

The amount of money the federal government spends and the amount of money it raises by taxing us, and the deficits it runs by spending more than it raises in taxes, are the result of careful, studied decisions taken with full knowledge of the consequences. Deficits don't just happen or grow like Topsy. They are made with loving care in Washington.

I have spent almost four years in the policymaking apparatus of the federal government, most recently as the domestic and economic policy adviser to President Reagan. I am always surprised when otherwise sophisticated, knowledgeable people—lawyers, businessmen, professors, reporters, doctors—bemoan what they see happening in Washington and say, "If they only knew what that policy is going to do."

Let me assure you. "They" know. The people in Washington, the congressmen, the senators, the president, White House aides, Cabinet heads, and high-ranking bureaucrats, are probably the best-informed people in the country on matters of public policy. The amount of accurate, detailed information that is available for their use is awesome. They admittedly don't know everything, or even all they would like to know, but they know far more than those who are not in policymaking positions.

Then why are we running triple-digit billion dollar deficits when everyone knows that large, sustained deficits will lead to economic disaster? Why don't we adopt responsible fiscal and monetary policies and balance the budget?

We don't because those with the power to make those decisions in Washington have collectively decided—Republicans and Democrats together—that the political consequences of adopting policies that would bring spending in line with revenue and balance the budget are more painful than those policies they are now following.

Large, continual deficits are a bad thing. You can make a nice theoretical argument that deficits don't matter if they are financed by borrowing in the private markets and not by the Federal Reserve creating money. But this sleek theory, as is often the case with theories, comes apart when its basic premise is undermined. In this case, the political pressures stemming from the high interest rates caused by massive federal borrowings in the private markets would force the Federal Reserve to do what it always has done, finance a substantial part of the deficit by creating money.

If you run large enough deficits for a long enough time, you will generate fierce inflationary pressures that will drive up the cost of living and interest rates and ultimately damage us all economically, especially those of us who are poor or trying to live on fixed incomes. No country has ever run large, sustained deficits without inflicting economic damage on itself, and no country ever will. It's a form of economic *seppuku* that always gives the country a bad bellyache.

Yet our Congress and our executive branch have run deficits for 23 of the past 24 years and have deliberately planned the most whopping deficits of all time for the next 5 years. Why?

There are only two ways to reduce or eliminate deficits. You must either increase future revenue or decrease future spending, or some of both.

On the spending side of the equation, there are three major elements: (1) interest payments, (2) spending for social programs, and (3) defense spending.

Interest payments are untouchable. They must and will be met for a simple reason. If for any reason the federal government were to repudiate the debt or declare a moratorium on interest payments, the creditworthiness of the federal government would plunge toward zero and the whole game would be up. A government that cannot borrow in the private markets cannot run a deficit without literally printing the money it needs to pay its bills. This would make everything so clear to so many that government officials could not tolerate or withstand the political reaction for long.

All new spending programs must have a source of funds. You can get the money to pay for them by raising taxes, or by taking money away from other programs, or by borrowing and thus increasing the deficit. Each of these sources of money has a political cost that is carefully weighed by the decision makers in Washington. It is a complex and difficult calculation. The bottom line is whether the net political advantages of the program to the person making the decision exceed the net political costs of the sources of money used to finance that program.

Few in Washington take a balanced overview of the question with the goal of what is best for the country uppermost in mind. Most approach the budgeting question with a clear bias that, in their own minds, is eminently defensible.

For those who are primarily concerned with social programs that provide money and services and goods to people with relatively low incomes, the issue is clear. They view welfare, Social Security, medical care, public housing, and dozens of other social programs as something to which low-income people have a right. The poor and the sick and the elderly are entitled to whatever resources are necessary to fund these programs in an adequate, comprehensive fashion. It is really unthinkable that anything else could have a higher claim. Higher taxes and deficits are a small price to pay to satisfy the claims of those who cannot fully care for themselves, and if fully satisfying those claims requires us to reduce the margin of safety in our national defense, then we should take the risk.

For those whose major concern is national security, the answer to the budget dilemma is simple. Given the enormous increase in the military strength of the Soviet Union and the thug-like mentality of the Soviet rulers who control that power, they see a clear and present danger to the United States that can only be diminished by a swift, sustained military buildup of our own. In their view, unless we can defend and protect our society, there will be no social programs to spend any money on, and questions of tax rates and deficits will be meaningless. They find the cost of spending less on social programs, of increasing taxes, and of borrowing money a real bargain if the result is sufficient military power to deter any aggressor.

For those who focus on taxation, the answer to the budget dilemma is also quite simple. If the level of taxation becomes too high and the degree of progressivity becomes too steep, the incentive of people to work, to save, and to invest is so diminished that our entire economy begins to falter. Productivity declines, economic growth slows, inflation rises, people lose their jobs, and government revenue falls, widening the deficit. If taxes are raised further to compensate for the fall in revenue, revenues only fall more, making the original problem worse. In their view, a weak economy makes it impossible to have either a strong defense or adequate social programs. They find that any effort to substantially raise taxes to pay for national defense or social problems or to eliminate the deficit will only have the opposite effect of what is intended. If we follow this path to get more security or more income transfers, we will just end up with less of both.

For those whose concern is fiscal responsibility, period, the balanced budget outweighs all other claims. Convinced that long-range deficits can only lead to economic weakness and stagnation and decline, it is clear to them that unless we begin to balance the budget now and do it quickly, in the long run we will have to sharply increase taxes, slash social programs, and permit our national security to depend on the goodwill of countries more militarily powerful than ourselves. We may have unbalanced our budget to achieve very important, very desirable goals, but if we continue to pursue our goals by using this path, we will sooner or later lose what we now think most important.

Social programs, national security, taxes, and deficits—they are all critically important and all totally intertwined. If spending on defense and social programs increases, so then must taxes or the deficit. If taxes decrease, then spending must decrease or the deficit must increase. The problem comes when we put constraints or limits on any one of the variables.

Ideally, taxes, especially tax rates, must be kept reasonably low. The deficit must be reduced to zero. We must spend what is necessary for defense and what is right for social programs. Unfortunately, it all doesn't fit.

It's as if we had a small ball filled with incompressible fluid that had four sticks pushed into it. If you push in one stick, the other three move out further. If you hold two and push on one, the fourth moves out a lot. There is no way that you can push in all four sticks at the same time.

National budget policy consists essentially of four policy sticks. One is the tax rate stick. The further we push it in, the lower tax rates are. Right now it is out as far as it should be, probably too far. Another stick is defense spending. The further in we push it, the more we spend on defense. Generally speaking, the more people know about our defense posture, the more they agree that the stick needs to be pushed in further. The third stick is social spending. The further in we push it, the more we spend on social programs. The political pressures are such that anyone who stops pushing on this stick is not apt to get re-elected. The last stick is the deficit stick. If we want to balance the budget, it has to be pushed in flush with the side of the ball. Right now it sticks out a lot.

Given our current values and priorities, there is no way we can eliminate the deficit and achieve our other goals. But it also true that if we do not eliminate the deficit, we will also fail to achieve those goals over a longer period of time.

The fundamental problem is that cutting spending for defense or social programs or increasing taxes all have immediate, very painful consequences. The consequences of a large, sustained deficit are also very painful, but they are not immediate. And the time preference of political decision makers is such that they will almost always heavily discount anything that happens in the future. When the future is defined as sometime beyond their next election, the discount is very nearly total. Thus in any serious contest between the costs of a deficit and the costs of a spending cut or a tax increase, the deficit will always lose.

We can say that politicians should not act that way, that they should be good enough and wise enough to consider the long run, to act statesmanlike, and to incur the short-run political cost. But they are also good enough and wise enough to know that if they do, they will probably not be re-elected. In effect, a vote for fiscal responsibility is a vote for political suicide.

And that is why it is useless to expect or to ask or to demand that congressmen and senators collectively take the necessary steps to curb spending, which is the root cause of our economic problems. They must be forced to do so. They must not have any say or choice in the matter, for if they do, the political pressures will in turn force them to act otherwise.

But how does one go about forcing our elected officials to take responsible positions on fiscal policy? We can reason with them, plead with them, exhort them, and we will have the same effect that we have had in the past—negligible. The structure of economic interest groups in this country has produced a fiscal stalemate. Our political institutions are unable to override the combined political power of people with special economic interests, even though taking the national point of view would benefit all. The current rules of the current economic political game make it impossible.

It is similar to the old economic example of six people who go out to dinner and beforehand agree to split the bill evenly among themselves regardless of what any particular person orders. Given these rules, each dining partner has a powerful incentive to order the most desirable, most expensive dish on the menu, even though the total bill may far exceed what any one of them wishes to pay. The solution, of course, in this case is to change the rules so that each person only pays for what he orders.

In national economic policy, we have been groping for years for some way to cope with the vastly increased size of the federal government and the political forces for spending that have grown up as a consequence. For the past several years, we have tried a new, more rational budget process in the U.S. Congress. Though well intentioned, the main result is that to a large degree we have no budget at all. We rely more and more on "continuing resolutions" just to keep the government operating. To provide more and better budget information to the Congress, we established the Congressional Budget Office and increased the power and size of the Office of Management and Budget for the president. The main result is that we now follow irresponsible fiscal policies with a much clearer and more comprehensive knowledge of just how bad these policies are.

Some have suggested that a budget cycle of one year is simply too short, that it should be at least two years. The main result of that kind of change would be that we will make irresponsible budget decisions half as often for twice as much money. Others have suggested a capital budget as a solution, somehow believing that changing the accounting techniques for reporting on what the government spends will change the amount of what the government spends.

In desperation it has even been suggested that we turn to the field of international policy and borrow one of the techniques used to try to settle international conflicts, that we have our own "national summit." In 1983, Alan Greenspan, chairman of the Council of Economic Advisers under President Ford, urged that a national summit including the president and top congressional leaders be held to make the necessary "hard political trade-offs."[1] But as is so often true in international politics, the problem is not one of communication. It is a problem of disagreement. The spectacle of a domestic "summit conference" of our highest political leaders to resolve our economic stalemate would be the ultimate confession of the failure of our established political institutions. It would be unlikely to have any more lasting effects on fundamental economic policy than international summits have had on foreign policy.

But something has to be done. In fact, something will be done regardless of the course we intentionally follow. Our economic system has built into it very powerful self-corrective measures. If we continue to abuse it the way we have for the past two decades, it will generate corrective actions automatically that will inflict a terrible toll, especially on those least able to withstand it.

The Constitution of the United States is a remarkable document, embodying a high order of political genius. It is truly remarkable when we consider how greatly this country has grown over the past 200 years or so, how much the world has changed, and how much of that original document still validly applies. But none of the Founding Fathers ever seriously thought this country would grow into the economic colossus it has become. While the Constitution is not bashful about treating economic issues, it is silent on many critical economic questions that developed with the growth of the country.

Changes in or additions to our Constitution should only be contemplated when important, fundamental questions cannot be dealt with in any other way. Part of the genius of our Constitution is that it clearly recognized that man, being slightly imperfect, could not foresee all the things that could occur in this country and, thus, made explicit provisions for changing the Constitution if, and when, it should become appropriate.

That time has come.

There are many things that we do not leave to the vagaries of the day-to-day political process, no matter how much faith we may have in its ultimate workings or in the goodwill of our elected officials. For example, we have felt since virtually the beginning of the country that certain civil rights were so important to the proper functioning of a free society that we eliminated the possibility of any future Congress's presuming to change them. Freedom of religion, freedom of speech, and freedom of the press were placed off limits for our elected officials.

In the Bill of Rights, the people speak as a whole, rising above any combination of interest groups, and prohibit any tampering with basic personal freedoms. The framers of the Constitution wisely did not trust elected officials, not because they were not honorable men and women, but because they realized that political forces could be generated that would cause them to act against the national interest when it was in their own self-interest to do so.

There are certain elements of economic policy that are so crucial and fundamental to the proper functioning of a free economy in this century that they should not be left to the tender mercies of any particular Congress or president.

Martin Anderson

Early in 1979, I took a leave of absence from the Hoover Institution at Stanford University and moved to Los Angeles, California, to coordinate the development of policy positions for Ronald Reagan's pending presidential campaign in 1980. There were many important issues discussed during that campaign, but, in retrospect, it is clear that one issue—economic policy—dominated the others and was the pivotal issue. Over the course of his long political career and before then, when he was lecturing on public issues around the country, Reagan had addressed virtually every substantial economic issue that we had. The positions he had taken were clear and consistent, but he had never spelled out in detail a comprehensive economic program for the country, a national economic policy.

As the campaign developed, the demands for such an economic program became more insistent and more frequent. As many times as one pointed out to the press the wide scope of economic issues that Reagan had addressed, it was never clear to them that he had any kind of an economic program.

In the summer of 1979, I decided to draw together the various economic positions that Reagan had taken. As the list took shape, it struck me that he had indeed developed a comprehensive economic program. But no one was aware of it, essentially because it had never all been set down in one place and called an economic program. Drawing heavily on what Reagan had already said and done, adding a little here and there, and synthesizing complementary elements, I wrote what became known as Policy Memorandum #1.

Written in August 1979, the memorandum sketched out a national economic program that contained both short- and long-term economic policies. Most of the long-term prescriptions were summed up toward the end under what I called an "Economic Bill of Rights." However, as the campaign rolled on and we discussed the economic policy proposals with some of the most astute economists and politicians in the country, it became clear that the economic trouble we were in was so serious and the pessimism of the electorate was so deep that we must focus on what could be done in the short term—within the next year or two. There were very few people that had any faith whatsoever in nice-sounding constitutional amendments that would have to clear the hurdle of the approval of 38 state legislatures, to say nothing of the possibility of having to call a constitutional convention. So a decision was made to forgo any consideration of long-term economic policy changes until a more promising time.

Similar ideas were being considered by others at about the same time. As the economic troubles of this country deepened, more and more economic experts were beginning to believe that the basic political institutions of the country contained serious economic policy flaws. The clearest, and most complete, exposition of that view was published in early 1980 by Milton and Rose Friedman in their powerful and persuasive best-seller, *Free to Choose*.[2] After tracking and explaining how we had managed to get ourselves into such an economic mess, they ended their book with a suggestion on how we might cope with the gigantic task of restoring and then maintaining the long-run economic health of the country.

After dismissing the conventional way of trying to work within the established political institutions ("It is doomed to failure. Each of us would defend our own special privileges and try to limit government at someone else's expense. We would be fighting a many-headed hydra that would grow new heads faster than we could cut old ones off."),[3] they instead suggested that major additions be made to the Constitution. They argued that "we need, in our opinion, the equivalent of the First Amendment to limit government power in the economic and social area—an economic Bill of Rights to complement and reinforce the original Bill of Rights."[4]

As with so many things the Friedmans have thought about and made recommendations on in the past, they were absolutely right. The amendment they proposed included major provisions to limit taxes and spending and sections to guarantee free trade, prohibit wage and price controls, eliminate licensing for the professions, establish a flat tax rate, introduce indexing, and to guarantee sounder money by controlling the rate of monetary growth.[5] If we had followed that prescription then, we would be better off now.

The Friedmans recognized that much of what they suggested then would not be acted on. For example, after they stated their suggested amendment that would guarantee a totally free trade policy for the United States, they admitted that "it is visionary to suppose that such an amendment could be enacted now."[6] And they were right once again. The early 1980s were not a propitious time for proposing apparently complex constitutional amendments.

But times do change, and the past few years have witnessed changes in fundamental attitudes toward matters of politics and economics that few would have fantasized about five years ago. That movement continues, hastening the ripening of the opportunity to achieve some lasting improvements in economic policy.

The list of desirable sections to be included in an economic bill of rights is a long one. In seriously proposing important changes in the

Constitution, it is critical that such changes have deep, underlying political support from the people of the country. Changing the Constitution, for whatever purpose, is a uniquely political process, and for it to have any chance at success, it must have substantial political support. Any proposed amendment to the Constitution should be judged by the criterion of political possibility as well as by the criterion of economic importance. For example, one I would personally put at the end of the list is a provision calling for totally free trade. The economic case for free trade is clear, and it is critically important—but those facts are fully understood by very few. The political case for totally free trade has not yet been established, and we have a long way to go before it is.

On the other hand, there are some elements of economic policy that are not only critically important to the effective functioning of a free economy, but also seem to enjoy a substantial, and growing, amount of support from the people of this country.

Fiscal Policy

The most critical element of economic policy is fiscal policy, and in fiscal policy, the basic problem is government spending. Spending more than we should prudently spend puts pressure on the government to tax more than it should tax and to run up deficits. Large, continuing deficits eventually cause powerful inflationary pressures, driving up interest rates and the cost of living. Deficits make it extremely difficult for the monetary authorities to pursue a predictable, steady policy, and they generate strong political pressure for wage and price controls and new government regulation of the economy.

The seed of virtually all our economic woes is simply that most of our elected officials want to spend more than the revenue received from the taxes they are willing to vote for. This, of course, is true for all of us. Unfortunately, the federal government does not yet have the constraints that bind private citizens. Government can, and does, spend more than it should, and there is no effective way to prevent this within current government institutions.

This is why we must add a provision to our Constitution that requires the federal government to balance the budget.

We have already taken some major steps toward accomplishing this. First, the general public has clearly understood for some time the importance of balancing spending and taxing. National opinion polls show overwhelming majorities in favor of balanced budgets. Second, very powerful political support for calling a constitutional convention to propose such an amendment has already built up in the states. Partly due to the reluctance of Congress to pursue anything that would limit the power or prerogatives of its members, and partly due to the persuasive efforts of the National Taxpayers Union, 32 states had passed, by early 1983, a resolution calling for a constitutional convention on the question of a balanced budget amendment.

Limiting Federal Spending

If we introduce a balanced budget requirement into our Constitution, there is one thing that we must be very careful about. Overspending, not undertaxing, is the basic cause of our growing deficit problem. A balanced budget amendment could prohibit deficits, but it would not specify how to eliminate them. And, as Milton Friedman has often indicated, one way to balance a budget is to raise taxes. A bare, balanced budget amendment could be used as a very effective excuse to raise taxes to sustain an even larger amount of government spending. Under certain circumstances, this could produce worse economic consequences than the deficit itself.

For this reason, we need some provision that will limit the amount that the federal government is allowed to spend, to limit the share of the gross national product that can be taken in taxes. Such provisions have been proposed in a number of states, and, spurred by the National Tax Limitation Committee, a sophisticated constitutional amendment that combined a provision for tax limitation with the provision for a balanced budget was actually approved by the full Senate Committee on the Judiciary in 1981 and by the entire Senate (69–31) in August 1982.[7]

The case for fiscal responsibility has been made, the people want it, and Congress shall surely follow. It is only a matter of time.

The Presidential Veto

There is one other item that is crucial to achieving fiscal responsibility in the United States, a form of veto authority for the president that would allow him to selectively delete specific spending measures sent to him by the Congress, spending measures that could only be reinstituted by a two-thirds vote of the Congress.

Ever since this country was founded, Congress has jealously

guarded its power to send the president large appropriation packages, often forcing him to accept spending proposals he does not favor in order to get the ones he does favor. The president should have the power to pick and choose, to veto any spending program that he opposes, no matter how small.

The case for the so-called line-item veto was eloquently set forth in a recent article by Russell Ross, a professor of political science, and Fred Schwengel, the president of the United States Capitol Historical Society:

> It has been asserted that nothing is so powerful as an idea whose time has come. The item veto for the President of the United States is not a new idea but it well may be an idea whose time has finally arrived. With the federal budget exceeding six hundred billion dollars annually it is imperative that greater fiscal controls be exercised. One of the best methods of achieving fiscal responsibility may well be to grant the President of the United States this item veto authority.
>
> Every President with one exception during the twentieth century that has expressed himself on the question has requested the veto. In forty-three of the fifty states the chief executive has been granted such a fiscal tool. Many members of Congress have been on record as believing that it is a necessary part of the presidential power. Numerous scholars have testified to the desirability of the item veto. Seventy percent of the American citizens as reported by the latest Gallup survey on the subject likewise favor granting this authority to the nation's chief executive. The three principal arguments favoring the plan are: 1) it has worked successfully in the states, 2) it would help to reduce extravagance in public expenditures by curbing logrolling and pork barrel appropriations, and 3) it would restore the veto power to the office of the president.[8]

Under current arrangements, the president must submit his budget proposals to the Congress, which can then add or delete as it wishes. What it deletes cannot be put back by the president, but deletions are rare. The Congress is much better at adding to the budget, and when the additions to line items in the budget are sent back to the president in several large appropriation packages, it is impossible for him to veto relatively small items without vetoing the entire appropriation.

With "line-item veto" authority, the president would have the capacity to veto specific additions to any part of his budget. The only way Congress could put these deletions back in would be by the two-thirds vote necessary to override any presidential veto.

The idea of a line-item veto was first proposed in 1876. Since then it has been formally proposed 140 times, with the majority of the bills proposing some form of a constitutional amendment. During the Eighty-sixth Congress, 24 such bills were introduced.[9]

The time is long overdue for us to give the president of the United States the budget power he needs to counter the runaway spending of the Congress. Congress has always had the power to counter any runaway spending tendencies a president might have. We should now balance the scales by adding a presidential line-item veto to the Constitution. Coupled with measures limiting overall spending and requiring balanced budgets, the "pork barrel" veto would greatly facilitate the task of gaining control of the budget.

Monetary Policy

Monetary policy is a critical component of economic policy. A free economy is lubricated by money, and the quality and quantity of that money can have a profound effect on how well that economy works.

Today, monetary policy is determined by the Federal Reserve, independent of the other economic policy domains within the federal government, with virtually total power to control and manipulate the money supply. As Paul Samuelson once wrote in his famous introductory economics text, "A Central Bank is . . . a legal counterfeiter. Its power comes from its ability to expand its liabilities—its notes and deposits. These liabilities are the assets of the public and the bank. The history, therefore, of the Fed is to be found in the history of its changing balance sheet. The Fed is a free will. Its own actions form its balance sheet and cause changes in bank reserves."[10] Today an increasing number of experts are questioning whether the Federal Reserve is too much of a free will.

Since 1971, when President Nixon took the United States off the gold standard by executive order, we have been plagued by inflation and economic stagnation. This has been caused primarily by excessive spending and massive, continuing deficits. But a substantial contributor to this problem has been the ability of the Federal Reserve, unconstrained by the limitations of gold convertibility, to create money.

Few would argue that the restoration of some form of gold standard would solve all of the difficult economic problems we face today, but as Alan Greenspan recently stated,

> The increasingly numerous proponents of a gold standard persuasively argue that large budget deficits and large federal borrowing requirements would be difficult to finance under such a standard . . . with unlimited dollar conversion into gold, the ability to issue dollar claims would be severely limited. Obviously if you cannot finance federal deficits, you cannot create them. Either taxes would then have to be raised or expenditures lowered. The restrictions of gold convertibility would therefore profoundly alter the politics of fiscal policy that have prevailed for half a century.[11]

The pros and cons and all the ramifications of restoring the gold standard are voluminous, and the passionate defense of and opposition to this idea have created an intense controversy that often sheds more heat than light on the issue. But there is one aspect of a gold standard that no one seems to argue with. If the United States were on some form of a gold standard, it would be politically more difficult to run large, continuing deficits. Because if we did, we would arouse inflationary fears and erode confidence in the value of the dollar. Some people holding dollars would choose to turn them in for gold. And as our gold supply became depleted, elected officials would be under increasing pressure to adopt economic policies that would restore confidence in the dollar and stop the gold drain.

Then why didn't this happen in 1971 when diminishing faith in the value of the dollar led to a massive outflow of gold from the United States? The reason it didn't happen is that there is a giant loophole in our political institutions that permits the president of the United States, all by himself, to order the secretary of the Treasury to buy and sell gold, or not to. A presidential order not to in effect repudiates the gold standard. In 1971, a clear decision was made that it was better to go off the gold standard and bear the increased risks of inflation and economic stagnation than to restrain government spending or raise taxes to eliminate the growing deficits. As usual, urgent, immediate political pressures overpowered the case for responsible economic actions that would ensure lasting economic prosperity.

The establishment of some form of a gold standard will not magically cure our economic problems. But the existence of a gold standard can be a powerful inhibition against irresponsible economic policies that can ruin an economy in the long run. When you cut through the luxuriant foliage of monetary policy debates, this is what the struggle is really all about. Politicians do not want to be constrained in the kind of short-term political actions they believe they must take to remain in office. And that is precisely why they should be restrained in these critical matters of economic policy.

There are many arguments for and against a gold standard, all of them eloquently and concisely set forth in the report of the Gold Commission to Congress in 1982.[12] But, given the kinds of economic problems we face today, only one argument is really necessary to justify its restoration—that it would make it difficult for politicians to spend and tax more than they should.

Actually, the gold standard could be restored by President Reagan as swiftly as it was taken away by President Nixon. What an executive order can take away, an executive order can bring back. If political support continues to grow for such a move, it is possible that President Reagan, who has always had a keen appreciation for the discipline of a gold standard, might issue that order.

But that does not solve the real problem. The very fact that such a fundamental part of national economic policy can be whisked away or returned with the stroke of a pen causes widespread uncertainty about any future economic policy. Business confidence is critical to a free economy. As John Maynard Keynes wrote in *The General Theory*,

> The state of confidence, as they term it, is a matter to which practical men always pay the closest and most anxious attention . . . economic prosperity is excessively dependent on a political and social atmosphere which is congenial to the average business man. If the fear of a Labour Government or a New Deal depresses enterprise, this need not be the result either of a reasonable calculation or of a plot with political intent;—it is the mere consequence of upsetting the delicate balance of spontaneous optimism.[13]

Businessmen tend to assume that the government will do what is politically popular rather than what is economically right, and businessmen and others make this assumption with a great deal of historical evidence to support them.

What we should do is to return to some form of effective gold standard in a phased manner that does not unduly upset our current economic institutions and then, once we have achieved a reasonable degree of economic prosperity, lock in the gold standard so that it will be very difficult for our elected officials to opt out of it. If we can do that, we will have created an effective political device for helping to maintain economic prosperity. If the world was convinced that this course of events would actually come to pass, it might also help us to achieve economic prosperity.

It seems that there is only one way that this could be accomplished. We need to make a gold standard part of our Constitution.

Government Regulation

Another area of government activity that has a profound effect on how well the economy performs is regulation. Most regulations that affect the economy have a purpose other than economic—the achievement of better health, safety, and cleaner air and water, for example. Every effort should be made to carefully evaluate the economic impact of these regulations and weigh any negative consequences against the expected benefits in other areas.

But there is one very powerful set of regulations that has an economic purpose. Those regulations are wage and price controls, and their purpose is to contain the symptoms or results of bad economic policies.

To the economically ignorant, it is not clear why prices and wages inflate. They are simply concerned with stopping the inflation, and to many, passing a law seems as good a way as any. And to many politicians, the call for wage and price controls is politically irresistible, even though they know such controls will only temporarily halt the increase in prices, will cause shortages, introduce damaging distortions into the economy, and ultimately fail. History has proven time and again that wage and price controls are counterproductive, that they always hurt more than they help. But history has also proven that politicians will grab at them for short-term political gain.

President Nixon, largely at the urging of the business community, was the last president to try them. As usual, they failed miserably. Fortunately, that lesson lasted a few years, and buttressed by the unanimous judgment of professional economists, no major politician has called for them since—even during the late 1970s when the economy began to career out of control.

But people have a fairly short memory about the efficacy of wage and price controls. The possibility that those controls could be imposed in time of future inflationary pressures is a clear and present danger that hangs threateningly over the prospects of long-term economic prosperity. That possibility has a particularly paralyzing effect on those making business decisions. Most businessmen believe that our government would not hesitate to reimpose wage and price controls if inflation reignited, and they plan accordingly.

The only effective way to preclude the use of wage and price controls is to make it impossible for our elected officials to impose them. And that is why the prohibition of general wage and price controls should be another economic addition to our Constitution.

An Economic Bill of Rights

Too much federal spending has been the main cause of the economic problems we have had during the past decade or two. We have labored mightily through the normal political channels to control and limit this spending. The results have been disappointing. In spite of all the effort to control spending, we are now predicting deficits of $200 billion a year and more for as far into the future as we can see. Many have become discouraged and seem resigned to accepting the fact that the budget is "uncontrollable."

And yet we all know what could and should be done.

To achieve it, though, we are going to have to elevate the importance of certain key economic policies, elevate them to the constitutional level safely out of the grasp of our elected officials.

First, we are going to have to require them to balance the budget, period. Then we are going to have to make sure they do it the right way by limiting spending, not raising taxes. To help Congress achieve this, we will have to improve the budgetary balance of power by giving the president a line-item veto. To make the whole thing as fail-safe as possible, it will also be necessary to eliminate two courses of action open to governments bent on running deficits as easily and as long as possible. We should return to the discipline of a gold standard and eliminate the president's ability to cut the link between the dollar and gold with a stroke of the pen. And we should prohibit wage and price controls to eliminate the possibility that politicians can use them to temporarily mask the damaging impact of inflation.

Basically what we need is an economic bill of rights, an amendment to the Constitution that would guarantee responsible economic policies in the same way that certain personal freedoms are guaranteed by the Bill of Rights. These economic guarantees should be set forth in a single amendment, with appropriate sections. The relevant sections would include provision for the following:

Section 1. A balanced federal budget;

Section 2. A limit on the amount that the federal government can spend;

Section 3. A line-item veto power over the budget for the president;

Section 4. A gold standard;

Section 5. A prohibition on the imposition of wage and price controls.

Such an economic bill of rights, with the proper safeguards for exceptions in time of war, would go a long way toward ensuring the future economic prosperity of this country for us and for our children.

Constitutional Convention

All the steps that are necessary for lasting responsible economic policy can only be achieved by taking away power from our elected officials or by seriously limiting their freedom of political action in certain economic areas. It is not in the nature of things for them to do this voluntarily, so it is not reasonable to expect them to press for such a constitutional amendment. They will do so only if they have to.

And the only way we have to get their serious attention is to call for a constitutional convention to propose the amendment. If it looked like there were actually going to be such a convention, Congress would almost certainly pre-empt it by proposing the amendment itself and submitting it to the states for ratification. But there must be a real possibility of a constitutional convention before Congress will act to limit its own power. Of course, if it does not act, the constitutional convention can supersede Congress and initiate the amendment itself.

If we really want a reliable national economic policy, one that we can count on in the years ahead, we are going to have to hammer it into the Constitution of the United States.

Like certain civil liberties, some economic powers are too important to entrust to elected officials and must be retained by the people themselves.

Notes

1. *U.S. News & World Report*, June 13, 1983, p. 88.
2. Milton Friedman and Rose Friedman, *Free to Choose: A Personal Statement* (New York: Harcourt Brace Jovanovich, 1980, 1979), 338 pp.
3. Ibid., p. 299.
4. Ibid.
5. Ibid., pp. 301–9.
6. Ibid., p. 304.
7. Alvin Rabushka, "A Compelling Case for a Constitutional Amendment to Balance the Budget and Limit Taxes," in Richard E. Wagner et al., eds., *Balanced Budgets, Fiscal Responsibility, and the Constitution* (Washington, D.C.: CATO Institute, 1982), p. 74.

8. Russell M. Ross and Fred Schwengel, "An Item Veto for the President," *Presidential Studies Quarterly* 12 (Winter 1982): 66.
9. Ibid.
10. Paul A. Samuelson, *Economics: An Introductory Analysis* (New York: McGraw-Hill, 1958), p. 316.
11. Alan Greenspan, *Wall Street Journal*, September 1, 1981, op-ed page.
12. Commission on the Role of Gold in the Domestic and International Monetary Systems, *Report to the Congress* (Washington, D.C., March 1982), 2 vols.
13. John Maynard Keynes, *The General Theory of Employment, Interest, and Money* (New York: Harcourt, Brace, 1936), pp. 148, 162.

2
Monetary Policy for the 1980s

Milton Friedman

Monetary policy can be discussed on two very different levels: the tactics of policy—the specific actions that the monetary authorities should take; and the strategy or framework of policy—the ideal monetary institutions and arrangements for the conduct of monetary policy that should be adopted.

Tactics are more tempting. They are immediately relevant, promise direct results, and are in most respects easier to discuss than the thorny problem of the basic framework appropriate for monetary policy. Yet long experience persuades me that, given our present institutions, a discussion of tactics is unlikely to be rewarding.

The temptation to concentrate on tactics derives in considerable part from a tendency to personalize policy: to speak of the Eisenhower, Kennedy, or Reagan economic policy and the Martin, Burns, or Volcker monetary policy. Sometimes that approach is correct. The particular person in charge may make a major difference to the course of events. For example, in *Monetary History*, Anna Schwartz and I attributed considerable importance to the early death of Benjamin Strong, first governor of the Federal Reserve Bank of New York, in explaining monetary policy from 1929 to 1933. More frequently perhaps, the personalized approach is misleading. The person ostensibly in charge is like the rooster crowing at dawn. The course of events is decided by deeper and less visible forces that determine both the character of those nominally in charge and the pressures on them.

Monetary developments during the past few decades have, I believe, been determined far more by the institutional structure of the Federal Reserve and by external pressures than by the intentions, knowledge, or personal characteristics of the persons who appeared to be in charge. Knowing the name, the background, and the personal qualities of the chairman of the Fed, for example, is of little use in judging what happened to monetary growth during his term of office.[1]

If the present monetary structure were producing satisfactory results, we would be well advised to leave it alone. Tactics would then be the only topic. However, the present monetary structure is not producing satisfactory results. Indeed, in my opinion, no major institution in the United States has so poor a record of performance over so long a period yet so high a public reputation as the Federal Reserve.

The conduct of monetary policy is of major importance: monetary instability breeds economic instability. A monetary structure that fosters steadiness and predictability in the general price level is an essential precondition for healthy noninflationary growth. That is why it is important to consider fundamental changes in our monetary institutions. Such changes may be neither feasible nor urgent now. But unless we consider them now, we shall not be prepared to adopt them when and if the need is urgent.

Overview of Federal Reserve Performance

In *Monetary History*, Anna Schwartz and I examined the performance of the Federal Reserve System in great detail from 1914, when it began operation, to 1960. Here, I shall touch on only a few highlights and then examine more closely the period since 1960.

From 1914 to 1960

The Federal Reserve was established to prevent banking panics, not to control the quantity of money. When the Fed began operations in 1914, the gold standard reigned supreme, and it was taken for granted that it would continue to do so. However, the breakdown of the gold standard during World War I drastically changed the role of the Federal Reserve. It quickly became the full-fledged monetary authority, with power to determine the quantity of money, that it has remained ever since—despite the temporary reinstatement of an anemic gold standard during the 1920s and the link between the dollar and gold forged at Bretton Woods after World War II.

During World War I, the Fed mediated wartime inflation—a development that would have occurred with or without the Fed. However, under earlier monetary arrangements, rapid monetary expansion would have ended with the war. This time, the Fed continued an "easy" money policy, creating reserves to finance business rather than government. The result was that monetary growth continued, indeed accelerated, after the end of the war and inflation did not peak until eighteen months later. The postwar price rise accounted for something like one-third of the total inflation of about 150 percent associated with World War I. By comparison, the Civil War inflation peaked in January 1865, a few months before the end of the war.

In 1920, the Fed for the first time acted in a way that later came to be a common feature of its behavior: it went from one extreme to the other, stepping sharply on the monetary brakes, so that the monetary growth went from +15 percent per year to −6 percent per year. The resulting contraction of 1920–21, though relatively brief, was one of the most severe in business cycle annals.

Schwartz and I characterized the years from 1923 to 1929 as the "high tide" of the Federal Reserve System. During this period, it gained the great prestige at home and abroad that it has never lost.

The years from 1929 to 1939 could be characterized as the low tide of the Fed. From 1929 to 1933, the Fed permitted the quantity of money to decline by one-third. A system established largely to prevent banking panics presided over by far the worst series of panics in the country's history. During the long, extended course of those panics, one-third of the country's banks went out of business. The process ended in an unprecedented banking holiday in which the central bank itself closed its doors. It is easy to sympathize with Treasury Secretary Ogden Mills's 1932 comment: "For a great central banking system to stand by . . . without taking active steps in such a situation was almost inconceivable and almost unforgivable"; and with Herbert Hoover's comment in his *Memoirs*: "I concluded [the Reserve Board] was indeed a weak reed for a nation to lean on in time of trouble" (*Monetary History*, pp. 385, 328). Our own view was that "if the pre-1914 banking system rather than the Federal Reserve System had been in existence in 1929," the crisis would have been much less severe, would have ended much earlier, and would not have been accompanied by the collapse of the banking system.

During the rest of the 1930s, the system was largely passive. Active monetary policy was conducted by the Treasury, with one notable exception: the use of newly granted powers to double reserve requirements in 1936, which led to another shift from rapid monetary growth to sharp decline and produced, or at least intensified, the severe contraction of 1937 to 1938.

World War II was largely a replay of World War I. The Fed again presided over a rapid wartime expansion in the quantity of money and again continued the expansion after the war ended. As a result, the wartime inflation did not peak until August 1948, 36 months after the end of the war—twice as long a delay as after World War I—and the postwar rise accounted for an even larger part of the total inflation.[2]

The Korean War was accompanied by another burst of inflation—but this time, one that cannot be attributed to Federal Reserve action. The Korean inflation is the only inflationary episode I know about, in the United States or any other country, that reflected primarily an autonomous rise in velocity rather than prior excessive monetary growth. The outbreak of war only five years after the end of World War II and less than two years after the peak of the World War II inflation reawakened fears of inflation, which in turn produced a flight from money—that is, a sharp rise in velocity.

The Korean War episode helped to produce the famous Treasury–Federal Reserve Accord, which ended the Fed's commitment to pegging the prices of U.S. government securities and enabled the Fed to become largely independent of the Treasury for the first time since 1933. It also paved the way for a continuation of a relatively stable rate of monetary growth.

From 1960 to October 1979

Monetary restraint, encouraged by President Eisenhower's willingness to tolerate two recessions within four years (1957–58 and 1960–61) in order to bring down inflation, eliminated inflation by 1960. The end of inflationary expectations laid the groundwork for a long expansion from 1961 to 1966—the postwar "high tide" of the Federal Reserve System comparable to the 1923–1928 period.[3] As then, this proved a passing phase, although the immediate aftermath was inflation rather than depression. The rate of monetary growth roughly doubled after 1960. At first, the effect was rapid economic growth, but then inflation started to gain ground, leading to a brief period of monetary restraint and a mini-recession from 1966 to 1967.

This episode was the beginning of a roller coaster of monetary growth, inflation, and unemployment that dominated the 1960s and 1970s. Each increase in monetary growth was followed by a rise in inflation, which led the authorities to reduce monetary growth sharply, which in turn produced economic recession. The political pressures created by rising unemployment led the Fed to reverse course at the first sign that inflation was tapering off. The Fed took its foot, as it were, off the brake and stepped on the gas. After an interval of about six months, the acceleration in monetary growth was followed by economic recovery, then a decline in unemployment, and, after another year or so, by accelerated inflation.

This roller coaster was superimposed on a rising trend. Each peak in monetary growth was higher than the preceding peak; each trough in monetary growth higher than the preceding trough. Each inflationary peak was higher than the preceding peak; each inflationary trough higher than the preceding trough. Similarly, at each peak in the economy, unemployment was higher than at the preceding peak, and at each trough in the economy, unemployment was higher than at the preceding trough.

Monetary growth during the 1960s, while high enough to rekindle inflation, was nonetheless relatively stable, which explains why there was only a mini-recession during the decade. But then it became decidedly more erratic, with sharp ups and downs. The result was a more erratic economy as well.

Rising concern about inflation, and growing recognition of the role played by monetary growth in producing inflation, led Congress in 1975 to require the Federal Reserve to specify targets for monetary growth. However, the Federal Reserve, which had opposed the congressional action, succeeded in rendering the requirement largely meaningless by (1) introducing a multiplicity of monetary aggregate measures; (2) specifying targets in terms of a range of growth rates, rather than dollar levels; and (3) shifting the base to which it applied its growth rates every quarter.

In practice, it continued to target interest rates, specifically the federal funds rate, rather than monetary aggregates, and continued to adjust its interest rate targets only slowly and belatedly to changing market pressure. The result was that the monetary aggregates tended on average to rise excessively, contributing to inflation. However, from time to time, the Fed was too slow in lowering rather than in raising the federal funds rate. The results were a sharp deceleration in the monetary aggregates and an economic recession. The time duration of these swings was relatively long—short gyrations lasting about six months; longer waves rising for two to three years and falling for a year or less. Changes in rates of monetary growth were followed by changes in the same direction in both interest rates and economic activity after

October 1979 to Summer 1982

By 1979, inflation and interest rates had both reached double digits, and a flight from the dollar, which had begun in 1978, accelerated. On October 6, 1979, following pressure at an International Monetary Fund meeting in Belgrade, Paul Volcker announced a major change in monetary policy "to support the objective of containing growth in the monetary aggregates" by "placing greater emphasis in day-to-day operations on the supply of bank reserves and less emphasis on confining short-term fluctuations in the federal funds rate."[4] The change was intended to produce lower and steadier monetary growth, at the cost, it was believed, of more variable short-term interest rates.

Unfortunately, while the objective was excellent, the execution was not. The Fed tried to achieve its new objectives by modifying its earlier procedures without changing its regulations. In particular, lagged reserve requirements, which had hindered the achievement of earlier objectives to a minor extent, proved an extremely serious hindrance to achieving the new objectives.[5]

As a result, while average monetary growth was lower after the change than before—which accounts for the subsequent decline in inflation—monetary growth became much more variable after the change rather than steadier. The period of the gyrations also shortened. The short gyrations lasted about one quarter, the longer waves about one year or less.

Interest rates and economic activity followed suit, fluctuating more violently and over shorter periods than earlier. In addition, the lag between changes in monetary growth and subsequent changes in interest rates, economic activity, and inflation shortened: from six months to about three months for interest rates and economic activity; from two years to a little more than one year for inflation.

Table 2.1, based on quarterly data, summarizes the experience since the change in monetary policy. To the best of my knowledge, no earlier three-year period since the Fed was established shows such wide fluctuations in either monetary growth or economic activity.

Since Summer 1982

Around July 1982, the Federal Reserve again appears to have made a major change in its operating procedures. By contrast with October

Table 2.1
The Impact of Changes in Monetary Growth on Nominal and Real GNP and the Three-Month Treasury-Bill Rate

Period for monetary growth (year and quarter)	No. of quarters	$M1^a$ (percentages)	$M2^b$	Annual Rate of Growth GNP (percentages) In current dollars	In 1972 dollars	Change in three-month T-Bill rate (percentage points)	Period for GNP and T-bill rate
					One quarter later		
79:4 to 80:2	2	1.8	6.5	5.3	−4.1	−4.2	80:1 to 80:3
80:2 to 81:2	4	10.1	10.5	12.8	+3.2	+5.9	80:3 to 81:3
81:2 to 81:4	2	3.0	8.9	2.9	−5.2	−2.1	81:3 to 82:1
81:4 to 82:1	1	10.9	10.1	6.8	+2.1	−0.4	82:1 to 82:2
82:1 to 82:3	2	3.4	9.9	4.2	−0.2	−4.5	82:2 to 82:4
82:3 to 83:2	3	13.8	13.9	10.9	+5.4	+0.3	82:4 to 83:2
79:4 to 83:2	14	7.9	10.2	7.7	+0.4	−5.0	80:1 to 83:2

[a] Currency and all checking-account deposits.
[b] M1 plus savings and small time deposits.

1979, however, it made no public announcement. On the contrary, it stated that it had not changed its procedures, but was giving less attention to M1 (currency and checking-account deposits) simply because institutional changes were introducing erratic disturbances into M1.

To judge from its behavior, the Fed reverted to its pre–October 1979 policy of targeting interest rates and of delayed adjustment to market pressures affecting interest rates. The result, as earlier, was surrender of control over the monetary aggregates. In the twelve months from July 1982 to July 1983, M1 rose at a rate of 13.5 percent per year.

The shift to the earlier policy appears to have been accompanied by a return to the earlier relation between monetary growth and interest rates and economic activity. Money growth accelerated in July 1982. On the 1979–1982 pattern, interest rates might have been expected to decline for about one to three months thereafter and then start rising. On the pre-1979 pattern, the lag was about six months. After money growth accelerated in July 1982, interest rates did decline sharply for about two months. But they were stable for the next few months and then started to rise.

Similarly, on the 1979–1982 pattern, the economy might have been expected to begin recovering about three months after money accelerated, or in October 1982; in the pre-1979 pattern, not until six months later, or January 1983. The economy apparently reached its trough and started recovering in November 1982, or four months after the acceleration in monetary growth—moving toward the earlier pattern but still closer to the later one.

Summary

To summarize this 69-year record: two major wartime inflations; two major depressions; a banking panic far more severe than was ever experienced before the Federal Reserve System was established; a succession of booms and recessions; a post–World War II roller coaster marked by accelerating inflation and terminating in four years of unusual instability—the whole relieved by relative stability and prosperity during the two decades after the Korean War.

Granted, the Fed alone is not to blame for this dismal record. Yet it is—to put it mildly—hardly an impressive performance compared either to our nation's experience before the Federal Reserve System was established or to the record of some other nations with a different monetary structure. It is time for a change.

Economic Stability and Monetary Stability

Is monetary stability important? For that we turn to the evidence on the relation between stability in the rate of growth of the quantity of money, on the one hand, and stability in the economy, on the other.

The evidence consists of two parts: (1) the systematic cyclical behavior of the quantity of money and its relation, on a cycle-by-cycle basis, to the subsequent behavior of the economy; (2) the linkage over time between instability in monetary growth and instability in the economy.

Anna Schwartz and I have examined the cyclical behavior of the quantity of money in the United States for the whole period since 1867. Throughout that period, monetary growth has risen and fallen not with but before economic activity. The cyclical peak of monetary growth regularly precedes the cyclical peak of economic activity by an interval that varies a good deal, but on the average is something like six to nine months; the cyclical trough of monetary growth regularly precedes the cyclical trough of economic activity by an average interval of roughly the same length. Moreover, sizable monetary accelerations and decelerations tend to be followed by sizable expansions and contractions in economic activity; modest accelerations and decelerations, by modest expansions and contractions.

The evidence is particularly strong for such major movements in income as occur during major contractions and major booms—the contractions of 1873 to 1879, 1892 to 1894, 1895 to 1896, 1907 to 1908, 1920 to 1921, 1929 to 1932, 1937 to 1938, and all the major inflationary expansions. For these, the evidence is extremely strong that large changes in monetary growth are both a necessary and a sufficient condition for large changes in nominal income.[6]

Further evidence for the importance of monetary stability is the comparison between the variability in money and in income over more than a century presented in Figure 2.1, which plots moving standard deviations for four-year periods of annual rates of change in money and in income, as measured by the net national product. This chart slightly revises and updates a chart prepared more than two decades ago, yet the description of the earlier chart will do for this one as well:

> The two curves parallel one another with a high degree of fidelity, expecially when it is borne in mind that standard deviations based on only four observations (three degrees of freedom) are subject

Figure 2.1
Monetary and Economic Volatility: Moving Four-Year Standard Deviations of Annual Rates of Change in Money and in Income, 1869–1981

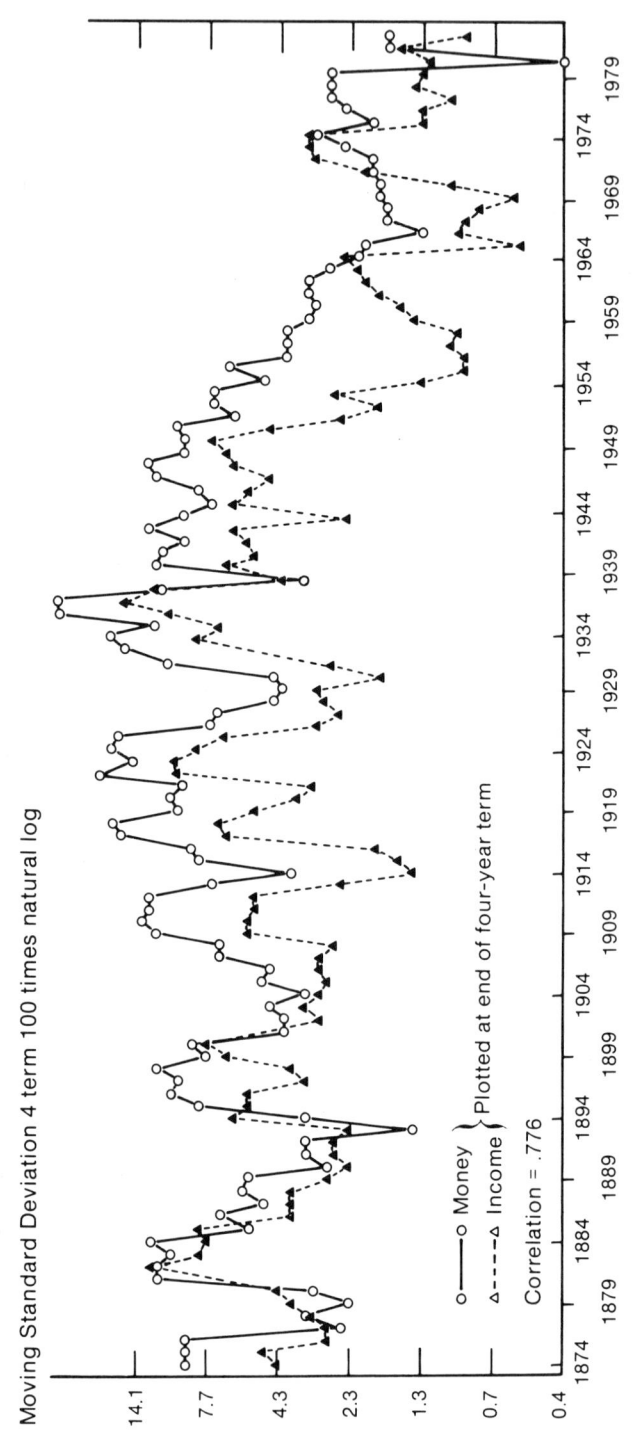

to a good deal of sampling variation, that the net national product and money series are, so far as we know, wholly independent in their statistical construction, and that both are subject to an appreciable margin of error.[7]

For the 114 years as a whole, the correlation between the two series is .776. Omitting the years before 1898, when the statistical quality of the income data improved, gives an even higher correlation, .858. For the period since 1898, monetary variability is highly correlated with the variability both of real income (correlation = .767) and prices (correlation = .706).

In a recent paper, Robert J. Gordon presented evidence on the variability of money, nominal income, real income, and prices from 1908 to 1980.[8] His basic data are the same or closely related to those we used and hence do not represent independent additional evidence on the relation between monetary and economic variability. However, he converted the original data to deviations from trend, or, as he described them, "natural" growth rates, and calculated standard deviations for seven distinct periods, rather than moving standard deviations. Some of his results are presented in Table 2.2, as a supplement to Figure 2.1. They clearly reinforce the evidence from our cor-

Table 2.2

Monetary and Economic Variability in Seven Subperiods, 1908 to 1914
(calculated from quarterly data)

Period (year and quarter)	Standard deviations of deviations of quarterly growth rates from trend or natural growth rate			
	Money (M2)	Nominal GNP	Real GNP	Implicit Price Index
1908:4 to 1914:4	2.9	8.3	6.4	4.3
1915:1 to 1922:4	10.1	21.4	14.4	15.4
1923:1 to 1929:3	4.1	9.9	9.0	3.7
1929:4 to 1941:4	12.3	24.1	19.4	7.8
1942:1 to 1953:4	8.5	11.6	11.4	8.1
1954:1 to 1967:2	2.6	3.9	3.8	2.0
1967:3 to 1980:4	3.5	3.9	4.0	2.2

SOURCE: Robert J. Gordon, "Price Inertia and Policy Ineffectiveness in the United States, 1890-1980," *Journal of Political Economy* 90 (1982): 1100, Table 1. Copyright 1982 by The University of Chicago Press. All rights reserved.

relations: periods of high monetary variability are periods of high variability in nominal and real income and, with one exception, of prices. His data also reveal an important detail that comes out less clearly in our chart: during and after World War II, the variability of nominal income was decidedly less relative to that in money than earlier. In each earlier period, the variability of nominal income was twice or more that in money; thereafter, between one and one and a half times. I have no good explanation for this change but suspect that it may result more from changes in the statistical quality of the income data than from a structural change in economic relationships.

Quarterly data for the period since the end of World War II yield similar, though less striking, results, as Table 2.3 shows for four-quarter and twelve-quarter moving standard deviations. In general, the correlations are decidedly lower for the period as a whole than for each part separately. The reason is a sharp drop in the variability of GNP between the first period and the second—a phenomenon that I am tentatively inclined to attribute to the effect of the Korean War, which, as noted earlier, produced unusually wide movements in velocity.

The evidence is clear: variability in the rate of monetary growth is associated with variability in economic growth. High monetary variability accompanies high economic variability, and vice versa.[9]

It is important to stress two points about this relationship. First, it has persisted despite substantial changes in monetary institutions: from a fairly rigorous gold standard before World War I to a much looser gold standard followed by a purely fiduciary standard; from the period before to the period after the establishment of the Federal Reserve System. The implication is that the direction of influence is from monetary variability to economic variability, not the reverse—a conclusion that Schwartz and I have documented repeatedly on the basis of very different evidence.[10]

The second point is related to the first. The Federal Reserve has sought to use monetary policy to stabilize the economy—that is, to vary monetary growth in order to offset forces introducing disturbances into the economy. Had it succeeded, high monetary variability would have been associated with low economic variability, not with high economic variability. The correlations between the moving standard deviations that we have calculated would have been negative or zero, rather than systematically positive.[11] The implication is again that monetary variability has been a source of economic variability, not an offset.

These two points buttress a single conclusion: it is important to reduce monetary variability. In considering proposals for monetary reform, we should give that objective high priority.[12]

Table 2.3

Monetary and Economic Variability, Post–World War II Quarterly Data
(correlations between logarithms of moving standard deviations)

Period[a]	Item	Correlation with					
		GNP		Real GNP		Implicit price deflator	
		M1	M2	M1	M2	M1	M2
Four-Quarter Moving Standard Deviations							
1947–1963	Maximum correlation	.461	.461	.468	.350	.207	.289
	Lead of M (quarters)	0	−1	0	1	9	9
1963–1982	Maximum correlation	.432	.390	.384	.378	.260	.375
	Lead of M	0	2	−1	1	4	3
1947–1982	Maximum correlation	.694	.325	.344	.265	.120	.158
	Lead of M	6	0	0	1	4	3
Twelve-Quarter Moving Standard Deviations							
1947–1963	Maximum correlation	.582	.517	.671	.541	.330	.257
	Lead of M	0	−1	0	−1	8	9
1961–1982	Maximum correlation	.505	.531	.531	.620	.104	.471
	Lead of M	0	0	0	0	7	9
1947–1982	Maximum correlation	.305	.042	.254	.221	.223	.305
	Lead of M	2	2	1	2	7	9

[a]Period refers to dates of rates of change used in calculating the moving standard deviations.

The Tactics of Monetary Policy

Three issues are involved in the tactics of monetary policy: adopting a variable or variables as intermediate target or targets; choosing the desired path of the target variables; devising procedures for achieving that path as closely as possible.

The Intermediate Targets

The Fed has vacillated between using one or more interest rates or one or more monetary aggregates as its intermediate targets. In the past decade, however, it joined monetary authorities in other countries in stressing monetary growth. Since 1975, it has been required by Congress to specify explicit numerical targets for the growth of monetary aggregates. Although many proposals have recently surfaced for the substitution of other targets—from real interest rates to sensitive commodity prices to the price of gold to nominal GNP—I shall assume that one or more monetary aggregates remains the intermediate target.[13]

In my opinion, the selection of a target or of a target path is not and has not been the problem. If the Fed had consistently achieved the targets it specified to Congress, monetary growth would have been highly stable instead of highly variable, inflation would never have become the menace it did, and the United States would have been spared the worst parts of the punishing recession (or recessions) from 1979 to 1982.

The Fed has specified targets for several aggregates primarily, as I have argued elsewhere, to obfuscate the issue and reduce accountability.[14] In general, the different aggregates move together. The exceptions have essentially all been due to the interest rate restrictions imposed by the Fed under Regulation Q and the associated development of new forms of deposit liabilities. And they would not have arisen if the Fed had achieved its targets for any one of the aggregates.

The use of multiple intermediate targets is undesirable. The Fed has one major instrument of monetary control: control over the quantity of high-powered money. With one instrument, it cannot independently control several aggregates. Its other instruments—primarily the discount rate and reserve requirements—are highly defective as instruments for monetary control and of questionable effectiveness in enabling it to control separately more than one aggregate.[15]

It makes far less difference which aggregate the Fed selects than that it select one and only one. For simplicity of exposition, I shall assume that the target aggregate is M1 as currently designed. Selection of another aggregate would alter the desirable numerical targets but not their temporal pattern.

The Target Path

A long-run growth rate of about 1 to 3 percent per year for M1 would be roughly consistent with zero inflation.[16] That should be our objective. Actual growth in M1 was 8.5 percent from fourth quarter 1981 to fourth quarter 1982. A crucial question is how rapidly to go from that level to the 1 to 3 percent range. In my opinion, it is desirable to proceed gradually, over something like a three- to five-year period, which means that the rate of growth should be reduced by about 1 to 1.5 percentage points a year.

The Fed has consistently stated its targets in terms of a range of growth rates. For example, its initial target for M1 for 1983 was a growth rate of 4 to 8 percent from the fourth quarter of 1982 to the fourth quarter of 1983. That method of stating targets is seriously defective. It provides a widening cone of limits on the absolute money supply as the year proceeds and fosters a shift in base from year to year, thereby frustrating accountability over long periods. This is indeed what happened. In July 1983, Chairman Volker announced a new target of 5 to 9 percent for the second quarter of 1983 to the second quarter of 1984 but from the second quarter 1983 base, which is 3 percent (6 percent at an annual rate) above the top of the earlier range.

A better way to state the targets is in terms of a central target for the absolute money supply plus or minus a band of, say, 1.5 percent on either side—about the range the Fed has specified for annual growth rates.

Figure 2.2 exemplifies monetary targets stated in this way for a five-year period. The actual values of M1 available in mid-1983 are also plotted on the chart. The United States is heading either for a renewed upsurge of inflation or for a sharp monetary—and therefore probably economic—contraction.

Procedures for Hitting the Target

There is widespread agreement both inside and outside the Federal Reserve System that current procedures and reserve regulations make accurate control of monetary growth over short periods difficult or impossible. These procedures and regulations do not explain such long-

Figure 2.2

Proposed Monetary Targets for M1, December 1982 to December 1987

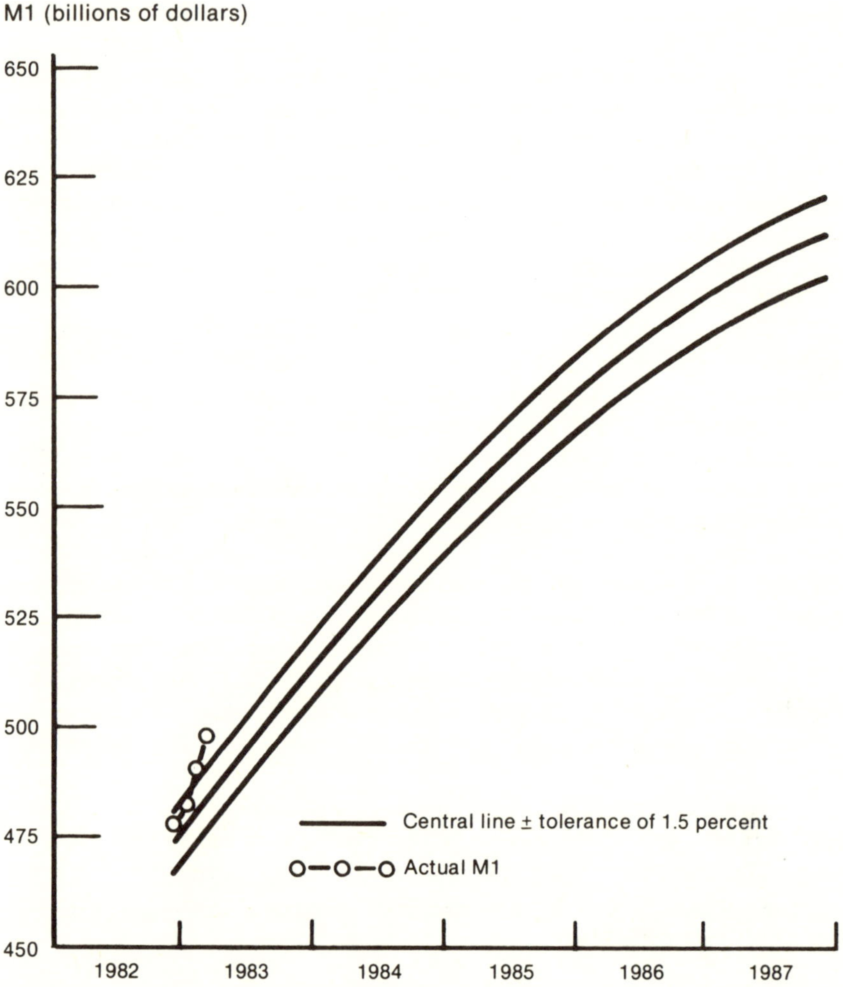

NOTE: 1. Initial rate of growth: actual 8.5 percent, 4th quarter 1981 to 4th quarter 1982.
2. Terminal rate of growth: 2 percent.

sustained departures from the targets as the monetary explosions from April 1980 to April 1981 or July 1982 to July 1983 or the monetary retardations from April 1981 to October 1981 or January 1982 to July 1982. However, they do explain the wide volatility in monetary growth from week to week and month to month, which introduces undesirable uncertainty into the economy and financial markets and reduces Fed accountability for not hitting its targets.

There is also widespread agreement about the changes in procedures and regulations that would enable the Fed to come very much closer to hitting its targets over fairly short periods. The most important such change is the replacement of lagged reserve accounting, introduced in 1968, by contemporaneous reserve accounting comparable to that prevailing from 1914 to 1968. The obstacle to controlling monetary growth posed by lagged reserve accounting has been recognized since 1970 at the latest.[17] Unfortunately, the Fed did not act until 1982, when it finally decided to replace lagged by contemporary reserve requirements. However, it has delayed implementation until February 1984—the longest delay in implementing a changed regulation in the history of the Fed. There was no insuperable technical obstacle to implementing the change more promptly. However, given the Fed's past resistance to change, it cannot be taken for granted that implementation of contemporary reserves will not be further delayed, or even occur.

The other major procedural changes needed are:

1. Selection by the Fed of a single monetary target to end the Fed's juggling between targets;
2. Imposition of the same percentage reserve requirements on all deposit components of the selected target;
3. The use of total rather than nonborrowed reserves as the short-term operating instrument;
4. Linking of the discount rate to a market rate and making it a penalty rate (unfortunately, neither this change nor the preceding is feasible for technical reasons under lagged reserve accounting and hence must await the implementation of contemporaneous reserve accounting);
5. Reduction of the churning in which the Fed engages in the course of its so-called defensive open-market operations.[18]

Even without most of these changes, it would be possible for the Fed to put into effect almost instantaneously a policy that would pro-

vide a far stabler monetary environment than we have at present, even though it would by no means be ideal. The obstacle is not feasibility but bureaucratic inertia and the preservation of bureaucratic power and status.

A simple example will illustrate. Let the Fed continue to state targets for M1 growth. Let it estimate the change in its total holdings of U.S. government securities that would be required in the next six months, say, to produce the targeted growth in M1. Divide that amount by 26. Let the Fed purchase the resulting amount every week on the open market, in addition to any amount needed to replace maturing securities, and make no other purchases or sales. Finally, let it announce this schedule of purchases in advance and in full detail and stick to it.

Such a policy would assure control over the monetary aggregates, not from day to day, but over the longer period that the Fed insists is all that matters. It would enable the market to know precisely what the Fed would do and adjust its own actions accordingly. It would end the weekly guessing game that currently follows each Friday's release of figures on the money supply. The financial markets have certainly demonstrated that they have ample flexibility to handle whatever day-to-day or seasonal adjustments might be needed. It is hard to envisage any significant adverse effects from such a policy.

A few numbers will show how much difference such a policy would make to the Fed's open-market activities. In 1982, it added an average of $176 million a week to its total holdings of government securities—an unusually high amount. In the process of acquiring $176 million, it purchased each week an average of $13 *billion* of securities and sold nearly as much. About half of these transactions were on behalf of foreign central banks. But that still leaves roughly $40 of purchases or $80 of transactions for every one dollar added to its portfolio—a degree of churning of a customer's account that would send a private stockbroker to jail, or at least to limbo.

Increased predictability, reduced churning, the loss of inscrutability—these are at the same time the major reasons for making so drastic a change and the major obstacle to its achievement. It would simply upset too many comfortable dovecotes.

The Framework of Monetary Policy

The chief problem in discussing the framework of monetary policy is to set limits. The subject is old, yet immediately pertinent;

numerous proposals have been made, and few, however ancient, do not have contemporary proponents. In view of my own belief that the important desiderata of structural reform are to reduce the variability of monetary growth, to limit the discretion of the monetary authorities, and to provide a stable monetary framework, I shall limit myself to proposals directed at those objectives, proceeding from the least to the most radical.

Imposing a Monetary Rule on the Fed

I have long argued that a major improvement in monetary policy could be achieved without any significant change in monetary institutions simply by imposing a monetary rule on the Fed. From an economic point of view, it would be desirable to state the rule in terms of a monetary aggregate such as M1 that has a close and consistent relation to subsequent changes in national income. However, recent years have demonstrated that the Fed has been unable or unwilling to achieve such a target, even when it sets it itself, and that it has been able to plead inability and thereby avoid accountability. Accordingly, I have reluctantly decided that it is preferable to state the rule in terms of a magnitude that has a somewhat less close relation to national income but that unquestionably can be controlled within very narrow limits within very brief time periods, namely, the Fed's own non-interest-bearing obligations, the monetary base.

In *Free to Choose*, my wife, Rose, and I proposed a specific form of rule as a constitutional amendment:

> Congress shall have the power to authorize non-interest-bearing obligations of the government in the form of currency or book entries, provided that the total dollar amount outstanding increases by no more than 5 percent per year and no less than 3 percent.
>
> It might be desirable to include a provision that two-thirds of each House of Congress, or some similar qualified majority, can waive the requirement in case of a declaration of war, the suspension to terminate annually unless renewed.[19]

A constitutional amendment would be the most effective way to establish confidence in the stability of the rule. However, it is clearly not the only way to impose the rule. Congress could equally well legislate it, and, indeed, proposals for a legislated monetary rule have been introduced in Congress.

This proposal has the merit that it minimizes the extent of institutional change. However, that is also its chief shortcoming. So long as the current institutional arrangements remain in being, strong pressure will be brought to bear to use them in ways that would avoid or evade the rule. Moreover, as a political matter, a constitutional amendment is unlikely to attract support sufficient for passage except under circumstances of deep and widespread dissatisfaction with monetary arrangements. Since such circumstances would also permit more far-reaching and fundamental changes, why settle for a half-measure?

I remain persuaded that a monetary rule that leads to a predictable long-run path of a specified monetary aggregate is a highly desirable goal—superior either to discretionary control of the quantity of money by a set of monetary authorities or to a commodity standard. However, I am no longer so optimistic as I once was that it can be effected by either persuading the monetary authorities to follow it or legislating its adoption. Congressional attempts in the past decade to push the Fed in that direction have repeatedly failed. The Fed has rhetorically accepted monetary targets but never a firm monetary rule. Moreover, the Fed has not been willing even to match its performance to a rhetorical acceptance of monetary targets. All this suggests that a change in our monetary institutions is required in order to make such a rule effective.

An International Monetary Rule

Some economists, in particular Ronald McKinnon, have accepted the case for a monetary rule but have argued that if applied on a national basis, it would be rendered largely ineffective by substitution of other market currencies for the one being controlled by the rule. Hence they propose the adoption of a rule by a group of countries with respect to an aggregate of their money supplies, which implies, of course, some agreement on the exchange rates at which the monies will be combined. McKinnon has suggested that Japan, the United States, and Germany should adopt such a rule for a total including the yen, the dollar, and the mark.

This proposal has received considerable attention, particularly with respect to the substantive contention that even under floating exchange rates currency substitution renders control of the U.S. money supply "increasingly inefficient for . . . stabilizing American income and prices."[20] The bulk of the evidence does not support McKinnon's contention.[21] Rather, it suggests that substitution of other currencies for the dollar is a trivial impediment to the effectiveness of a monetary rule for the dollar alone.

The economic objections to the proposal are dwarfed by the political objections. A verbal agreement is possible, but a credible and enforceable one, next to impossible.[22] But even if it were, the proposal involves giving great and essentially discretionary powers to an international body independent of any political control by citizens of each member-country short of withdrawal from the agreement. As I indicate below, I regard the independence in a democracy of a national central bank as highly objectionable on political grounds. The objection is vastly stronger to an independent world or tri-country central bank.

Separating Regulatory from Monetary Functions

A modest institutional reform that promises considerable benefits is to separate the regulatory from the monetary functions of the Fed. Currently, regulatory functions absorb most of the attention of the Fed. Moreover, they obscure accountability for monetary control by confusing the two very separate and to some extent inconsistent functions.

As has recently been proposed in a study of the Federal Deposit Insurance Corporation (FDIC), the Fed should be stripped of its regulatory functions, which would be combined with the largely overlapping functions of the FDIC, the Federal Savings and Loan Insurance Corporation (FSLIC), and the comptroller of the currency. Such a combined agency should have no monetary powers. It also might well include the operating functions of the Federal Reserve Banks—the monitoring of reserve requirements, issuance of currency, clearing of checks, reporting of data, and so forth.[23]

A separate monetary control agency could be a very small body, charged solely with determining the total quantity of high-powered money through open-market operations. Its function would be clear, highly visible, and subject to effective accountability.

Ending the Independence of the Fed

An approach that need involve relatively little institutional change—although it is far more drastic than the preceding—and that could be implemented by legislation would be to end the independence of the Fed by converting it into a bureau of the Treasury Department. That would end the present division of responsibilities for monetary and fiscal policy that leads to the spectacle of chairmen of the Fed blaming all the nation's ills on the defects of fiscal policy and secretaries of the Treasury blaming them on the defects of monetary policy—a phenomenon that has prevailed for decades. There would be a single locus of authority that could be held responsible.

The immediate objection that arises is that it would make monetary policy a plaything of politics. My own examination of monetary history indicates that this judgment is correct, but that it is an argument for, not against, eliminating the central bank's independence.

I examined this issue at length in an article published more than two decades ago entitled "Should There Be an Independent Monetary Authority?"[24] I concluded that it is

> highly dubious that the United States, or for that matter any other country, has in practice ever had an independent central bank in [the] fullest sense of the term . . . To judge by experience, even those central banks that have been nominally independent in the fullest sense of the term have in fact been closely linked to the executive authority.
>
> But of course this does not dispose of the matter. The ideal is seldom fully realized. Suppose we could have an independent central bank in the sense of a coordinate constitutionally established, separate organization. Would it be desirable to do so? I think not, for both political and economic reasons.
>
> The political objections are perhaps more obvious than the economic ones. Is it really tolerable in a democracy to have so much power concentrated in a body free from any kind of direct, effective political control? A "liberal" often characterizes his position as involving belief in the rule of law rather than of men. It is hard to reconcile such a view with the approval of an independent central bank in any meaningful way. True, it is impossible to dispense fully with the rule of men. No law can be specified so precisely as to avoid problems of interpretation or to cover explicitly every possible case. But the kind of limited discretion left by even the best of laws in the hands of those administering them is a far cry indeed from the kind of far-reaching powers that the laws establishing central banks generally place in the hands of a small number of men.
>
> One [economic] defect of an independent central bank . . . is that it almost inevitably involves dispersal of responsibility . . .
>
> Another defect . . . is the extent to which policy is . . . made highly dependent on personalities . . .
>
> A third technical defect is that an independent central bank will almost inevitably give undue emphasis to the point of view of bankers . . .
>
> The three defects I have outlined constitute a strong technical

argument against an independent central bank. Combined with the political argument, the case against a fully independent central bank is strong indeed.[25]

The experience of the past two decades has led me to alter my views in one respect only—about the importance of personalities. They have on occasion made a great deal of difference, but additional experience and study has impressed me with the continuity of Fed policy, despite the wide differences in the personalities and backgrounds of the persons supposedly in charge.

For the rest, experience has reinforced my views. Anna Schwartz and I pointed out in *Monetary History* that subservience to congressional pressure in 1930 and 1931 would have prevented the disastrous monetary policy followed by the Fed. That is equally true for the past fifteen years. The relevant committees of Congress have generally, though by no means invariably, urged policies on the Fed that would have produced a stabler rate of monetary growth and much less inflation. Excessively rapid and volatile monetary growth from, say, 1971 to 1979 was not the result of political pressure—certainly not from Congress, although in some of these years there clearly was pressure for more rapid growth from the administration. Nonetheless, no political pressures would have prevented the Fed from increasing M1 over this period at, say, an average annual rate of 5 percent—the rate of increase during the prior eight years—instead of 6.7 percent.

Subordinating the Fed to the Treasury is by no means ideal. Yet it would be a great improvement over the existing situation, even with no other changes.

A Gold Standard

Superficially, there appears to be widespread support for a "gold standard." However, as the report of the Gold Commission demonstrated, the apparent consensus disappears when the question is what kind of gold standard.[26] Some who refer to themselves as proponents of a gold standard simply want the Fed to use the price of gold as a guide to increasing or decreasing the growth rate of the money supply without buying or selling gold and without committing itself to keeping the price of gold within any specified limits. Others want to add a commitment by the Fed to specific numerical limits on the price of gold. Still others want to fix dollar prices at which the Fed—or the Treasury—will buy and sell gold, generally with the proviso that other major countries agree to do the same in terms of their own currencies. Finally, a small minority wants a "real" gold standard in which the Fed and the Treasury would cease issuing any non-interest-bearing obligations other than, perhaps, warehouse certificates for specified physical amounts of gold, and in which gold coins or warehouse certificates, or their equivalent, would be the circulating medium.

For reasons that I have spelled out elsewhere, I regard only the last—a real gold standard—as constituting an improvement rather than a deterioration in our monetary arrangements. And that alternative, which is by no means ideal, has minuscule political support.[27]

Competitive Issue of Money

Increasing interest has been expressed in recent years in proposals to replace governmental issuance of money and control of its quality by private market arrangements. One set of proposals would end the government monopoly on the issuance of currency and permit the competitive issue of currency. Another would eliminate entirely any issuance of money by government and, instead, restrict the role of government to defining a monetary unit.

Choice in Currency and a Tabular Standard. This set of proposals derives largely from a pamphlet by F. A. Hayek entitled *Choice in Currency: A Way to Stop Inflation*.[28] Hayek proposed that all special privileges (such as "legal tender" quality) attached to government-issued currency be removed, and that financial institutions be permitted to issue currency or deposit obligations on whatever terms were mutually acceptable to the issuer and the holder of the liabilities. He envisaged a system in which institutions would in fact issue obligations expressed in terms of purchasing power either of specific commodities, such as gold or silver, or of commodities in general through linkage to a price index. In his opinion, constant-purchasing-power moneys would come to dominate the market and largely replace both obligations denominated in dollars or pounds or other similar units and in specific commodities.

The idea of a currency unit linked to a price index is an ancient one—proposed in the nineteenth century by W. Stanley Jevons and Alfred Marshall, who named it a "tabular" standard—and repeatedly rediscovered.[29] It is part of the theoretically highly attractive idea of widespread indexation. Experience, however, has demonstrated that the theoretical attractiveness of the idea is not matched by practice. Nothing has prevented the widespread use of indexation in one form or another—indeed, the voluntary adoption of the equivalent of a tabular standard—in the United States, Britain, or other capitalist countries. Yet indexation has been extensive only when inflation has been extremely high and variable, as in some South American countries and Israel. Indexing, though frequent, is of minor importance except in labor contracts, and even in that area, it is far from dominant.

I approve of Professor Hayek's proposal to remove restrictions on the issuance of private moneys to compete with government moneys. But I do not share his belief about the outcome. Private moneys now exist—traveler's and cashier's checks, bank deposits, money orders, and various forms of bank drafts and negotiable instruments. But these are almost all claims on a specified number of units of government currency (of dollars or pounds or francs or marks). Currently, they are subject to government regulation and control. But even if such regulations and controls were entirely eliminated, the advantage of a single national currency unit buttressed by long tradition will, I suspect, serve to prevent any other type of private currency unit from seriously challenging the dominant government currency, and this despite the high degree of monetary variability many countries have experienced over recent decades.

The recent explosion in financial futures markets offers a possible new road to the achievement, through private market actions, of the equivalent of a tabular standard. This possibility is highly speculative—little more than a gleam in one economist's eye. It involves the establishment of futures markets in one or more price indexes—strictly parallel to the markets that have developed in stock price indexes. Such markets, if active and covering a considerable range of future dates, would provide a relatively costless means of hedging long-term contracts against risks of changes in the price level. A combination of an orthodox dollar contract plus a properly timed set of futures in a price level would be the precise equivalent of a tabular standard, but would have the advantage that any one party to a contract, with the help of speculators and other hedgers in the futures market, could have the benefit of a tabular standard without the agreement of the other party or parties.

Recent changes in banking regulations have opened still another route to a partial tabular standard on a substantial scale. The Federal Home Loan Bank has finally authorized federally chartered savings and loan associations to offer price-level-adjusted mortgage (PLAM) loans. Concurrently, the restrictions on the interest rate that can be paid on deposits by a wide range of financial institutions have been eased and removed entirely for deposits of longer maturities.

This would permit financial institutions simultaneously to lend and borrow on a price-level-adjusted basis: to lend on a PLAM and borrow on a price-level-adjusted deposit (PLAD), both at an interest rate specified in real rather than nominal terms. By matching PLAM loans against PLAD deposits, a bank would be fully hedged against changes in inflation, covering its costs by the difference between the interest rate it charges and pays. Similarly, both borrowers and lenders would be safeguarded against changes in inflation with respect to a particular liability and asset.

As yet, I know of no financial institutions that have proceeded along these lines. I conjecture that no major development will occur unless and until inflation once again accelerates. When and if that occurs, PLAMs and PLADs may well become household words and not simply mysterious acronyms.[30]

Eliminating Government Money. A number of economic theorists who have been re-examining the foundations of monetary systems have recently offered a new set of proposals. The basic idea is that the government simply define a monetary unit—for example, the value of a specified basket of goods—and play no other role in the monetary system. Private institutions would issue claims denominated in the officially defined unit (as, in futures markets, they now issue promises to deliver wheat or gold or silver specified in officially defined units). The role of government would be restricted to enforcing such contracts, preventing fraud, and the like.[31]

The set of ideas underlying these proposals are intellectually exciting and will contribute to a fuller understanding of the role and value of money. But, as yet, they seem too radical, too unsupported by evidence, to be regarded as a practical proposal for institutional reform. As Robert Hall, one of the main contributors to these developments, states, "All of these proposals share a basic microeconomic goal—full deregulation of transaction services and intermediation [borrowing from some and lending to others]. None of them would rely on the concept of a money stock or its stability relative to total income. Whether their macroeconomic performance would equal that of a simple money growth rule is still a matter of controversy."[32]

Freezing High-Powered Money

The final proposal combines features from most of the preceding. It is radical and far-reaching, yet simple.

The proposal is that, after a transition period, the quantity of high-powered money—non-interest-bearing obligations of the U.S. government—be frozen at a fixed amount.[33] These non-interest-bearing obligations now take two forms: currency and deposits at the Federal Reserve System. The simplest way to envisage the change is to suppose that Federal Reserve deposit liabilities were replaced dollar for dollar by currency notes, which were turned over to the owners of those deposits. Thereafter, the government's monetary role would be limited to keeping the amount constant by replacing worn-out currency. In effect, a monetary rule of zero growth in high-powered money would be adopted. (In practice, it would not be necessary to replace deposits at the Federal Reserve with currency; they could be retained as book entries, so long as the total of such book entries plus currency notes was kept constant.)

As noted above, the Fed currently has two roles: determining the quantity of money; and regulating banking institutions and providing such services as collateralized loans, check-clearing, wire transfers, and the like. Under this proposal its first role would be eliminated. In this sense, the proposal would end the independence of the Federal Reserve System. Its second role could, if desired, be continued, preferably by combining it with the similar roles of the FDIC, the FSLIC, and the comptroller of the currency, as suggested earlier.

This proposal would be consistent with, indeed require, the continued existence of private institutions issuing claims to government currency. These could be regulated as now, with the whole paraphernalia of required reserves, bank examinations, limitations on lending, and the like. However, they could also be freed from all or most such regulations. In particular, the need for reserve requirements to enable the Fed to control the quantity of money would disappear.

Reserve requirements might still be desirable for a different though related reason. The new monetary economists argue that only the existence of such government regulations as reserve requirements and prohibition of the private issuance of currency explains the relatively stable demand for high-powered money. In the absence of such regulations, they contend, non-interest-bearing money would be completely dominated by interest-bearing assets, or, at the very least, the demand for such money would be rendered highly unstable.

I am far from persuaded by this contention. It supposes a closer approach to a frictionless world with minimal transaction costs than seems to me a useful approximation to the actual world.[34] Nonetheless, it is arguable that the elimination of reserve requirements would introduce an unpredictable and erratic element into the demand for high-powered money. For that reason, although personally I would favor the deregulation of financial institutions, thereby incorporating a major element of Hayek's proposed competitive financial system, it would seem prudent to proceed in stages: first, freeze high-powered money; then, after a period, eliminate reserve requirements and other remaining regulations, including the prohibition on the issuance of hand-to-hand currency by private institutions.

Why zero growth? Zero has a special appeal on political grounds that is not shared by any other number. If 3 percent, why not 4 percent? It is hard, as it were, to go to the political barricades to defend 3 rather than 4, or 4 rather than 5. But zero is—as a psychological matter—qualitatively different. It is what has come to be called a Schelling point—a natural point at which people tend to agree, like "splitting the difference" in a dispute over a monetary sum. Moreover, by removing any power to create money it eliminates institutional arrangements lending themselves to discretionary changes in monetary growth.

Would zero growth in high-powered money be consistent with a healthy economy? In the hypothetical long-long-run stationary economy, when the whole economy had become adjusted to the situation, and population, real output, and so on were all stationary, zero growth in high-powered money would imply zero growth in other monetary aggregates and mean stable velocities for the aggregates. In consequence, the price level would be stable. In a somewhat less than stationary state in which output was rising, if financial innovations kept pace, the money multiplier would tend to rise at the same rate as output and again prices would be stable. If financial innovations ceased but total output continued to rise, prices would decline. If output rose at about 3 percent per year, prices would tend to fall at 3 percent per year. So long as that was known and relatively stable, all contracts could be adjusted to it, and it would cause no problems and indeed would have some advantages.[35]

However, any such outcome is many decades away. The more interesting and important question is not the final stationary-state result but the intermediate dynamic process.

Once the policy was in effect, the actual behavior of nominal income and the price level would depend on what happened to a monetary aggregate like M1 relative to high-powered money and what happened to nominal income relative to M1—that is, on the behavior of the money multiplier (the ratio of M1 to high-powered money) and on the income velocity of M1 (the ratio of nominal income to M1).

Given a loosening of the financial structure through continued deregulation, there would be every reason to expect a continued flow of innovations raising the money multiplier. This process has in fact occurred throughout the past several centuries. For example, in the century from 1870 to 1970, the ratio of the quantity of money, as defined by Anna Schwartz and me in *Monetary History*, to high-powered money rose at the average rate of 1 percent per year. In the post–World War II period, the velocity of M1 has risen at about 3 percent per year, and at a relatively steady rate. This trend cannot of course continue indefinitely. Above, in specifying a desirable target for the Fed, I estimated the rise in velocity would slow to about 1 or 2 percent per year. However, a complete end to the rapid trend in velocity is not in sight.

There is no way to make precise numerical estimates, but there is every reason to anticipate that for decades after the introduction of a freeze on high-powered money, both the money multiplier and velocity would tend to rise at rates in the range of historical experience. Under these circumstances, a zero rate of growth of high-powered money would imply roughly stable prices, though ultimately, perhaps, slightly declining prices.

What of the transition? Over the three years from 1979 to 1982, high-powered money grew an average of 7.0 percent a year. It would be desirable to bring that rate to zero gradually. As for M1 growth, about a five-year period seems appropriate—or a transition that reduces the rate of growth of high-powered money by about 1.5 percentage points a year. The only other transitional problem would be to phase out the Fed's powers to create and destroy high-powered money by open-market operations and discounting. Neither transition offers any special problem. The Fed, or its successor agency, could still use part of the existing stock of high-powered money for similar purposes, particularly for lender-of-last-resort purposes, if that function were retained.

The great advantage of this proposal is that it would end the arbitrary power of the Federal Reserve System to determine the quantity of money and would do so without establishing any comparable locus of power and without introducing any major disturbances into other existing economic and financial institutions.

I have found that few things are harder even for knowledgeable nonexperts to accept than the proposition that twelve (or nineteen) people sitting around a table in Washington, subject to neither election nor dismissal nor close administrative or political control, have the power to determine the quantity of money—to permit a reduction by one-third during the Great Depression or a near doubling from 1970 to 1980.[36] That power is too important, too pervasive, to be exercised by a few people, however public-spirited, if there is any feasible alternative.

There is no need for such arbitrary power. In the system I have just described, the total quantity of any monetary aggregate would be determined by the market interactions of many financial institutions and millions of holders of monetary assets. It would be limited by the constant quantity of high-powered money available as ultimate reserves. The ratios of various aggregates to high-powered money would doubtless change from time to time, but in the absence of rigid government controls—such as those exemplified by Regulation Q, fortunately being phased out—the ratios would change gradually and only as financial innovations or changes in business and industry altered the proportions in which the public chose to hold various monetary assets. No small number of individuals would be in a position to introduce major changes in the ratios or in the rates of growth of various monetary aggregates—to move, for example, from a 3 percent per year rate of growth in M1 for one six-month period (January to July 1982) to a 13 percent rate of growth for the next six months (July 1982 to January 1983).

Conclusion

Major institutional change occurs only at times of crisis. For the rest, the tyranny of the status quo limits changes in institutions to marginal tinkering—we muddle through. It took the Great Depression to produce the FDIC, the most important structural change in our monetary institutions since at least 1914, when the Federal Reserve System began operations, and to shift power over monetary policy from the Federal Reserve Banks, especially that in New York, to the board in Washington. Since then, our monetary institutions have been remarkably stable. It took the severe inflation of the 1970s and accompanying double-digit interest rates—combined with the enforcement of Regulation Q—to produce money market mutual funds and thereby force a considerable measure of deregulation of banking.

Nonetheless, it is worth discussing radical changes, not in the expectation that they will be adopted promptly but for two other reasons. One is to construct an ideal goal, so that incremental changes can be judged by whether they move the institutional structure toward or away from that ideal.

The other reason is very different. It is so that if a crisis requiring or facilitating radical change does arise, alternatives will be available that have been carefully developed and fully explored. An excellent example is provided by international monetary arrangements. For decades, economists had been exploring alternatives to the system of fixed exchange rates, in particular, floating exchange rates among national currencies. The practical men of affairs derided proposals for floating rates as unrealistic, impractical, ivory tower. Yet when crisis came, when the Bretton Woods fixed-rate system had to be scrapped, the theorists' impractical proposal became highly practical and formed the basis for the new system of international monetary arrangements.

Needless to say, I hope that no crises will occur that will necessitate a drastic change in domestic monetary institutions. The most likely such crisis is continued monetary instability, a return to a roller coaster of inflation about an upward trend, with inflation accelerating to levels of 20, 30, or more percent per year. That would shake the social and political framework of the nation and would produce results none of us would like to witness. Yet, it would be burying one's head in the sand to fail to recognize that such a development is a real possibility. It has occurred elsewhere, and it could occur here. If it does, the best way to cut it short, to minimize the harm it would do, is to be ready not with Band-Aids but with a real cure for the basic illness.

As of now, I believe the best real cure would be the reform outlined in the preceding section: abolish the money-creating powers of the Federal Reserve, freeze the quantity of high-powered money, and deregulate the financial system.

The less radical changes in policy and procedures suggested in the section on tactics seem to me to offer the best chance of avoiding a crisis. They call for the Fed to change its procedures so as to enable it to control more accurately a chosen monetary aggregate; to choose a single monetary aggregate to control; and to specify in advance, and adhere to, a five-year path for the growth of that aggregate that would bring it to a rate consistent with a healthy noninflationary economy. Figure 2.2 shows an illustrative path.

These tactical changes are feasible technically. However, I am not optimistic that they will be adopted. The obstacle is political. As with any bureaucratic organization, it is not in the self-interest of the Fed to adopt policies that would render it accountable. The Fed has persistently avoided doing so over a long period. None of the tactics that I have proposed is new. The proposed changes would have made just as much sense five or ten years ago—indeed, if adopted then, the inflation and volatility of the past ten years would never have occurred. They have had the support of a large fraction of monetary experts outside the Fed. The Fed has resisted them for bureaucratic and political, not technical reasons.[37] And resistance has been in the Fed's interest.

By keeping monetary policy an arcane subject that must be entrusted to "experts" and kept out of politics, incapable of being judged by nonexperts, the Fed has been able to maintain the high public reputation of which I spoke at the outset of this paper, despite its poor record of performance.

One chairman after another, in testimony to Congress, has emphasized the mystery and difficulty of the Fed's task and the need for discretion, judgment, and the balancing of many considerations. Each has stressed how well the Fed has done and proclaimed its dedication to pursuing a noninflationary policy and has attributed any undesirable outcome to forces outside the Fed's control or to deficiencies in other components of government policy—particularly fiscal policy. Even the few excerpts from the testimony of the four most recent chairmen of the Fed that are given in the appendix to this essay suffice to document their pervasive concern with avoiding accountability—a concern with which it is easy to sympathize in view of the purely coincidental relation between their announced intentions and the actual outcome.

Clearly the problem is not the person who happens to be chairman, but the system.

Appendix

Excerpts from Congressional Testimony of Recent Federal Reserve Chairmen

WILLIAM McCHESNEY MARTIN, JR.

"The flexible monetary policy that has been in effect now for a full decade . . . is one of leaning against the winds of inflation and deflation alike—and with equal vigor" (Joint Economic Committee, March 7, 1961).[38]

"Monetary policy, which had carried the brunt of the battle to restrain inflationary pressures in 1966, moved promptly toward a position of ease last fall, as soon as it became evident that inflationary pressures were coming under control" (House Ways and Means Committee, September 14, 1967).

"Inflation is no longer just a threat—it is a reality . . . Vigorous fiscal action . . . offers the best hope" (House Ways and Means Committee, November 29, 1967).

"I am optimistic about the prospects for gradual success of the stabilization policies now in force" (Joint Economic Committee, February 26, 1969).

[INFLATION DURING THE PRECEDING TWO YEARS, 4.0 PERCENT; DURING THE NEXT TWO YEARS, 5.7 PERCENT.]

Arthur Burns

"The appropriate course for monetary policy . . . is to tread cautiously the narrow and slippery path that lies between too much restraint and too much ease . . . success in our efforts to regain full employment without inflation will depend principally on the conduct of monetary and fiscal policies" (Joint Economic Committee, July 23, 1970).

"While a high rate of growth of the narrowly defined money supply may well be appropriate for brief periods, rates of increase above the 5 to 6 percent range—if continued for a long period of time—have typically intensified inflationary pressures . . . the Federal Reserve will not become the architects of a new wave of inflation" (Joint Economic Committee, February 19, 1971).

[M1 GROWTH DURING THE NEXT TWO YEARS, 8.1 PERCENT; DURING THE NEXT SEVEN YEARS, 6.4 PERCENT; INFLATION DURING THE NEXT TWO YEARS (UNDER PRICE CONTROLS), 3.5 PERCENT; DURING THE NEXT SEVEN YEARS, 6.8 PERCENT.]

G. William Miller

"The Federal Reserve continued to pursue the objective of fostering financial conditions consistent with expansion of economic activity and moderation of inflationary pressures." "One of the great disappointments . . . has been the lack of progress in reducing the rate of inflation" (House Committee on Banking, Finance, and Urban Affairs, March 9, 1978).

"I must emphasize, however, that the solution to the Nation's problems of high unemployment and rapid inflation does not rest with monetary policy alone . . . Clearly other tools of public policy must be marshalled in the effort to improve economic performance" (Senate Committee on the Budget, March 15, 1978).

"Monetary policy has been—and will continue to be—designed to restrain inflation. But monetary policy cannot do the job alone" (House Banking Committee, July 28, 1978).

"You can be assured that monetary policy will do its part in achieving that objective" (House Banking Committee, November 16, 1978).

[M1 GROWTH DURING MILLER'S TERM IN OFFICE (MARCH 1978 TO AUGUST 1979), 8.6 PERCENT PER YEAR; INFLATION, 11.1 PERCENT.]

Paul A. Volcker

"The suggestion has been made that . . . [we set] out a specific target path for future growth in the money stock over a number of years . . . However, experience shows that many forces can affect the financial requirements of the economy at any time . . .

"For all these reasons—and despite the underlying element of truth in the broad proposition relating inflation to excessive monetary growth—I think that it would be a mistake to attempt to set rigid and narrow long-range monetary targets. Further, a legislative approach . . . would raise the basic question as to whether the Congress would want to inject itself so directly into these judgments, filled with technical complexity and doctrinal controversy. It does not seem to be consistent with the approach . . . that these decisions should emerge from a dispassionate, professional, deliberative process and be shielded from partisan pressures.

"We are now placing more emphasis on controlling the provision of reserves to the banking system . . . to keep monetary growth within our established targets" (Subcommittee of House Banking Committee, November 13, 1979).

"We should not rely on monetary policy alone, critical as disciplined monetary policy is, to solve our economic problem" (Joint Economic Committee, October 17, 1979).

"In terms of the broad nature of monetary policy; these considerations translate into a prescription for persistently working toward non-inflationary growth of the money supply" (Joint Economic Committee, February 1, 1980).

[M1 GROWTH TARGET, FOURTH QUARTER TO FOURTH QUARTER: 1979-80, 4 TO 6.5 PERCENT (ACTUAL 7.2 PERCENT); 1980-81, TARGET 6 TO 8.5 PERCENT (ACTUAL 5.1 PERCENT); 1981-82, TARGET 2.5 TO 5.5 PERCENT (ACTUAL 8.5 PERCENT). TIMES AT BAT, 3: HITS, 0; RUNS, 0; ERRORS, 3.]

"Our objective is easy to state in principle—to maintain progress toward price stability while providing the money and liquidity necessary to support economic growth. In practice, achieving the appropriate balance is difficult—and a full measure of success cannot be achieved by the tools of monetary policy alone."

"I appreciate the complexity—for the Federal Reserve and for those observing our operations—of weighing performance with respect to a number of monetary and credit targets, of taking account of institutional change, and of assessing the possibility of shifts in relationships established earlier."

"That objective [price and financial stability] . . . will require that we avoid excessive growth of money and credit" (Senate Committee on Banking, Housing, and Urban Affairs, February 16, 1983).

[AVERAGE GROWTH IN M1: JULY 1982 TO JUNE 1983, 13.9 PERCENT PER YEAR.]

Notes

1. Robert E. Weintraub has suggested that learning the name of the president is of somewhat more value. See his "Congressional Supervision of Monetary Policy," *Journal of Monetary Economics* 4 (April 1978): 341-62.
2. The fraction of the inflation that occurred after the end of the war is hard to

estimate because wartime and early postwar price controls distort the reported figures. According to the official estimates of the price index implicit in deflating the GNP, nearly 60 percent of the total wartime inflation occurred after the end of the war; according to estimates adjusted for the effects of price controls constructed by Anna Schwartz and me, slightly over 40 percent. Both estimates exceed the one-third of the World War I inflation that came after the end of the war. (See Milton Friedman and Anna J. Schwartz, *Monetary Trends in the United States and the United Kingdom* [Chicago: University of Chicago Press, 1982], p. 107.)

3. The rates of growth of money in the successive five-year periods 1950–1955, 1955–1960, and 1960–1965 were 3.2, 1.0, and 2.9 percent for M1; 4.0, 3.0, and 6.4 percent for the monetary aggregate we used in *Monetary History* and *Monetary Trends*, equivalent to the former Federal Reserve M2; and 5.2, 4.6, and 8.4 percent for the current Federal Reserve M2 (our M4 in our *Monetary Statistics of the United States*). It is interesting to compare these numbers with those in the earlier periods. The rates of growth of the monetary aggregate we used in *Monetary History* from 1918–1920, 1920–1922, and 1922–1927 were +14.1, −1.6, and +5.8 percent. The periods preceding the "high tide" were shorter and more extreme, but the earlier high-tide period itself had roughly the same growth rate as the later one.

4. *Federal Reserve Bulletin*, Ocotber 1979, p. 830.

5. Lagged reserve requirements referred to a procedure that was adopted in 1968 under which banks calculate, on the basis of their deposits two weeks earlier, the reserves they are required to hold. Its effect was to convert the technique the Fed now proposed to use (controlling nonborrowed reserves) into the equivalent of an earlier and discredited guide, free reserves.

6. For the evidence for 1867 to 1960, see Milton Friedman and Anna J. Schwartz, "Money and Business Cycles," *Review of Economics and Statistics* 45, no. 1, part 2: supplement (February 1963), reprinted in M. Friedman, *The Optimum Quantity of Money and Other Essays* (Chicago: Aldine, 1969), pp. 189–235. Evidence for the more recent period is available in many publications by many authors.

7. Ibid., pp. 234–35.

8. "Price Inertia and Policy Ineffectiveness in the United States, 1890–1980," *Journal of Political Economy* 90 (1982): 1087–116.

9. Christopher A. Sims questions this proposition on the basis of evidence on the variability of money and industrial production over two decades and in five countries. However, the evidence he presents is seriously flawed. For the United States, his monetary series consists of the average of daily figures, for the other countries of figures for one day a month. As I have demonstrated elsewhere, the standard deviation of monthly growth rates (or annual averages of monthly growth rates) is more than twice as large for one-day figures as for averages of daily figures. When his estimates are corrected for this bias, the standard deviations are roughly the same for all the countries. I do not know the details of the industrial production indexes he uses and so have no

judgment on their comparability among countries. His one comparison for the United States (for 1960–1971 compared with 1971–1982) seems inconsistent with the results in Table 2.2. (See Sims, "Is There a Monetary Business Cycle?" *American Economic Review: Papers and Proceedings* 73 [May 1983]: 228–33, especially Table 1, p. 231; and M. Friedman, "Monetary Variability: U.S. and Japan," *Journal of Money, Credit, and Banking* [August 1983].)

10. See Milton Friedman, "Monetary Studies of the National Bureau," in *Optimum Quantity of Money and Other Essays*, pp. 265–77.
11. See Levis Kochin, "Judging Monetary Policy," in Federal Reserve Bank of San Francisco, *Proceedings of the Third West Coast Academic/Federal Reserve Economic Seminar* (Fall 1979), pp. 143–84.
12. A. J. Schwartz and Michael Bordo reach a similar conclusion on the basis of overlapping yet somewhat different evidence in their forthcoming paper, "The Importance of Stable Money. Theory and Evidence."
13. For a thoughtful evaluation of proposed price rules, see R. E. Hafer, "Monetary Policy and the Price Rule: The Newest Odd Couple," *Federal Reserve Bank of St. Louis Review*, February 1983, pp. 5–13.
14. See Milton Friedman, "Monetary Policy: Theory and Practice," *Journal of Money, Credit, and Banking* 14 (February 1982): 98–118.
15. See my *Program for Monetary Stability* (New York: Fordham University Press, 1959), chap. 2.
16. Over the past three decades, M1 velocity has risen about 3 percent a year. Given a long-term rate of real growth of about 3 percent per year, continued velocity growth of 3 percent a year would mean that zero M1 growth would be required for zero inflation. However, part of the velocity growth has been a reaction to rising inflation and interest rates, which have made it more costly to hold cash. Successful disinflation has the opposite effect. Since the third quarter of 1981, M1 velocity has declined (by 6 percent to the second quarter of 1983) rather than risen. In addition, technological improvements in cash management cannot continue indefinitely. It therefore seems safer to suppose that M1 velocity will cease rising as rapidly as in the past, which explains the 1 to 3 estimate in the text. It implicitly allows for about a 1 to 2 percent per year velocity growth.
17. George Kaufman warned of the problem before lagged reserve accounting was introduced. See my "Monetary Policy," pp. 110–13, for a detailed discussion of lagged reserve requirements.
18. For a fuller discussion, see my "Monetary Policy."
19. Milton and Rose Friedman, *Free to Choose* (New York: Harcourt Brace Jovanovich, 1980), p. 308.
20. Ronald I. McKinnon, "Currency Substitution and Instability in the World Dollar Standard," *American Economic Review* 72 (June 1982): 332.

21. Henry N. Goldstein and Stephen E. Haynes, "A Critical Appraisal of McKinnon's World Money Supply Hypothesis" (unpublished paper, March 1983), conclude, "In a number of important respects ... his interpretation seems strikingly at odds with the empirical evidence." A similar negative conclusion is reached by Thomas D. Willett, "U.S. Monetary Policy and World Liquidity," *American Economic Review* 73 (May 1983): 43–47.
22. See George M. von Furstenberg, "Internationally Managed Moneys," *American Economic Review* 73 (May 1983): 54–58.
23. See Federal Deposit Insurance Corporation, *Deposit Insurance in a Changing Environment* (April 15, 1983), esp. pp. xxi–xxiv and chap. 6.
24. In Leland B. Yeager, ed., *In Search of a Monetary Constitution* (Cambridge, Mass.: Harvard University Press, 1962), chap. 8; reprinted in M. Friedman, *Dollars and Deficits* (Englewood Cliffs, N.J.: Prentice-Hall, 1968), chap. 6.
25. Ibid., pp. 180, 184, 186, 188, 190.
26. See *Report to the Congress of the Commission on the Role of Gold in the Domestic and International Monetary Systems* (March 1982), vols. 1 and 2.
27. See my "Real and Pseudo Gold Standards," *Dollars and Deficits*, chap. 11; and "The Role and Value of Gold," *Reason*, June 1975, pp. 87, 91–94.
28. Institute of Economic Affairs, Occasional Paper 48 (London, 1976).
29. For an interesting recent rediscovery, see the article by R. W. R. White, governor of the Reserve Bank of New Zealand, on a proposed purchasing-power-adjusted money of account that he termed the "Real" (*Reserve Bank of New Zealand Bulletin*, October 1979, pp. 371–74). This article was followed by a series of five articles in successive monthly issues of the *Bulletin* dealing with the possible effects of the Real on various aspects of the economy.
30. See J. Huston McCulloch, "PLAMs: Affordable Mortgages from Inflation-Proof Deposits," *Quarterly Review* (Federal Home Loan Bank of Cincinnati), 3 (1982): 2–6. Also see my *Newsweek* column, "PLAM's and PLAD's," June 13, 1983.
31. See Robert E. Hall, "*Monetary Trends in the United States and the United Kingdom*: A Review from the Perspective of New Developments in Monetary Economics," *Journal of Economic Literature* 20 (December 1982): 1552–556, for a succinct and authoritative summary of recent ideas. Robert L. Greenfield and Leland B. Yeager, "A Laissez Faire Approach to Monetary Stability," *Journal of Money, Credit, and Banking* (August 1983), is an excellent analysis of the theoretical basis of this collection of proposals.
32. Hall, "New Developments in Monetary Economics," p. 1555.
33. In deference to tradition, I designate currency and deposits at the Federal Reserve as "obligations," but they are not in any meaningful sense obligations of the U.S. government, or, indeed, anyone else. They are simply pure fiat money.

34. The empirical issue is the same as that embedded in the extreme form of the rational expectations hypothesis, which asserts the complete inability, even over short periods, of perceived changes in monetary policy to affect real magnitudes.
35. See my "The Optimum Quantity of Money," *Optimum Quantity of Money and Other Essays*, chap. 1.
36. The Open Market Investment Committee, which has the power, consists of the seven members of the Board of Governors plus five of the twelve presidents of Federal Reserve Banks; hence the number twelve. However, all twelve presidents attend the meetings of the committee and engage in the discussions of policy, although only five vote; hence the number nineteen.
37. See George Kaufman, "Monetarism at the Fed," *Journal of Contemporary Studies* (Winter 1983).
38. This and all subsequent quotations of the chairmen are taken from relevant issues of the *Federal Reserve Bulletin*.

3
Monetary Policy for Noninflationary Growth

Robert E. Hall

Monetary policy faces more serious problems than ever as the United States emerges from the depressed conditions of the beginning of the decade. Somehow, monetary policy has to lock in the progress the nation has made toward long-run price stability without choking off growth. Recent major changes in monetary regulations and institutions have substantially complicated the conduct of monetary policy. It is not my intention to review these changes and make a detailed recommendation for modifications in monetary growth targets in their light. Rather, I want to comment on how the basic setup of monetary policy needs to be changed to deal more adequately with the evolution taking place in money markets and with the very serious problems that may accompany price stabilization.

From late in 1979 until the middle of 1982, the Federal Reserve adhered to the monetary principle of setting the growth of the money stock at a predetermined level, without adjustment for actual economic conditions. The result was a period of zero growth in real output and rapid growth in unemployment, together with rapid progress toward price stability. Real GNP in 1979 was $1,479 billion in 1972 prices; in 1982, it was $1,475 billion. Unemployment averaged 5.8 percent in 1979 and 9.7 percent in 1982. The cost of living rose 13.3 percent in the course of 1979 and 3.9 percent in 1982.

In the middle of 1982, the Federal Reserve abandoned the principle of predetermined money growth and permitted growth well above its announced targets. Many economists have applauded the expansionary impact of the turnaround. Real growth resumed early in 1983, unemployment began to fall, and forecasters predicted a continuation of the recovery at least through 1984. Other economists are concerned that the United States is in just another go-phase in the sad history of stop-go monetary policy.

Earlier go-phases produced the inflation of the late 1960s and 1970s. Is the United States headed for high levels of inflation like that experienced in the past decade? Or can it achieve a reasonable recovery leading to noninflationary growth?

The framers of monetary policy must recognize that it determines price stability in the long run and profoundly affects the level of real activity in the shorter run. With unemployment over 10 percent in the United States and even higher elsewhere, it is not surprising that during the depths of the last recession the Fed devoted most of its attention to expansion.

What is missing now is any sense that Fed policy will fulfill its responsibility for longer-run control of inflation. High rates of money growth are acceptable only if they are part of a coherent program of price stability. As yet, neither the Fed nor the Reagan administration has announced any program for stability. The demise of strict control of money growth literally leaves the nation without a policy for price stabilization.

Stable money growth is not the solution when deregulation is changing the nature of money altogether, blurring the distinction between checking accounts and long-term investments. The way out of this problem is to recognize that constant money growth is not an end in itself. The fundamental goal of monetary policy should be to provide a currency and a unit of account of maximum usefulness. The dollar ought to be a standard of value for financial planning over the length of a whole lifetime. Its usefulness for this purpose was sadly eroded by the inflationary surge of the past two decades. Although the United States has made outstanding progress toward reversing this surge since 1980, it needs to stabilize the purchasing power of the dollar in a long-run sense. Restoration of a truly useful dollar requires more than eliminating inflation—Washington must do as much as possible to limit uncertainty about the future value of the dollar. This can be done, but a rule prescribing constant money growth is not the way. Nor, for that matter, is linking the dollar to gold. Prospective shifts in the purchasing power of the dollar would be even larger under a gold standard than under a constant money growth rule.

One principle has wide and growing support among economists; namely, the Fed should conduct monetary policy so as to keep the dollar value of total output in the economy on a prescribed growth track. In short, it should set a course for growth in nominal GNP.

If a boom pushes the dollar value of output above the track through a combination of higher prices and more physical output, then the Fed should step on the brakes. Contracting the money supply and raising interest rates will cool the economy off and bring nominal GNP back down to the target. In the case of a recession, the Fed should accelerate money growth and bring down interest rates. This stimulus will raise nominal GNP back to the target.

Under this strategy, the Fed decides the degree of expansion or contraction necessary to keep nominal GNP on the predetermined track. Its responsibility can be spelled out very precisely: keep nominal GNP as close to the track as possible, and don't worry about other aspects of the economy. The evidence suggests that the economy is sufficiently responsive to monetary policy that the Fed can keep the dollar value of output within 1 or 2 percent of the goal.

The rule of stabilizing the dollar value of the growth of total output embodies just the right combination of attention to the price level in the long run and employment in the short run. If, in the long run, the dollar value of output is kept on track, the purchasing power of the dollar cannot get out of control. A burst of inflation would raise nominal GNP and automatically bring a contractionary response from the Fed. The policy also counteracts recessions in the short run. When the economy entered a recession, nominal GNP would drop below its target. An expansionary policy would then go into effect to limit the severity of the recession.

Under the principle of keeping nominal GNP on track, the monetary ease of late 1982 and early 1983 made sense. The recession brought nominal GNP growth down to only 4.1 percent in 1982, far below any reasonable target. A move toward stimulus was clearly in order.

As an example of how a policy of targeting nominal GNP might work, let me introduce a recommendation I presented to the Federal Reserve Board in the fall of 1980 (see Table 3.1). My recommendation called for setting the targets shown for nominal GNP. The target was based on slowing nominal GNP growth by 1 percent per year; it would have phased out inflation gradually by 1987. Actual policy was slightly

Table 3.1

Nominal GNP Targets
(U.S.$ billions)

Year	Target	Actual	Percentage above or below target
1980	2,659	2,633	−0.98
1981	2,899	2,938	+1.34
1982	3,131	3,059	−2.30
1983	3,350	3,322[a]	−0.84

[a]Forecast

too contractionary in 1980, a little too expansionary in 1981, much too contractionary in 1982, and just a little too contractionary in 1983, if the forecasts made in the summer of 1983 turn out to be right. Except for the lapse in 1982, policy has pretty much followed my recommendation.

The Advantages of Nominal GNP Targeting

Why is it desirable to keep nominal GNP on a predetermined growth track when it would not be desirable to keep either the price level or real output on a predetermined track? The answer is that targeting nominal GNP is the best compromise between price targeting and real targeting. Price targeting gives a guarantee against inflation, but can bring severe fluctuations in real activity and unemployment. Real targeting can bring unlimited inflation. Nobody has yet come up with a monetary policy that guarantees perfect price stability and a full-employment economy. The best available is a "fail-soft" policy—one that guarantees that the situation will not get too bad no matter what happens.

Nominal GNP targeting is a fail-soft policy. With respect to inflation, it does not promise perfectly stable prices, but it does prevent serious inflationary spirals. The inflation of the 1970s and early 1980s could not have occurred under nominal GNP targeting. If inflation started, nominal GNP would exceed its target. The Fed would immediately begin to lean against inflation. If inflation persisted, the Fed would intensify its contractionary policy. Within a year or two, inflation would respond to monetary contraction, just as it responded from 1981 to 1983. Persistent inflation would be impossible. If some force perturbs the price level upward, eventually prices will revert to their original level. A period of inflation will be followed by a period of deflation to keep the price level stable.

As for real output, nominal GNP targeting is also fail-soft. Again, the policy does not promise no recessions. Instead, monetary policy will act to offset recessions and prevent them from becoming serious. When output falls in a recession, nominal GNP falls by at least as much. The value of output falls because output falls and may fall even further if prices fall as well. Expansionary policy is set in motion automatically if nominal GNP targeting is in effect.

The nominal GNP target solves a problem that vexed monetary policy in 1982 and 1983: How can a responsible monetary policy generate expansion to offset a recession without kindling inflation? Nominal GNP dropped below target in early 1982. The United States could have had an even stronger expansionary response than the one chosen by the Fed, without alarming financial markets and the public that the expansion represented an abandonment of the underlying anti-inflationary policy.

Politics of Nominal GNP Targeting

The Federal Reserve is an independent body, and I think it should remain that way. If adopted, nominal GNP targeting should not prescribe to the Fed exactly how to keep the economy on track. That is a technical question, much like the issue of keeping monetary aggregates on track between 1979 and 1982 when the Fed followed a policy of keeping those aggregates on a prescribed track.

How should existing procedures for governing monetary policy be modified? First, Congress should adopt a permanent target path for nominal GNP, not to be reconsidered in the future. The path should start at 7 percent annual growth and decline 1 percent per year until it reaches the noninflationary level of 3 percent per year. This path takes into account the state of the economy in 1983 and the evidence about how rapidly the remaining inflation can safely be phased out.

Congress should instruct the Fed that it is to be single-minded in keeping nominal GNP as close as possible to the track. No other aspect of the economy's behavior should influence monetary policy.

When the chairman of the Fed makes his periodic report to Congress, there should be only one question on the agenda: How close is nominal GNP to the target? If nominal GNP is above the target, the chairman should explain what recent surprise led to the error and how the Fed has contracted the money supply to offset the error. If it is below target, the chairman should explain how the Fed is bringing the economy back up to the target.

Congress should judge the Fed's performance by the following criteria: if nominal GNP is within 2 percent of the target, the Fed's monetary policy is appropriate and the chairman should be applauded. If nominal GNP is 2 to 4 percent above or below target, something may be wrong; the chairman should be expected to explain how it will be corrected soon. Even with the best policy, errors in that range will occur every five years or so. If nominal GNP is more than 4 percent off target, and especially if it has been off target for a year or more, something is seriously amiss. The chairman should be called in for a public accounting. If the problem persists, the chairman and perhaps the entire board should be replaced.

One item should definitely not be on the agenda: amendment of the nominal GNP target. It will always be tempting to raise the target rather than contract the economy after an inflationary episode. But tampering with the target defeats the fundamental purpose of nominal GNP targeting—to assure the public that the dollar will have a predictable value decades in the future.

Our philosophy about the nominal GNP target should be the same as our philosophy about the length of the yard. No matter how inconvenient some people find the definition of the yard, we do not contemplate changing it. We recognize the advantages of a completely stable yard, and so we ignore proposals for changing its length. Our attitude toward changing the nominal GNP target should be exactly the same.

The Mechanics of Targeting

There is no point in extolling the virtues of keeping the economy on a predetermined path of nominal GNP growth unless the policy can actually be implemented. Of course, the Fed is not capable of keeping exactly on a prescribed nominal GNP path—it is bound to be off by a percentage point or two on either side, even if it is doing the best possible job. But it is important to be confident that the Fed can keep the economy within these bounds.

Fundamentally, the Fed controls its own portfolio. Its influence on the economy derives from its purchase and sale of securities from its portfolio and the consequent changes in its liabilities (namely, reserves and currency). To control nominal GNP, ultimately the Fed must develop a strategy that tells it how much reserves and currency should be outstanding at each moment in time.

Each month, the Fed gets a new reading from the Commerce Department on the level of nominal GNP in the most recent quarter. The first reliable information does not arrive until almost a month after the end of the quarter; at that time, the information refers in part to economic events of four months earlier. The Fed also has a large amount of more up-to-date information—interest rates, other financial data, industrial production, retail sales, wholesale and consumer prices. Moreover, it can consult a number of forecasts of the likely behavior of the economy over the succeeding year or two.

Armed with all of this information, the decision makers at the Fed should issue instructions to the portfolio managers. These instructions, issued at, say, monthly intervals, can have one of two forms: a level for the Fed's total liabilities, or a level for the short-term interest rate. A policy is expansionary if it calls for an increase in liabilities or a decrease in interest rates; it is contractionary if it calls for a decrease in liabilities or an increase in interest rates. The technicians at the Open Market Desk who buy and sell the Fed's holdings will have no problem executing the instructions precisely, whichever form they have.

The Fed's general strategy should be to expand whenever nominal GNP is below target and threatens to remain there or to contract whenever nominal GNP is above target and threatens to remain there. The Fed's action should not be a purely mechanical reaction to the most recent level of nominal GNP. If nominal GNP is a bit below target but forecasters agree that it is headed above target, the Fed should not expand.

How should the Fed determine the magnitude of the expansion or contraction? Congress should not try to answer this question; it is one that is best left to the technicians. The success of the policy does not depend on choosing exactly the right rule. The policy is like the thermostat in a house. When the furnace is installed, the builder has only a vague idea of the amount of heat that will be necessary to keep the house warm. But as long as the thermostat turns the furnace on when the house is a little cool and off when it is a little warm, the house will stay at the right temperature. The Fed can keep nominal GNP close to the target by an analogous policy. Even if it steps on the gas or on the brake a little too hard, the policy will work because it is self-limiting—any excess response will be cut off as soon as nominal GNP reaches the target amount.

Of course, if the Fed is much too timid, it may take many years to get nominal GNP back on course. The Fed needs to review its record after a few years for evidence that a more aggressive policy would have kept nominal GNP closer to the track. If there have been a number of lengthy episodes persistently above or below target, the Fed should change its operating rules to move more decisively toward expansion or contraction when the economy is off track.

A more serious danger is that policy will be too aggressive. It is possible for the Fed to expand the money supply so vigorously when the economy is below target that its momentum carries it far above target. Worse yet, if the overshooting calls forth an even more forceful contraction, the economy could go into an unstable spiral of ever-worsening departures from target.

Some overshooting is inevitably part of a stabilization policy. Under a successful policy, the economy will spend half its time above the target and half the time below the target. What the Fed must avoid is a pattern of severe and growing overshooting. To avoid the problem, the Fed should be conservative in its response, especially in the early years of the policy.

For example, a cautious policy, based on the total liabilities of the Fed, would set the liabilities each month at a level as many percentage points above their level of a year earlier as nominal GNP was currently below the target. If nominal GNP were 2 percent below target, the Fed would set liabilities 2 percent higher than they had been a year before. If it were 3 percent above target, the Fed would make liabilities 3 percent below their level of a year before.

This policy is tailored for an economy where the average monetary policy over the preceding year influences the current level of nominal GNP. The evidence supports that kind of relationship for the United States. However, such a policy is very cautious compared with the policy that would be best if we were absolutely confident that was the way the economy responded to monetary policy.

Another example of a cautious policy would operate on interest rates. Each month, monetary policy could be stated in terms of a desired level of the short-term interest rate—say, the federal funds rate. Within the month, the traders at the Fed would buy and sell the amount of government debt necessary to keep the rate at the prescribed level. Each month, the level should be changed to keep the economy on the nominal GNP track. A conservative rule for changing the interest rate is for each percentage point nominal GNP is above target, raise the interest rate by two-tenths of a percentage point. Lower the interest rate in the same way when nominal GNP is below target.

Both of these policies have the same character. The Fed should step gently on the brake when nominal GNP goes above target and keep stepping harder until nominal GNP begins to return to the target. The Fed should step on the gas if nominal GNP goes below target. The two examples differ slightly in the definition of what it means to step on the brake and on the gas.

Alternatives to Nominal GNP Targeting

Monetary policy will emerge from its present state of total confusion only when some guiding principle is chosen. If not nominal GNP targeting, it will be some other principle. Ideas that have been put forward include:

1. Setting a target for a broad monetary aggregate and ignoring the instabilities in that aggregate associated with deregulation;
2. Setting a target for the liabilities of the Fed (the monetary base);
3. Setting a target for some price index;
4. Adopting some form of the gold standard.

None of these alternatives has the fail-soft features of nominal GNP targeting.

Putting a broad monetary aggregate on a predetermined growth path is one of the more attractive second choices, primarily because it would give results similar to a policy based on nominal GNP. The broadest aggregate, called total credit, has historically moved very closely with nominal GNP. As long as this relationship persists, controlling the growth of total credit is much the same as controlling the growth of nominal GNP. Total credit is the sum of all liabilities of the banking system. It is unaffected by forms of deregulation that cause bank deposits to swell at the expense of other bank liabilities, but it is sensitive to the overall size of the banking sector compared with that of other financial institutions. If Sears Roebuck and American Express grow as financial intermediaries in the way they would like, the banking industry may shrink in a way that alters the relation of total credit to nominal GNP. If that were to happen under a total credit target, the result would be unwanted inflation as the Fed tried to keep total credit along its normal growth track even though demand had shifted away from credit.

Another type of monetary targeting would put the monetary base on a predetermined growth path. One of the virtues of this policy is that since the Fed has immediate control over its own portfolio, it can achieve the target for the monetary base exactly, day by day. However, the relations of the base to the price level in the long run and the level of income in the short run are quite unstable. Most of the base is currency. The demand for currency has shifted erratically for the past thirty years, especially recently. There is over $1,400 in currency in circulation for each family in the United States. Because few families actually hold that much currency at any one time, much currency is apparently held in large hoards. Fluctuations in the desire of a few people to maintain large holdings of currency, not the overall level of nominal activity, are the principal determinant of the demand for currency. Under a policy of keeping the monetary base on a predetermined growth path, every shift of currency out of hoards would be inflationary and every shift in would be deflationary.

Targeting the price level itself is much in the spirit of this essay. Since the fundamental objective of monetary policy is long-run price stability, why not make that the operating rule of the Fed? The main reason why direct price targeting is undesirable is that it lacks the failsoft feature in the short run. If a burst of inflation hits the economy, price targeting tells the Fed to step on the brakes immediately. There is no limit to the severity of the recession that would accompany a price shock. The United States learned in 1974–1975 and again in 1979–1980 that price shocks bring recession. But in those cases, the Fed did not step on the brake; rather, it accommodated a good deal of inflation. Had price targeting been in effect, those recessions would have been even more severe.

Finally, the gold standard is a special form of price targeting where the price of gold, not the general cost of living, is the target of monetary policy. In all variants of the gold standard, monetary policy is to be used as necessary to keep the dollar price of gold at a predetermined level. The gold standard exposes the U.S. economy to the instabilities of the world gold market, which have been frequent in the past decade. When oil wealth flows into the gold market, as it did in 1980, the dollar price of gold skyrockets under the current system. Under a gold standard, the same shift in demand would severely depress the U.S. economy. It would be completely irresponsible to expose the economy to this risk or to the opposite risk: when the world demand for gold declines, inflation would occur in the United States.

Nominal GNP targeting will not solve all macroeconomic problems. It would not prevent recessions. It would not even prevent inflation. But it is a better compromise than any other policy. It is fail-soft—under nominal GNP targeting, neither deep recession nor chronic inflation is possible. Monetary policy automatically turns expansionary if the economy begins to contract and automatically slows the economy down if inflation threatens.

The time has come for the United States to adopt a new principle for monetary policy. Today there is no guiding principle. Financial markets are operating on generous expectations of future inflation in interest rates even though enormous progress has been made in reducing actual inflation since 1980.

The president and Congress should announce a coherent policy for noninflationary growth. They should set up a long-run growth track for nominal GNP and establish a framework under which the Fed is held accountable for keeping the economy on that track year after year.

4
Supply-Side Economics, Growth, and Liberty

Paul Craig Roberts

The elections of the Thatcher, Reagan, and Kohl governments are signs that despite the appeal of envy, free electorates are coming to the realization that the emphasis of economic policy must be changed from redistribution to economic growth because today only economic growth can solve the problems that afflict the countries that are the reservoir of liberty. The industrial democracies, by introducing broad-scale welfare programs, have created new property rights in the form of entitlements and transfer payments. Millions of people can now claim rights to income that they did not produce. The transfer societies, which grew up on the backs of strong and growing economies, now burden the economies that permitted that growth. As a result, only three choices remain for the future: to default on the promises of future transfer payments; to confiscate even more from the producers in society; or to encourage economic growth, which, together with restraint in the growth of entitlements, would maintain a dynamic economic base for society.

For a fuller treatment of the issues discussed here, see Paul Craig Roberts, *The Supply-Side Revolution* (Cambridge, Mass.: Harvard University Press, 1984).

In the United States, the problems stemming from the growth of the transfer society have been compounded by a fiscal policy that attended to only one side of the economy. For nearly fifteen years fiscal policy was used as a tool to manipulate the level of aggregate demand, or total spending, in the economy. Policymakers and economists believed that the production side would respond automatically to demand. They ignored the effects of tax rate changes on relative prices and the supply-side of the economy.

It is important to understand these relative price effects. Relative prices influence people's decisions to allocate income between consumption and saving. The cost to an individual of allocating a dollar of income to current consumption is the future income stream forgone by not saving and investing that dollar of income. The higher the tax rate, the less the value of the income stream. Thus, high tax rates make consumption cheap in terms of forgone income and reduce the saving rate, resulting in less investment.

The 98 percent marginal income tax rate on investment income that applied in Great Britain until a few years ago was a startling example of this. Anyone in that high bracket trying to decide whether to buy a Rolls Royce with $100,000 or invest that money at 17 percent interest quickly perceived that on a pretax basis the cost of the Rolls Royce was a forgone income stream of $17,000 per year, a relatively high price for a car. But after tax the value of that additional income stream was only $340 per year (the 2 percent of the $17,000 remaining), which was all that had to be given up to enjoy a Rolls Royce—a very low price indeed. This explains the paradox of why there are so many Rolls Royces on London streets at a time when England is in economic decline. The Rolls Royces are signs not of prosperity but of high tax rates on investment income. The principle involved is most vividly illustrated by this extreme example, but it operates across the spectrum of tax rates.

Relative prices also govern people's decisions regarding how they divide their time between work and leisure or between leisure and education to improve employment skills. The cost to a person of allocating another hour of time to leisure is the current earnings given up by not working (for example, overtime on Saturday) or the future income given up by not investing in human capital by taking courses and improving work skills. The value of the forgone income is determined by the rates at which the additional income is taxed. The higher the marginal tax rates, the cheaper the price of leisure. Absenteeism rates go up, willingness to accept overtime declines, and people spend less time improving their work skills.

For example, a physician who encounters the 50 percent tax rate after six months of work faces working another six months for only 50 percent of his or her earnings. Such a low reward for additional effort encourages doctors to share practices, reduce working hours, and take longer vacations. The high tax rates shrink the tax base by discouraging doctors from earning additional amounts of taxable income. The high tax rates also drive up the cost of medical care by reducing the supply of medical services. A tax rate reduction would raise the relative price of leisure to doctors and result in more taxable income earned as well as a greater supply of medical services.

The effect of tax rates on the decision to earn additional taxable income is by no means limited to doctors in the top bracket. Even a carpenter facing a 25 percent marginal rate finds for every additional $100 he earns, he is allowed to keep only $75. Suppose that his house needs painting and he can hire a painter for $80 a day. Since the carpenter's take-home pay is only $75, he would save $5 by painting his own home. In this case the tax base shrinks by $180—the $100 that the carpenter chooses not to earn and the $80 that he does not pay the painter.

To be effective, supply-side economics does not require large individual responses to improved incentives. With a work force of 100 million people, small individual responses result in a large aggregate effect. If the average number of hours worked per week, for example, rises from 35 to just 35.5, GNP rises by about $30 billion.

Every year the Tax Foundation reminds us that American taxpayers have on average to work the first four months and several days of the year for the government in order to pay their taxes and only then start working for themselves. But in fact it is the other way around. The first part of the year taxpayers work for themselves. They only begin working for the government when their income reaches taxable levels. Once that has happened, the more they earn, the more they work for the government—until rising marginal tax rates discourage further work. The progressive income tax is perverse: it penalizes effort and rewards underexertion. Since each additional effort comes on top of existing effort, the disutility to the individual of additional effort is high. But since the income from the additional effort is added to existing income, it is taxed at higher rates. So as efforts rise, rewards fall.

The progressive income tax was implemented to "soak the rich" and redistribute income. In practice it works as a barrier to upward mobility and discourages people from making their best effort. In pandering to envy, the tax system has made it almost impossible for the average taxpayer to obtain financial independence.

It is this barrier to success that supply-side economists want to remove. Without proper rewards for individual success, a society sets its own course for failure. The greater the extent of private success, the smaller the need for public assistance and the lower the burden of government on the economy. Supply-side economics is not an antigovernment position. It simply acknowledges that by robbing people of the incentive to produce, government destroys the economic base on which society thrives. If income redistribution is necessary, it should be achieved through the expenditure side of the budget, not through the rising marginal tax rates of a progressive income tax.

The relative price perspective allows supply-side economists to broaden the discussion about "crowding out." When most people think of private investment being crowded out by fiscal policy, they think of upward pressure on interest rates as a result of government borrowing to finance budget deficits. But investment is also crowded out by taxation, whether the budget is in balance or not.

Consider a simple example. Suppose that to be undertaken, an investment must earn a 10 percent rate of return. If the government imposes a 50 percent tax rate on investment income, investments earning 10 percent before tax will no longer be undertaken. Only investments earning 20 percent before tax will return 10 percent after tax.

Taxation crowds out investment by reducing the number of profitable investments. When tax rates are reduced, aftertax rates of return rise, and the number of profitable investments increases.

The experience of the past twenty years provides important empirical evidence for supply-side economics. It is clear that the economy's performance has been declining for over a decade. Economic performance previously deemed unacceptable became unattainable as both inflation and unemployment rates rose. As an example, 1979 capped a four-year period of expansion, but the unemployment rate in that year was nearly one full percentage point higher than in the recession year of 1970.

Productivity is a useful measure to determine how well the supply-side of the economy is performing. Judging by the trends in productivity during the 1960s and 1970s, the supply-side of the economy did not do very well. As Figure 4.1 shows, the rate of growth of labor productivity declined precipitously beginning in the latter part of the 1960s. The annual growth of output per worker averaged 3.1 percent between 1948 and 1968 but declined to 2.1 percent between 1968 and 1973. From 1973 to 1980, productivity growth in the private business sector averaged only 0.6 percent per year, or one-fifth of the rate over the twenty-year period ending in 1968. Productivity actually

Figure 4.1
Rates of Growth in the Capital-Labor Ratio, Productivity, and Real Net Capital Stock

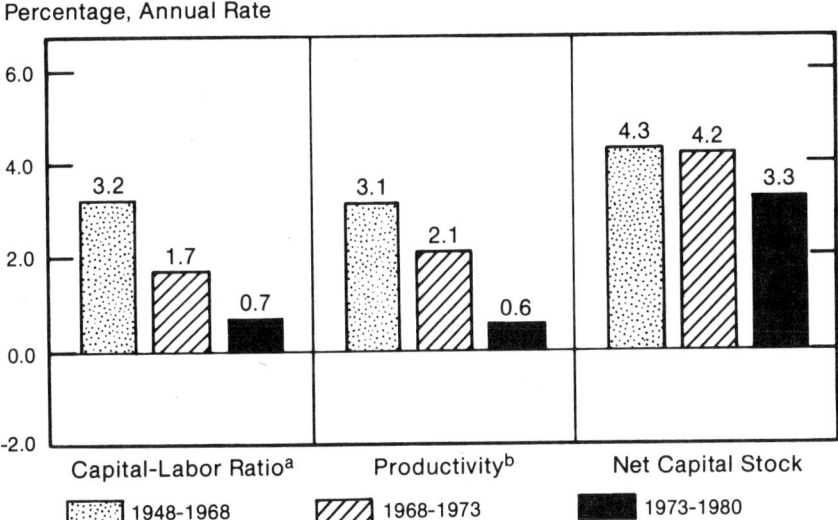

NOTES: [a] Real net capital stock (gross stock less replacement requirements and pollution abatement expenditures) in the private business sector divided by the civilian labor force (excluding government).
[b] Output per hour of all persons in the private business sector.

declined in 1979 and 1980, when cyclical developments combined with a declining trend in productivity growth.

Not only has productivity growth slowed from the early postwar pace, but it has lagged far behind the performance of the United States' leading trading partners. International productivity data for the manufacturing sector prepared by the U.S. Labor Department show a 1.7 percent rate of growth for the United States between 1973 and 1981 compared with 6.8 percent for Japan, 4.6 percent for France, 4.5 percent for Germany, 3.7 percent for Italy, and 2.2 percent for the United Kingdom. The United States and Canada, with a 1.4 percent rate of growth, were the clear-cut laggards in productivity performance among the leading industrialized nations.

The consequences of sluggish or nonexistent productivity growth are well known. A country's products first become less competitive and then uncompetitive in markets both at home and abroad, and pressures for protectionism rise. Productivity is the font from which improved standards of living flow. Declining productivity makes it difficult for living standards to rise, and when a decline is combined with *taxflation*—the combination of inflation and rising marginal tax rates—it becomes a fight just to hold on to existing standards. The result is often social tension, divisiveness, and demoralization.

The causes of the slowdown in growth of productivity can be examined at two levels: (1) the more or less direct causative factors, for example, the rates of capital formation and technological advance; and (2) government economic policy and the set of incentives that determine rates of capital formation and technological change.

Foremost among the factors directly affecting productivity growth is the rate at which the nation's stock of plant and equipment per worker increases. Slow capital growth means not only that less capital is available for each worker, but also that the newest technology is incorporated less rapidly into the production process.

The decline in growth of the capital-labor ratio can be traced not only to the well-publicized speedup in growth of the labor force, but also to the less well-known slowdown in the rate of capital formation. That slowdown occurred even though the ratio of gross business fixed investment to GNP has been creeping upward over the years—a statistic often cited by defenders of past policies. The measure of gross investment is misleading, however, because an increasing share consists of capital replacement. The composition of capital spending has shifted over the years to shorter-lived assets, which depreciate at a faster rate.

The gross investment measure also reflects a larger volume of capital being depreciated. The share of *net* real investment in overall activity has trended downward, and a portion of that net investment has been directed at meeting federally mandated environmental standards. Annual growth of real productive capital stock averaged only 3.3 percent over the 1973–1980 period, one percentage point less than earlier in the postwar period.

The decline in productivity is not unrelated to economic policy. "Demand management," which manipulated taxes and expenditures in order to move the economy toward target levels of spending, took the supply-side of the economy for granted.

By focusing on demand, policymakers overlooked the rising disincentives to produce additional income. The combination of inflation and a progressive income tax pushed potential savers into higher tax brackets and reduced incentives to save. A median-income family of four faced a federal marginal tax rate on personal income of 17 percent in 1965. By 1981, the rate was 24 percent—a 41 percent increase in the tax rate on additions to the family's income. If Social Security taxes and state income taxes are included, the median-income family is in the 40 percent bracket or higher. A family with twice the median income saw its federal marginal tax rate nearly double, rising from 22 percent in 1965 to 43 percent in 1981. The sharp upward rise in marginal tax rates had an adverse effect on saving because income from saving and investment is added to wage and salary income and is automatically taxed at the taxpayer's top rate.

The adverse effect on saving was compounded by government-imposed ceilings on interest rates. Many households could obtain only negative real aftertax rates of return on their savings; that is, they got less than the inflation rate. The personal saving rate averaged only 6.1 percent between 1976 and 1980—one of the worst five-year periods of the postwar era and substantially below the 7.8 percent average from 1966 to 1975. This decline reduced funds available to the capital market by $130 billion over those five years.

Rising marginal tax rates also undermined work attitudes and the incentive to invest in human capital by upgrading skills because the aftertax rewards for extra effort were low. The results were a rise in absenteeism, growing unwillingness to accept overtime work, and a decline in the effectiveness with which the existing capital stock was utilized. In a hearing before the Joint Economic Committee of Congress on May 21, 1980, Representative Bud Brown, a Republican from Ohio, took issue with the Keynesians' claim that tax rates do not significantly affect work attitudes among full-time employees. During a recent, six-month-long strike at International Harvester in Ohio, one of the issues had been whether the company could assign overtime and expect its employees to show up for work. The employees did not want overtime because it pushed them into higher tax brackets and was not worth the additional effort. Brown said he knew tax rates affected employees' work attitudes because "I have had them explain this issue to me on a very personal basis in short Anglo-Saxon expressions."

Business saving was also impaired. The combination of inflation and the tax depreciation law caused the cost of replacing the plant, equipment, and inventories used up in production to be understated. In the nonfinancial corporate sector, the replacement values of inventories and fixed assets were understated by $262 billion over the 1976–1980 period. This reduction in business saving, together with the decline in personal saving, reduced funds available to the capital market by an amount larger than the accumulated federal budget deficits over the five-year period. The decline in saving is one way in which taxation crowds out investment.

Understating depreciation overstated corporate profits, raising the effective corporate tax rate above the statutory rate. When book depreciation allowances are adjusted to a replacement cost basis, corporate profits have been taxed at a higher rate than the statutory rate for more than a decade, averaging 56 percent in the 1970s and reaching 77 percent in 1974 (see Table 4.1).

The "stop-go" demand management policies during the 1970s created additional uncertainty. No one knew for sure when the policy of expanding demand would give way to one of contracting demand, or vice versa. This additional element of uncertainty compounded the difficulties of planning, thus raising the "hurdle rate of return" that must be met before new investment commitments are made. All these factors, along with excessive government regulation and inflationary money growth, combined to reduce the rate of private capital formation, to curb business investment in research and development, and to direct resources to nonproductive purposes or into the underground economy. The overall result was a marked deterioration in our productivity performance (see Figure 4.1).

The tax system together with inflation encouraged the accumulation of debt instead of equity. Many people found that the only way to "save" at all was to go into debt and rely on taxflation to push up the value of their homes and depreciate the value of their mortgages. Businesses were equally encouraged by the tax system into becoming debt

Table 4.1

Effective Corporate Tax Rates
(percentage)

Year	Rate	Year	Rate
1960	54.1	1970	58.4
1961	53.4	1971	53.6
1962	47.0	1972	50.4
1963	46.2	1973	55.9
1964	43.3	1974	76.8
1965	42.0	1975	53.9
1966	43.3	1976	53.6
1967	43.3	1977	49.7
1968	49.3	1978	50.9
1969	53.8	1979	56.4
		1980	58.6

NOTE: Nonfinancial corporate profits tax liabilities as percentage of corporate profits with inventory valuation adjustment and depreciation of fixed assets adjusted to replacement costs at double-declining balance over 75 percent of Bulletin F service lives.

junkies. Their depreciation allowances were confiscated by taxflation, which reduced their cash flow and curtailed internal financing. Since payments to equity must be made from taxable income but debt service is tax deductible, business became increasingly debt dependent.

Until recently, the United States was unquestionably the world's richest nation. But the 1981 *World Bank Atlas* (published in early 1982) ranked the United States ninth in terms of per capita income, a fall of three places from the previous year's report. There are problems with the conventional measures of international per capita income comparisons, and it is probably not true that the United States is only number nine on the list of richest nations. Nevertheless, the World Bank report challenges the perception of Americans as the people of plenty.

If there is decline, it is not irreversible. Economic performance is affected by policy. Pessimists argue that there is no evidence that supply-side economics can do any better than the Keynesian policies that led the economy into decline. Actually, there is strong evidence in behalf of supply-side economics. The Mellon tax cuts of the 1920s, named after Treasury Secretary Andrew Mellon, produced a noninflationary economic boom. Tax revenues increased, particularly from the rich, and Mellon was able to pay off 36 percent of the national debt during the 1920s.[1]

Closer to our time were the Kennedy tax cuts. The economic boom that resulted from them has been misinterpreted by Keynesian economists as a consumption-led expansion caused by higher spending. In actual fact, after the tax cut went into effect, people spent a *smaller* percentage of their income. Figure 4.2 relates consumer spending to disposable income. The dotted line shows the path consumer spending would have taken if people had continued consuming the same percentage of their incomes after the tax cut as before. The solid line shows actual consumption expenditures. By 1967 consumption was at least $17.5 billion below the previous trend—a sum larger than the size of the personal income tax cut (measured in constant dollars).

If consumers were spending a smaller percentage of their income, they had to be saving a larger share. And, indeed, the empirical record shows that personal saving rose sharply. Figure 4.3 shows the behavior of personal saving and the saving rate. There was a marked increase in the real volume of personal saving following the tax cut, and the saving rate, which had been declining during the early 1960s, rose sharply. It remained high for a decade until rising marginal tax rates pushed it down.

Table 4.2 shows an estimate of the impact of the Kennedy tax cut

Figure 4.2

Real Consumer Expenditures: Actual Compared with Predicted Values from a Keynesian Consumption Function

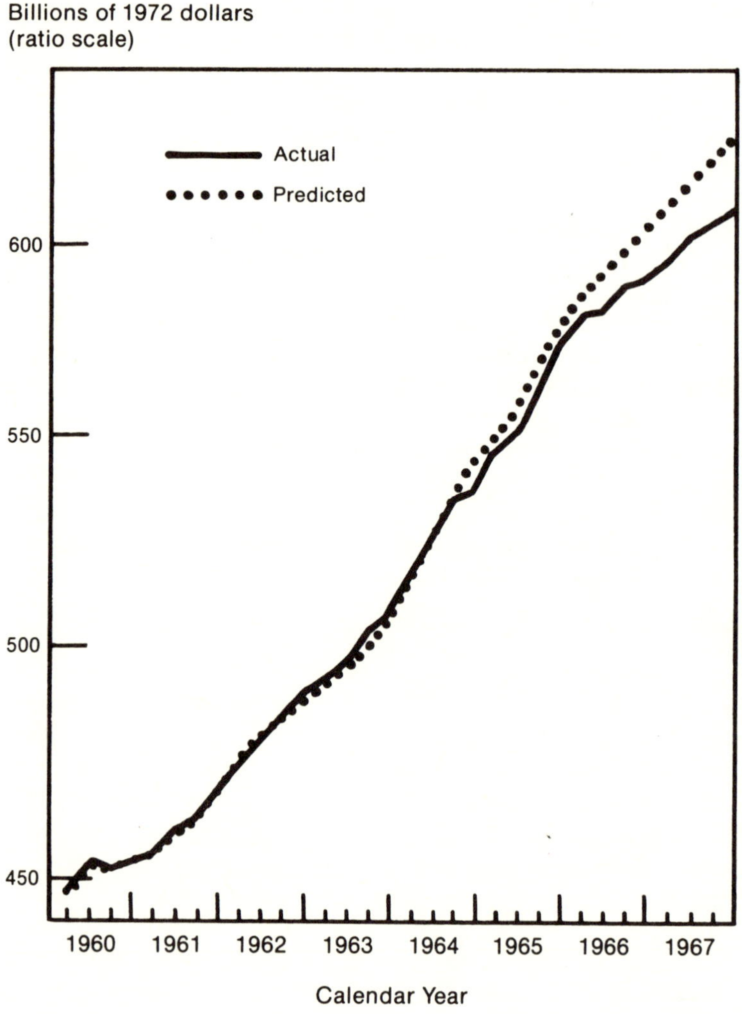

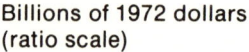

Figure 4.3
Personal Saving Before and After Kennedy Tax Cuts

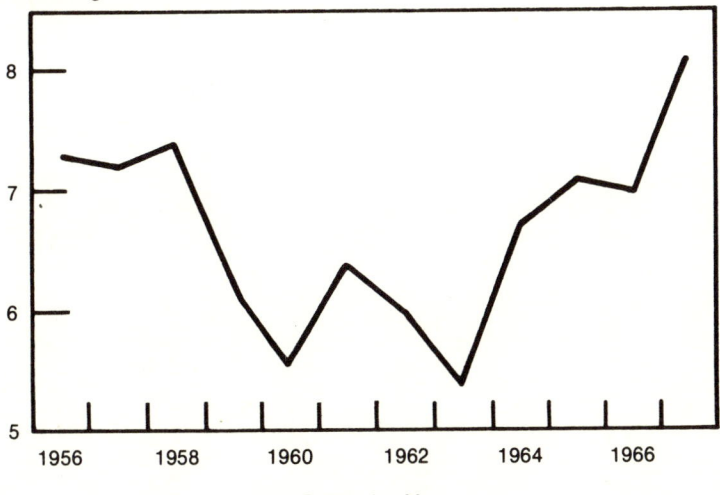

Table 4.2

Gains Above Trend in Real Personal Saving Following the 1964 Tax Cut

Year	Trend Real Disposable Income Without Tax Cut[a]	Trend Real Personal Saving Without Tax Cut[b]	Actual Real Personal Saving	Gain over Trend in Real Personal Saving with Tax Cut[c]	Gain in Real Personal Saving as Percentage of Tax Cut[d]
	(billions of 1972 dollars)				(percentage)
1964	$559.1	$32.4	$39.0	$ 6.6	74
1965	576.4	33.4	43.6	10.2	72
1966	594.3	34.5	45.3	10.8	72
1967	612.7	35.5	54.5	19.0	121

NOTES: [a]Values of real disposable income that would have developed had the trend of 1959 to 1963 been maintained.
[b]The real personal saving that would have been associated with that income path had households maintained the 5.8 percent saving rate of the 1960–1963 period.
[c]The difference between actual real personal saving and the calculated values of the pre-tax cut trend (second column).
[d]The ratio of the gain in saving above trend to the real value of the personal tax cut. The saving gain in the years 1964–1966 was about three-fourths of the tax cut, while the increment to saving in 1967 exceeded the value of the tax reduction by 21 percent.

on personal saving. In 1964 real personal saving rose $6.6 billion above the trend growth prior to the tax cut. The gain in saving was 74 percent of the size of the tax cut. In the next two years saving increased $10.2 and $10.8 billion above the previous trend, a gain equal to 72 percent of the tax cut. In 1967 saving was $19 billion above the previous trend—a gain equal to 121 percent of the size of the tax cut.

The rise in saving, by releasing real resources from consumption, assisted a rapid growth of business investment. In real terms, capital spending (for both the expansion of the capital stock of the economy and the replacement of worn-out capital stock) had grown at an annual rate of 3.5 percent during the 1950s and the early 1960s through 1962. During the remainder of the 1960s, real capital spending rose over twice as fast, increasing 7.2 percent annually; the rate of growth from 1963 through 1966 was especially rapid. While growth was high in the corporate sector, small-business investment posted the greatest acceleration.

The acceleration in investment greatly enhanced the economy's ability to produce. The net stock of capital had grown by 3.8 percent annually between 1949 and 1963, but with the tax cuts it rose to 5.5 percent for the remainder of the 1960s. Keynesians claim that the investment boom resulted from the investment tax credit, but the sharp rise in investment could not have taken place if consumers had not released resources from consumption by saving a larger share of their incomes.

The saving response makes clear that had the budget deficit widened as a result of the tax rate reduction, the larger saving pool would have financed it. As it turned out, the federal budget moved close to balance in 1965. It was only after the expansion of federal expenditures to pay for the Vietnam war and the Great Society programs that the budget moved into deficit. Figure 4.4 shows why the budget position was favorable in spite of—or rather because of—the tax cut. In real terms federal revenues increased sharply and far outdistanced the trend growth in revenues.

In testimony before the Joint Economic Committee of Congress on February 7, 1977, Walter Heller, chairman of the Council of Economic Advisers under President Kennedy, made these same points, though arguing from the demand side. He told the committee that the 1964 tax cut

> was the major factor that led to our running a $3 billion surplus by the middle of 1965 before escalation in Vietnam struck us. It was a $12 billion tax cut which would be about $33 or $34 billion in today's terms, and within one year the revenues into the

federal Treasury were already above what they had been before the tax cut.

He concluded: "Did it pay for itself in increased revenues? I think the evidence is very strong that it did."

Figure 4.4

Real Federal Receipts in the Kennedy Tax-Cut Years

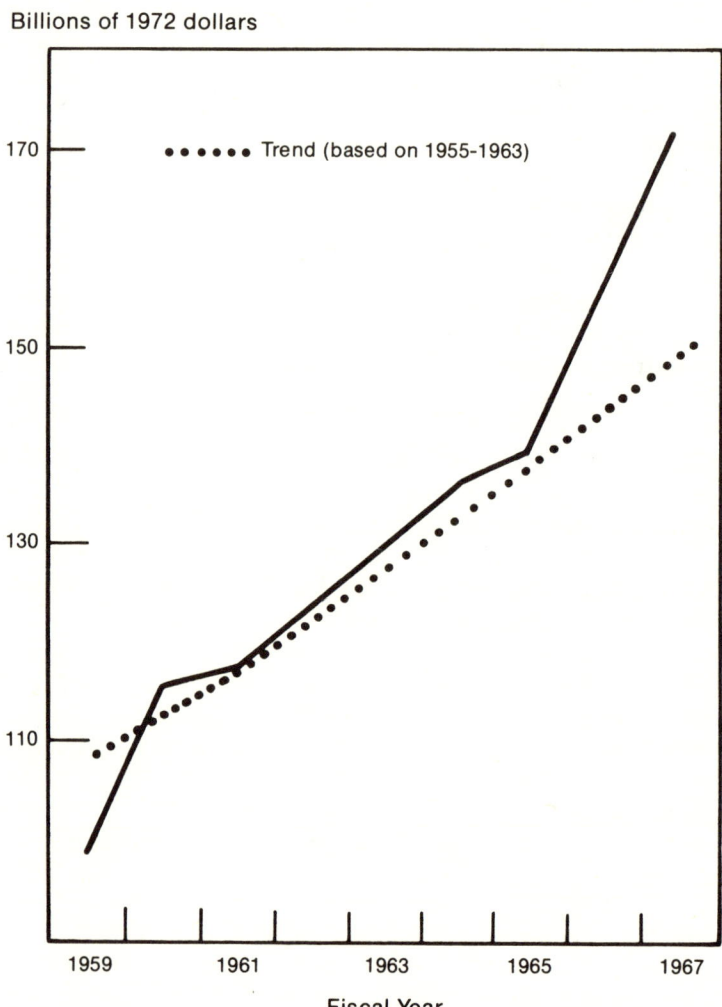

Keynesians credit the 1964 tax cut with raising GNP by $25 billion by mid-1965 and by $30 billion by the end of the year. Yet, one Keynesian, Edward Denison of the Brookings Institution, estimated the gap between actual and potential GNP to be only $12 billion—the size of the Kennedy tax cut. Obviously, a $12 billion gap does not leave enough room for a $30 billion expansion based on increased demand and unused capacity. Denison is an expert at estimating these gaps. If his estimate is a ball-park figure, the substantial expansion that followed the Kennedy tax cut had to be based on a supply-side response to the higher aftertax rates of return to productive activities.

The Keynesian advisers to President Kennedy wanted to stimulate the economy to its full potential. They chose a policy that they thought would stimulate consumer spending, and the conventional wisdom today still holds that the resulting boom was a consumption-led expansion. However, the evidence shows that what the policymakers really got was a burst of saving and investment activity that spurred the economy beyond fuller utilization of existing resources to faster growth of the ability to produce. Far from being a consumption-led expansion, real consumer spending actually declined as a percentage of income. Saving, investment, and tax revenues rose strongly. As Stanford economics professor Paul Evans has said, "the critics who assert that there is not a shred of evidence [for supply-side economics] just have not looked for it."[2]

Higher real economic growth is needed more today than at any other time in post–World War II history. In just twenty years, federal transfer payments have nearly doubled as a share of total federal outlays, rising from 27.3 percent in 1963 to an estimated 48.7 percent in 1983. The growth of transfer payments has changed the face of our economic institutions and brought us to a policy watershed. Of the three choices facing society—to default on future transfer payments, to confiscate still more from producers, or to encourage economic growth in the private sector while restraining the growth of entitlements—only the last holds out the hope of rising standards of living in the future.

Since its inception, the United States has been known as the land of liberty. It has attracted and absorbed into the stream of progress wave after wave of penniless immigrants because it provided the opportunity to work, accumulate, and advance. Immigrant factory workers saw their children become professionals without the benefit of government welfare and income-support programs.

The United States became an economic miracle because of the opportunities people found in a free economy. The American free enterprise system works by allowing individuals to make the decisions that affect their own lives. It is these myriad decisions, made every day of the year, that have produced the economic growth, technological innovation, and rising standards of living that have made America famous. As these decisions become inhibited by bureaucracy and red tape, and as their outcome becomes less certain because of the gradual erosion of private property rights, the efficiency of our economy declines.

In the United States the momentum toward a government economy is proving difficult to change despite a determined president. Ronald Reagan was elected by an overwhelming majority of Americans after campaigning on a platform of lower taxes and spending. Nonetheless, according to the administration's 1984 budget, taxes will average 19.2 percent of GNP for fiscal years 1983–1986, higher than the 18.6 percent average for the 1960s and the 18.9 percent average for the 1970s, although down from the 1981 peacetime peak of 20.9 percent. Spending is exploding as a percentage of GNP, rising from an average of 20.8 percent during the 1970s to 22.9 percent in 1981 to a projected 25 percent in 1983.

In the industrial democracies, government has gradually assumed a greater responsibility for people, and as a result people are losing the opportunity and the inclination to take responsibility for themselves. As more people come to depend on the state for their income, political activity crowds out productive activity and the dynamics of society change. To quote former Treasury secretary William E. Simon, government suffers from the illusion that it "can substitute for the billions and trillions of decisions that go on in a free market."[3]

The governments of the United States and other industrialized democracies cannot continue to promise future benefits independently of economic growth, and they cannot provide economic growth by curtailing the opportunities that reside in self-reliance. A successful society is not one that achieves the maximum in income redistribution, but one that allows people to achieve financial independence on their own. Financial independence does not come easily, and governments impatient to redistribute income have tended to implement policies that retard rather than encourage the progress of individuals.

Economic and political liberty are inextricably linked and are requisites for prosperity. This relationship is most evident in communist countries, where both economic and political liberty are absent, along with prosperity. To "solve" problems by expanding government crowds out both liberty and prosperity. Supply-side economics recognizes these critical links and encourages the incentives that spur economic achievements.

It was not so long ago that Alexis de Tocqueville warned the fledgling United States, and other democracies to come, that pressures for unbridled equality would eventually threaten liberty. Equality of opportunity benefited the millions of penniless immigrants to the United States and their children, just as it enriched society as a whole. But the United States would never have become a leader if equality had not been tempered with a generous dose of merit and individual liberty. People must be allowed to succeed on their own merit. When equality crowds out liberty, society devours itself. Without free economic institutions, merit and vision have no opportunities, and humanity's natural inclination to truck, barter, and trade is confined to an illegal existence. The growth of underground economies is clear evidence that governments have already infringed the property rights of labor and capital more than the market will bear. Supply-side economics restores incentives to economic policy and redresses the imbalance that has developed between the individual's just rewards and the demands of the state. And it provides the opportunity for countries that have improvidently built up the burden of government to produce their way out of their difficulties.

Notes

1. See Bruce Bartlett, *Reaganomics* (Westport, Conn.: Arlington House, 1981), p. 103.
2. See Paul Evans, "Kemp-Roth and Saving," *Weekly Letter* (Federal Reserve Bank of San Francisco), May 8, 1981, p. 3.
3. William E. Simon, *A Time for Truth* (New York: Reader's Digest Press, 1978), pp. 34–35.

5
Social Security Reform: A Mature System in an Aging Society

Rita Ricardo-Campbell

The U.S. Social Security system is nearly fifty years old. It is mature in the sense that everyone who now retires at the age of 62 or later has paid, if work has been in covered employment, Social Security taxes all of his or her working life. It is also mature because about 95 percent of all jobs are covered today. The major exclusions are federal workers who are not newly hired and some state and local government employees and workers in nonprofit institutions who have not elected coverage. Over thirty years ago, in 1950, the coverage of farm and domestic workers resulted in about 90 percent coverage of the private sector occupations.

The gradual extension over occupations has added slightly to the size of the total intergenerational transfer, from young to old. In a mature system the size of commitments for future benefits should be approaching a balance with the individual and matching payroll taxes paid and interest forgone. This usually takes place 40 to 45 years after coverage begins. Increasingly, workers are retiring at age 62, and many do not enter the labor force until after they graduate from college. The full working through of the coverage additions in 1950 has added to the financial problems of the 1980s.

The additional coverage of newly hired federal workers in 1983 will not have a similar effect because 80 percent of all retired federal employees are already drawing a Social Security benefit and also because this uniquely slow phase-in is so gradual that no one future year is especially hurt by new financial commitments.

The Social Security program absorbs about one-fourth of the U.S. budget, but the payments are made to only about 16 percent of the U.S. population. It clearly transfers income from young to old and not necessarily from rich to poor. The aged are no poorer than other age groups. The after-tax, per capita average income of persons 65 years and older is greater than the after-tax, per capita average income of persons under 65 years. Young heads of households do not own their homes free of mortgage and do not have investments in household goods—cars, refrigerators, washing machines, and dryers. Seventy percent of the aged own their own homes with 80 percent of these owning them free of mortgage. Young workers are, on the average, borrowers not lenders. In 1980, 66 percent of all aged reported income from assets, and this income represented 22 percent of their aggregate income. Concomitant with the rise in unearned income to the aged is the decline of their participation in the labor force. In 1980, their incomes from earnings were only 19 percent of their aggregate incomes.

A mature social security system ideally should not have an independent effect on the demographic and economic factors that underlie its stability. The U.S. system does affect both demographic and economic trends. The U.S. Social Security system probably encourages divorce because, since 1977, it has awarded sizable spousal benefits after ten years of marriage. The 1983 legislation taxes half the benefit of retired individuals with $25,000 adjusted gross income including their Social Security benefit, but taxes married couples similarly, beginning at $32,000. Because these limits are not indexed, by year 2020 these new taxes will be paid by, depending on inflation, half of all aged beneficiaries. Couples with over $32,000 adjusted gross incomes have an incentive for divorce if they can adjust their income flows, and younger working wives with retired husbands have an incentive to divorce or, alternatively, to leave the labor force.

Other demographic and economic effects are more pervasive. Because the benefits are indexed to the cost of living, the system helps feed inflation. Higher inflation means that more married women work. If they work, they have fewer children and the demographic tax base shrinks. Thus, countries with such schemes are entering a downward spiral of economic growth. Benefits indexed to the cost of living contribute to budget deficits and higher taxes. As populations age, taxes per capita increase and/or benefits are contained below previously anticipated levels. Fewer dependent children partially offset more dependent older persons. Although in the immediate period there are more resources per capita, the downward spiral of the population decline means eventual societal extinction. West Germany has a completed birthrate of 1.4 children per woman. Demographer Mikhail Bernstam estimates that in 200 years, all things being equal, West Germany will be extinct.

A mature social security system should ideally be self-supporting through recessions and in periods of potential imbalance because of demographic changes created by the system. Financial stability does not characterize the U.S. system, even after the 1983 legislation.

Without that legislation, the Old-Age and Survivors Insurance (OASI) trust fund would have been out of money in July 1983. Moreover, for the first time, the other two trust funds from which it has borrowed in the past, the Disability and the Medicare, Part A, Hospital Insurance funds, were both too low to tide OASI over much beyond mid-1984. In the popular literature, Social Security is usually used to cover only the old age and survivor's benefits (OASI) and sometimes also the permanent disability benefit (OASDI). Viewed as the latter, there are two funds, one that acts to pay out pensions and a form of term life insurance benefits and one that pays benefits to permanently disabled individuals. It is these two funds, the combined OASI and DI funds, that, in every year after 1974, have paid out more than they have received.

The 1983 Amendments

The 1983 legislation found major sources of new funds for OASI in the 1980s from what might be called "creative accounting," backdoor general revenue financing, a six-month delay in the cost-of-living increase in the benefits of already covered workers, new taxes paid by newly covered workers, and an increase in the taxes paid by already covered workers. The new tax on half the benefits of higher-income persons has a relatively low short-run yield, but its long-run yield is high; about one-third of the long-run deficit of 1.82 percent of covered payroll estimated by the 1982–83 National Commission on Social Security Reform (hereafter, the Reform Commission). The long-run tax yield is double the long-run gain from the six-month delay in the cost-of-living adjustment (COLA). The expansion of coverage over new federal employees and the removal of opting-out by nonprofit organizations was anticipated to raise only about 0.3 percent of long-run payroll. Thus, 0.58 to 0.85 percent of the 1980s deficit was to be selected from alternative methods.[1] The 1983 act is estimated to raise $166.2 billion during the 1980s. There were several inexpensive items that were added to costs in order to make entitlement equal for men and women. For example, divorced or disabled widows and dependent widowers who are beneficiaries and remarry after age 60 remain eligible for a survivor's benefit based on their deceased ex-spouse's primary earned benefit. The change was made to bring the statutory law in accord with judicial rulings that men are equally entitled to the same benefits as women.

It was estimated that OASI would need a total of nearly $200 billion during the 1980s in order to meet payments of the benefits. The 1983 legislation is expected to raise $160–170 billion under the probable best of circumstances. Thus, there is a standby provision to index benefits by the lower of the rise in the consumer price index (CPI) or a wage index, triggered during the period 1985–1988 if the trust fund falls below 15 percent of the annual payout. After 1988, the trigger is 20 percent. The 1983 legislative provisions that postpone the entitlement age for the full benefit affect only the long-run financial status of the trust funds and are discussed in a separate section of this essay.

Social Security Administration Projections

Once the system gets through the 1980s, and any recession would place this in doubt, the Social Security Administration (SSA) states that for the next 35 years, the OASDI funds will receive in taxes and interest more than they pay out. Deficits are projected for each year after 2020 by the SSA's actuaries, using Intermediate II-B assumptions of the 1983 Trustees' Report. The assumptions behind their estimates are discussed in depth later in this essay. They estimate only a 0.33 percent of long-run payroll balance in the OASI fund for the period 2008–2032, nearly fifty years into the future. This is a precarious situation because projections of economic trends for even 25 years into the future are uncertain. In the period 2005–2010, when the baby boom generation begins to retire, the size of the age cohorts that enter the labor force will be lower, reflecting the declining fertility rates of the late 1960s and subsequent years.

The long-run revenues and costs of Social Security are usually expressed as percentages of the covered payrolls. This is because the system is financed by a 6.7 percent tax of the employee's wages up to an annual base of $35,700 and 6.7 percent paid by the employer on the matching payroll (in 1983). The estimated, long-run deficit just prior to the 1983 legislation was 2.1 percent of long-run covered payroll.

In Washington, D.C., it was the new estimate of a long-run, overall, 75-year projection of a *precise* balance of revenues against expenditures—0.0 percent of payroll for OASDI—that was being touted early in June 1983. This was somewhat revised to plus 0.02 percent in the printed 1983 Trustees' Report. Although I have my doubts about any 75-year projection being precise to the second decimal point, it is obviously important to discuss the assumptions by which this more or less happy circumstance of a near "balance" is reached. A trust fund with a 0.0 percent balance has no reserve money to weather economic adversity or unperceived demographic changes.

Even with the passage of the 1983 Social Security Reform legislation, I believe that the trust funds of Social Security will not be in balance at the end of the next 25 years; some persons estimate an imbalance even as early as 1988. The latter date is clearly accurate if the Hospital Insurance fund, or Part A of Medicare, is included as part of Social Security. This is because prospective Diagnosis Related Groups (DRGs) payments will not contain hospital costs. At most, this approach is expected to save $11 billion over fiscal years 1983–1987. No other federal legislation to contain hospital costs under Medicare had passed by mid-1983, although the Reagan administration has proposed three other major reforms. The administration might, however, also use the stricter Tax Equity and Fiscal Responsibility Act of 1982 (TEFRA) provisions on top of DRGs, and this would result in substantial savings.

The 1983 Trustees' Hospital Insurance Trust Fund Report estimates that costs will exceed revenues in every year through 2005 with an average deficit (Intermediate II-B) for the 25-year period 1983–2007 of −1.24 percent of payroll.

The SSA had estimated (February 18, 1982) that over the first 25-year period, 1983–2007, a 0.58 percent of covered payroll OASDI surplus; for the second 25-year period, 2008–2032, an OASDI −1.89 percent of payroll deficit; and in the third 25-year period, 2033–2057, a −4.96 percent of payroll deficit. The 1983 legislation, SSA claims, wipes out the estimated deficit for the first 50 years. Although the last 25-year deficit is claimed to be halved, a deficit of −1.01 percent is estimated to persist from 2033–2057. Prior to the legislation, SSA's

1983 estimate for the usually computed whole 75 years, was a deficit of –2.09 percent of covered payroll; after the legislation, a surplus of 0.02 percent. The 1982–83 Reform Commission used a –1.82 percent deficit for its deliberations. The long-run estimates were changed as early as February 1983 because SSA changed its assumptions that lie behind its mid-range Intermediate II-B estimates. The major changes were a decrease from 2.1 to 2.0 completed or ultimate births per woman, an increase in the assumed long-term unemployment rate from 5.0 to 5.5 percent, and, for the first time, a factor for the negative impact of withdrawals.

I agree with those who argue that it is impossible to project precisely these kinds of data far into the future. However, because such projections are made and used by the federal government, it behooves interested parties to check on the probability of any such existing estimates. A "Sensitivity Analysis of Assumptions . . ." behind the II-B Intermediate estimates was made in memorandum number 7 to the Reform Commission (March 15, 1982) by Robert J. Myers, who had been the system's actuary for over 30 years. In this analysis, one question addressed was "How much better would the Alternative II-B (Intermediate) assumptions of the 1981 Trustees' Report have to be in order to have actuarial balance during the third 25-year period?" Part of the answer was "an ultimate fertility rate of 3.2 births per woman (per lifetime) would be necessary, keeping all other assumptions unchanged." The same question was asked in respect to the other key assumptions. Manipulating the assumptions, rather than seeking the scientific basis of assumptions through presentation of data, does not seem professional.

I question whether the SSA Intermediate II-B assumptions are still too optimistic and note that SSA actuaries are fully aware that by slightly changing the assumptions they can "eliminate" a projected deficit.

Although the projected SSA deficits, made prior to the 1983 legislation, were not as large as those computed by actuary Geoffrey Calvert and myself in 1981, they are important for two reasons. It was the first time that SSA had attempted to project the hospital trust fund for Medicare for any period longer than 25 years. Second, the estimates illustrate what Calvert and I are most disturbed about, and that is the deficit increases with the years, culminating in our estimates made before the 1983 legislation, at –8.94 percent of payroll during the last, or third, 25-year period, nearly double SSA's estimates. The SSA's estimates after the 1983 legislation more than halved their earlier estimates, but still found a substantial deficit in the third 25-year period.

The Assumptions Behind the Estimates

In 1975, in my dissent to the Report of the Quadrennial (1974) Advisory Council on Social Security, I protested that there was only one set of assumptions underlying the estimates of the financial status of Social Security over the next 75 years. In response to this criticism, not only three, "low, medium, and high," but four sets—optimistic, Intermediate II-A, Intermediate II-B (the latter slightly more pessimistic), and pessimistic—are now developed, with the mid-range Intermediate II-B accepted as "probable" by most government officials and bodies. There is also a "worst possible case" estimate for the near future. In Table 5.1, the long-run level assumptions (1981–2055), used by the Reform Commission, are the same as in the 1981 Trustees' Report. The table has, side-by-side, the author's assumptions that were developed in 1981 with Geoffrey N. Calvert,[2] and SSA's 1981 and 1983 assumptions, before and after the legislation.

Fertility Rate

Calvert's and my arguments for our more pessimistic assumptions are stronger today than in 1981. The lowest ultimate fertility rate reached after a secular 200-year decline was 1.738 births in 1976. The rate subsequently has been slowly rising. Although SSA has reduced its birthrate assumption from 2.1 average births over a woman's lifetime to 2.0, the Census Bureau uses an intermediate assumption of 1.9 births. I find it puzzling that SSA now places the optimistic rate at 2.3, both intermediate rates at 2.0, and the pessimistic rate as low as 1.6. These assumptions give the nonactuary little help in estimating the effect of the more probable rates of either 1.9 or 1.85.

There has been a recent, slight upward blip in the total fertility rate because a higher proportion of better-educated women have postponed having a child until they were in their thirties. These women are now bearing their first child. The usual result of delayed births is that the total number of births per woman over a lifetime falls and, therefore, larger families tend to disappear. In 1979, 28 percent of white women at age 30 were childless, compared with only 14 percent in 1970.[3] However, the increase in births among nonwhite women and the recent large increase in the number of all women 30–34 years, reflecting the earlier baby boom, were sufficient to override the postponement of births by younger women. It is estimated that the number of women in the childbearing years will stop increasing and begin to stabilize in

Table 5.1
Long-run Level Assumptions

	1981		1983	
			Before	After
	SSA	Calvert/RRC	Legislation	
Total fertility rate (Average number of births over a woman's lifetime)	2.1	1.85	2.0	2.0
Mortality rate (annual improvement compared with 1900-1978 average)	0.5	0.75	36%	0.5[a]
Disability rate (annual increase compared with 1978-1980 average)	15%	15%	15%	15%[b]
Inflation	4%	5%	4%	4%
Real wage differential	1.5%	1%	1.5%	1.5%
Unemployment	5%	6%	5.5%	5.5%

[a]The base becomes 1900-1981.
[b]The base becomes 1980-1982.
SOURCES: 1981, SSA: *1981 Annual Report of the Board of Trustees of the Federal Old-Age and Survivors Insurance and Disability Insurance Trust Funds*, preprint copy (July 1981), pp. 29, 72, 73, 81.
1981, Calvert/RRC: Geoffrey N. Calvert, "What Really Lies Ahead?" (New York: Alexander & Alexander Services, 1981), n.p.
1983, Before: John A. Svahn, letter to Daniel Rostenkowski, February 18, 1983.
1983, After: *1983 Annual Report of the Board of Trustees of the Federal Old-Age and Survivors Insurance and Disability Trust Funds*, preprint copy (June 1983), pp. 38, 85, 86, 94.

about 1988. Even though in 1979, 20 percent of all births were to women 30 years and older; in 1960, 27 percent of all children had been born to this age group, illustrating the strength of the long-run (over 200 years) downward trend.[4]

Working women, on the average, bear fewer children than nonworking women. In 1960, only 38 percent of women worked for pay. In 1982, 53 percent of women 16 years and over worked, but 66 percent of women 20 through 44 years worked. In 1960, the percentage of younger women 25-34 years, the primary childbearing years, who were working was sharply less than among women 20-24 and 45-54 years. However, by 1980, labor force participation among women 25–34 years was equal to that for women 35–44 years.[5] Working women no longer routinely plan to quit work when they have a child.

The use of effective contraceptive methods to prevent births is likely to increase. Recent research indicates that the usual oral contraceptive drug protects women who do not smoke from heart disease and cancer and also osteoporosis (loss of calcium leading to the breaking of bones). There is even recent evidence that the estrogen component reduces the incidence and possibly the severity of rheumatoid arthritis, a disease to which women are especially at risk. Thus, the slight decline in the use of oral contraceptives that occurred in the 1970s, in response to medical opinion that their use creates undesirable side effects, is expected to reverse and the rate of use even to increase. The oral contraceptive is a more reliable method of birth control than any other method except sterilization.

The percentage of married couples where one individual is surgically sterile rose from 16 percent in 1965 to 28 percent in 1976. The increase reflects primarily an increase of those sterilized for contraceptive purposes and may have been, in some part, a substitute for the oral contraceptive. "In 1976, one-half of all couples with three or more children, and one-third of those with two, were surgically sterile."[6] Large families are becoming extinct.

Nonsurgical infertility has also been increasing primarily among younger, ages 20–24, black couples and also among younger white couples. The reasons for this are not fully understood. The most often cited contributing cause is the increase in reported cases of gonorrhea and pelvic inflammation, the latter stemming from the use of intrauterine devices (IUD) to prevent pregnancy. Additionally, fewer females relative to males are being born in the United States than in earlier years. The decline in this ratio appears to correlate with the decline in birthrates. The fertility rates in many advanced countries of the world are lower than in the United States. Examples are 1.6 births per woman in Austria, Denmark, Finland, and the Netherlands; 1.5 in Switzerland; and 1.4 in West Germany (all 1979 data). Except for Ireland and New Zealand, countries with a larger rural component than the United States, I know of no country classified as "industrialized" that has a 2.1 or greater fertility rate. The weighted average for the European population of the USSR is 1.9.

There are some economists who believe that there is a cyclical relationship between the relative size of a birth cohort (all those in the same age group) and the fertility rate of the cohort. Large cohorts, such as that of the baby boom period after World War II, have fewer babies because they have to compete more intensely for jobs and a share of the national income. But their children will, because of their relative scarcity, fare better economically and thus will bear more children. This theory is supported by only one full cycle in the United States, and the cycle does not occur in all countries. I believe that other socioeconomic factors will override this economic, cyclical effect.

The Trustees' 1983 Report for the first time adjusts for immigration, estimated at 400,000 persons per year under its Intermediate II-B assumptions. The Spanish-surname and other recent immigrant groups have higher birthrates than the U.S. population as a whole; however, their numbers are small relative to the total U.S. population (232 million). Additionally, these newer groups will gradually adopt the attitudes of their new neighbors and co-workers, and their children, those of their schoolmates.

Mortality Rate

SSA's 1981 assumption that the continuing downward trend in mortality would level at one-half the average rate of decrease, 1900–1978 and their February 1983 assumption at 36 percent seem astonishing.

The July 1983 Trustees' Report uses "about half the average rate of decline observed during 1900–1981" (p. 86). It is true that antibiotics were very instrumental in increasing life expectancy in the early period, but mortality rates, especially from cardiovascular disease, continue to decline sharply. New fields of research, such as recombinant DNA gene-splicing, and improvements in medical diagnostic technology, such as the sharp imaging of nuclear magnetic resonance machines, are just now opening up. These and other advances promise continuation of substantial increasing life expectancy. Moreover, it is life expectancy at age 65, not at birth that is the more relevant figure for social security systems. Recent data indicate that life expectancy at age 65 is increasing faster in the United States than life expectancy at birth. Thus, I continue to believe that *three-quarters*, not one-half or 36 percent, of the 1900–1978 average rate is the more plausible assumption.

Disability Rate

Because of the 1983 legislation, I revise my estimate that the rate of disability will level at a 15 percent increase over the high 1978–1980 average. The 1983 Trustees' Report uses 15 percent above the 1980–1982 experience, which is slightly lower than 15 percent above the 1978–1980 experience. However, the 1983 legislation gradually delays entitlement to the full Social Security benefit to age 67 by 2027. Disability rates are higher among older people. There will be a greater temptation for those who cannot obtain a retirement benefit to seek a disability benefit. However, there are offsetting factors that will delay the onset of disability: improvement in nutrition, advances in medical science, and disease prevention. I, therefore, increase the level disability rate to 20 percent above the 1978–1980 average.

Unemployment Rate

Additionally, although the Calvert–Ricardo-Campbell estimates "settled for 6 percent unemployment rate" rather than my preference of 6.5 percent, I return to the 6.5 percent (and even possibly 7 percent) as the more probable long-run level rate. The SSA increased its estimate after the 1983 amendments from a 5.0 to a 5.5 rate.

The increase in structural unemployment because of robotics and other technological change has pushed up the foreign trade imbalance, which increases unemployment. Two-worker families now outnumber one-worker families. It seems reasonable to expect that "seeking work" by an unemployed person receiving unemployment compensation may, on the average, be less intense in families where one paycheck is still being received. For these and other reasons, I concur with the observation in the 1983 *Report of the Council of Economic Advisers* that the 6.1 percent unemployment rate of 1978 is "close to most observers' estimates of full employment" (p. 31) and also that the inflation-threshold unemployment rate "probably lies between 6 and 7 percent" (p. 37).

I do not believe that the long-run unemployment rate will level at below the current full employment rate, but rather above it. Technological change will continue to occur, and entitlement programs such as Social Security that have indexed benefits help to create government deficits, inflationary pressure, and unstable employment.

Inflation and Real Wage

Although the 1982 inflation rate was less than 5 percent and the real wage differential rose by 2.0 percent, output fell. Others have stated "that an annual ultimate real wage assumption of 1.25 percent is much more realistic than SSA's 1.5 and is not inconsistent with the experience of the last thirty years. An annual growth of 1.25 percent in real wages over a period of 50 years will increase the purchasing power of workers by 86 percent, certainly not an overly pessimistic outlook."[7] My estimate of the long-run real wage differential at 1.0 percent rather than 1.5 percent remains defensible.

Usually SSA's estimates and those of the Trustees of the funds are identical. Because the estimates of the future financial status of the Social Security trust funds are very sensitive to economic projections and the long-run estimates especially sensitive to projected birth and mortality rates, some deviation in estimates by independent actuaries and economists would be expected. Because there are no deviations between SSA and the Trustees' estimates, the belief that the latter act as a separate, independent review of the financing of the system seems to be an illusion.

Ronald Reagan's Social Security Task Force 1980

Aware of the political forces involved and also seeking informed opinion about the Social Security system, Ronald Reagan, as candidate for the presidency, appointed a task force in the fall of 1980 with the statement that he regarded it "a sacred obligation to make certain that the integrity of this [Social Security] system is defended and that the benefits of those individuals on social security are protected" (September 22, 1980).

The final report of Ronald Reagan's 1980 Social Security Task Force has never been made public. Seven of the eleven members of that task force were, in contrast to the Reform Commission of 1982–83, academic economists. The commission had only one economist, its chairman. The task force stressed the restructuring of benefits, while the more politically oriented Reform Commission relied on tax increases, leaving the benefit structure intact.

The task force's recommendations were considered, after the election, to be politically too "hot" to release. However, it is interesting, now that legislation has been enacted, to compare the 1983 legislation with the task force's recommendations.

The Social Security Task Force considered that President-elect Reagan's statement quoted above was a mandate to make recommendations that would ensure the continuing payment of future Social Security benefits to all persons then receiving or soon to receive them. The task force recognized that there was no easy solution to the *short-run* imbalance of the OASI fund and that it would exist through most of the 1980s.

The task force recommended several actions, a surprising number of which were followed, although in a watered-down version. For example, the task force recommended that the president seek on a crisis basis "a special interim report (preferably within six months) on three questions: (1) how best to implement universal coverage, (2) how best to phase in later ages for entitlement to the full retirement benefit (now age 65) by the year 2000 or shortly thereafter, and (3) how best to phase out over a long period of time the secondary benefits of spouses in order to correct the current, inequitable treatment of two-worker families that, in practice, creates an inequity between married, working women and married, non-working women."

A special "Reform Commission" was appointed. The 1983 Congress enacted legislation dealing with the first two items. The task force had recommended, as a start toward universal coverage, that all new federal employees be covered under Social Security. They also had recommended that the entitlement age to benefits be increased, but there was no agreement on precisely how this should be implemented. The task force observed that "a 3 percent increase per year in the primary benefit for each year that persons continue to work after age 65 and do not draw a benefit will not have a great effect on retirement decisions." The 1983 legislation phases in, starting in 1990, an 8 percent increase for each year of delay in receiving a full benefit, for a maximum of five years. This could be a financial disaster, if individuals take advantage of this provision. The self-employed, who are likely to have relatively higher incomes, are those who have the greatest opportunity to continue working.

The task force had recommended "that all social security monthly cash benefits be indexed by the lower of the changes in the consumer price index (CPI) *or* a suitable wage index." The 1983 legislation made this a safeguard provision triggered when the OASI trust fund fell below 15 percent of annual payout during 1985–1988 and below 20 percent in subsequent years. President Reagan has been successful in making Social Security a nonissue for the 1984 campaign. It is not, however, clear within the context of the president's overall philosophy and legislative program that the 1983 legislation evolved in a manner consistent with the tax posture of the Reagan administration.

The 1983 Legislation and Retirement Age

The 1983 legislation improved on the Reform Commission's recommendations in several ways, but most important was the gradual delaying of entitlement to a full benefit to age 66 in 2009 and age 67 in 2027, and the reduction from 80 percent to 70 percent in 2027 of the full benefit at age 62. To what degree the new table of benefit amounts scheduled for 2027 reflects the actuarial data and to what degree it adds on inducements for persons to retire later than 62 years are not clear. At 62 years, a worker will receive 70 percent of the full benefit; 63 years, 75 percent; 64 years, 80 percent; 65 years, 86.7 percent; 66 years, 93.3 percent; 67 years, 100 percent; 68 years, 108 percent; and for each successive year (5 years maximum) of delayed receipt of benefits, an additional 8 percent.

By retaining the 86.7 percent and 93.3 percent of the current formula, albeit at different ages, the SSA missed the opportunity to simplify the percentages so that individuals might remember them more easily. When one is talking about 40 years hence, the exactitude of decimal points is superfluous. The varying intervals with an 8 percent return starting at age 67 contrast with the province of Quebec's recently adopted even 6 percent gradation from age 60 through 65, starting with 70 percent at age 60, then 76 percent at age 61, and so forth.

Even though lower benefit amounts may not affect many retirement decisions, they will reduce the payout total because the benefits are reduced. In 1980, only 20 percent of males 65 years and older were still working. This compares with nearly 40 percent in 1950. Only about 60 percent of males aged 60 to 64 are working today. During the 1970s, the trend toward early retirement among men increased. However, women retire earlier than men do.

The mere existence of any Social Security benefits at age 62 encourages early retirement. It will in the future be more costly to firms to retain older workers because employers can no longer exclude, under the amended 1982 Federal Age Discrimination in Employment Act, employees 65–69 years and their dependents from health insurance plans that cover younger workers. This means increases in health insurance premiums paid by companies. Where the plans do not cover part-time workers, older persons who work part-time also would not be covered. There will be a greater availability of part-time work and work-sharing for older workers to supplement OASI benefits by the 1990s, when workers will begin to be in short supply related to demand.

Because large companies have pension plans that shelter early retirees against the reduced benefit at age 62, it is probable that many companies will make up some or all of the reduction with increases in private pensions, and employees will continue to retire early. Overlooked is that the effective or usual age of retirement increasingly is age 62. Private pension plans encourage individuals to retire early. Many of the integrated direct-offset plans give a full pension at age 62 and then offset the pension at age 65 by a percentage of the employee's Social Security benefit. The 1983 legislation will probably increase the costs of private pension plans that partly shelter employees against this change in Social Security. The interface between private pensions and Social Security deserves more attention from the media than it gets.

Congress, unlike the Reform Commission, addressed in statesman-like fashion the long-run financial problems by gradually increasing the entitlement to a full benefit from 65 to 67. Congressman J. J. Pickle, a Democrat from Texas and chairman of the House Ways and Means Committee's Subcommittee on Social Security, led the fight for this important reform, passed in the House by a 228 to 202 vote. Although this measure will clearly save money, it will not save as much as would have the elimination of receipt of any retirement benefit prior to age 64. The amount of the early retirement benefit was somewhat reduced, but the decision to retire at different levels of the full benefit remains with the individual. That surviving spouses, living with the worker at time of death or divorce, receive a benefit at age 60 makes mandating a later entitlement age for workers at 64 years politically difficult. This is an inequity that the new legislation exacerbates.

If, as I expect, few persons will retire later as a result of the new economic inducements, Congress may, some years down the road, need to enact a gradually phased-in later entitlement to any retiree benefit before age 64. At such time, age 60 for survivors might also be reassessed. Older persons who have retired from one job, often after an extended vacation, seek new, less demanding jobs. The labor shortage beginning in the 1990s will encourage the latter.

There is the beginning of a revolutionary change of attitude toward work that is not recognized by the Social Security system. As older persons retain better health into later ages, many will prefer to work part-time rather than retire. Already many persons who retire seek less demanding and lesser paid work in new jobs, often in self-employment, after a lengthy vacation.

I recognize that any government program that promises benefits to persons when they reach a given age must give those persons early warning of future change, so that during those years when they are still working they can plan income flows for their own retirement. If there is a strong possibility that the Social Security benefits of today's younger workers will be lower in real terms than they anticipated, these individuals need time to change their saving habits. The spring 1983 budget estimates of the Office of Management and Budget (OMB) indicate that there would be an unanticipated $4.8 billion general revenue loss due to higher than anticipated sheltering of personal income under the new individual retirement accounts (IRAs) in that fiscal year alone. The increase in personal savings occurred even though no one over the age of 45 is affected by the 1983 legislation. Faith in the Social Security system has been shaken. Younger persons are saving not only for down payments on houses but also for their own old age.

The Japanese rate of savings is about 21 percent—more than three times the savings rate in the United States. Although there are several reasons for this large difference, one reason is the greater gap in Japan between the usual age of retirement at 55 from one's lifetime job and the first receipt of a government benefit at age 65. In the United States, the male retirement age peaks at age 62. In 1979, 73 percent of retired workers benefits initiated that year went to workers aged 62-64 years. Forty-six percent of the newly available benefits went to persons 62 years and only 25 percent to those who were 65 years.[8]

How the 1977 Social Security Amendments Affect Benefit Amounts

A "Dear Abby" letter published nationwide, Sunday, September 4, 1983, made clear to the public how changes in the benefit formula create new inequities. This short section explains why the 1977 changes were made and who are most adversely affected.

The 1977 Social Security amendments corrected the 1972 legislative error that permitted inflation to count twice in the computation of Social Security benefits. The old computation method counted both the increases in prices and the increases in workers' earnings that were also usually rising with the cost of living.

The 1977 revision, which is the current computation method, counts the increases in average indexed wages prior to age 62 and then indexes the derived benefit to the cost of living.

To make more gradual the transition from the old to the new method, a five-year "notch group," that is, persons who became age 62 during the years 1979-1983, is permitted to use a special formula that yields a benefit between the old and new (1977) computation methods. Because the 1977 revision does not apply to persons who reached age 62 prior to 1979, many persons who are retiring in 1983 at age 67 or later are receiving extraordinarily high benefits that reflect the double count of double-digit inflation prior to 1981 and the 1981 price rise over 1980 of 9.6 percent. Their benefits are high because they became 62 prior to 1979 and not because they worked until age 67 or later.

Persons retiring at age 65 in 1982 receive much lower benefit amounts than those who retired at age 65 in 1981. The unanticipated double-digit inflation makes the differences greater than initially projected. Even if those who became 62 after 1978 continue to work and retire after age 65, the difference will not be made up. Until 1990, each additional year worked adds only 3 percent to the benefit. Beginning in 1990, each additional year adds 8 percent. By 1990, those who were 62 in 1983 will be 69 years old.

The transitional provisions for persons who reach age 62, 1979 through 1983, and also retire then or very shortly thereafter yield somewhat higher benefits than the new method. These provisions help very little those who continue to work. Cost-of-living increases from 1979 (the year the amendments were first implemented) through the year the worker reaches age 61 are not permitted under the "notch" formula, nor are they under the new law. The CPI rose 12.7 percent in 1979 over 1978, 12.6 percent in 1980 over 1979, and 9.6 percent in 1981 over 1980. These increases are counted for those who were age 62 prior to 1979.

Dollars earned after workers reach age 62 cannot be used to compute their benefits in the manner permitted under the old law. Both the transition provisions and the 1977 amendments permit all persons to substitute higher earnings at age 62 and later for lower-earning years. The transition provisions appear to help only those who quit work at age 62. Most severely penalized are those who work beyond age 62, and especially those whose earnings usually peak in their later years. The 1977 amendments, by replacing actual earnings with average indexed earnings in the computation method, decreased benefits (compared to the old law) to those persons who increased their earnings faster than the average earner. Because of budget shortfalls and the sizable costs of phasing in more smoothly the 1977 benefit formula, new legislation to correct this inequity is not anticipated. The value of this exposition is that it illustrates the complexity of the system and some of its relatively unknown effects.

Women and Social Security

For many years I have argued that the fundamental problem of Social Security is that it taxes on the basis of the individual, but pays benefits on the basis of a family unit. Single persons and two-worker families are less favorably treated than one-worker families. ("Worker" is used throughout this paper to mean a "paid worker" or "earner.")

Although there may be some societal reasons to favor marrieds over singles and one-worker families over two-worker families, these reasons and the degree depend on value judgments.

The United States has a costly and generous retired spousal benefit equal to one-half the worker's earned benefit. Among the earnings-related programs worldwide, only Switzerland has as generous a benefit. The United States' surviving spousal benefit is the most generous in the world. It equals 100 percent of the worker's earned benefit. Most countries have a survivor's benefit equal to 60 percent or less of the worker's earned benefit.

Several countries have a two-tier system of benefits. Everyone who has proof of residence for a set number of years (40 years in Canada and Denmark) receives at a given age a low monthly sum (A) with earners receiving an additional wage-related pension amount (B). (This "A plus B" system that treats all individuals the same whether married or not is discussed in depth at the end of this essay.)

The numbers of nonmarried individuals and two-worker families in the United States are increasing, and one-worker families are decreasing. These numbers have political meaning. The economic status of married working women influences two votes: wife and husband. Politics influences Social Security policy more than financial analysis does.

Apparently at no time during the Reform Commission's discussions or in the staff memorandums was the connection made between the U.S. method of adding spouses' benefits and the degree of the subsequent financial imbalance. If a worker who is entitled to a private pension also elects a spousal benefit under a private plan, then the retired worker's pension is usually reduced. Currently under Social Security, surviving spouses receive at age 60 the 71.5 percent of the worker's benefit and continue to receive it even if they remarry. Originally this benefit was awarded for humanitarian reasons, not because it was "paid for." It is assumed that the spouse is dependent. In many cases, that is not true today. Most survivors receive insurance benefits, and some surviving spouses are working. Increasingly, women who have worked will have earned a private or government pension. Others, including housewives, are saving via the new IRAs for their own old age. For those who are poor, there are the 1974 Supplemental Security Income (SSI) benefits supported by general revenues.

The earliest age at which workers receive a Social Security benefit at retirement is 62, and then 80 percent of the full benefit. The 1983 legislation reduces that amount to 70 percent gradually in an attempt to encourage later retirement.

The 1983 legislation provides that divorced spouses who have been married ten years receive a retirement benefit even if the earner or previous spouse has not retired. Until 1972, a dependency test had to be met by divorced women. In 1977, the 20-years-of-marriage requirement was reduced to 10 years. The 1983 legislation liberalized entitlement to dependency benefits, but did nothing to make a two-worker family's combined benefits equal to a one-worker family's combined benefits, which are based on identical earnings.

Benefits paid to divorced spouses do not come under the family maximum cap of 175 percent of the primary benefit. Thus, 300 percent or more can be paid out on one worker's earnings record. Although one person is entitled to only one benefit, the trend is to pile up benefits based on high earners. Clearly, rewards from Social Security are greater for married workers with dependents than for the single individual who does not later acquire a spouse. It is also clear that under the present structure of benefits, a two-worker family earning precisely the same total amount as a one-worker family in covered employment, at the same ages and paying the same taxes, will receive benefits on retirement that average 17 percent less for the two-worker family than those for the one-worker family; their survivor's benefits will average 25 percent less. This largely unknown inequity has been labeled by a conservative academic economist in a 1983 book as "ferocious discrimination against working women."[9]

The U.S. system pays benefits to spouses, but no one who has worked for the required ten years can receive a spousal benefit plus his or her earner's benefit, but rather is entitled only to the higher benefit. Because women usually have lower average lifetime earnings than men, their earned benefits usually do not equal the 100 percent surviving spousal benefit, and sometimes not even half of the retired spouse's earned benefit. Most working women receive no more, and often less, than if they had never worked.

Because this gross inequity is not readily understood, there follows a simplified, *hypothetical* example.

A one-worker family has average, indexed monthly earnings of $200. Upon retirement the earner's benefit is 80 percent of the first $100 and 30 percent of the next $100, yielding $110. The spouse, assumed age 65, receives $55 (half of the primary benefit) and the total family benefit is $165.

An identically situated two-worker family, where each earns $100, has an $80 primary benefit for each worker, totaling a $160 benefit, or $5 less. Another, more typical but otherwise identically situated two-worker family is where one worker earns $140; the other $60. The family chooses between the higher of the two earned benefits and an earned plus the derivative benefit. The family, of course, chooses the higher: $140 (both earned benefits) and not the $138, where one is a derivative benefit. At first glance, the two-worker family believes that it has gained $2 monthly. But if only one worker had earned $200, the benefit, as indicated in the preceding paragraph, would have been $165, or a comparative loss to the two-worker family of $25 monthly.

The main body of the Reform Commission's report ignored this problem. None of the over sixty internal memorandums addressed directly how to give married working women some return on the OASI taxes that they pay above the very small return in the form of term life insurance. This has never been recognized as an inequity by Robert Myers, who had been the chief actuary for many years for the system and who was chosen, unwisely I believe, the executive director of the National Reform Commission. I say "unwisely" because Robert Myers is saturated with the dogma that underlies the existing system and the executive director's job is a full-time job, while most of the members of any such commission have a very part-time involvement because their primary working hours are devoted to other matters. It is the full-time head staff person who is responsible for the option papers. The staff head and the chairman of a commission usually set the agenda, and the latter has final responsibility for the selection of subjects about which staff memorandums are written. However, Myers, in addition to Robert Ball, a former Social Security commissioner and a member of the Reform Commission, were the only persons who fully understood this complex system, and they support the *status quo*.

Myers states in his "The Basis of the Social Security Program, Especially as It Affects Married Couples" (undated, mimeo., nine pages, 1980) that there is no discrimination by sex implied in the distinction made between one-worker and two-worker families; it just happens to work out that way. "The present basis is reasonable and fair, especially when one fully understands the underlying social-adequacy nature of OASDI" (p. 7). The usual argument for some correction, Myers states, is some persons' beliefs that each individual should receive "an actuarial deal," which is "equally good" as others in their same age cohort. Myers dismisses the concept of equity among individuals in the same generation with "there is no reason to be disturbed about this. There is the important social principle that a non-working spouse who is taking care of the home and raising children should have a benefit. Then, if such a spouse also has a benefit based on own earnings, it is only fair that the larger of the two available benefits should be paid—no consideration need be given to the taxes that were or were not paid" (p. 6). But he does not address the problem that even with this choice the benefit of the two-worker family is always less than that of an identical family where the same total dollars are earned by one person.

Inequities between generations have been extensively documented in the economic literature. The social-adequacy argument seems more applicable within this context than for intragenerational inequities, or inequities within the same age group. Under any *new* social security system, earlier generations will always benefit at the expense of later generations, but it is not necessary and it is not usual to favor one group over another in the same age cohort.

The U.S. system is now fifty years old. Yet in recent years, the anticipated benefits for the elderly continue to be greater than what they and their employers, on their behalf, have paid in—and this also holds even if the estimated, forgone interest payments on all the taxes are included. This remains true under the 1983 amendments for all individuals, 55 years and older, except for the single male who has no spouse or dependent children who may claim benefits. Prior to the new legislation, such a single, 55-year-old man with total earnings in 1983 of $15,000, anticipated a net lifetime loss of $1,000 and at earnings of $35,700, a net loss of $21,325.[10] Single women fare better than single men because women live longer. The number of single men who have no claims by previous spouses or dependent children is probably much smaller than the number who have not remained single all their lives.

One-earner couples at age 40 continue under the 1983 legislation to experience lifetime gains; two-earner couples at age 40 with $20,000 or higher incomes continue to experience lifetime losses. Among those age 25 in 1983, however, one-worker couples earning $30,000 in 1983 will have a net lifetime loss of $132, and those 25-year-old single males earning at the maximum, who of course may marry, have about an $86,000 loss; the single woman, a $62,000 loss; and the two-worker couple, a $32,800 loss. Only the latter cannot escape the redistributional effect by marrying. They do have the additional alternative that one person may leave the labor force. However, the 1983 act is supposed to encourage later retirement, not induce even earlier retirement.

Moreover, a one-worker family usually produces larger amounts and a higher quality of household goods and services than the two-worker family. Household-produced goods and services are not included in the national income accounts and are not included in the income levels given above. The value of goods and services produced in the household are usually referred to as imputed income and include such items as home-baked bread, personal child care, home upkeep and repair, including wall papering, painting, sewing curtains, upholstering, and other time-consuming items that two-worker families are likely to purchase rather than produce because of the lack of time that can be allocated for household needs. Economists more precisely point out that the price of leisure hours of two-earner couples earning the same total income as a one-earner couple is, on the average, higher than that of one-earner couples.

The working young must, in some manner, help take care of the nonworking aged when the latter are poor. However, in the 1970s and early 1980s, real weekly earnings declined, while the real value of Social Security benefits was increased. In many cases, it is the retired aged who are helping to support the working young or more recently some unemployed young.

The social-adequacy argument for benefit amounts greater than taxes paid and the interest forgone has been weakened because the aged in the United States *as a group* are no poorer than the younger age cohorts who are parents or potential parents of future generations. The new tax on half the benefits recognizes this. It is a value judgment to what degree the welfare components of the benefit structure should be retained. I support the heavier weights for benefits of low lifetime earners.

The Myers option paper "Possible Solutions to Long-Range Financing Problems of OASDI Program" dismisses any savings from changing entitlement rules or the level of the secondary or derivative spouses' benefits. Myers writes that "reduction in auxiliary benefit amounts" ("auxiliary" is new terminology for Social Security) would reduce costs only by "a small extent." The same option paper dismisses earnings-sharing between spouses that includes "hold-harmless" features (some features that leave those already entitled to a benefit no worse off) as too costly. Specific estimates are not given. Earnings-sharing does increase costs in the U.S. system because it increases the number of the heavily weighted benefits based on low lifetime earnings and simultaneously reduces the number of low-weighted benefits based on high lifetime earnings. The Reform Commission apparently never discussed any proposal to add a portion of an earner's benefit to the spousal benefit or permit workers already entitled to a benefit to stop paying taxes after a number of years. Omitting options can shift the true center of a range of choices so that the compromise takes place to the left or right of true center.

The complete lack of redress in the final recommendations of the majority report of the Reform Commission for working married women would probably not have occurred if there had been an option paper and if some members of the commission had been articulate advocates of some reform.

Benefits to spouses were originally added on the basis of the presumed need of a nonearning wife when the earning husband had died or retired. The philosophy that justified spouses' benefits was one of social adequacy, but without any use of a means test to determine the need. Today, most women work, and men are entitled to spouses' benefits under the same rules as women. Supreme Court decisions require equal entitlement by sex to spouses' benefits. The 1977 legislation liberalized entitlement by men to secondary benefits on the basis of their "presumed dependency," rather than the alternative of deliberalizing entitlement by women to proof of need. If one's "earned" benefit is less than one's spouse's benefit, the latter is awarded. Apparently, requiring proof of need for a spouse's benefit was considered to be politically impossible.

Supplemental Security Income (SSI) was enacted in 1974 to help those in need. It is financed out of general revenues. The Social Security benefits were sold by SSA's literature as "insurance"—"you paid for them"—but the system now provides many welfare-type benefits and without any required proof of actual need. This is costly.

The Reform Commission states (Statement 7, p. 11-4) that it "identified 12 options that address the issue of making Social Security equitable for women." However, the options appear only in the appendix to its report. The first six items deal with dependent spouses' benefits. The next two would allow "child care drop-out years." The use of "child care" rather than "birth of child" drop-out years underplays that which is fundamental to society—its survival. The last four deal with earnings-sharing, one version of which, according to the Report, would actually save, not cost, about 0.06 percent of long-run payroll. These options were taken from the February 1979 Department of Health, Education and Welfare report "Social Security & the Changing Roles of Men and Women." No mention is made of the more recent Health and Human Services Department (HHS) internal memorandum entitled "Options to Improve Protection for Women Under Social Security" (1982). This in-depth study gives many more options to increase equity for married working women than the earlier 1979 report.

I have estimated that as high as 3.5 percent of the long-run covered payroll comes in recent years from the excess Social Security taxes paid by and on behalf of married women who work (*Washington Post*, September 20, 1982, p. 15). I do not know the percentage of long-run payroll that the spouses' benefits absorb, but it must be considerably higher than 3.5 percent.

Although most Social Security benefits are paid on a family basis, divorced spouses' benefits are paid on an individual basis because they are not under the family maximum cap of 175 percent of the earner's benefit. The concept of social adequacy underlies the presumed need of all surviving divorced women and dependent men, 60 years old, even if they remarry. However, remarriage usually changes the economic status of women and dependent men. The argument that older persons might "live in sin" in order to save their Social Security benefits prevails over requiring proof of need. A similar concern that working women already married to retired men might choose "to live in sin" was not expressed during the congressional debate, resulting in very unequal trigger points by singles and marrieds for payment of taxes on half the benefits.

Because an individual may collect only one benefit and because most men earn more than women do, few men, in practice, collect spouses' benefits. The percentage of all men in the labor force is declining. Men are increasingly retiring earlier. Many are married to younger women who continue to work. This could increase the number of men entitled to spouses' benefits in future years.

Ricardo-Campbell's 1983 Proposal

My 1983 proposal is fashioned to give some return in the amount of the retirement benefit and the survivor's benefit to working married women by at least correcting the existing inequities of a 17 percent lesser average benefit at retirement and a 25 percent lesser average benefit to the surviving spouse of two-earner couples as compared to one-earner couples of the same age and with the same amount of earnings subject to the payroll tax. In doing this, I try to meet the following criteria: not to increase the dollar costs of the total OASDI package, to improve individual equity, and not to sacrifice the social adequacy of benefits for those aged who are poor. The proposal has perforce several parts. Additionally, the proposal package is intended to encourage not discourage the birth of children.

My proposal also speaks to, but does not correct, the inequities of return to singles as compared to married couples. There is a societal reason to favor married over singles because, on the average, married persons bear more children than singles. In a period in which our society has a birthrate below replacement rate, 2.1 births completed per woman, society has an interest in favoring marrieds for self-preservation. Therefore, I couch my recommendations, which slightly compromise my original proposal of 1974–1975, in terms of paid one-worker and paid two-worker couples.[11]

These recommendations follow a direct approach. By presenting the proposal in several parts, I make clear the serious degree of inequity that exists for married working women. However, politically, a more radical approach might be preferable, and this method is briefly detailed in a later section of this essay. The 1983 legislation acts as a guide to imply that twenty years might suffice for the suggested changes.

1. Working married women and dependent men (Social Security is now sex-neutral) on retirement may add part of their earned benefits to their derivative benefits, the total being capped by 125 percent of the earned benefit, or three-fourths rather than one-half of the spousal benefit, whichever is higher. Although alternatively the retirement spousal benefit might be phased out, increasingly women are earning their own primary benefit. It is estimated that the long-run costs would be about 0.5 percent of payroll.

2. The spouse married to a worker at the time of the latter's death would be entitled to one-half of the worker's benefit and additional amounts on a prorated basis of one-quarter of that benefit for each 10 years of marriage above 20 years, but with a maximum cap of 100 percent of the earned benefit, as now exists. For example, 25 years of marriage would yield one-half plus one-eighth of the earned benefit; 40 years of marriage, 100 percent of the earned benefit.

3. This prorated approach would apply also to divorced spouses' derivative benefits: for each ten years of marriage, one-quarter of the earned benefit. In mid 1983, the average monthly benefit paid to surviving divorced women with no worker's benefits of their own was $383. The governing Social Security rule is that an individual may have only one benefit, and that benefit is the highest to which they have legal entitlement. The estimated savings from prorating are 0.19 percent of payroll.

4. An integral part of my recommendation is to allow two years of earnings credit for each child born, at a cost of 0.07 percent of payroll. Similar provisions are in social security programs in other countries. Although some argue that this is sex discrimination because men do not bear children, I do not view it as such. Those who do, substitute earnings credit for care of children under three years in the home by the otherwise employed parent.

5. The surviving spouse may add 25 percent of an earned primary benefit to the spousal benefit, the total being capped by 133 percent of the earned benefit or 125 percent of the spousal benefit, whichever is higher.

6. If the costs of the above are deemed too high, the benefit paid to retired spouses (half of the worker's benefit) should be means-tested, as was recently enacted in France. Additionally, spousal survivor benefits might be means-tested.

7. The age for entitlement to a benefit by a surviving spouse should be made to conform to the age of entitlement for all workers and their spouses at retirement, that is, 62 years. It is difficult to tell nonmarried working women that they must wait until age 62 before receiving even a reduced benefit, while nonworking widows, many with sizable benefits from their deceased husbands' life insurance, may get a benefit at age 60.

Two-Tier or "*A* Plus *B*"

There is an alternative, but more radical reform that would reduce some of the intragenerational inequities. It has been suggested over the years, even before the U.S. system was begun. This plan would award everyone at a given age who has proof of U.S. residence for 40 years (a common requirement in other countries) the same monthly benefit, without a means test. This is the first tier or A of the two-tiered system used today in some countries. A could be set at $150 per month, and to this would be added a strictly earnings-related amount, or B. As in most countries that use this type of formula, there must be a long residency period required for the A benefit. The Netherlands is phasing in a 50-year coverage requirement for a full benefit. The U.S. ten-year coverage requirement is too low for our current system and, if used in a two-tier system, would encourage a greater flow of illegal residents.

The original objection to this system in the United States (with the A amount set at a low level) was that without a requirement of earnings for A; the A part is "welfare." However, we now have many "derivative" Social Security benefits for which the recipient has no past earnings record, and also lower lifetime average earnings yield proportionately higher benefits. If an A plus B approach were adopted, workers, regardless of marital status, could receive returns that were related more closely to the individual taxes that they and their employers pay and not to their marital status. It also could be popular politically, as nonearners and those who do not meet an earnings requirement would get some benefit in their own name and not as a derivative benefit.

Many who know the history of social insurance in other countries, however, are wary of this approach because the welfare component A is subject to political pressure for increases. The two-tier approach also makes it easier to argue for general revenue funding of A. It brings into the open the welfare component of social insurance.

Today, the A plus B concept may be preferable to tinkering continually with the system, which has made so numerous the entitlement regulations and the rules that govern the determination of the level of benefits that their complexity is not understood except by a few experts.

For those who believe that the system should become more of an individual equity system, the two-tier approach may be a transitional method of moving toward that goal. However, the eventual outcome of the Social Security system will depend on the distribution of political power among demographic groups. Women are not a homogeneous group in respect to Social Security. If the working married woman can achieve some degree of equity under the system only at the expense of the nonworking married woman, then divisiveness is created between working and nonworking women. A plus B is radical, but because it can be tailored to yield large political gains, for minimal dollar costs, it has appeal to political parties.

Supportive Analysis for True Reform

Today, more women are working than not working. This was not true even in 1960, 25 years after Social Security legislation was passed. About 65 percent of women in their prime working years, ages 20 to 60, are today in the labor force. Among women in childbearing years, the percentage working is even higher: ages 20–24 years, 68.9 percent; ages 25–34, 65.5 percent; and ages 35–44, 65.5 percent. Almost 50 percent of mothers with children under six years old are working, as are 66 percent of mothers with children six to seventeen years. Women today are not bearing as many children as they used to, and women who do have children do not always leave the labor force.

In Sweden, 85 percent of women ages 35 to 44 years are in the labor force. This is higher than the percentage of men in the labor force in the United States. In Sweden, however, 55 percent of women work part-time. In the United States, only about 30 percent of women work part-time.[12]

There are as yet no historical data about the health of married working women who have basically carried two jobs over their working lives, one paid job and one often a less than full-time, unpaid job at home. This creates a type of stress for full-time working women who also have children at home that may contribute to ill health of the mothers and even shorten life expectancy. Because high numbers of working women are so recent in the United States, there are no historical data to prove whether this effect exists. Moreover, because of the changing variables over time, it will be a statistically difficult problem to resolve.

Under the U.S. Social Security system, many women have an earned primary benefit greater than the spousal benefit (half of the husband's earned benefit). There are probably more women 62 years and over who have a primary benefit larger than their secondary or spousal retirement benefit. In the five-year period ending in 1982, more than 1.5 million women 65 years and over were added to the already 7.5 million women 65 years and older who are fully insured—that is, those who have already met the years of covered earnings requirement for their own primary benefits. Table 5.2 shows the percentages of women by age categories who were fully insured in 1982.

Additional published data to document the actual and the anticipated percentages of women who receive an amount equal only to their earned primary benefits are not readily available. Thus, it is impossible for me to cost all the various options of my detailed reform proposal.

Over 90 percent of women today have worked for ten years during their lifetime. Some of these women have worked only prior to marriage, but increasingly women continue to work after marriage and after having a child. By year 2000, few healthy women will not have earned a Social Security benefit if *all* jobs are covered by the system. The dramatic increase in the number of women working is a result of economic forces—for example, the recent rapid inflation and the increasing expansion of the service industries that traditionally employ women. Most women work to maintain a family life-style that they perceive to be desirable.

The overall labor supply will shrink when the low-birthrate population of the 1970s and, especially, the 1980s enters the labor market and the baby boom generation begins to retire. This will occur in the 1990s. It is logical to assume as the labor supply shrinks and the demand in women-dominated occupations increases that the historically constant ratio of average earnings of full-time working women to the average earnings of full-time working men will increase beyond the historical limit of 60 percent. As that occurs, women's Social Security

Table 5.2
Percentage of Women Fully Insured, by Age

Ages	Percentage[a]
20–29	88
30–39	83
40–49	71
50–59	67
60–64	65
65 and older	58

[a]Ten years (40 quarters of coverage) or quarterly coverage "equal to years elapsed after 1950 (or year age 21 attained) and before year of death" or age 62.
SOURCE: *Social Security Bulletin, Annual Statistical Supplement, 1981* (Washington, D.C.: Government Printing Office, 1982), Table 45, p. 100.

benefits will also rise relative to men's because the benefits are related to lifetime earnings.

Divorced women who are supporting children are an increasing percentage of the poor. These economic trends will help them because a large proportion of them are working. Very few countries other than the United States provide non-means-tested social security benefits for divorced women, except as part of a two-tier, *A* plus *B* system.

The extraordinary returns to couples with a dependent spouse are primarily because 100 percent of the earner's benefit is also the amount of the secondary or derivative benefit for the surviving spouse. I use the word "extraordinary" also because the benefits replace a very high amount of net earnings after taxes for retired workers with dependent spouses. In 1972, a married worker with spouse retiring at age 65, with a lifetime low level of earnings had a 112.1 percent net (after taxes "and work expenses") replacement rate;[13] in 1975, this was as high as 122.2 percent. For average earners, comparable data in 1972 were 97.9 percent and in 1975, 105.1 percent. For earners at the maximum, these ratios were 82.1 and 82.6. The initial benefit awarded was decreased in relation to taxes by the 1977 legislation, and replacement rates fell by 1981 to 89.9 percent for the low earner, 76.8 percent for the average earner, and 57.2 percent for earners at the maximum. The data do not include payments to divorced spouses. The comparable replacement rates for singles in 1981 were 65.1 percent, 54.9 percent, and 42.2 percent.[14]

Everyone (if the two-worker family is considered as a unit) already retired or soon to retire receives back within two to two and a half years the total taxes paid by them and their employers and even the forgone interest on the amount of these taxes. Although the 1983 legislation does increase somewhat the time-frame over which these high average returns are paid, it is obvious that in periods of declining population and declining economic growth, everyone cannot get more than was paid in. However, individuals of a two-earner couple not only continue to receive a lesser return than individuals of a one-earner couple, but many more of them than previously will experience actual lifetime losses. Because the rates of return to the young have been reduced by the 1983 legislation, inequities within a generation will be more sharply felt and protested. It is obvious that any social insurance system will initially treat the nearly retired more favorably than the working young, but at maturity the degree of favoring of elders should diminish. Otherwise the system will always be running out of money. The United States and many other nations have a long way to go in this area.

Although some steps to reduce the intergenerational transfer payments were made by the 1983 legislation, no steps were taken to resolve differences in returns among individuals in the same age cohorts who pay the same tax. Indeed, the transfers from singles, two-worker families, and blacks to one-worker families and whites were noticeably increased.

The poor among older persons who receive Social Security benefits today are primarily those widows, 80 years or older, dependent on derivative benefits based on their spouses' low earnings during the Depression and into the 1950s and 1960s. The number of these widows is decreasing. SSI started in 1974 to pay benefits on a needs basis to the very poor. New widows today and in the near future will receive benefits based on their spouses' higher earnings of the 1970s and 1980s. The primary benefit awards made during the 1970s are relatively very high compared to earlier and later awards.

Why did the Reform Commission and Congress propose no changes that addressed the issue of inequity to married working women? The commission members believed that any meaningful changes would be too costly either in dollars or in political votes. If a working married woman receives an additional return above that of the derivative spouse's benefit, it is costly in money. To phase out any portion of the very high, by worldwide standards, retirement and surviving spousal benefits was deemed too costly in a political sense. For example, the HHS in-house option paper to which I have referred has a proposal to reduce the spouse's benefit upon the worker's retirement from half the primary benefit amount to one-third. It alternately proposes capping the dollar amount of the spouses' benefits of high earners. Both of these proposals would have saved money, but both were deemed politically too costly.

However, Congress did add to dollar costs by providing that divorced spouses may collect the one-half retirement benefit whether or not the earning spouse has retired. This was not costly in dollars because of the few numbers affected and was not costly politically because it is not widely known.

The HHS option paper also has various combined-earnings proposals that might have been seriously considered. Congress in 1983 directed HHS to develop the various earnings-sharing proposals further. On March 23, 1983, the Senate passed two years of earnings credit for parents who leave the work force to care for children under the age of three at home. The provision, however, was dropped in conference with the House on March 24.

The commission has pointed the way to a trade-off approach toward restraining costs while making reforms: some reduction in spouses' benefits and some return related to the taxes paid by and on behalf of married working women. The 1983 legislation, however, helps only dependent spouses and thus increases the inequity perceived by working women, whose husbands will vote with them on this issue.

Overall Assessment

Social Security has been increasingly adding to the budget deficit. As more women work, fewer children per woman are born. Thus, the demographic base for paying taxes shrinks, and pressure for inflation begins. It is important for aging societies to recognize this resulting downward spiral induced by heavy transfer payments and not attribute declining birthrates resulting in negative population growth solely to the urbanization of once rural societies. Children in rural societies are investments for one's old age; in urbanized societies, children are primarily a consumption expense. A final word—*it is important* not to push downward the birthrate via inflation and taxes so far below the replacement rate that it leads to a negative rate of population growth even with immigration. This has already occurred in some societies. In these societies, expectations of government services must drastically decrease. The current U.S. rate is 1.8 births per woman; the replacement rate is 2.1 births per woman. There are mature societies that have a birthrate as low as 1.4 children per woman.

In the words of a demographer who protests, "The more somebody else's parents, and somebody else's children and the bureaucracy in between, that a present-day parental generation has to support, the fewer of its own children this generation can afford to have."[15]

Because of the 1983 legislation, no new legislation concerning the OASI part of Social Security can be expected for several years, unless there is a depression. However, in the area of hospital insurance, new legislation is pending. As the system moves closer, however, to the period when both the baby boom generation retires and the number of new workers added to the labor force declines, about 25 years hence, there should be a reassessment of what then lies immediately ahead. In other words, probably 8–10 years from now, new legislation can be anticipated. The legislative and administrative branches of the federal government have learned that gradual phasing-in or -out of changes in the system is the only way that the public will accept change. We cannot wait until disaster is imminent because, as we have learned, compromise, not true reform, occurs.

Notes

1. John A. Svahn, former SSA commissioner, letter to Congressman Daniel Rostenkowski, chairman of the House Ways and Means Committee, February 18, 1983.
2. Geoffrey N. Calvert, "The Social Security System: Long Term Outlook—What Really Lies Ahead" (New York: Alexander & Alexander Services, 1981), pp. 2–5.
3. Stephanie J. Ventura, "Trends in First Births to Older Mothers, 1970–79," *Monthly Vital Statistics Report* 31, no. 2 supplement 2 (May 27, 1982): 3.
4. Ibid.
5. Constance Sorrentino, "International Comparisons of Labor Force Participation," *Monthly Labor Review* 106, no. 2 (February 1983), p. 32.
6. William Mosher, "Infertility Trends Among U.S. Couples: 1965–76," *Family Planning Perspectives* 14, no. 1 (January/February 1982): 22.
7. Gregory J. Savord, "Discussion . . . ," *Transactions of the Society of Actuaries* 33 (1981): 96.
8. *Social Security Bulletin: Annual Statistical Supplement, 1981* (Washington, D.C.: Government Printing Office, 1981), Table 74, p. 141.

9. Gordon Tullock, *Economics of Income Redistribution* (Boston: Kluwer-Nijhoff, 1983), p. 131.
10. Anthony J. Pellechio and Gordon P. Goodfellow, "Individual Gains and Losses from Social Security Before and After the 1983 Social Security Amendments," preliminary draft, prepared for the CATO Institute, San Francisco, forthcoming, Tables 3–5, pp. 13–22.
11. Rita Ricardo-Campbell, *Social Security: Promise and Reality* (Stanford: Hoover Institution Press, 1977), pp. 309–14.
12. Sorrentino, "International Comparisons," p. 27.
13. National Commission on Social Security Reform, "History of Net Replacement Rates for Various Amendments to the Social Security Act," memorandum no. 14 from Robert J. Myers, April 22, 1982 (Washington, D.C. mimeo.). The assumed "minimum necessary work expenses for the 1977 Act, one-worker family, was $220 a year plus two percent of earnings, with a $500 maximum" (p. 3).
14. Ibid.
15. Mikhail Bernstam, "Demography of Soviet Ethnic Groups in World Perspective," typed draft, March 1983, Hoover Institution, Stanford, Calif., p. 69.

6
Health Policy in 1984: The Crisis in Costs

Patricia Munch Danzon

Health care is absorbing an ever-increasing percentage of national income and of government budgets. Between 1965 and 1980, health expenditures grew at an average annual rate of 12.5 percent, a rate one-third higher than the growth in GNP, and hence increased from 6 to 9.4 percent of GNP. Between 1970 and 1980, federal health expenditures quadrupled, while state and local health expenditures more than tripled, adding to the burden on budgets already plagued with expanding deficits. Now that access to medical care for all citizens has largely been achieved, the primary concern of health policy has shifted to cost control.

An increase in expenditures on health is not in itself cause for concern if it represents an efficient allocation of resources. But no such presumption is valid in the health care sector. For most goods and services, competition in private markets ensures efficient allocation. Health care has two intrinsic features that prevent fully efficient markets. First, health insurance, while providing protection against the unpredictable and potentially large costs of health, creates a risk of "moral hazard": the insured patient is insensitive to price and tends to utilize services excessively. Second, patients lack the information necessary to make optimal choices and to judge quality. They must rely on physicians to act as their agents. A fundamental problem in medical care is structuring payment mechanisms such that physicians have incentives to act as patients would wish, if they were as knowledgeable as physicians.

With moral hazard and imperfect information, some inefficiencies—gaps in coverage, unnecessary utilization—in health care markets are inevitable. But because inefficiency is costly to consumers, competing insurance companies have incentives to devise methods of health care financing and delivery that minimize these inefficiencies. The perceived defects of the health care system today are not evidence that private markets cannot work, because they have not been tried. Tax and regulatory policies have undermined the incentive and ability of consumers and health insurers to act as prudent buyers. Consequently, providers have had little incentive to compete on price and every incentive to order any procedure that promises any medical benefit, regardless of cost. Regulatory policy in the 1970s attempted to contain the resulting cost increases by direct controls on facilities, utilization, and prices. These measures have been largely ineffectual, not surprisingly, because they restrict supply without changing the consumer and provider incentives driving the cost spiral.

In the face of the widely admitted failure of direct controls, there is a growing consensus in support of an incentive-based approach in the health care sector. Incentive-based reform sounds painless, but it will not be. The potential savings from eliminating pure waste are small.[1] Significant cost containment therefore requires forgoing services that, though medically efficacious, yield benefits less than costs. If all medically efficacious procedures are available as a right to all who derive any benefit from them, there will be no limit to the explosion of health costs. The competitive or incentive-based approach to health policy therefore aims at confronting consumers, providers, and insurers with incentives to weigh benefits against costs.

The Private Sector

Tax Policy

Almost 85 percent of private health insurance is employment related.[2] Under current law, employer contributions to employee health insurance are tax exempt. This regressive subsidy, which benefits most those in high tax brackets, cost an estimated $31 billion in forgone tax revenues in 1983. More important, preferential tax treatment distorts the perceived price of health insurance. To an employee with a marginal tax rate of 40 percent, $100 of tax-free health insurance effectively costs only $60. This subsidy has encouraged the purchase of excessive health insurance, which has undermined cost-consciousness on the part of consumers and providers, destroyed competition in health care markets, and fueled the explosion of prices and technology.

It is now widely recognized that some limit on the amount of tax-free health insurance is essential to effective cost containment.[3] The lower the cap, the greater the savings in tax revenues and the larger the fraction of subscribers who will face an increase in the marginal cost of health insurance. The Reagan administration's proposal to limit tax-free contributions to $175 per month for a family ($70 a month for an individual) would affect less than 30 percent of subscribers initially, but over time an increasing percentage would be affected if the limits are not indexed to health care prices.[4]

Regulatory Policy in the Private Sector

Private sector initiatives to control costs are burgeoning. The major insurance companies are experimenting with a variety of innovative programs, including prepaid group practices or health maintenance organizations (HMOs), preferred provider organizations (PPOs), and primary care networks (PCNs). Although differing in detail, these experiments all look to two basic sources of savings: (1) limiting patients to less costly providers, and (2) creating incentives for providers to control costs by their participation in financial liability, through a prepaid, capitation form of reimbursement in place of the traditional fee for service. Other employer initiatives include incentive plans (which share with employees the savings from choosing cheaper insurance options or provide cash rebates for reduced utilization), "stay well" programs (to encourage healthier life-styles), and the direct provision of medical services.

These initiatives are currently impeded by a variety of laws and regulations. A majority of states have freedom-of-choice laws. Although apparently designed to guarantee the patient free choice of providers, in practice the main beneficiaries have probably been providers rather than consumers. Such laws have restricted the ability of insurers to contract with providers who cooperate in containing costs. In California, for example, special legislation was required to enable insurers to enter into exclusive or preferred provider agreements, at negotiated rates, with individual hospitals. Moreover, free-choice laws have also been used to require insurers to cover nontraditional providers, such as midwives, chiropractors, and podiatrists. There may once have been a legitimate concern that private insurers, in association with physicians and hospitals, would boycott nontraditional practitioners. But with free competition among the several hundred insurers in the market, nontraditional services that are worth their cost to consumers will be covered voluntarily and do not need protective legislation.

Another obstacle to fair competition in health financing is the unequal regulatory treatment of nonprofit Blue Cross and Blue Shield plans, commercial insurers, and self-insured firms. The Blues are exempt from state premium taxation and are subject to different capital requirements and rate regulation than the commercials. The evidence on the impact of this favorable regulatory treatment of the Blues is mixed, but to the extent that they are affiliated with provider organizations, it can only hinder, not help, competition in insurance and health care markets. In many states Blue Cross is the largest insurer and has been able to negotiate preferential discounts on hospital rates, sometimes with the support of state rate-setting programs. To encourage competition, commercial insurers should be granted antitrust exemption for joint negotiation with providers for special rates and other activities, provided that dominant market shares are not involved. Granting insurers, individually or jointly, the right to negotiate rates with providers is a far more promising means of controlling hospital costs than the alternative of comprehensive rate regulation, which simply eliminates all competition.

Fair competition between traditional insurers and self-insured plans poses special problems. Self-insurance grew from 5 percent of the market in 1975 to nearly 20 percent in 1981.[5] In part this is the result of favorable treatment of self-insured plans under section 514(c) of the Employment Retirement Income Security Act (ERISA), which exempts self-insurers not only from state premium taxes and solvency regulations, but also from mandated benefits, free-choice provisions, and continuation of coverage and conversion options. Since self-insurance is a valuable competitive force, it should be encouraged. It should not, however, be subsidized. A reasonable compromise would be to retain the preferential treatment of self-insurers with respect to solvency requirements (since such requirements are less necessary for self-insurers, which are typically large firms), but extend to all insurers the exemption from free-choice laws, mandated benefit laws, and the like. Similarly, to promote fair competition between alternative forms of health care financing, Congress should eliminate the subsidies and mandatory coverage requirements imposed on HMOs.

Antitrust Policy

The immunity from the antitrust laws enjoyed by the medical and other learned professions ended in 1975 with the Supreme Court's ruling in *Goldfarb v. Virginia State Bar*.[6] Similarly, the insurance industry's exemption from antitrust scrutiny under the McCarran-Ferguson Act has been narrowed by recent rulings.[7]

The application of antitrust law to the health care sector is not an unmixed blessing. On the one hand, it will deter collusive agreements among providers, which in the past have obstructed cost-reducing innovations.[8] But if tax and regulatory policies were designed to encourage competition between providers and insurers, the monolithic power of professional organizations would be drastically curtailed, even without antitrust action.

On the other hand, exposure to antitrust may discourage precisely the types of restrictive contract between insurers and providers necessary for effective cost control. Exclusive provider agreements and maximum fee schedules have been challenged on grounds of boycott and price fixing, both of which are normally per se violations of the Sherman Act (that is, illegal without regard to their purpose or effect).[9] For the most part, the courts have entered the health care field with caution, eschewing application of strict per se illegality in favor of a rule of reason approach, which weighs pro-competitive effects against anticompetitive effects to determine whether a particular restraint is on balance unreasonable. Nevertheless, a case can be made for legislation explicitly authorizing joint activities necessary for cost containment.[10] But market-wide agreements among health care providers to restrict the supply of services in the name of health care planning should not be encouraged. The 1974 Planning and Resources Development Act explicitly authorized the voluntary cooperation of health care providers with health system agencies (HSAs) to prevent unnecessary duplication of health facilities. The presumption underlying this act, that planning is necessary because competition does not work, is premature. In light of the evidence that planning has been at best ineffectual, at worst counterproductive,[11] it is worth giving the competitive alternative a try.

Mandatory Benefits and Coverage

In recent years, federal and state legislatures have intervened to mandate additional coverages (home health care, chemical abuse, and mental health) and have restricted underwriting discretion by requiring coverage, among others, of newborns, the handicapped, pregnant women, and the aged.[12] Several of the "pro-competition" proposals under consideration include similar minimum benefit and open enrollment requirements.

The exclusion of particular benefits in voluntary contracts suggests they are not economically feasible because, due to moral hazard and adverse selection, the cost would exceed the price consumers are willing to pay.[13] However, as a matter of public policy, we may wish to subsidize insurance for high-risk individuals. A major shortcoming of our private, employment-based system of health insurance is that individuals who are identifiably high-risk and thus most in need of insurance because of disability or chronic disease face an unaffordably high price of insurance and may face discrimination in employment because of the load they would place on an employment-based insurance program.

Granted the political decision to cover high-risk individuals, there remains the question of how to provide such coverage. Legislation to mandate benefits and nondiscriminatory underwriting may in fact jeopardize the employment possibilities of the high-risk individuals intended to benefit. Moreover, it undermines the competitive approach to health care reform by curtailing competition on two important dimensions. An alternative approach is a comprehensive health insurance availability plan, such as those enacted in Connecticut, Indiana, Minnesota, North Dakota, and Wisconsin. These plans create an assigned risk pool, which offers a prescribed level of coverage to individuals unable to obtain insurance in the voluntary market. Private carriers share the excess losses of these pools. Such pools, which are common for automobile insurance, may be a reasonably efficient method of subsidizing high-risk individuals.

Public Programs: Medicare and Medicaid

Medicare and Medicaid finance medical services for the aged and disabled and for the poor, respectively. Since their inception in 1965, these programs have greatly improved access to medical care for the needy, but at a cost that has soared beyond initial projections. Between 1979 and 1982, Medicare expenditures rose 19 percent annually, due primarily to an increase in benefits per enrollee. Current projections see the Hospital Insurance (Part A) trust fund, which is funded by Social Security payroll taxes, as depleted by 1987 or 1988.[14]

Medicare Part B, which covers physician and other outpatient services, competes with other programs for general revenue funds. Among the factors contributing to the cost spiral are the open-ended entitlement structure of the programs; copayment and reimbursement provisions that do little to promote cost-consciousness by beneficiaries and providers; and in the case of Medicaid, the federal matching grant formula, which subsidizes the marginal cost to the state of additional Medicaid outlays.[15]

The 1970s witnessed a proliferation of regulations concerning provider charges and utilization and cutbacks in eligibility criteria and scope of benefits. To the extent these controls have slowed the growth in expenditures, it is through eliminating services rather than increasing efficiency. If the public programs retain their open-ended entitlement and service-benefit structure, several incentive-based reforms could improve efficiency.

Medicare

Copayment provisions for hospital care should be restructured to provide less complete coverage of short stays, but more complete coverage of truly catastrophic losses.[16] To prevent undue hardship to low-income beneficiaries, coinsurance rates could be varied with income. To prevent the nullification of incentive effects of copayment, a tax on supplementary coverage is necessary. Currently, more than half of Medicare beneficiaries purchase private supplementary coverage, and an additional sixth are eligible for general revenue–supported Medicaid coverage.[17] Supplementary coverage is effectively subsidized because Medicare bears part of the costs of the additional utilization encouraged by supplementation. This subsidy is estimated at more than $3 billion per year.[18] A tax on supplemental coverage, equal to about 35 percent of the private plan's premium, could offset this added cost to Medicare and restore the incentive effects of Medicare copayment provisions.

Since patient copayment must remain limited if the program is to continue to provide real insurance, government reimbursement policies must bear the brunt of creating efficient incentives for providers. The traditional system of retroactive cost-based reimbursement for hospitals creates no incentive for efficiency since most costs are automatically reimbursed. In response to the requirements of the 1982 Tax Equity and Fiscal Responsibility Act (TEFRA), the administration has proposed the nationwide application of the New Jersey system of prospective payment based on Diagnosis Related Groups (DRGs).[19] Patients would be categorized into 467 DRGs based on diagnosis, procedure, age, and discharge status. Medicare would pay a fixed rate for each DRG, modified by an index of local labor costs.[20] Since the hospital retains any surplus between the payment rate and its actual cost, cost minimization is encouraged—perhaps to excessive levels.

Whether prospective reimbursement will reduce the rate of inflation depends on how DRG prices are adjusted over time. If allowed to rise less rapidly than costs in the private sector, problems of access and cost shifting from public to private patients will remain. Moreover, even if DRG prices are controlled, total expenditures may continue to rise because of "DRG creep" (artificial inflating of diagnoses) or unnecessary hospital admissions.

It is easier to point to the defects of DRG reimbursement than to identify a superior alternative. As a multidimensional service, medical care is inherently ill-suited to price regulation. Payment on a per admission, per diem, or per service basis creates incentives for unnecessary admissions, extended lengths of stay, or unnecessary services, whether rates are set prospectively or retrospectively. A ceiling on total hospital budgets, as implemented in New York, controls expenditures by fiat, but does nothing to assure that the arbitrarily limited resources are efficiently allocated.

Because the federal government is inherently ill-suited to run an insurance program, the voucher option deserves serious consideration. The current entitlement to medical services would be replaced by a voucher that could be used to purchase any qualified private health plan. Beneficiaries would have an incentive to choose cost-effective coverage, since they would retain any difference between the voucher amount and the cost of the plan, and could supplement the plan if desired. Although the voucher does not offer immediate budget savings, it does provide control over total Medicare outlays, more freedom of choice for beneficiaries, and an end to the distinction between private and public patients.

Medicaid

Spurred on by reduced federal participation and by budget deficits, several states have initiated a fundamental redesign of their Medicaid programs. Common features of these experiments are prepayment, to involve providers in the financial risk, and restricted patient choice to an HMO or a PCN of primary care physicians who make referrals to designated specialists. These experiments resemble private sector initiatives by insurers and employers to act as prudent buyers on behalf of patients—a necessary condition for efficiency in the health care sector. The role of the federal government should be to remove unreasonable obstacles. Some progress was made by the Omnibus Budget Reconciliation Act of 1981, which permitted waivers from the federal requirement of freedom of choice for Medicaid recipients and granted the states more freedom to require copayment. As in the private sector, this sacrifice of free choice may be a price worth paying for improved efficiency, particularly if the alternatives are unlimited cost inflation or restrictions on covered services.

Long-Term Care

Spending on nursing homes is rising faster than any other component of health costs and is expected to absorb over 11 percent of personal health expenditures by 1990. But it occupies a much more dramatic percentage of public budgets. The share of nursing home care exceeds 40 percent of Medicaid budgets on average and is over 60 percent in some states.[21]

Long-term care has several unique features. Private insurance coverage is virtually nonexistent—less than 5 percent of all private spending on nursing homes is financed through insurance. Thus the effective options for the functionally limited are being cared for at home by family or friends, paying the full cost of nursing home care, or spending down to the point of eligibility for public support. The comprehensive package of medical care, housekeeping, and recreational services provided by all nursing homes exceeds the needs of a substantial fraction of the nursing home population. But publicly supported patients have no incentive to select a low-cost facility because there is no copayment, although there is a substantial implicit deductible since persons admitted to a nursing home under Medicaid must forgo all their income minus a small personal allowance.

Public policy toward long-term care must face difficult allocative and distributive questions. Currently, families of the noninstitutionalized bear the cost of their care, but the state bears the cost of the institutionalized. Requiring some copayment by families who place elderly relatives in homes would allocate costs more equally and discourage utilization, at some cost in terms of public intervention in private family decision making. Several studies indicate that the present system of heavy subsidy exclusively to institutionalized care results in unnecessary services for a substantial fraction of the nursing home population who could be cared for at lower cost through home help services, while denying needed services to the more numerous, noninstitutionalized disabled. A top priority is to find some way of providing noninstitutionalized care without incurring large increases in program costs because of the moral hazard posed by a service-benefits approach to home health care. One promising approach is the use of vouchers based on health status, local costs, and possibly income. This would discourage individuals who can be more efficiently helped at home from seeking more expensive institutional care.

Health care cost containment will not be painless. It requires sacrifices by patients and providers. Some inefficiencies are inevitable because of the moral hazard and imperfect information problems inherent in health care delivery. The challenge is to make the sacrifices where they hurt least. That requires creating incentives to eliminate inefficiencies in production and services worth less than cost. Competition in free markets generally gives individual decision makers incentives to eliminate such inefficiencies. Competition has not yet been given a fair chance in the health care sector, but there is movement in that direction. Private sector insurers and individual states in operating their Medicaid programs are experimenting in innovative methods of health care delivery and financing designed to improve consumer and provider incentives. In view of the dismal failure of the regulatory approach to cost control in the 1970s and promising evidence of the effects of incentive-based reforms, the primary role of public policy should be to remove tax and regulatory obstacles to such reforms and to move toward incorporating them into public sector programs.

Notes

1. William B. Schwartz and Paul L. Joskow, "Duplicated Hospital Facilities: How Much Can We Save by Consolidating Them?" *New England Journal of Medicine* 303 (1980): 1149–157.
2. Amy K. Taylor and Gail R. Wilensky, "The Effect of Tax Policies on Expenditures for Private Health Insurers," in Jack A. Meyer, ed., *Market Reforms in Health Care* (Washington, D.C.: American Enterprise Institute, 1983), pp. 163–84.
3. For example, S. 433, introduced by Senator David Durenberger (R., Minn.), and H.R. 850, introduced by Representative Richard A. Gephardt (D., Mo.).
4. Taylor and Wilensky, "Effect of Tax Policies." The authors estimate the elasticity of coverage purchased in response to price to range from -0.2 in the short run to -0.5 in the long run. For a person in the 50 percent marginal tax bracket, a cap on the tax-deductible status of health insurance implies a

100 percent increase in the effective price. With an elasticity of -0.5, this would imply a 50 percent reduction in the amount of coverage purchased.
5. Patricia W. Samors and Sean Sullivan, "Health Care Cost Containment Through Private Sector Initiatives," in Meyer, *Market Reforms in Health Care*, pp. 144-62.
6. 421 U.S. 773 (1975). In ruling the Virginia Bar Association minimum fee schedules illegal, the Supreme Court stated: "The nature of an occupation, standing alone, does not provide sanctuary from the Sherman Act."
7. In *St. Paul Fire and Marine Insurance Co. v. Barry*, 98 S. Ct. 2923 (1978), the boycott exception to the exemption was expanded to include refusal by insurers to write policyholders, in contrast to the refusal to deal with other insurance companies or their agents. In *Group Life and Health Insurance Co. v. Royal Drug Co., Inc.*, 99 S. Ct. 1067 (1979), the Court narrowed the definition of "business of insurance," as distinct from "business of insurers." Only activities whose indispensable characteristic is the spreading of underwriting of risk are entitled to the McCarran exemption.
8. Lawrence G. Goldberg and Warren Greenberg, "The Effect of Physician Controlled Health Insurance: *U.S. v. Oregon State Medical Society*," *Journal of Health Politics Policy and Law* 2 (1977): 48-78.
9. For example, *Sausalito Pharmacy v. Blue Shield of California*, no. C-78-2196 RFP (N.D. Cal., May 12, 1980); and *Arizona v. Maricopa County Medical Society*, 102 S. Ct. 2466 (1982).
10. See William G. Kopit, "Health and Anti-trust: The Case for Legislative Relief," in Meyer, *Market Reforms in Health Care*, pp. 323-29.
11. Frank A. Sloan and Bruce Steinwald, *Insurance, Regulation and Hospital Costs* (Lexington, Mass.: Lexington Books, 1980).
12. George Heitler and Mary Ader, "Blue Cross and Blue Shield Plan Contracts with Providers," *Journal of Legal Medicine* 2 (1981): 265-96.
13. "Moral hazard" refers to the tendency for insurance to increase the likelihood of the risk being insured against. "Adverse selection" refers to the propensity of high-risk individuals to seek insurance or to select high levels of coverage.
14. *Changing the Structure of Medicare Benefits: Issues and Options* (Washington, D.C.: Congressional Budget Office, March 1983).
15. Medicaid is administered and partly financed at the state level. States have some flexibility in setting eligibility standards and covered services, and in structuring provider reimbursement. The federal government pays from 50 to 77 percent of expenditures depending on per capita income in the state. With a federal match of 50 percent, for example, the cost to the state of one dollar of Medicaid expenditure is effectively 50 cents. Until recently, Medicaid had no copayment in many states.
16. The Reagan administration has proposed a low copayment rate for 60 days but zero thereafter, in place of the traditional system of a deductible for the

first day of hospitalization ($304 in 1983), no copayment for the next 59 days in the hospital, but substantial payments thereafter ($76 per day for days 61–90).
17. Paul B. Ginsburg, "Market Oriented Options in Medicare and Medicaid," in Meyer, *Market Reforms in Health Care*, pp. 103–18.
18. Ibid., p. 106.
19. U.S. Department of Health and Human Services, *Report to Congress: Hospital Prospective Payment for Medicare* (Washington, D.C., December 1982).
20. Teaching and capital costs are reimbursed separately.
21. U.S. Department of Health and Human Services, Health Care Financing Administration, *Medicaid Statistics, Fiscal Year 1978*, DHEW publication no. (HCFA) 78–03154 (Washington, D.C., 1978).

7

Poverty and Welfare

John C. Goodman

In 1982, more than $403 billion was spent in the United States on social welfare programs at the federal, state, and local level.[1] This amounts to $2,117 for every "nonpoor" man, woman, and child in the country, or $8,468 for a family of four.

Since the advent of the War on Poverty, the poverty industry has been a growth industry. Today it employs more than five million public and private workers and provides benefits to between 50 and 60 million people. The social welfare budget has grown by more than 400 percent over the last decade—about 43 percent faster than the rate of inflation. At the federal level, social welfare spending now consumes almost 50 percent of the federal budget and is twice the size of the defense budget.

Despite these facts, in fall 1983 the U.S. Bureau of the Census made an amazing announcement. According to the Census Bureau, there were 34.4 million Americans living in poverty in 1982. This is more than the number of people who were living in poverty in 1965 when the War on Poverty was just getting started!

To see how utterly shocking this revelation was to many people, consider the following fact. Had the $403 billion in social welfare spending simply been given to people officially classified as living in poverty, it would have amounted to $11,730 per poor person—more than the U.S. per capita income—or $46,920 for a family of four. Such a gift would propel a poverty level family of four into the upper 20 percent of the distribution of family income. Viewed another way, $403 billion is enough money to support almost 60 percent of U.S. households at the poverty threshold disregarding all other sources of income.

Is it possible that we could spend so much money eliminating poverty and not even put a dent in the poverty level population? Not only is it possible, but there is probably no limit to the extent of such failures. Were a benevolent deity to bestow on Congress an extra $400 billion to spend on social welfare programs, I have no doubt that Congress could exhaust the entire amount without eliminating poverty. Indeed, if we doubled the poverty budget, it is possible, even likely, that the number of persons classified as poor would rise, not fall.

In order to see why this is true, it is necessary to understand three facts about the U.S. welfare system. First, the official poverty statistics have only a scant relationship to the actual incidence of human need in our society and are a totally inaccurate account of the real incidence of poverty. Second, while the official designations of poverty bear virtually no relationship to reality, these designations are highly valuable to individuals. Individuals who become certified as poor become eligible for one or more of 49 major entitlement programs, including Medicaid, the most complete and comprehensive health insurance policy to be found anywhere in the world. Third, individuals by the millions are responding to this incentive and are being classified as poor.

Paying People to Be Poor

Since the time of Adam Smith, economists have known that subsidizing an activity encourages it; taxing an activity discourages it. The United States subsidizes poverty and taxes nonpoverty. In some cases, it subsidizes poverty lavishly.

The fact that the poverty population rose in 1982 was surprising only to those who do not follow Census Bureau statistics.[2] Those who track these numbers know that since 1973 there has been a steady, almost unbroken upward trend in the number of persons living below the poverty level. By 1982, the number was 50 percent higher than in 1973, and this was not the result of population growth. Over the same period of time, there was a steady, almost unbroken upward trend in the *percentage* of people living in poverty. What these statistics reveal more than anything else is that the more you subsidize poverty, the more poverty you will have.

To say that the government subsidizes poverty is only a first-order approximation. To be more specific, government welfare programs in the United States are subsidizing divorce, unwed teenage pregnancies, the abandonment of parents, and the wholesale dissolution of the family.

The dissolution of the family is best illustrated in the Census Bureau statistics on unrelated individuals, persons living apart from a spouse or other family members. In an earlier era, if such individuals were in financial trouble many would have lived with relatives. Not so in the modern welfare state. Since 1959, the number of unrelated individuals living below the poverty level has increased by 31 percent.

A popular conception of the poverty population is that of a large family with many children. In fact, almost a third of poverty families consists of unrelated individuals. Families with incomes in the lowest fifth of the income distribution contain only 13.8 percent of the population. By contrast, families in the highest fifth of the income distribution contain twice that many people.

Most people are aware that a large number of female heads of households rely on the welfare state. It is not generally appreciated, however, that since 1959 the number of these women living in poverty has increased by 79 percent. Among black women, the increase is 179 percent. This is due partly to the fact that the welfare state makes divorce increasingly financially attractive. But it also is due to the fact that the welfare state subsidizes teenage pregnancy. In the 1940s, less than 10 percent of all black babies were illegitimate. Today over half of all black babies are born to unwed mothers.

During the 1970s, there probably was no other group in America that received more government largesse than the elderly. Social Security and Medicare benefits grew at a rate that far surpassed the rate of inflation, and today more than 25 percent of the federal budget is spent on the elderly. Despite this fact, there were more elderly persons living in poverty in 1982 than there were in 1972.

The trend toward poverty status is especially pronounced among elderly women living without a man in the household. In 1982, there were more of these women living in poverty than there were in 1959. Among elderly black women, the number living in poverty in 1982 was 90 percent higher than in 1959.

Can the trend toward an increasing number of Americans officially classified as poor continue much further? According to George Gilder, we have barely scratched the surface:

AFDC (Aid to Families with Dependent Children) offers a guaranteed income to any child-raising couple that is willing to break up, or to any teenage girl over sixteen who is willing to bear an illegitimate child. In 1979 there were some 20 million families that could substantially improve their economic lot by leaving work and splitting up. Yet they did not. Three-fifths of eligible two-parent families even resist all the noxious advertising campaigns to apply for food stamps, which they can have merely by the asking. Millions of qualified couples continue to jilt the welfare state. Only in the ghetto, among the most visible, concentrated, and identifiable poor, have the insidious seductions of the War on Poverty and its well-paid agents fully prevailed over home and family.[3]

The Benefits of Being Poor

To be officially poor in 1982, a family of four had to have an income of less than $9,862. At first glance, it would appear that such an income would support only a very meager standard of living. The official statistics, however, count only *money* income. They conveniently ignore the value of housing, food, medical care, and a great many other items that most people pay for out of their own budget.

In the U.S. welfare system, the key to being classified as poor is to have a low money income, or at least to have a low *reported* money income. Even if this involves a substantial sacrifice, the sacrifice may well be worth it financially. In the 1970s, a congressional committee found that among families receiving Aid to Families with Dependent Children (AFDC) benefits, 99 percent were covered by Medicaid, 60 percent got food stamps, and 14 percent lived in public housing.[4]

To see how lucrative these and other benefits can be, consider the case of a welfare mother reported in the *Boston Globe* in 1975:

> The mother is well-organized. She buys food stamps twice a month, refuses to live in a housing project, is a member of a community women's group at Catholic charities, and is studying for her high school diploma. Her bimonthly cash grant is $466; she gets a flat grant every three months of $142; and her monthly savings from food stamps amount to $86. Her cash income [earnings] may be given at $599 monthly, or $7,188 a year. If she and her family spent the average amount paid personally for health care in this country (and the mother gets some psychiatric care), this would amount at full costs to an additional $1,750 in health

care expenses. Since there are no financial restrictions for this family on the use of health care, and the mother is intelligent and knowledgeable, one may assume that full use of this opportunity is taken. The three older children go free of charge to an alternative school which costs paying pupils $2,000 a year, and another child goes to a day care center whose cost for a paying child would be $1,000 a year. Cash income and free health and education services to this family thus amount to $16,028. The older children work summers, and I will not cost that out. The family pays no taxes, and need put nothing aside for savings, as the welfare department is committed to meeting its needs. A working head of family would have to earn at least $20,000 to match this standard of living.[5]

In 1975, about three-fourths of the families in the United States had incomes below $20,000.

Charles Hobbs has estimated that in 1976 the average welfare family of four received $15,000 in government subsidies. In 1979, the amount was close to $18,000. These figures compare with the U.S. median family income of $14,500 in 1976 and $16,500 in 1979. They are about twice the level of full-time earnings at the minimum wage.[6]

As Gilder has noted, "The fundamental fact in the lives of the poor in most parts of America today is that the wages of common labor are far below the benefits of AFDC, Medicaid, food stamps, public housing, public defenders, leisure time and all the other goods and services of the welfare state."[7]

Viewed in strictly material terms, in the United States today enormous benefits flow from being classified as poor. Poverty pays, and in some cases, it pays very well.

The Real Incidence of Poverty

As noted earlier, Census Bureau statistics on the number of Americans living in poverty count only money income. They ignore the value of food, housing, medical care, and other goods and services given in-kind. However, as Table 7.1 shows, this method of counting seriously distorts the true picture. In 1976, families in the lowest fifth of the income distribution received on the average 43 cents in the form of in-kind income for every dollar of welfare benefits they received in the form of cash. Among families in the second fifth of the income distribution, for every dollar received in cash, another 28 cents was received in in-kind income.

Table 7.1

Distribution of Welfare Benefits, 1976
(U.S. $ billions)

Family Income	Cash Benefits	In-Kind Benefits	Total Benefits	Total Benefits as a Percentage of Pre-Tax Income
Lowest fifth	$50.7	$21.8	$72.5	96
Second fifth	38.9	10.8	49.7	39
Third fifth	21.8	4.3	26.1	13
Fourth fifth	15.8	2.2	18.0	6
Highest fifth	15.0	1.8	16.8	3

SOURCE: Congressional Budget Office, "Poverty Status of Families Under Alternative Definitions of Income," Background Paper No. 17 (Washington, D.C., January 13, 1977), Table A-4; and Edgar K. Browning and Jacqueline M. Browning, *Public Finance and the Price System* (New York: Macmillan, 1979): Table 7–8, p.204.

There is some question about how much value to attach to goods and services received in-kind. This question will be examined later. For the moment, it is sufficient to note that food, shelter, and medical care surely have some value and that to ignore them altogether, as the Census Bureau does, is indefensible.

It is not surprising that official statistics exaggerate the extent of poverty. After all, the vast welfare state bureaucracy has a vested interest in maintaining and expanding the extent of poverty. The result is a major distortion of the truth. While Census Bureau statistics point to an ever increasing number of people living in poverty, virtually all scholarly studies of the incidence of real poverty point in the opposite direction.

> "In a meaningful sense poverty had become virtually nonexistent in America by 1973" (Edgar Browning, University of Virginia, 1975).[8]
>
> "Only 3 percent of Americans were poor in 1975" (Morton Paglin, Portland State University, 1977).[9]
>
> "If poverty is defined as a lack of basic needs, it's almost been eliminated" (Sar Levitan, George Washington University, 1977).[10]

"The war on poverty has been won, except for perhaps a few mopping-up operations. The combination of strong economic growth and a dramatic increase in government spending on welfare and income transfer programs during the last decade has virtually wiped out poverty in the United States" (Martin Anderson, Hoover Institution, 1978).[11]

Most scholarly studies show that the inclusion of in-kind benefits reduces the poverty rate from one-half to two-thirds of the level that is officially reported by the Census Bureau. These figures could be further modified to take into account the large amount of unreported income among low-income families. Some estimates of the underground economy place it between 10 and 25 percent of GNP. And one study concluded that individuals with reported incomes under $1,000 were spending $224 for every $100 of reported income.[12]

Add to this consideration the fact that among low-income individuals there are would-be writers, artists, and actors—people whose potential earning ability is actually quite high. In addition, there apparently are many people who refuse public assistance, regardless of the personal cost.

Can we then conclude that the problem of poverty is virtually nonexistent? Before we do, let's take a look at where the welfare dollars go.

Where the Welfare Dollars Go

In 1981, almost $300 billion was taken out of the pockets of some Americans and given to other Americans in the form of income transfers. These transfers now amount to 10 percent of the GNP, and transfers in the form of cash now go to 42 percent of all U.S. households.

Most income transfer programs enjoy widespread support because they are thought to assist low income families. Yet only 24 percent of these transfers actually go to poor families because they are poor. That is, only 24 percent of the funds are *means-tested* benefits. The bulk of transfer income goes to families that are solidly middle class. Social Security is an example. A number of Social Security recipients have low incomes. But, partly because of Social Security, the per capita aftertax income of the elderly now exceeds the per capita aftertax income of those under 65 years of age. In addition, the elderly, on the average, are more wealthy than those under 65 years of age.

Another interesting fact is that almost two-thirds of the income transfers that are now means-tested are given in in-kind transfers. Only one-third is given in cash.

There are two important differences between cash and in-kind benefits. First, in-kind transfer funds eventually end up in the pockets of people who are not poor. Money spent on Medicaid, for example, goes to doctors, hospitals, and nursing homes. Money spent on food stamps goes to farmers. Money spent on housing goes to landlords and contractors. The poor, in other words, are a mere way station or conduit through which money is channeled from taxpayers to a nonpoor receiving group.

The second important difference is that when transfers are made in-kind, there is no assurance that those same goods and services would have been purchased by poor persons had they been given the cash instead. In other words, the goods and services received may be less valuable to the recipients than the price paid for them. If an elderly person has $10,000 in cash, for example, would that person really spend it to stay in a nursing home? Would poor families spend their own money to visit "Medicaid mills"? In-kind transfers are ideal if the objective is to divert income to the medical, farming, and housing industries. But, in general, they are defective vehicles for raising the standard of living of low-income families.

Not only are in-kind transfers the primary method of assisting the poor under means-tested programs, but the vast majority of the increase in means-tested spending has been in in-kind transfers. Means-tested cash transfers have increased about fourfold since 1965, while means-tested in-kind transfers have increased by more than fiftyfold (see Table 7.2).

In fact, when the numbers are adjusted for the effects of inflation, it is clear that the amount of cash given to the poor because they are poor has barely changed in real terms since 1965. While Social Security benefits have seen a real growth rate of 55.7 percent, and other non-means-tested cash benefits have increased by over 65 percent, the real increase in means-tested cash benefits has increased at less than one-fifth the rate of increase in household income.

In his classic book, *Welfare*, Martin Anderson wrote:

> The growth of social welfare programs—AFDC, SSI, food stamps, child nutrition, day care, public housing, medicaid and medicare, tuition aid, and social security—has been so comprehensive and diffuse that there is virtually no person in the United States needing help who is not eligible for some form of government aid.[13]

Table 7.2

Growth of Means-Tested Benefits
(U.S. $ billions)

Benefit	1965	1981	Percentage Increase
Cash transfers[a]	$6.70	$26.9	402
In-kind transfers[b]	0.84	43.9	5,226

[a]AFDC, SSI, general assistance, and pensions to needy veterans.
[b]Medicaid, food stamps, and housing assistance.
SOURCE: Based on Sheldon Danziger, Robert Haveman, and Robert Plotnik, "How Income Transfer Programs Affect Work, Savings and the Income Distribution: A Critical Review," *Journal of Economic Literature* 19 (September 1981): 977, Table 1.

The great variety of benefit programs is not in doubt. But there may be one thing that a poor individual cannot get from the welfare bureaucracy—cash. Indeed, among families that are truly needy and not adept at manipulating the welfare system to get in-kind benefits, it appears that public assistance has been relatively stingy. In 1981, about 9 percent of all income transfers and less than 7 percent of all social welfare spending were given in the form of cash to poor people, because they were poor.

It is sobering to realize that almost all transfer income in the United States goes to special interest groups, for which poverty status is not a condition for aid, or to some group that is providing a good or service in-kind that may or may not be highly valued by the people who consume it.

Undesirable Side Effects of the Welfare System

Even if true poverty has been eliminated, or at least held to a bare minimum, we are paying a very heavy price for achieving this goal. The American welfare bureaucracy is slowly changing our economic system and threatens to change our entire culture.

Penalizing Productive Work

It is now recognized by almost every student of the subject that welfare undermines personal incentives to become self-sufficient. That the welfare system reduces productive work was once a hotly debated issue, but is now recognized as a fact of life.

During the late 1960s and early 1970s, there were six major guaranteed income experiments conducted by the federal government. The results of these experiments varied from case to case, but a rough summary of the results is as follows: male heads of households reduced their work effort by 5 percent; female heads of households reduced their work effort by 8 percent; wives reduced work efforts by 22 percent; and dependents by 46 percent. Moreover, these results may significantly understate the negative effects of welfare on willingness to work.[14]

A survey article in a recent issue of the *Journal of Economic Literature* summarized the results of the latest econometric estimates of reduced work incentives under all major income transfer programs. On the average, the studies suggest, income transfers reduce aggregate production in the economy by an amount equal to 3.5 percent of total household earnings. This was about $62 billion in 1981—an amount equal to more than one-fifth of the total income transfers that year.[15]

Part of the reason for reduced work incentives is that it is virtually impossible to construct a welfare system that does not penalize the welfare recipient who earns more in the marketplace. After all, few of us would want to subsidize welfare recipients regardless of their private sector earnings.

The American welfare system, however, erects such penalties in the worst possible way. When a low-income family receiving welfare benefits earns an additional dollar of income, it is penalized in two ways. The family not only faces income and payroll taxes, but also a reduction in welfare benefits. For each additional dollar of earned income, low-income families lose 27 cents in taxes. However, the family also loses an additional 35 cents in reduced welfare benefits. The combined effect of these two penalties is an effective marginal tax rate of 62 percent. As a result, low-income families face a higher effective marginal tax rate than any other income group.[16]

The effective marginal tax rate of 62 percent is only the average for low-income families. For particular families at particular income levels, the tax rate can be much higher. Henry Aaron of the Brookings Institution has explained why: "On earnings from $576 to $8,390 per year, the family eligible solely for AFDC and Medicaid faces a tax rate of 67 percent. Eligibility for food stamp and housing assistance raises the tax rate as high as 80 percent, and brings it to 73 percent over the income range from $4,000 to $8,300."[17] When earnings reach $8,390, the family is removed from the welfare rolls, and as a result of the last dollar earned, loses $1,000 in Medicaid benefits and a $288 food stamp bonus. At $8,389, in other words, the family faces a marginal tax rate of 1,288 percent!

Discouraging Savings

The United States has one of the lowest rates of personal savings among developed countries, and many believe that our welfare system contributes to this low savings rate. For example, when people know that they can rely on transfer income, particularly Social Security retirement income, they have less incentive to engage in personal savings for retirement or other adverse contingencies. There is considerable debate over the magnitude of this effect, but some recent estimates suggest that income transfer programs may reduce the personal savings rate by as much as 20 percent.[18]

Encouraging the Breakup of Families

It is generally well known that the welfare system has traditionally encouraged the breakup of poor families. As Gilder put it, from a financial viewpoint an indexed welfare benefit for the mother is "more preferable in every way to the taxable, inflatable, losable, drinkable, druggable, and interruptible earnings of a man."[19]

What is less well known is that a guaranteed income from welfare apparently encourages divorce even when there are no financial incentives to break up. The results of the Seattle-Denver guaranteed income experiment, for example, show that the incidence of divorce among whites increased 430 percent during the first six months of the experiment. Over a two-year period, the incidence of divorce relative to a control group increased 244 percent for whites, 169 percent for blacks, and 194 percent for Hispanics. Apparently, economic necessity is a strong force holding marriages together.[20]

Gilder has proposed a persuasive theory of why this is true:

> The combination of welfare and other social services enhance[s] the mother's role and obviate[s] the man's. As a result, men tend to leave their children, whether before or after marriage. Crises that would be resolved in a normal family may break up a ghetto family. Perhaps not the first time or the fifth, but sooner or later the pressures of the subsidy state dissolve the roles of fatherhood, the disciplines of work, and the rules of marriage.[21]

Encouraging Dependence

One of the remarkable facts about U.S. family income is that 20 percent of all U.S. families depend on government welfare for 96 percent of their income (see Table 7.1). Much has been made of the fact that only 20 percent of those on public assistance accept it as a more or less permanent way of life. This figure, however, is apparently much higher than it was formerly. One study found that permanent dependency, which characterized only 5 percent of the welfare recipients 20 years ago, now has reached 30 percent in Los Angeles, and predicts that it will rise to 40 percent over the next ten years.[22]

The Distribution of Income

A natural question to ask about the welfare system is: To what extent has it reduced inequality of income in our society? After surveying the results of a number of econometric studies, one team of authors concluded that the cumulative effect of all income transfer programs has been a reduction in poverty of 74 percent and a substantial reduction in inequality of income distribution.[23]

Before accepting this conclusion, however, consider the statistics

Table 7.3

Distribution of Family Income in the United States
(percentage)

Year	Lowest Fifth	Second Fifth	Third Fifth	Fourth Fifth	Highest Fifth
1947	5.1	11.8	16.7	23.2	43.3
1952	4.9	12.2	17.1	23.5	42.2
1962	5.0	12.1	17.6	24.0	41.3
1972	5.4	11.9	17.5	23.9	41.4
1982	4.7	11.2	17.1	24.3	42.7

SOURCES: U.S. Bureau of the Census, "Money Income in 1972 of Families and Persons in the United States," *Current Population Reports*, Series P-60, No. 90 (1973), Table 16 for 1947, 1952, 1962, and 1972. For 1982, U.S. Bureau of the Census, "Money Income and Poverty Status of Families and Persons in the United States: 1982," *Current Population Reports*, Series P-60, No. 140 (1983), Table 4, p. 11.

on family *money* income in Table 7.3, which clearly indicates that there has been little change in the U.S. distribution of money income since 1947. Indeed, were it not that 1982 was a recession year, one might conclude that there is less equality of income in the United States today than at any time since World War II.

Econometric models are designed to estimate the effects on behavior of marginal changes. They are not designed to measure large institutional changes in the economy or in the culture. Clearly, we have had such large institutional changes. For example, in 1935 about 50 percent of all welfare was private charity. Today, private charity accounts for about 1 percent. The broad picture presented in Table 7.3 suggests that if we had never created the welfare state, the distribution of family income today would not be much different from what it actually is. We have paid a heavy price for the institutional changes of the welfare society. Yet it is not clear what we have gained in return.

Toward Welfare Reform

Welfare reform is urgently needed. But to achieve reform there first must be widespread agreement on the general principles that shape and govern the welfare system. The following four principles seem eminently reasonable:

1. *Most people can and should take responsibility for supporting themselves and their families.* In the absence of physical or mental impairment, individuals should perceive that society expects them to support themselves and their families, and this perception should be reinforced by the operation of the welfare system.

2. *Short-term help should be available to many; long-term help should be reserved for a few.* A humane welfare system is one that readily provides temporary and emergency help to those in need. A responsible welfare system is one that provides permanent aid to only the very few who cannot support themselves.

3. *The welfare system should not encourage the breakup of the family.* Family members should not find it in their economic self-interest to dissolve the family unit. One of the reasons why families exist in every culture is that there are economic advantages to specialization and division of labor within the family. The welfare system should not undermine these advantages.

4. *The goals of the welfare system should be achieved at minimum*

cost. As with every other social goal, it is in our self-interest to find the most cost-effective ways of operating welfare based on these principles.

While these goals may seem acceptable on the surface, if they are to be adopted and pursued vigorously they will necessitate radical reform of the U.S. welfare system. Here are just a few of the reforms implied by these principles:

1. *Welfare should be separated from social insurance.* This is implied by Principle 4. Under the current system, the working poor are paying taxes under Social Security and Medicare programs to fund the retirement pensions and medical care of retired millionaires. Yet these programs enjoy widespread support because they are thought to benefit many needy individuals. By separating social insurance from welfare, we can greatly lower the cost of achieving legitimate welfare objectives.

2. *All welfare benefits should be means-tested.* This is implied by Principles 1 and 2. There is no legitimate reason for welfare benefits except to provide for needs that otherwise will go unmet. In order to ensure that the objectives of a rational welfare system are achieved, there must be evidence that genuine needs exist.

3. *It should be easy to enter the welfare system, but difficult to remain there.* This is implied by Principle 2. As Gilder has pointed out, this change would move us in the opposite direction of many recent reforms, especially those in New York and California.[24]

4. *Welfare should be dispensed at the state and local levels rather than at the federal level, preferably by private, voluntary organizations.* This reform is dictated by Principles 1, 2, and 3. It is beyond the capability of the national welfare bureaucracy to distinguish between real need and the lack thereof, or between short-term and long-term needs. Moreover, it is in the self-interest of the bureaucracy at every level of government to expand both the number of welfare recipients and their duration time on welfare. By contrast, private charitable organizations in this country have traditionally focused on short-term emergency relief.

What could be expected as a result of such reforms? From an economic standpoint alone, the potential savings are enormous. Jonathon Hobbs has estimated, conservatively, that simply by handing money to poor families we could bring every family in America up to the nonpoverty threshold for a cost of about $100 billion—one-fourth of current social welfare spending.²⁵

This estimate ignores the vast amount of unreported income, and it does not consider the goal of dispensing welfare benefits in a way that does not encourage the dissolution of the family. These two considerations would probably cut the $100 billion figure in half.

In other words, there is every reason to believe that we could solve the problem of real poverty in America for as little as 1 to 2 percent of the GNP.

Notes

1. This estimate of Jonathon Hobbs includes all major income transfer programs as well as programs such as child nutrition and youth job training. See "Welfare Need and Welfare Spending," *Heritage Backgrounder* (Washington, D.C.), October 13, 1982.
2. The most recent Census Bureau estimates are in Bureau of the Census, "Money Income and Poverty Status of Families and Persons in the United States: 1982," *Current Population Reports*, 1983.
3. George Gilder, *Wealth and Poverty* (New York: Basic Books, 1981), p. 123.
4. Martin Anderson, *Welfare* (Stanford: Hoover Institution Press, 1978), p. 32.
5. Reprinted in Anderson, *Welfare*, p. 36.
6. Charles D. Hobbs, *The Welfare Industry* (Washington, D.C.: Heritage Foundation, 1978), pp. 83–84.
7. Gilder, *Wealth and Poverty*, p. 122.
8. Edgar K. Browning, *Redistribution in the Welfare System* (Washington, D.C.: American Enterprise Institute for Public Policy Research, 1975), p. 2.
9. Quoted in Anderson, *Welfare*, p. 24.
10. Ibid., p. 25.
11. Ibid., p. 37.
12. Edward C. Banfield, *The Unheavenly City: The Nature and Future of Our Urban Crisis* (Boston: Little, Brown & Co., 1970), p. 116.
13. Anderson, *Welfare*, pp. 36–37.
14. Ibid., chap. 5.
15. Sheldon Danziger, Robert Haveman, and Robert Plotnik, "How Income Transfer Programs Affect Work, Savings, and the Income Distribution," *Journal of Economic Literature* 19 (September 1981): 999.
16. Edgar K. Browning and William R. Johnson, *The Distribution of the Tax Burden* (Washington, D.C.: American Enterprise Institute for Public Policy Research, 1979), Table 17, p. 70.

17. Henry J. Aaron, *Why Is Welfare So Hard to Reform?* (Washington, D.C.: Brookings Institution, 1973), pp. 33–34.
18. Danziger et al., "Income Transfer Programs," p. 1006.
19. Gilder, *Wealth and Poverty*, p. 18.
20. Anderson, *Welfare*, p. 149.
21. Gilder, *Wealth and Poverty*, p. 122
22. Ibid., p. 124, *n*12.; p. 278.
23. Danziger et al., "Income Transfer Programs," p. 1014.
24. Gilder, *Wealth and Poverty*, p. 126.
25. Jonathon Hobbs, "Welfare Need and Welfare Spending," Table 1, p. 3.

8

Insurance in the Workplace: Experience Is the Best Guide

Daniel K. Benjamin

There is growing evidence that public insurance programs suffer from a fundamental defect: virtually uncontrollable costs. Social Security and Medicare are the best-publicized examples of this defect, yet lesser-known programs designed to insure against risks in the workplace could ultimately be even more troublesome.

This paper examines three types of workplace risks and the public insurance programs developed to compensate losers: (1) temporary unemployment, insured by the federal-state unemployment insurance system; (2) work-related injuries and diseases, largely covered by state workers' compensation programs but supplemented by a federal program that covers black lung, a disease suffered by coal miners, and other federal programs that protect several special groups, such as long-

---

All production processes of which I am aware involve the application of multiple inputs. The production of this paper was no exception. William Barnes, Robert Copeland, Gary Hendricks, and Gary Reed were the most important inputs. Credit for the desirable attributes of the final product belongs to them and other members of my staff who have contributed. Errors, omissions, and deficiencies—both factual and analytical—are solely my responsibility.

shoremen; and (3) the loss of retirement benefits through pension plan terminations, which is insured under a federal program created in 1974 as part of the Employee Retirement Income Security Act (ERISA).

The size and costs of these programs have been growing rapidly. Over the past two decades, benefits paid under workers' compensation systems have increased threefold, from $3.6 billion in 1960 to over $13 billion in constant 1980 dollars.[1] More than 90 percent of this growth occurred during the 1970s. Benefit increases have been reflected in payroll costs, which have risen from less than 1.0 percent of payroll in 1960 to nearly 2.0 percent of payroll in 1980, *despite* substantial contributions from general revenues.

Pension termination insurance is an equally dramatic example of a program whose costs are, and could continue, exploding. Between 1979 and 1982, the deficit of this relatively small, nine-year-old program jumped from $146 million to over $300 million and is projected to exceed $1.0 billion by 1988. Although this program is now minuscule by megabuck standards, the potential for growth in a program covering some 36 million workers in over 92,000 separate pension plans is staggering. Indeed, the program's current premium income of under $100 million a year pales in comparison with potential liabilities well in excess of $50 billion.

The problems in unemployment insurance (UI) are different but nonetheless serious. Over the past decade, the program has been expanded to provide federally subsidized extended and supplementary benefits during periods of high unemployment. This has not only increased the cost of insuring unemployment (federally subsidized benefits totaled over $9.0 billion in 1982 and 1983 alone) but has also increased the rate of unemployment by encouraging longer durations of unemployment.

In addition to federal cost increases, many states have borrowed heavily in recent years to finance their UI programs. As a result, five states now have loan balances of over $2 billion, and ten other states have outstanding UI debts in excess of $100 million. Total state UI indebtedness now exceeds $13 billion. At current UI tax rates, many states will not be able to pay off these debts for a decade or more, even with sustained economic growth.

The costs of work-related public insurance programs tend to be excessive for two reasons. First, expenditures under these programs are generally considered "uncontrollable" since benefit payments can change without any legislative action altering the schedule of benefits. Thus budget makers frequently accept expenditure changes passively rather than fighting to contain them.

Even more important, while typically characterized as "insurance" programs, these programs, by failing to allocate costs more precisely to participants, become transfer programs. Simply stated, contributing employers and those insured perceive little if any cost to themselves of using the programs or even expanding coverage and benefits. The creation of programs in which participants' costs are insensitive to their own use reflects in part a concern for keeping costs low for parties hit by damages or losses. Examples include keeping unemployment contributions low for businesses that suffer sales declines and keeping pension insurance costs low for employers whose pension plans have large unfunded liabilities. However, this concern has resulted in programs that are susceptible to unchecked growth.

The problems that arise when insured parties perceive little cost in making liberal use of their insurance are well known and ones that private insurers have solved by making premiums risk- and experience-related. Prominent examples include automobile insurance and insurance against theft.

Risk and experience rating is as essential to public insurance programs as it is to private ones. The reason for having publicly mandated insurance programs is that those who should insure are the least likely to. However, once insurance is mandated there is no reason to ignore the costs imposed on the system by individual parties. To the contrary, to the extent that events are, or could be, under the control of the insured, risk- and experience-related premiums not only contain costs but improve equity and the efficiency of resource allocation. Indeed, the very existence of publicly mandated insurance for a work-related risk implies that the risk is appropriately a part of the cost of production and properly should be borne by consumers of products in relation to how the cost is actually distributed among products.

In short, risk and experience rating is essential in fostering the efficiency of public work-related insurance programs, would improve the equity of these programs, and is a crucial tool for ensuring fiscal restraint in these important programs.

Unemployment Insurance

Unemployment insurance (UI) is designed to partially compensate workers for earnings lost through temporary unemployment either while laid off from their current job or during the period between leaving one job and finding another. In 1932, the first statewide UI program was enacted, and in 1935 federal legislation was passed as part of the Social Security Act. The Social Security Act provided for a federal unemployment tax of 3 percent of an employer's payroll, against which a tax credit of up to 2.7 percent would be granted for taxes paid under a qualifying state unemployment insurance law.[2] Moreover, an employer could pay less than 2.7 percent in state taxes and still receive the full federal tax credit if the employer's tax rate was based on his experience with unemployment among his workers. Thus, states that incorporated this "experience-rating" provision could have an average state tax of less than 2.7 percent and still afford employers protection from the full 2.7 percent in federal taxes. All states had enacted UI laws by mid-1937, and most incorporated some type of experience rating in their financing structure.

The UI system today comprises three components, each of which is financed somewhat differently. The main component, the regular state UI programs, generally provides up to 26 weeks of benefits to unemployed workers and is financed through state payroll taxes. Due to experience rating, state tax rates vary to some degree according to employer experience in generating insured unemployment, with higher taxes levied on employers responsible for more unemployment. The specific type and degree of experience rating, along with program features such as weekly benefit amounts, number of weeks of benefits, and benefit eligibility requirements, are set by specific state laws and differ significantly among states.

The second component of the UI system, extended benefits (EB), was enacted in 1971 and provides up to thirteen weeks of benefits beyond regular state benefits in states with unusually high unemployment. The EB program is financed by a combination of experience-rated state payroll taxes (one-half) and a federal payroll tax levied uniformly across employers, independently of their unemployment experience.

In addition, in each of the last two recessions, the regular state and EB programs have been supplemented by a temporary program to extend benefits exhausted under the other programs. This temporary program, now referred to as federal supplemental compensation (FSC), is financed out of general revenues and lacks any experience-rating features.

In fiscal 1983, the UI system paid out $29.4 billion in benefits. Of this, $21.5 billion was paid under regular state programs, $2.3 billion through the EB program, and $5.9 billion from FSC and other federally funded programs. Thus, nearly one-fourth of total UI benefits in fiscal 1983 was financed through federal revenues.

Employers influence the incidence and duration of unemployment through decisions on how to respond to changes in product demand. Incomplete experience rating induces employers to react to declines in product demand by decreasing the number of employees rather than the number of hours employees work. If employers do not pay the full cost of UI benefits collected by their employees (incomplete experience rating), they more readily accede to layoffs than they would if they paid the full cost of those benefits (complete experience rating). Employees generally prefer layoffs to reduced hours of work since UI benefits are paid only for complete days or weeks of unemployment and not for reduced hours of work. Incomplete experience rating creates a "moral hazard" for employers, making it profitable for them to create more unemployment through temporary layoffs than would otherwise occur.

Throughout its history, the UI program has attempted to limit the moral hazard problem for employers and more efficiently and equitably distribute costs by incorporating experience rating in the financing structure. Experience rating has generally been accepted as a solution to inducing more appropriate employer behavior, such as fewer layoffs for shorter durations. It is also intended to reduce interfirm and interindustry subsidies, thereby achieving a more efficient allocation of labor. Moreover, it provides incentives for firms to challenge benefit claims they feel are unwarranted, thus providing some self-policing of the system.

Despite the general acceptance of experience rating as a tool to modify employer behavior, two factors have limited its success. First, the provision of extended benefits during recent recessions has increased the share of UI benefits financed from federal revenues and thus not subject to state experience-rating systems. Second, federal UI tax provisions provide an incentive to states to have some experience rating, but do little to encourage *more complete* experience rating. Instead, the specific method and extent of experience rating has largely been left to the states to determine. The result has been a significant variation among state UI systems in the degree of effective experience rating.

Experience rating is less than complete in all states because of minimum and maximum tax rates provided for in state laws. Only those employers with tax rates between the minimum and maximum are appropriately experience rated. Employers paying the minimum tax cannot lower their tax rate by reducing layoffs, while employers paying the maximum tax will not face a higher tax rate if they further increase layoffs. In addition, experience rating is less than complete because of noncharged benefits (benefits not charged against the UI recipient's employer). The major source of noncharged benefits arises when an employee quits; although the employee may be eligible for benefits, those benefits will not be charged to the employer's account.

Any decline in the level of experience rating can have an important impact both on the behavior of individual employers and on the amount to which some industries subsidize the unemployment of others. For example, one recent study showed that almost all employers in the relatively high unemployment industries of manufacturing and agriculture were subsidized during 1977–78.[3] The industries paying the largest subsidies were the relatively low unemployment trade, finance, insurance, and real estate industries. Cross-subsidization like this encourages the production of "unemployment intensive" goods, thereby distorting resource allocation and raising the unemployment rate.

Two recent studies indicate that the level of experience rating has been declining. Topel and Welch conclude that this has resulted from the failure of maximum tax rates and the taxable wage base to keep up with increases in benefits.[4] Wandner and Crosslin found that less than 60 percent of total benefits paid in nine states during 1971–1978 was effectively charged to former employers, with the proportion effectively charged varying markedly over the business cycle.[5]

Studies of the impact of incomplete experience rating on employers' behavior have turned up even more important findings. Brechling estimated that at a 6 percent unemployment rate, 2 percentage points are the result of layoffs, and if the maximum tax rate were doubled, the layoff rate would fall to one percentage point.[6] Hence, a doubling of the maximum tax rates would have the effect of reducing a 6 percent unemployment rate to 5 percent. A study by Halpin indicated that an increase of one percentage point in the maximum tax rate would result in a decrease of 0.14 percentage point in the temporary layoff unemployment rates, or a cut of approximately 10 percent.[7] Studies by Feldstein and Topel have shown similar results.[8]

The importance of experience rating in encouraging fiscal responsibility is equally significant. During the 1981–82 recession, many states found themselves with inadequate UI tax revenue to cover UI benefit payments and were forced to borrow from the federal government. Foreseeing the implications of this for future UI tax rates, the business community exerted considerable pressure for UI reforms. In many states this effort was successful, resulting in significant tightening of eligibility and work test requirements and reductions in UI benefits. At the same time, just the opposite was happening with the introduction and expansion of FSC, which is funded out of general revenues. From September 1982 to September 1983 alone, $5.6 billion was spent on FSC. While the total lack of experience rating in FSC does not completely explain either the program's existence or largesse, it is clear that the general revenue financing of FSC was important in dampening the business community's opposition to the program. It is equally clear that expensive programs like FSC will be a recurring feature of future recessions, largely because they will be operated as transfer programs rather than as true insurance plans.

In short, the EB and FSC federal extensions of UI have substantially reduced experience rating within the overall program, and recent evidence indicates that experience rating within the regular state programs probably has been on the decline as well. These developments make the system less efficient and more susceptible to expansion. In addition, the current trend toward erosion of UI experience rating is likely to generate pressure for even less experience rating in the future, especially from states that have borrowed heavily to subsidize their programs and employers within these states. The outcome is likely to be significant growth in a program that is increasingly coming to resemble a transfer program rather than the insurance program it was intended to be and should be.

Work-Related Injuries and Diseases

The first system for dealing with work-related injuries in the United States was the legal system of fault determination based on the common law. At its simplest, the party found to be at fault (the tortfeasor) had to pay for any damage he caused, providing employers (among others) with an economic incentive not to cause damage. Under common law, compensation for damages is total, with whatever harm can be shown compensated in full by whoever caused the damage.

Beginning in the early 1900s, workers' compensation programs began to replace the common law for most work-related injuries. Currently nearly all workers are covered by state systems, although a few are covered under federal statutes. The early programs were designed to cover traumatic injuries on a no-fault basis and were a radical departure from the fault-oriented common law. The programs shifted the risk from total compensation when the employer was at fault to employer liability for more limited compensation of all workplace injuries, regardless of fault.

The program structure and financing arrangements for workers' compensation are mandated by the states, and the states regulate the methods of insurance that employers use. Insurance can take the form of self-insurance by the employer, purchase of coverage from an insurer (either a private carrier or, in eighteen states, a state fund), or some combination of the two. Private insurers may have some form of deductible amount in their policies and thus a limited amount of self-insurance.

Experience rating is complete for self-insurers because they pay directly for damages suffered by their employees. Larger employers who purchase insurance are usually experience rated by the insurer. In addition, rebates or dividends may be paid back to the employer after the premium year if safety performance exceeds expectations. For smaller employers, premium rates in most states are developed by the National Council on Compensation Insurance and approved by state commissioners of insurance. The rates are based on past industry and occupational injury experience, not on an individual business's experience, although small employers with a bad injury record may be placed in higher risk categories with some increase in premium rates.

There are no generally accepted estimates of the amount of experience rating in the state systems. However, a reasonable guess based on indirect evidence is that 20 to 30 percent of covered workers are employed by firms with complete experience rating. Another 55 to 60 percent are with employers with partial experience rating, and about 15 percent are in firms with no experience rating. Hence, as much as 80 percent of the work force is employed under conditions of less than complete experience rating.

The lack of more complete experience rating causes overuse of the system because employers' incentives for assuring and enforcing safe work practices are reduced, leading to increases in accidents and other work-related injuries. In addition, statistics on the prevalence of experience rating exaggerate its actual extent. Under all systems, employers' liabilities are capped and thus are sometimes far less than the total loss.

Various developments in recent years have tended to undermine further the efficient allocation of workers' compensation costs. Growing social insurance programs, particularly Social Security, have picked up some costs originally intended to be borne by workers' compensation. The Social Security Disability Program, for example, was expanded dramatically in the early 1970s. Although this program has an offset for workers' compensation benefits, a number of states have been allowed to *reverse* the offset. In such cases, workers' compensation payments, which have some experience rating, are replaced by Social Security Disability insurance, which has no experience rating. Old Age and Survivors Social Security benefits and programs such as Medicare, Medicaid, and vocational rehabilitation are also used as substitute sources of benefits that more appropriately should be paid by workers' compensation. Allowing these general revenue programs to spill over into work-related disability compensation increases the costs of the broader social insurance programs, which are already in serious financial trouble, and simultaneously reduces employers' incentives to assure safe working conditions.

The most significant development related to workplace risks in recent years has been the growing importance of long-latency occupational diseases. These diseases present unique technical difficulties that make evaluating damage and allocating costs extremely difficult. Although workers' compensation does not require a showing of employer fault, it *does* require that the workplace be the cause of the condition. The current state of medical and scientific knowledge about the toxicity of various substances often permits the demonstration that a particular agent is, for example, carcinogenic. However, the fact that exposure to asbestos, for example, can cause cancer does *not* prove that a particular case of cancer was in fact caused by asbestos. This makes the link between the disease and the workplace tenuous at best and thus makes workers' compensation as yet ill suited as a remedy. One symptom of this is that workers' compensation awards in occupational disease cases have generally been both relatively infrequent and meager.

The fact that occupational diseases often appear only after long latency periods creates further problems. Few cancers are likely to show up within ten years of exposure, and many may not show up for thirty or more years. Moreover, knowledge of a substance's toxicity is often discovered only many years after the substance has been introduced into society. By that time, the exposed population can be large, and the ability to prevent disease extremely limited. As a result it is difficult, and perhaps impossible, to structure an experience-rated compensation system because knowledge of the risks does not exist when the harmful exposure occurs. Finally, long latency periods make identification of which employer, insurer, or other party should pay for a given case difficult at best.

Because of these problems, workers' compensation has been slow to adapt to providing compensation for occupational diseases. Although all state systems cover occupational diseases, the state systems have substantial barriers to occupational disease recoveries, including requirements that the worker have been recently exposed or that the disease not be an ordinary disease of life such as lung cancer. Pressures have mounted to create new programs to compensate those with such diseases. In response to earlier pressures along these lines, Congress enacted the black lung program in 1969. Initial estimates of total costs for the black lung program varied between $135 million and $1 billion (in 1982 dollars). In fact, the program had cost $14.5 billion through the end of 1982 and was expected to cost another $5.6 billion by the end of 1985.

Various factors have contributed to the explosion of costs in the black lung program. All of them are tied to the lack of risk or experience rating in the program. Eligibility for benefits was originally to be limited to the most serious cases coming from underground coal mines. The criteria for eligibility have been liberalized many times, often relying on presumptions of disability based on the number of years an individual had worked in the mines. Much of the liberalization of eligibility took place chiefly in the early years of the program when it was funded totally out of general revenues. The lack of a specific revenue source (such as a tax on coal production or employment) created a political imbalance; there simply was no coalescent political force to counter the strong push by miners for liberalization of eligibility.

Another important problem has been that, given the mobility of workers among mines, there was no way to determine which operator might have caused a particular case of the disease. This dilemma and the eligibility problems discussed in the previous paragraph led ultimately to a flat tax on coal production. This method of financing is certainly superior to the use of general revenues since it allows for a better balancing of political forces. Nevertheless, it is virtually devoid of risk- or experience-related components. As a result, mine operators have no financial incentives to contest possibly erroneous or fraudulent claims, or to seek better means to reduce the incidence of black lung except in the relatively few cases where they are made specifically liable.

In short, the black lung program has become largely an income transfer program with inadequate experience rating of employers, inappropriate financial incentives, and belated fiscal restraint. Indeed, critics of the program allege that it amounts to little more than a pension program for miners rather than a responsible means of compensating for an occupational disease.

The huge costs of the black lung program demonstrate the danger of creating special compensation programs to deal with specific occupational diseases. Nevertheless, the sluggish response of the workers' compensation system has created strong pressures to do just that. These pressures have been intensified by the seeming inability of the tort system to deal with the problem—either because of the bankruptcy of alleged tort-feasors such as the Manville Corporation or the staggering legal fees associated with bringing and defending lawsuits. The result of these pressures has been the development of proposals to create special compensation schemes for victims of occupational diseases. The potential costs of such schemes are staggering. Compensating asbestos victims, for example, could cost half a *trillion* dollars over the next thirty years under one widely discussed 1982 legislative proposal. Since asbestos is but one of many disease-causing agents in the workplace (including those as yet unknown), the inescapable conclusion is that hasty action in dealing with compensation for victims of occupational diseases is likely to be disastrous action.

Whether the ultimate response to the problem takes the form of fundamental reform of tort law or the development of alternative compensation systems, the experiences of the workers' compensation system and the black lung programs suggest some guidelines. First, the identities of the parties responsible for paying the cost of compensation must be clear from the outset. Any program predicated on general revenue financing will face a set of political forces so unbalanced as to ensure virtually uncontrollable costs. Second, whether through some form of comparative negligence or through risk- or experience-rated insurance premiums, parties must perceive the true costs of their actions. Only if this principle is followed will the incidence and costs of occupational diseases be minimized. Finally, and this is more speculative, the past failures of the federal government to follow the first two guidelines suggest that the states and not the federal government should take the lead in developing solutions.

Pension Termination Insurance

As part of ERISA, two programs were enacted in 1974 to insure benefits when a private pension plan terminates with inadequate funds to meet its future commitments. The first program insures benefits of plans that cover the workers of only one employer. The second program insures benefits under collectively bargained plans that cover the workers of several different employers. In addition, each program applies only to defined-benefit pension plans (plans where the monthly benefit received is based on a formula typically related to the number of years with an employer, with a specific monthly amount payable for each year of employment).

Both programs are operated by the Pension Benefit Guaranty Corporation (PBGC), a public corporation created by Congress. The two programs are structured differently, and only the program that covers single employers is discussed here. This program insures the benefits of more than 90,000 pension plans covering over 28 million workers.[9] These plans currently have unfunded liabilities of over $45 billion, which are insured by the PBGC.

Prior to ERISA, pension plan terminations were reasonably rare, and the proportion of benefits for which funds had already been set aside was reasonably high. During the 1960s only a little over one-tenth of 1 percent of plans terminated in a given year, and there was only a 2.5 percent chance that a plan would terminate in a given 25-year period, the typical tenure of a worker receiving a private pension benefit. Moreover, throughout that decade, pension plans were about 85 percent funded in the aggregate.

With generally high funding rates and low termination rates, Congress anticipated that insuring pension plan terminations would be inexpensive. The initial annual premium for the program was set at a flat $1.00 per plan participant. For most, if not all, plans this was an imperceptible increase in plan costs. Furthermore, the act placed no restrictions on the circumstances under which an employer could terminate his pension program. Thus, as was the case prior to ERISA, an employer could voluntarily terminate a pension plan at any time.

In the case of pension termination insurance, as in other public insurance programs, events subsequent to the program's enactment demonstrated the hazard of failing to adjust premiums in accordance with risks. From 1975 to 1979, the proportion of pension benefits that were funded dropped from its pre-1970s level of nearly 85 percent to a little under 65 percent. The annual termination rate for pension plans, on the other hand, jumped from its 1960s level of a little over 0.1 percent to over 0.5 percent, a fivefold increase. As a result, workers in the late 1970s faced a risk of one in eight that their pension plans would terminate within a given 25-year period. Workers in the 1960s had faced a termination risk of but one in forty.

The substantial increase in terminations in the late 1970s occurred despite a provision in ERISA to prevent this. In an attempt to ensure that poorly funded plans would not immediately terminate in order to unload their substantial liabilities on the insurance system, ERISA included a provision that allowed the PBGC to attach up to 30 percent of a firm's net worth to cover any insufficiency in the assets of a terminating pension plan. This provision was considered a sufficient disincentive to prevent ongoing employers from terminating a pension plan. However, the experience of the late 1970s, as well as more recent experience, demonstrates the provision's ineffectiveness.

During previous recessions, employers had some incentive to hold on to their pension plans if only to maintain their promises to long-term employees. Under the pension termination insurance system, however, recessions and other periods of high debt-to-equity ratios are ideal for the termination of poorly funded pension plans. Employees' benefits are largely guaranteed by the PBGC, the firm can rid itself of a troublesome and large liability, and the employer can make a fresh start by establishing a new pension plan to insure continuation of employees' accruals of pension benefits.

The extent to which the pension insurance system is used in this way is reflected by the fact that two-thirds of the pension terminations for which the PBGC incurs a loss are plans of ongoing businesses. The potential for program growth here is staggering. In 1982, the PBGC identified some 90 to 95 employers who would gain by terminating their pension plans and paying the PBGC 30 percent of their net worth. If these employers all terminated their plans, the PBGC's deficit would jump from its 1982 level of around $300 million to over $3.0 billion.

As the PBGC's single-employer program costs have continued to grow, the congressionally set premium has had to be revised upward. The flat $1.00 per participant rate set in 1974 was raised to a flat $2.60 in 1977. This soon proved inadequate. By 1982, the PBGC was experiencing serious financial difficulties. In that year, assets plus premium income were estimated to fall $400 million short of the amount required to meet future obligations for plans that had already terminated. Thus, in early 1982 a flat-rate premium of $6.00 per participant was proposed. Almost two years later, Congress had not yet acted on this premium increase, and recent events indicate that it will be inadequate if it is enacted.

Since the $6.00 premium was proposed in early 1982, the PBGC has experienced 58 percent more in losses than projected. Its deficit grew by 90 percent in 1982, and an increased deficit in 1983 appears likely. In any event, the PBGC will have a negative cash flow in 1984 unless the $6.00 premium increase is made retroactive to January 1983. In addition, no allowance has been made in the premium increase or the PBGC's deficit projections for a major termination, such as would occur if a large corporation, such as financially troubled International Harvester, were to fail. One such termination would double the PBGC's deficit and almost immediately cause a negative cash flow. In short, the $6.00 per participant premium is inadequate to fund the single-employer program. Further premium increases are inevitable, and even without a single major plan failure, another doubling of the premium will probably occur by the end of the decade.

Policymakers are not unconcerned about the growing deficits in this program. On the contrary, the PBGC's problems have received a great deal of attention. However, what is most startling about the proposals to control program costs is the lack of attention to introducing a risk-related premium. Virtually all proposals focus only on ways of preventing plans from terminating or of forcing plans to fund at the time of termination. Although implicitly reducing insurance in these ways is clearly one way of getting costs under control, it does nothing to improve the private pension system fundamentally in the longer run. In fact, it is likely to damage it.

With each new premium hike, the flat-rate premium will become more inequitable for employers of well-funded plans. Increasingly these employers will be penalized by paying for risks they did not create. In addition, each rate hike will further discourage the formation of new defined-benefit plans and give the best-funded plans a larger incentive to terminate. Developing risk-related premiums that reflect the amount of the unfunded liability, industry and firm health, a plan's financial well-being, and the soundness of plan management would allow the costs to be better assigned to potential beneficiaries of the coverage. This would result in a fairer rate structure that would not contain counterproductive incentives.

What many policymakers do not seem to understand is that the current system is a transfer program for workers covered by private defined-benefit pension plans. There is no incentive to fund and no reward for doing so. Moreover, the current system lacks any incentive to treat unfunded liabilities as a true liability in financial planning.

Unlike many other transfer programs, the losers (the well-funded plans) under this transfer scheme have the option of withdrawing by terminating their plans. This would leave the system with only the most poorly funded, high-risk plans. It seems unlikely that it was the intent of the framers of this program to discourage defined-benefit pension plans, particularly well-funded ones.

Perseverance will be required to maintain a sensible and affordable network of public and private programs to insure against workplace risks. While there are shortcomings in existing programs, potential problems threaten to be even more serious. This is especially the case for the compensation of occupational disease.

Prudent policy dictates that publicly sponsored workplace risk programs be fashioned as insurance programs. These programs need a strong element of risk-related financing to impose a price that discourages excessive program use and encourages fiscal restraint. In practice, these goals can usually be achieved by allocating costs appropriately through experience- and risk-related premiums. While the importance of this policy is quite clear, too often the principle of risk-related financing has been ignored. Short-term political considerations, veiled as compassion for program users by keeping costs low, threaten the financial integrity of the programs. Insolvency already has threatened the UI and black lung programs; it casts a shadow over the PBGC.

Past experience is discouraging. The two programs established fifty years ago or more—workers' compensation and unemployment insurance—contain at least some element of experience rating. In contrast, the programs established roughly a decade ago—PBGC and black lung—have no experience rating. Our political process appears to be unable to absorb the lessons of history or economics.

It is instructive that the two programs incorporating experience rating were fashioned by state governments rather than the federal government. Moreover, the financially strongest program, workers' compensation, is entirely a state program. Both factors support the notion that the state role should be a strong one.

The most pressing problem in the workplace-risk arena is that of developing a means for dealing effectively with long-term occupational disease. The technical difficulties of identifying causes and linking them to the workplace are substantial. However, the concern here is comparatively new, and these difficulties will be eased with additional attention and experience. Perhaps the most serious immediate danger is that programs will be enacted that reflect an irrational fear of the unknown—that is, too much income protection will be purchased under a financing structure that masks costs.

Notes

1. Total program costs in 1980 were $22 billion, including private insurers' claims adjustment costs, business expenses, and profits.
2. All states design their systems to enable employers to get full 2.7 percent credit. Hence, net federal tax is only 0.3 percent. Proceeds are used to finance EB and various administrative costs. FSC is funded out of general revenues.

3. Raymond C. Munts and Ephraim Asher, "Cross-subsidies Among Industries from 1969 to 1978," in *Unemployment Compensation: Studies and Research* (Washington, D.C.: National Commission on Unemployment Compensation, 1980), 2:299–314.
4. Robert Topel and Finis Welch, "Unemployment Insurance: Survey and Extensions," *Economica* 47 (1980): 351–80.
5. Stephen A. Wandner and Robert L. Crosslin, "Measuring Experience Rating," in *Unemployment Compensation: Studies and Research*, 2:271–76.
6. Frank Brechling, *Unemployment Insurance Tax and Labor Turnover: Further Empirical Results* (Alexandria, Va.: Public Research Institute, 1979).
7. Terrence C. Halpin, "Employment Stabilization," in *Unemployment Compensation: Studies and Research*, 2:415–24.
8. Martin Feldstein, "The Effect of Unemployment Insurance on Temporary Layoff Unemployment," *American Economic Review* 68 (1978): 834–46; and Robert Topel, "Unemployment Insurance Financing and Unemployment: Empirical Investigation of Adverse Incentives" (paper prepared for Assistant Secretary for Policy, U.S. Department of Labor, Washington, D.C., 1982).
9. The program that insures multiemployer plans covers about 8 million additional participants in another 2,000 plans.

9
Farm Policy at a Crossroads: Critical Choices Facing U.S. Agriculture

Stuart B. Hardy

Nineteen hundred eighty-three marked the fiftieth anniversary of the Agricultural Adjustment Act—a measure that initiated the crop price support and production control programs that still constitute the core of the federal farm program. The years since the Dust Bowl days of the Great Depression have witnessed mechanization and the introduction of hybrid crop varieties, new production methods and technologies, and fundamental changes in marketing conditions and the entire structure of agriculture. These changes have rendered the farm program increasingly obsolete. Recent escalating costs of the farm program and the dramatic response of the Reagan administration through the Payment-in-Kind (PIK) program have focused public attention on the inadequacies of stabilization programs that have governed agriculture for two generations. This critical public scrutiny provides a timely opportunity to undertake major reforms and bring federal farm policy into line with marketplace realities.

During the fiscal year that ended on September 30, 1983, farm support programs cost taxpayers a record amount of approximately $22 billion—nearly twice the 1982 expenditure, itself a record.[1] This vast investment of tax dollars has done little to cure the ailing farm economy. Farm income remains at depressed levels, well below the prosperous years of the mid-1970s. Aggregate farm indebtedness stands at $216 billion, the highest in our history, and the debt-to-asset ratio is 20 to 6, also a record.[2] The farm parity index, a rough but useful measurement of farm purchasing power, fluctuated during fiscal 1983 in the 55 to 60 percent range, a level approaching the 50-year low set in 1933.

The Scarcity Syndrome

How did American agriculture—reputed to be the most efficient and productive in the world—sink to such depressed levels? The recent history of federal farm policy illustrates the failure of farm programs and government planners to cope with the new realities and rapidly changing conditions of the agricultural economy.

The story begins during the 1970s, a decade that seemed to many policymakers to usher in a new era of food scarcity, world hunger, and a shrinking capacity to produce food. Rising energy costs seemed to halt the march of the Green Revolution in developing countries already suffering from a series of poor grain harvests. The Soviet entry into U.S. grain markets in 1972–73 and the rapid annual growth of U.S. exports for the remainder of the decade suggested the growing dependence of a hungry world on American agriculture. The problem of endemic crop surpluses during the 1950s and 1960s became a dim memory as Washington policymakers geared up to meet the challenge of food shortages.

This "scarcity syndrome"—as Secretary of Agriculture John R. Block termed it[3]—pervaded government and academic circles. It was clearly evident, for example, in the findings of President Carter's Commission on World Hunger, in the concern of resource planners over the conversion and erosion of farmland, and in the alarm of research scientists over the lack of new breakthroughs in crop yields and productivity.

Congress was also alarmed. Assuming the need for greater production, the Omnibus Farm Bills of 1973, 1977, and 1981 set high support levels for major commodities. In many instances, programs were indexed to assure annual increases in support levels.

Farmers responded to the incentives provided by these government actions. More than 60 million acres of new cropland were brought into production from 1971 to 1982, and crop production per acre rose 17 percent during the same period.[4] Meanwhile, rising land values during that inflationary decade meant more credit, and aggregate debt tripled as farmers and ranchers made heavy capital investments.[5] These trends were accelerated during the Carter administration by the easy credit policies of the Farmers Home Administration. Excessive debt was secured by land values that had risen, in part, because the value of crops was guaranteed by the government.

Scarcity Turns to Surplus

The consequences of the full production, high support policy were not immediately apparent. Strong domestic and international demand for U.S. food and fiber generally kept market prices at or above support levels, and annual government outlays—in the $3 to $4 billion range during the late 1970s—were relatively modest.

By autumn 1981, however, the situation had clearly turned around. The economic recession had caused a leveling-off of domestic demand for farm products. But the real pinch came in foreign markets, which had accounted for the lion's share of growth in U.S. agriculture during the preceding decade. During the fiscal year ending September 30, 1982, the value of farm exports, which had reached a record level of almost $44 billion in 1981, declined 11 percent.[6]

At home, favorable weather conditions and attractive government support prices spurred grain farmers to set all-time production records in 1981 and, again, in 1982. While the marketplace signaled less production, the support programs signaled more production, and producers were encouraged to invest and to make production decisions that made the situation even worse. Surplus stocks of wheat, corn, rice, cotton, and other commodities began to pile up at an alarming rate.

These surpluses loomed over the marketplace and resulted in sharply lower commodity prices, depressed farm income, and higher government farm program expenditures. From mid-1981 to late 1982, the prices farmers received for wheat, corn, and cotton fell 10 to 25 percent.[7] Farm income declined from $26.7 billion in 1979 to about $19 billion in 1982. Government outlays to support commodity prices tripled in the fiscal year ending September 30, 1982, to set a $12 billion record.[8]

The Farm Program

The farm crisis that developed in 1981–82 illustrates, in part, certain chronic problems unique to agriculture. The vagaries of weather, pest and disease problems, technology breakthroughs, and other factors make supply highly uncertain. Shifts in production volume require a relatively long lead time in many commodities, particularly in the dairy and livestock sectors. The large number of producers and the highly competitive nature of the business make any concerted action extremely difficult. Moreover, since farmers and ranchers possess fixed assets in land and machinery, they often continue to produce despite declines in commodity prices. In fact, the typical response of crop farmers to declining prices is to increase production in the hope of making up in volume what is lost in value.

The basic farm statutes of the New Deal era—the Agricultural Adjustment Act of 1933 and its successors, the Soil Conservation and Domestic Allotment Act of 1935, and the Agricultural Marketing Agreement Act of 1937—attempted to ease the problem of chronic disequilibrium in supply and demand by putting a floor under prices, establishing production control mechanisms such as marketing quotas and acreage allotments, and providing for the removal of surplus commodities from the marketplace.

The basic price support mechanism, the nonrecourse commodity loan program, is still in effect. The program provides growers of cotton, wheat, rice, soybeans, corn, and several other commodities with seasonal loans secured by the commodity itself. The U.S. Department of Agriculture's Commodity Credit Corporation (CCC) lends a specified amount per bushel or pound on a farmer's crop. If the market price goes higher than the loan level, the farmer sells his crop, repays the loan, and pockets the difference. If the market price falls below the loan level, the farmer turns the crop over to the CCC in full repayment with no further obligation.

In addition to nonrecourse loans, growers of cotton, wheat, rice, corn, and other feed grains are supported by "target prices." A target price is specified annually for each of these crops, and it is set higher than the loan level. If the market price falls below the target price, the government must pay the farmer a deficiency payment equal to the difference between the target price and the price the farmer actually received in the marketplace. The Agriculture and Food Act of 1981 (1981 Farm Bill) set the wheat loan level at $3.55 per bushel and the target price at $4.05 for the 1982 crop. The 1982 corn loan was set at $2.55 per bushel and the target at $2.70. These prices were well above market-clearing levels in 1982, and high deficiency payments were required.

The third major element of the crop price support mechanism is the Farmer-Owned Reserve. This program offers highly attractive nonrecourse loans and storage payments in exchange for keeping the collateral crop in the Reserve for three years, or until the market price reaches a certain, predesignated level.

Target prices and loan levels are set in law as part of the Omnibus Farm Bills usually enacted every four years. The House and Senate Agriculture Committees have made a conscientious effort in recent years to develop loan and target prices with reference to the cost of production. But the costs of producing a bushel of wheat or a pound of cotton vary enormously from farm to farm and region to region. In the end, support levels are more often the result of political trade-offs and commodity-group lobbying than the cost of production. Moreover, support levels reflect assumptions about future price and demand that may prove totally inaccurate.

The secretary of agriculture has relatively little flexibility to alter the program in response to changing conditions. One of the few tools at the secretary's discretion is the authority to require crop farmers to set aside or retire a certain percentage of their normal planted acreage as a condition for participation in the support program. Secretary Block exercised this option in 1981 by requiring a 15 percent acreage reduction for 1982 wheat, rice, and cotton and a 10 percent reduction of acres planted to corn. Some eleven million acres were retired, but grain farmers nevertheless produced record crops.

This is just one recent example in a long history of frustrating experiences with acreage reduction programs. Farmers retire their least productive land and farm the remainder intensively with generous applications of pesticides, fertilizers, and other inputs. Moreover, there is some evidence that other grain-producing nations have taken advantage of acreage reductions in the United States to increase their own production.[9]

Payment-in-Kind

As the 1982 crop came to harvest, Secretary Block spelled out the terms of the 1983 wheat, rice, cotton, corn, and feedgrain programs. Farmers who wished to receive nonrecourse loans and target price supports in 1983 would be required to idle from 10 to 20 percent of their cropland, depending on the crop. As a further incentive to reduce plantings, participating farmers were offered cash payments for idling an additional 5 to 10 percent of their cropland.

However, it was increasingly apparent that these production curbs would not be adequate. By autumn 1982, bin-busting stocks were piling up throughout the Grain Belt, and farm policymakers were in a difficult fix. With farm program incentives already locked into place as part of the 1981 Farm Bill, another bumper crop in 1983 appeared likely. Farm income was plummeting—in December, the Agriculture Department forecast net farm income in 1983 in the range of $15 to $19 billion[10]—and the costs to taxpayers had reached a level that embarrassed even the most cynical farm lobbyist.

Clearly, a drastic reduction of supply levels was needed. Some members of Congress proposed a massive expansion of the paid diversion program—cash payments in exchange for land retirement.[11] This proposal was deemed too expensive by the administration. Instead, the administration devised the PIK program, another method of paying farmers not to farm. The concept was simple. Producers of wheat, cotton, rice, corn, and grain sorghum were asked to cut production in 1983 in exchange for free commodities in amounts nearly equal to the amount of the reduction on each participating farm. This "crop swap" plan could be implemented with existing statutory authorities, and it was designed to operate in addition to the requirements of the acreage reduction and cash land diversion programs already announced for 1983. Altogether, this complex mechanism was expected to liquidate burdensome surplus stocks, bolster commodity prices, and end the hemorrhaging of government deficiency payments.

Farmers put a pencil to the numbers and responded with enthusiasm. In March 1983, the PIK sign-up figures were released. Some 83 million acres had been enrolled—about one-third of normal grain acres—and more than expected.[12] Crop estimates for 1983 were lowered, and prices were strengthened on the futures markets.

As the season progressed, an unusually wet spring and a severe summer drought throughout many growing regions further reduced the projected crop size. By September 1983, the Department of Agriculture's Crop Reporting Board was forecasting a two-thirds reduction in corn and sorghum carry-over stocks and similar cuts in cotton and rice stocks. Of all PIK commodities, only wheat, which was largely harvested in the spring and unaffected by the drought, failed to register a sharp decline in carry-over stocks.[13]

Administration officials argue with some justification that PIK, with the weather's cooperation, largely achieved its intended goal of bringing supply back into balance with demand. They point out that PIK, although drastic medicine, was the least costly and disruptive alternative available under the circumstances. The book value of PIK commodities—about $12 billion[14]—must be measured against the longer-term costs of price-depressing surpluses.

Critics of PIK have raised the specter of rising retail food costs, poked fun at the administration for paying farmers not to farm, and called attention to some logistical problems such as the shortages of upland cotton and long-grain rice.

However, the pertinent issue is much broader than PIK, and the PIK debate should not be allowed to obscure the real issue. What is at issue is the farm policies and programs that made PIK, or something like PIK, necessary by misallocating resources and destabilizing markets to the detriment of farmers, consumers, and taxpayers. The clumsy machinery of price support and supply management programs has grown increasingly unsuitable for a modern, dynamic, and rapidly changing agriculture.

Export Trade and Price Supports

Nowhere has change in the agricultural industry been more evident than in the dramatic expansion of export markets during the 1970s. The value of farm exports rose from about $7 billion in 1970 to more than $40 billion in 1980. The United States now accounts for 40 percent of world trade in wheat, 58 percent in coarse grains, and 84 percent in soybeans. According to the Agriculture Department, the produce from two out of every five acres of U.S. cropland ends up in export channels.[15]

The integration of U.S. agriculture into the world economy poses several new challenges: specifically, the need to become more competitive in price, more reliable in supply, and more responsive to the changing requirements of world markets. The export boom years of the 1970s, fueled by strong world demand and favorable currency exchange rates, have now ended. Today's more competitive atmosphere, reflected in a recent drop in farm exports, requires an examination of all factors[16] that inhibit export effectiveness. One such factor was identified by Secretary Block in a statement before the Joint Economic Committee of Congress on January 31, 1983:

> The artificial umbrella over world prices that we have created through the persistent upward ratcheting of our domestic support prices during the past inflationary spiral has served to encourage producers in other countries to increase production.[17]

Other grain-exporting nations, such as Canada, Argentina, Australia, and France, carefully track and applaud every increase in the U.S.

support levels, which promptly raises the ceiling over world grain prices and, at a stroke, renders them more competitive. Conversely, when President Reagan asked Congress to freeze target prices at 1983 levels, the Canadians and French protested. The Canadian Wheat Board called it "not good exporter cooperation."[18] Our competitors understand that the more we bring our support programs into line with market-clearing levels, the more it costs them to shield their farmers from the market.

Milking the Dairy Program

One major sector of the agriculture industry that has not participated in the export boom is the dairy industry. It provides a graphic example of a commodity sector, geared almost exclusively to stable domestic markets, which has experienced runaway surpluses stimulated by excessive support levels.

Dairy prices are maintained through the CCC's offer to purchase unlimited amounts of manufactured dairy products (butter, cheese, and nonfat dry milk) at specified prices. Fluid milk is regulated by 46 regional marketing orders, which set minimum prices that must be paid by handlers to dairy farmers.

In 1977, the dairy lobby persuaded Congress to increase the support level, from a price equivalent to 75 percent of parity to 80 percent, and to require an adjustment in the support price every six months to keep in step with the parity index. The impact on milk production was not apparent for many months. Program costs remained relatively modest, and in 1979 Congress extended the 80 percent of parity level (then $10.76 per hundredweight) for another two years.

However, dairymen had been responding all along with a gradual buildup in herd numbers, and some nondairymen were attracted into the business. The expanded production began to show up in late 1979. In the fiscal year ending September 30, 1980, the indexed support level went from $10.76 to $12.36, production rose by 4.7 billion pounds, and the government was forced to "remove" 8.2 billion pounds of surplus products at a cost of $1 billion. The following year, the support price, still indexed at 80 percent of parity level, had risen to $13.10 per hundredweight. Milk production increased another 4.4 billion pounds, and the government had to purchase and store 12.7 billion pounds at a cost of $1.9 billion.[19]

Congress froze the support level at $13.10 per hundredweight in 1981, but with little effect. Milk production continued to rise through 1983, and program costs are now in excess of $2 billion per year. As of September 1, 1983, government storage facilities contained 457.5 million pounds of butter, slightly more than one billion pounds of cheese, and 1.3 billion pounds of nonfat dry milk.[20]

Any remedy is certain to be painful to dairy farmers who made investments in their operations on the promise of high supports. The president, in seeming violation of his market-oriented philosophy, has signed into law a dairy lobby bill that provides cash payments to producers in exchange for a cut in base production levels.[21] Meanwhile, high supports have attracted foreign imports, encouraged the development of substitute products, increased retail prices, and contributed to a further decline in domestic dairy consumption.

Basic Choices

Farm policy is now at a crossroads of long-term significance. The signs point with increasing clarity to a fundamental, structural change in farm programs during the mid-1980s. Huge federal expenditures have focused public attention on farm policy, and if recent polls are accurate, the public is losing patience.[22] With only 3 percent of the total U.S. population now living on farms and ranches, the demographic base of the once powerful congressional farm bloc has shrunk in size and influence. The 1981 Farm Bill squeaked through the House of Representatives with only a two-vote margin, and other farm-related legislation has lately been treated to a degree of critical scrutiny unthinkable in the days of Congressman Bob Poage and Senator Allen Ellender.

New actors have come on the scene demanding a full voice in the policymaking process. These groups, including environmentalists, consumer advocates, the hunger lobby, and others, have little or no vested interest in the existing structure of support programs.

Divisions in the farm community are jeopardizing its political muscle in Washington, D.C. As agriculture has become more specialized, single-commodity organizations, such as the National Wheat Growers or the American Soybean Association, have taken on more influence. These organizations are not reluctant to press their own agendas even to the occasional detriment of other farm organizations.

All these factors raise questions about the ability of farm leaders in

Congress to extend the existing structure of farm programs when the current Farm Bill expires in 1985.

Farm, agribusiness, and food industry leaders are themselves voicing the need for fundamental changes in farm policy. This was evident, for example, at the Agricultural Summit Meeting in Washington, D.C., on July 12–13, 1983. While there was little consensus among farm and business leaders on a specific course of action, virtually everyone agreed on the need for basic changes. A return to business-as-usual in farm program management will jeopardize whatever good PIK has accomplished and result in another buildup of costly, price-depressing surplus stocks.

What are the options in the wake of PIK? Those who favor the continuation of price supports and an aggressive government role in agriculture generally agree that the problem can be remedied by stronger, more effective production controls. They suggest, for example, that acreage reduction programs could be strengthened through a carrot-and-stick combination of positive incentives (such as cash payments for idle land) and negative incentives (such as making conservation grants, crop insurance, and other government benefits contingent upon participation in the acreage program).

Production controls, however effective, are unlikely to keep supply in balance with demand because supply management programs are always predicated on the ability of government planners to anticipate supply and demand needs months in advance. Government would remain in the tractor seat, trying to second-guess the marketplace and paying the consequences when it calls the wrong shot. Farmers might gain a small measure of security, but they would lose a large measure of the freedom to pursue the full rewards of the marketplace. Moreover, domestic price supports would continue to undermine the competitive posture of U.S. commodities in world markets.

The Market Approach

A more promising alternative to the farm problem is put forward by proponents of greater market orientation in U.S. farm policy. This approach generally calls for the phased reduction or elimination of most price supports and supply management programs and strong emphasis on the expansion of export markets.

The first step toward a market approach should be the elimination, at the earliest possible date, of target prices for cotton and grains. The target-price mechanism was embraced by Congress in 1973 as a means of assuring minimum price levels that would not interfere with markets at home or abroad. However, as Secretary Block has convincingly argued, target prices have a significant effect on U.S. and foreign producers' supply decisions because producers know that budget exposure (that is, the higher the target level relative to the market level, the greater the exposure of the budget to mandated expenditures) and the prospect of huge deficiency payments will prompt the government to do everything possible to move farm prices up to the targeted levels.[23]

Nonrecourse commodity loans might serve a useful purpose as a safety-net support mechanism, but they must be set no higher than average market-clearing levels. Several economists have suggested that loan rates might be set annually at a certain percentage of a moving average of recent market prices for the commodity in question. They point to the example of the soybean loan program as a model for other commodities.[24] The secretary of agriculture has broad discretion to set soybean loan rates, and rates have generally been held below market levels. The method has proved acceptable to soybean growers who have no intention of encouraging the Brazilians and other soybean exporters to expand production. Consequently, soybeans have remained highly competitive in world markets.

The Farmer-Owned Reserve is a useful means of assuring a reliable supply for domestic and export markets and moderating wild fluctuations in price. Since 1980, however, the Reserve has been kept open for unlimited entry and pressed into service as a price support mechanism. As a result, farmers have been encouraged to produce for the Reserve. To correct this situation, the amount of commodities permitted into the Reserve should not exceed minimum quantities actually needed to offset a temporary shortfall.

The Agriculture and Food Act of 1981 expires in 1985 and must be replaced by a new farm bill. The elimination of target prices and the restructuring of nonrecourse commodity loans and the farmer-owned reserve are basic remedial measures that should be incorporated into the bill.

In the meantime, federal policymakers should consider the phased and orderly reduction of sugar import fees and quotas and domestic price supports that penalize our Caribbean allies and keep U.S. prices at about twice the world market level.

Other corrective steps might include a further examination of federal marketing orders for fruits, vegetables, and specialty crops. Marketing orders may be necessary to dampen the boom-and-bust price fluctuations endemic to those commodities. However, they should not be used to establish price cartels, restrict entry, or limit supply.

The 50 states should be encouraged to assume a greater share of the responsibility and cost of essential services in such areas as animal health and plant pest quarantines, market regulation and promotion, and soil and water conservation. The states have generally demonstrated an ability to carry out these functions at lower cost than the federal government and with comparable effectiveness.

Finally, producers should be encouraged to take fuller advantage of innovative marketing tools available in the private sector. The use of forward contracts, which lock in a price, is a well-established practice. More producers are also turning to the commodity futures markets to hedge price risks. Another attractive price-risk management tool—commodity options—has only recently become available. Unlike forward or futures contracts, options permit growers to buy the right or option to sell their crops at a specified price. There is no obligation to follow through. If the market goes up, the grower is free to walk away from the contract. If it declines, the grower can keep the contract and get the higher price.[25]

Excessive farm program costs have aroused public concern and created an opportunity to re-examine the basic principles and tools of federal farm policy. The presidential election in 1984 and the need to fashion a new farm bill in 1985 provide a timely forum for discussion of long-needed reforms in U.S. farm policy.

Agriculture is not the poor cousin of the American economy. It is an economic asset and a vast source of national wealth and prosperity. It has come of age as an efficient, dynamic, and aggressive force in U.S. and world commerce. The food and agricultural industry accounts for 20 percent of the gross national product, farm-related businesses employ 23 million people, and farm exports are the single largest factor in the balance of trade. Agriculture should be released from the straightjacket of antiquated policies and programs and allowed to share fully in the risks and rewards of the nation's economy.

Notes

1. In July 1983, the Office of Management and Budget (OMB) sent Congress the annual *Mid-Session Review* budget estimates, which projected an outlay of $21.8 billion to support commodity prices in fiscal year 1983, up from about $12 billion in fiscal year 1982.
2. U.S. Department of Agriculture, Economic Research Service, *Economic Indi-*

Stuart B. Hardy 181

    cators of the Farm Sector: Income and Balance Sheet Statistics, 1982 (Washington, D.C.: Government Printing Office, August 1983), ECIFS 2–2.
3. Testimony before the Joint Economic Committee of Congress, May 19, 1983.
4. Ibid., January 31, 1983.
5. Ibid.
6. U.S. Bureau of the Census, *FT-990: Highlights of U.S. Export and Import Trade* (Washington, D.C.: Government Printing Office, July 1983).
7. U.S. Department of Agriculture, Economic Research Service, *An Initial Assessment of the Payment-in-Kind Program*, 1309 (Washington, D.C.: Government Printing Office, April 1983), p. 5.
8. Ibid.
9. Block testimony of May 19, 1983.
10. Department of Agriculture, *An Initial Assessment of the Payment-in-Kind Program*, p. 15.
11. Perhaps the chief congressional spokesman for the paid diversion approach to the surplus problem was Congressman Glenn English (Dem., Okla.), who subsequently put this proposal in legislative form (H.R. 2634) and introduced it in the House of Representatives on April 20, 1983.
12. U.S. Department of Agriculture, Economic Research Service, *Outlook and Situation Summary: PIK Assessment* (Washington, D.C.: Government Printing Office, March 31, 1983).
13. U.S. Department of Agriculture, Crop Reporting Board, Statistical Reporting Service, *Crop Production* (Washington, D.C.: Government Printing Office, September 12, 1983).
14. U.S. Department of Agriculture, Office of Governmental and Public Affairs, *Backgrounder: The Cost of PIK* (Washington, D.C.: Government Printing Office, May 1983).
15. Department of Agriculture, *Economic Indicators of the Farm Sector*, August 1982.
16. They include, in part, three consecutive years of above average world harvests, a leveling off of world demand, a strong U.S. dollar, the lingering effects of the 1980 embargo of grain to the Soviet Union, and increased use by other food-exporting nations of export subsidies and other "unfair" trade practices.
17. Testimony of January 31, 1983, p. 12.
18. Senator Hazen Argue, minister responsible for Canadian Wheat Board, quoted in Bob Rupp, "Viewpoint and Comments," *The Farmer* 101, no. 15 (August 6, 1983): 6.
19. Testimony of Deputy Secretary of Agriculture Richard E. Lyng before the U.S. House of Representatives Subcommittee on Livestock, Dairy and Poultry, June 9, 1982.

20. U.S. Department of Agriculture, Commodity Credit Corporation, "Commodities in Storage" (unpublished monthly report, September 1, 1983).
21. This measure, S. 1521, provides for a diversion payment of $10 for every hundredweight of milk a dairyman cuts from his normal production level.
22. For example, a national opinion survey conducted in 1983 by Cambridge Reports, Inc., suggests an erosion of support for programs that provide cash or in-kind subsidies for not planting crops (see N. L. Reding, "The Problem Is Us," *Farm Chemicals* 147, no. 8 [August 1983]: 46–48).
23. Block testimony of May 19, 1983.
24. See, for example, Bruce Gardner, "Bringing a Free Market to the Farm," in Richard N. Holwill, ed., *Agenda '83: A Mandate for Leadership Report*, (Washington, D.C.: Heritage Foundation, 1983), p. 36.
25. An excellent summary of commodity options appears in Susan Lee, "Options and Farmers," *Wall Street Journal*, September 8, 1983.

10

The Federal Budget: Problems and Prospects

Annelise Graebner Anderson

As this is written, in mid-1983, prospects for controlling federal spending and reducing the federal budget deficit to anything much below 5 percent of GNP without major tax increases are dim. This is not an encouraging conclusion to arrive at two and one-half years into the term of a president elected on a fiscally conservative platform, especially since the election was followed by strenuous and sophisticated efforts by the Reagan administration to implement its policies and, for a time, by the partial support of the United States Congress.

The federal budget thus remains the nation's major macroeconomic problem. There is little wrong, and little that has been wrong, with the U.S. economy that cannot be traced to fiscal problems—to how much and for what the government spends, and to how much and how it taxes. There was a time, culminating in the 1960s, when economists believed they could fine-tune government taxing and spending to achieve beneficial effects on the economy. Instead, macroeconomic history since the 1960s has been a history of macroeconomic problems created by federal taxing and spending—problems of inflation, low productivity, high interest rates, unemployment, recession, and uncertainty about the future course of government action to deal with the yet-unresolved fiscal dilemma.

The essence of this dilemma is that we are spending more than we are willing to tax. As of July 1983, the federal government was expected to collect less than 19 percent of GNP in taxes in fiscal 1983 and spend over 25 percent—6.6 for national defense, 2.8 for net interest, and 15.7 for domestic program spending.[1] President Reagan has stated his unwillingness to raise taxes at all before fiscal 1986, and then only by 1 percent of GNP. The Congressional Budget Resolution for 1984 proposed minor (less than 0.4 percent of GNP) tax increases for 1984 and 1985—$12 and $15 billion, respectively—and $46 billion for 1986, an amount comparable to the president's proposal for that year.[2] But in terms of fiscal policy, these differences reflect no essential disagreement between the president and the Congress: neither is willing to recommend tax increases that would balance the budget at current or projected levels of spending. A tax increase of the magnitude involved would be politically and economically disastrous, requiring sharp increases in marginal tax rates and far higher average tax rates as well. In only four years since 1945 have budget receipts exceeded 20 percent of GNP.[3]

Sound fiscal policy—essentially, the problem of maintaining incentives to work, save, and invest—precludes taxes that would balance the budget at current spending levels. Increasing fiscal 1984 taxes to 23 percent of GNP would require, as an example, a surcharge on corporate and individual income taxes of over 40 percent. Such a surcharge—or some other tax increase to raise comparable amounts of revenue—would be required indefinitely to maintain receipts at 23 percent of GNP.

Although the receipts side of the budget is at least partly determined by considerations of fiscal policy, these considerations have less power to affect the spending side. National defense spending is determined primarily by the needs of the nation as seen by the president, even though the Congress seldom gives the president everything he asks for. Interest on the federal debt is largely a function of decisions made in the past and is not directly controllable by any action of the president or the Congress. And the politics of domestic program spending, at the margin where changes might be made, is almost entirely the politics of special interest groups rather than the consequence of any debate about whether a little more or less spending would be desirable from a fiscal standpoint. Budget outlays for domestic program spending have been 14 percent or more of GNP since 1975. With national defense expenditures approaching 8 percent by 1988 and net interest close to 3 percent, the federal government will be spending almost 25 percent of GNP in 1988 if domestic spending is at 14 percent of GNP.

The fundamental problem of the budget is thus the tension between spending as a macroeconomic problem and the pressures to spend for specific programs, especially domestic spending programs that affect specific groups of people. For 1984, the Congressional budget resolution included over $23 billion more for domestic programs than President Reagan requested.[4] In a budget of some $850 billion, this may not seem like much; but it would add two-thirds of a percentage point of GNP to domestic program spending.

The heavy demands on the budget for domestic program spending have crept upward gradually but steadily since the early 1950s, when they absorbed about 6 percent of GNP. By 1959, domestic spending was over 8 percent; it exceeded 9 percent by 1962, 10 percent by the late 1960s, and 12 percent by 1972.[5] It was a steady process of new programs, more beneficiaries, looser eligibility standards, automatic spending programs that bypassed the appropriations process, and automatic adjustments for increases in the cost of living that came to exceed the increases in the wages of the people who were paying the taxes to finance the programs.

The vast majority of domestic program spending is for human resources—those programs included in four of the functional categories of the budget—education, training, employment, and social services; health; income security; and veterans benefits and services. In 1983, spending for these programs will be almost 13 percent of GNP, the highest GNP share in U.S. history. The balance—all other—shows no growth trend and is most often between 2.5 and 3.5 percent of GNP, although Reagan budget proposals drive it below this level. In this category are most of the traditional or historical responsibilities of the U.S. government—federal law enforcement and administration of justice, international affairs, tax collection, land management, agriculture, and transportation; some of the newer activities, including science, space, energy, and the environment; and virtually all the independent regulatory agencies.

GNP shares are used throughout this essay as a means of measuring expenditures that avoids dealing with dollar amounts that have different meanings in different time periods. The problem with GNP shares, however, is that they are subject to cyclical fluctuations. In a year of high unemployment, for example, outlays for domestic spending will be relatively high owing to lower real GNP growth and increased outlays for unemployment insurance and means-tested entitlement programs—more people will qualify for benefits. High real growth over a period of years, without increases in inflation, will lower the GNP share of a program—such as national defense—without decreasing the real program level that can be bought with a given dollar amount. If interest rates do not increase, the burden of interest on the federal debt will also lessen. There is nothing better for the federal budget, as well as the American people and the national defense, than sustained, noninflationary economic growth.

At this point, federal spending is the major threat to sustained economic growth. It threatens federal borrowing that could drive up interest rates or tax rates that endanger incentives. The primary criterion by which any policymaker evaluates a proposal should therefore be its effect on real economic growth.

The Reagan Campaign Proposal

During the Reagan campaign, five basic economic policy actions were proposed:

1. Controlling the growth of government spending;
2. Reducing tax rates to remove disincentives to work, save, and invest;
3. Altering regulations to encourage economic growth;
4. Encouraging a stable, sound, and predictable monetary policy;
5. Restoring confidence by following consistent policies.

This was—and has continued to be—the heart of Reagan economic policy. During the campaign, Reagan was challenged on the "mirrors" question: How was it possible to balance the budget, increase defense spending, and cut taxes at the same time? A document demonstrating that this was indeed possible, given economic forecasts available at that time, was presented as Table II of the fact sheet accompanying Reagan's September 9, 1980, speech on economic policy.[6]

This document was extremely carefully prepared. To ensure that its credibility would not founder in wrangling over economic assumptions, it used the assumptions adopted by the Senate Budget Committee in its August 1980 mark-up of the budget resolution. From the committee's estimates of current-law tax receipts, the document deducted the Congressional Budget Office estimates of revenue losses from the Kemp-Roth reductions in individual income tax rates and the indexing of tax brackets. For the proposed reduction in business taxes from accelerated depreciation allowances, it used the cost estimates for Senator Lloyd Bentson's version of this legislation rather than the more generous version proposed by Congressmen Barber Conable, Jr., and James Jones (the 10-5-3 plan).

The campaign also used the Senate Budget Committee's dollar estimates for national defense, which allowed for a real growth of about 5 percent. Finally, from the committee's projected federal spending in the absence of policy changes, the document deducted savings of 2 percent in 1981, 4 percent in 1982, 5 percent in 1983, 6 percent in 1984, and 7 percent in 1985. It also projected, on an irregular path, additional revenues from higher economic growth. The budget balanced in 1983 and went into surplus in 1984 and 1985.

This demonstration was presented in current dollar amounts rather than GNP shares, but the campaign fact sheet provides enough information to convert it to GNP shares; the result is shown in Table 10.1. The GNP implicit in the additional revenue implies, using a Treasury rule of thumb that higher GNP generates revenues at about 25 percent of GNP, that the real growth forecast was about half a percentage point above the 3.8 percent rate used by the Senate Budget Committee. There is no implication whatsoever here that the tax rate

Table 10.1
Reagan Campaign Projection of the Federal Budget Converted to GNP Shares

Budget Category	Fiscal Years				
	1981	1982	1983	1984	1985
National defense/GNP	5.6	5.9	5.8	5.9	5.9
Net interest/GNP (estimated)	2.0	1.8	1.6	1.5	1.5
Domestic program spending/GNP	14.3	13.7	12.9	12.1	11.2
Total spending/GNP	21.9	21.4	20.3	19.5	18.6
Receipts/GNP	21.1	20.7	20.4	20.2	20.6

SOURCE: Based on Fact Sheet, Table II, to Reagan speech, September 9, 1980.

reductions, which reduced revenues from what they otherwise would have been but nevertheless allowed increased dollar receipts, were seen as self-financing.

The policy emphasis during the campaign was entirely on the importance of reducing marginal tax rates to eliminate disincentives to work, save, and invest; but the implicit average tax burden declines as well. As Table 10.1 shows, the receipts share of GNP declined from a projected 21.1 percent in 1981 to 20.7 percent in 1982, 20.4 percent in 1983, 20.2 percent in 1984 (a statistical quirk resulting from lower real growth projected in that year than in 1983 or 1985), and 20.6 percent in 1985.

There is nothing remarkable in the implicit proposal to reduce taxes to 20.5 percent of GNP. From 1953 through 1979, receipts averaged 18.6 percent of GNP. Until 1981, the federal government had taken more than 20.5 percent of GNP in taxes only at the peak war expenditure years of 1944 and 1945; the president and the Congress had always acted to reduce the average tax burden on the economy when inflation and the progressive tax code had projected increases. In his speech on September 9, 1980, Reagan called for additional rate reductions in the second half of the decade, and the campaign projection shows total spending at 18.6 percent of GNP in 1985, a level that would presumably have allowed further rate reductions resulting in a lower average tax take.

In the campaign projection, domestic program spending increases in dollar amounts but drops from 14.4 percent of GNP in 1981 to almost 11 percent by 1985; it is about 13 percent in the balanced-budget year of 1983. National defense outlays, increasing at a constant real growth rate, remain just under 6 percent of GNP—a substantial increase from the level proposed in the 1981 Carter budget.

The March 1981 Budget Revisions

During a term in office, the president sends four full budgets to the Congress. The first is sent to the Congress a year after he takes office, for the fiscal year beginning almost two years after his election; this budget is under consideration by the Congress in the months before the mid-term elections. The second budget follows the mid-term elections. The third budget is a re-election budget, assuming the president is running; in any event, his party will have a candidate. The fourth full budget is sent to the Congress just days before the end of his term; for a president not re-elected, it is an outgoing budget, and he has adequate time after the November elections to do with it what he wishes.

None of these required budgets is as important as the budget revisions a new president sends to the Congress just after taking office. President Reagan sent a fully revised budget for 1982 to the Congress on March 18, 1981, less than eight weeks after the inauguration.[7]

That budget differed from campaign proposals and projections in some significant respects:

1. Indexing of income tax brackets was dropped.
2. The business tax cut was far more generous, especially in later years.
3. Nominal GNP growth rates—incorporating the estimates of administration economists of rates of inflation consistent with the policies it would encourage the Federal Reserve Board to follow—were lower than the Senate Budget Committee's projections of nominal GNP growth.

As a result, estimated dollar revenues were lower than the campaign projection, and so was the receipts share of GNP. Reduced estimates of receipts were an experience the Reagan administration was to face repeatedly in the following two years, as both government and private forecasters repeatedly lowered their estimates of both inflation and real growth.

The March 1981 tax proposals produced receipts at about 19.5 percent of GNP, rather than the implicit 20.5 percent of the campaign. The legislation actually passed by the Congress—the Economic Recovery Tax Act (ERTA) of 1981—restored indexing and added some provisions the administration had not requested as well as some it favored but had proposed during the campaign to postpone until fiscal conditions permitted. Without legislative changes, ERTA would have reduced receipts in fiscal 1984 and future years to less than 19 percent of GNP according to 1983 budget estimates and less than 18 percent by 1984 budget reckoning.[8]

The Tax Equity and Fiscal Responsibility Act of 1982 reversed some of the consequences of ERTA. Nevertheless, projected revenues through fiscal 1988 under tax legislation in effect as of January 1983 average less than 19 percent of GNP. The contingent tax plan in the 1984 budget proposed to restore receipts to over 20 percent of GNP for fiscal 1986 and the following two years, in the event certain requirements were met. Had tax changes maintained the receipts share of GNP at the campaign level of about 20.5 percent, the 1983 deficit would have been over $60 billion lower, considering the actual economic events that occurred.

The March 1981 budget revisions also increased spending for national defense above the campaign projections, to just over 7 percent of GNP by 1986, instead of about 6 percent. Since then, dollar requests have been reduced by about $20 billion, but the July 1983 estimate of the 1986 GNP share increased to 7.6 percent owing to the lower GNP growth rate.

Outlays for domestic program spending were even lower than the campaign projections, declining to 11.2 percent of GNP in 1984 and 10.5 percent in 1986. While these projections included unidentified savings, they did not include the administration's Social Security proposals presented in May 1981.

National Defense

Spending for national defense averaged 8.9 percent of GNP from 1946 to 1973. It declined from 10.8 percent of GNP for the years 1952–1961 to 8.3 percent for 1962–1971 to 5.6 percent for 1972–1981. The downward trend in the national defense share of GNP since the late 1950s accompanied the upward trend in domestic program spending; the country was funding social programs out of the defense budget. The Carter 1981 budget, under consideration by the Congress during the election year of 1980, proposed defense spending at about 5.3 percent of GNP.

The bipartisan view that this was too low was reflected in the budget resolution prepared by the Senate Budget Committee in August 1980, where President Carter's request was ignored and national defense was increased to 6 percent of GNP. The Reagan administration proposed further increases in March 1981. Even by 1988, the administration's defense program leaves the national defense share of GNP under 8 percent.

The difficulty the administration has encountered in the Congress in increasing defense spending to a level that is still modest by historical standards reflects the consequences of baseline domestic program spending of 14 to almost 16 percent of GNP; this claim leaves little room for a national defense increase without major deficits or tax increases. During World War II, the country spent over 37 percent of GNP for national defense for three consecutive years, while decreasing domestic program spending from 7.5 percent of GNP in 1940 to 3.5 percent in 1945, a share that today would cover only about two-thirds of Social Security payments.

The impression one got from inside the administration was that by the time Reagan took office, the defense community felt it had been starved for funds for years. It seemed willing to support any expenditure that would increase national security in any way, regardless of cost—a strategy, perhaps, that funds should be gotten while the getting was good. The defense community seemed especially willing to support spending that might marginally increase national security if the funds were to be appropriated through domestic spending bills rather than national defense, as it appeared to be "free"—not to affect the national defense appropriations. This occurs in such programs on the domestic side of the budget as the Coast Guard, the national defense stockpile, subsidies for financing merchant shipbuilding, and civil defense. Because of President Reagan's commitment to national security, program proponents turned to the national defense rationale when all other arguments failed.

Two things are lost in this process: first, a careful setting of priorities—it may not be possible to do everything at once, and for some programs the marginal addition to national security is not justified by the cost; and second, the rejection of claims that masquerade as national defense but are in reality motivated by special interests—those of the armed services and domestic agencies as well as those of contractors, constituents of members of Congress, and specific industries.

Projected budget deficits and the large share of the budget committed to domestic program spending make it more difficult to increase the resources devoted to national security. To the extent that some overall constraint—on total spending or the deficit—operates in the budget process, leading the Congress to fund domestic programs out of the defense budget, the defense community would be well served by screening out its own weak claimants. It should refuse to accommodate special interests and assist the president in controlling domestic spending where it can, specifically spending for those programs weakly justified on national security grounds. The defense-domestic trade-off, reinforced by President Reagan's opposition to increasing taxes, suggests, for example, that the Defense Department's unwillingness to consider any changes in extremely generous military retirement benefits, in spite of the recommendations of the President's Private Sector

Survey on Cost Control, hurts the administration's efforts to reform the generous civil service retirement system. The lost savings may come out of the defense budget.

Net Interest

From 1951 through 1973, net interest on the federal debt varied from 1.2 to 1.5 percent of GNP. By 1980, it had reached 2 percent, and it is estimated to be 2.9 percent in 1984, 1985, and 1986, dropping a few tenths of a percentage point in later years only because interest rates are projected to decline, the real GNP is projected to grow, and the administration's proposals would limit accumulated deficits.

Interest on the federal debt depends on the amount of debt outstanding, its maturity structure, and interest rates. At high rates of interest, interest feeds on itself. Outstanding debt of $100 billion at 10 percent requires interest payments of $10 billion, but under current fiscal conditions the money to pay the interest must also be borrowed, and thus interest payments on the $100 billion will double every seven years or so. At 8 percent, it takes a little longer: closer to nine years. At 15 percent, it takes only five years. In the Reagan 1984 budget, net interest in 1988 is roughly equal to the deficit.

Most of the federal debt is short term; about 50 percent rolls over every fifteen months. Interest payments are therefore very sensitive to interest rates. Federal debt held by the public will be over $1.1 trillion by the end of fiscal 1983; financial data from President Reagan's 1984 budget project that by the end of 1988, the federal debt held by the public will be almost $2 trillion. A one percentage point increase in the rate of interest, over that forecast, would ultimately increase interest on the 40 percent or so of the debt refunded in a year by $8 billion; three percentage points would add $24 billion, or half a percentage point of 1988 GNP. The administration's July 1983 forecast for the 91-day T-bill rate in fiscal 1988 was 6.2 percent. It does not seem highly unlikely that it could be 9.2 percent. As debt held by the public is increasing as a percentage of GNP, net interest is a potentially increasing share of GNP as well.

Domestic Program Spending

Domestic program spending has been an area of explosive budget growth. Real growth rates have far exceeded real growth in GNP.

Domestic program spending increased at a 7.4 percent average annual compound real rate of growth in the 1952–1962 decade, 6.3 percent in the 1962–1972 decade, and 4.4 percent in the 1972–1982 decade, whereas real growth rates for GNP were 2.8 percent, 3.9 percent, and 2.6 percent, respectively.

Domestic program spending for 1983 was estimated in the July 1983 budget update at 15.7 percent of GNP, higher than it has ever been. When the final data on fiscal 1983 are in, the ratio may be lower, but still a record. President Reagan's 1984 budget requests nearly $500 billion for domestic program spending, as shown in Table 10.2.

This $500 billion is 14.3 percent of estimated 1984 GNP and includes everything but national defense and net interest. It is clearly dominated by large retirement and health programs. Other human resource programs covered by the $89 billion figure in Table 10.2 include all outlays for education, training, employment, and social services, as well as subsidized housing, food stamps and child nutrition, Supplemental Security Income (SSI), Aid to Families with Dependent Children (AFDC), railroad retirement, and additional health expenditures. The wide range of federal government functions included in the $75.9

Table 10.2

**1984 Outlays for Domestic Program Spending
President Reagan's 1984 Budget**

Human Resources	$ Millions	Percentage of GNP
Social Security (OASDI)	178,248	5.1
Medicare	59,829	2.3
Medicaid	20,799	
Federal employee retirement and disability	22,153	
Veterans benefits and services (primarily pensions and health)	25,724	2.2
Unemployment compensation	28,774	
Other human resources programs	88,522	2.5
Total, human resources	424,049	12.1
All other domestic program spending	75,949	2.2
Total	499,998	14.3

SOURCE: Fiscal year 1984 budget; fiscal 1984 GNP of $3,513.9 billion.

billion for all other domestic program spending was outlined earlier. Among these programs are the most fundamentally legitimate functions of government as well as programs that raise basic questions about the appropriate role of the federal government and its ability to accomplish its avowed purposes.

There is nothing that helps this part of the budget so much as real, sustained, noninflationary economic growth. This is reflected in current services estimates—estimates of what spending would be in the absence of further policy changes. The administration's estimates of current services spending for domestic programs, based on its July 1983 economic forecast, project a drop in human resources and all other spending of about 2.6 percentage points of GNP (about $130 billion) as a result of economic change alone—not policy changes—by 1988, from 15.7 percent in 1983 to 13.1 percent. The policy changes requested by President Reagan in the 1984 budget would further reduce this to 12.2 percent by 1988.

Current services estimates reflect what the budget would be if no policy changes were made, but they are based on the administration's economic forecast. There is an inconsistency here, in that economic projections assume full adoption of the president's proposals. The argument is that if the policy proposals reducing outlays from the current services level are not adopted, the deficit will be higher, interest rates will be higher than projected, economic growth will be lower, and the strong and sustained economic recovery with low inflation will not be accomplished; thus the current services estimates are too low in the absence of policy changes.

The drop in current services estimates illustrates how sensitive this major portion of the budget is to economic events. About 60 percent of spending for human resources and all other domestic programs is indexed for inflation by the consumer price index. Outlays for the many means-tested programs in this area depend heavily on the number of beneficiaries, which increases with unemployment—as does unemployment insurance itself.

About one percentage point of the 1983–1988 current services decline occurs in 1984, largely because of higher GNP growth and lower outlays for unemployment insurance and means-tested entitlements. The reverse relationship, an increase of a percentage point, is approximately what would occur over the peak-to-trough period of the business cycle.

The 1984 budget is not the first budget to project a decline in domestic program spending as a percentage of GNP; this has been characteristic of presidents' budgets since the mid-1970s. The problem is that the economic forecasts on which they were based, which uniformly predicted declining unemployment, declining inflation, declining interest rates, and sustained real growth, did not materialize, and the Congress often rejected major portions of the policy proposals, as it did with President Reagan's 1983 and 1984 budgets.

Administration Requests and Congressional Action

Given the record spending for domestic programs in fiscal 1983 and the widespread impression of substantial budget cutting by the administration, it may be useful to evaluate what the Reagan administration actually accomplished with respect to this component of the federal budget against two criteria: what it asked for and what would have occurred had nothing been done, given the actual economic events that took place and the administration's forecast as of July 1983. To do this, it is necessary to estimate what spending for these programs would have been had no policy changes been made, and what spending would have been had all policy changes requested in the March 1981 revisions of the 1982 budget been achieved—including enactment of unidentified savings.

Table 10.3 shows the results. Line 1, the February 1981 current policy baseline, is what spending for these programs would be, given the July 1983 economic forecasts and accounting practices, had no policy changes been made. The second line shows what spending would be, using today's prices, had all proposals been enacted, and thus the implied proposed savings, line 3, can be calculated. What was actually achieved is line 4, the July 1983 current services line; this is what domestic program spending would be were no further policy changes made.

The reduction in outlays from what they otherwise would have been—net savings achieved in comparison to the projected spending when President Reagan took office had no policy changes been made—is shown in line 5. It is far less than his originally proposed savings, for two reasons. First, in major areas including retirement and health programs, the Congress enacted only modest reforms. The GNP claim of Social Security, Medicare, and Medicaid is almost a full percentage point higher than it would have been had President Reagan's reforms been fully enacted. Second, in several areas President Reagan has requested, and the Congress granted, funding above his original request—sometimes even above the February 1981 baseline. Program

Table 10.3

Domestic Program Spending: Reagan Administration Requests Versus Savings Achieved
($ billions)

	Fiscal Years			
	1983	*1984*	*1985*	*1986*
1. Projected spending when Reagan took office assuming no policy changes	538	555	590	623
2. Projected spending assuming adoption of all March 1981 Reagan administration proposals	460	452	475	505
3. Savings proposed	78	103	115	118
4. Projected spending as of July 1983 without further policy changes	506	514	542	576
5. Net savings achieved	32	41	48	47

SOURCES: Office of Management and Budget, *March 1982 Budget Revisions* (March 18, 1981); OMB, "Current Services" (July 1983); and repricing estimates and accounting adjustments by OMB.

levels have increased for highways, modernization of the national airspace system, space and science, agricultural subsidies, public works, law enforcement, job training, and other programs.

The savings achieved amount to about 1 percent of GNP; President Reagan's original request was closer to 3 percent. The net effect of these changes is a domestic spending baseline that will remain well over 13 percent of GNP in 1988 even if the full effects of the projected recovery are realized.

A Crossroads

The economy and the budget stand at a crossroads. Economic recovery has begun, and sustained, noninflationary growth holds promise for reducing the burden of financing both national defense and domestic programs.

With sustained real growth, in five years the administration's national defense program could absorb only 7.5 percent of GNP; interest on the federal debt could, if the budget itself is controlled, be held to 2.5 percent; and domestic programs, with judicious paring, could be reduced to 12 percent. That would give us a budget of 22 percent of GNP.

But the economic recovery could be derailed or slowed down by high rates of interest fueled by financing the federal deficit and meeting the widespread financial demands of the federal government's off-budget credit programs. Less rapid or less sustained GNP growth could then put the administration's national defense program (were it to be achieved) at 8.5 percent of GNP, net interest at 3.5 percent or even 4.0 percent, and domestic program spending (in a nonrecessionary year) at 14.5 percent, with total spending at 26 to 27 percent of GNP. This is more likely than it seems. National defense spending is a rising GNP claimant; net interest, assuming constant rates of interest on an amount of publicly held debt increasing as a percentage of GNP, is a rising claim as well. So are some retirement and health programs under current legislation—a major portion of domestic program spending.

Eventually the country will have to choose whether it wishes to accept the tax burdens that go with even the most optimistic of these scenarios—the 22 percent version, requiring an increase in corporate and individual income taxes of about 30 percent—or whether it wants to require the Congress to make the difficult choices needed to reduce aggregate spending.

In the meantime, given the intimate interaction between the budget and the economy, what the administration and the Congress do with the federal budget—and federal credit—is critical to giving the country its best possible chance at sustained real growth.

Notes

1. Office of Management and Budget (OMB), *Mid-session Review of the 1984 Budget* (July 1983). Off-budget outlays of about half a percentage point of GNP are ignored here and throughout the text.
2. U.S. Senate, "Conference Report on the First Concurrent Resolution on the Budget," Report No. 98-155 (June 1983).
3. OMB, "Federal Government Finances: 1984 Budget Data" (February 1983). Used for historical data throughout the text.
4. "Conference Report on the First Concurrent Resolution on the Budget."
5. OMB, "Federal Government Finances: 1984 Budget Data."
6. "A Strategy for Growth: The American Economy in the 1980s," address by

Ronald Reagan, International Business Council, Chicago, Ill., September 9, 1980; and "Fact Sheet: Ronald Reagan's Strategy for Economic Growth and Stability in the 1980s," Reagan-Bush Campaign, Arlington, Va., September 9, 1980.

7. OMB, *Fiscal Year 1982 Budget Revisions* (March 1981).
8. OMB, *Budget of the United States Government, Fiscal Year 1983, Fiscal Year 1984.* Other fiscal year budgets are mentioned later in the text.

11
Controlling the Federal Budget

Alvin Rabushka

On November 26, 1798, a decade after the U.S. Constitution was written, Thomas Jefferson wrote, "I wish it were possible to obtain a single amendment to our Constitution. I would be willing to depend on that alone for the reduction of the administration of our government to the genuine principles of its Constitution; I mean an additional article, taking from the federal government the power of borrowing."

Today, the need for such an amendment is greater than ever. Large and protracted federal deficits have brought havoc to today's economy. The nation's trillion dollar debt represents a true and onerous burden to the average American citizen. The carrying cost on the debt has skyrocketed. The bill we pay arrives in several forms: higher taxes, declining real income, higher interest rates, and periodic recessions.

Of course, deficits are not the only cause of our economic troubles. Many of the undesirable consequences popularly attributed to deficits would have occurred even with a balanced budget if government spending and money creation had followed the path of the past twenty years. However, the burden of taxation on current and future generations would have been quantitatively different. Government debt would be lower, tax rates higher, and inflation about the same. The disincentive effects of taxes on investment and employment would not have been avoided. In order to preserve our economic and political freedom, it is necessary both to outlaw deficits and to place a cap on taxes such that the size of government, relative to the entire economy, does not increase.

The Flaws in Statutory Reform

Reforming the federal budgetary process has been and remains a popular topic with politicians, scholars, and taxpayers. Many reformers believe that statutory changes in the way Congress conducts its business can alone bring about a responsible federal budget. Proponents of this view claim that statutory reform would avoid the time-consuming and cumbersome process of amending the Constitution to achieve fiscal restraint. They believe that Congress is capable of drafting legislation that will put its fiscal house back in order. This view, however, has repeatedly been proven false.

Reform of the congressional budgetary process has been debated extensively since 1921. For example, the Revenue Act of 1964 stated: "To further the objective of balanced budgets in the near future, Congress by this action recognizes the importance of taking all reasonable means to restrain government spending." The Budget and Impoundment Control Act of 1974 enacted major reforms—the establishment of budget committees within each house, the creation of the Congressional Budget Office to supply timely information and analysis, and the development of a budgetary timetable—to enable Congress to consider individual spending measures in light of overall budgetary objectives. The Humphrey-Hawkins Full Employment Act declared a balanced budget a national policy priority. An amendment offered by Representative (now Senator) Charles Grassley and Senator Harry Byrd, Jr., to an International Monetary Fund loan program measure was enacted into law and required that, beginning with fiscal year 1981, total budget outlays of the federal government "shall not" exceed its receipts (P.L. 95–435). In 1979, a provision in a measure to increase the public debt limit stated that "Congress shall balance the federal budget" (P.L. 96–5) and required congressional budget committees to propose balanced budgets for fiscal 1981 and later years.

None of these measures has effectively constrained deficits. None has reduced the share of national income taxed or spent by government. The most obvious reason for this is that no Congress can bind a succeeding Congress by a simple statute. A balanced budget or tax limitation statute can itself be repealed by the simple expedient of adopting a new statute or new budget that conflicts with the earlier measure. The Byrd-Grassley amendment, which required a balanced budget for 1981, proved no deterrent to the adoption of a budget with a $40 billion deficit for that year.

Indeed, legislation passed by Congress has exacerbated the problem of runaway federal spending. A convincing case can be made that control over the budget has steadily declined since the 1974 act. Despite congressional adherence to the budget timetable, deficits have assumed record proportions: seven deficits exceeded $40 billion in the 1970s, and a regime of $200 billion deficits appears likely in the early 1980s. Control over off-budget outlays (for example, funds for the Federal Financing Bank, which loans money for subsidized housing, foreign military sales, the Tennessee Valley Authority, and other agencies; the Rural Electrification Administration; the Synthetic Fuels Corporation) has eroded even more sharply: off-budget outlays increased from less than $1 billion in fiscal 1973 to over $20 billion in fiscal 1982. Finally, those items in the budget known as "uncontrollables" have increased from 72 percent of the total in 1973 to 77 percent in 1983. (An uncontrollable is a budget authority or an outlay that would require substantive legislation to cancel. These consist chiefly of open-ended entitlements such as Social Security and Medicare, open-ended programs such as interest payments on the national debt and farm price supports, and contracts and obligations entered upon in the past and payable in the present.) Congress has thus been wholly unable to impose its own priorities on the budget.

The source of this failure lies in a structural bias within our political system that causes higher levels of spending, taxing, and deficits than are desired by the people, even though most members of Congress believe that large deficits and excessive government spending damage the economy. This spending bias has yet to be corrected by internal reform because none of these reforms allow members to cope with spending pressures. The removal of prior constraints calls for the imposition of a new constraint. A constitutional amendment would reimpose those constraints that the framers of the Constitution originally imposed or assumed. It would do much to correct the present defects in congressional operations.

Amending the Constitution

Article V of the Constitution provides two methods of proposing amendments. The first method (the only one ever used) requires the proposal of an amendment by two-thirds of each house of Congress, and ratification by three-fourths of the states. The second method allows for an amendment drawn by a constitutional convention, which must be called by Congress in response to the application of two-thirds of the states. Whichever method is invoked, the proposed amendment must be approved by three-fourths of the states (38).

Since 1975, the National Taxpayers Union has worked with state legislatures to pass resolutions calling on Congress to invoke Article V of the Constitution and convene a constitutional convention for the purpose of writing a balanced budget amendment. To date, 32 states have done so.

In early 1979, largely because of pressure being exerted by the states to convene a constitutional convention, the Senate Judiciary Subcommittee on the Constitution began to develop its own constitutional proposal to prohibit budget deficits. Senate Joint Resolution 58, a combined balanced budget–tax limitation amendment, was reported out of the full Senate Committee on the Judiciary on May 19, 1981. Its companion in the House of Representatives was House Joint Resolution 350. The measure passed the Senate in August 1982 by a 69–31 vote, but was defeated in the House two months later. Slightly modified, it was reintroduced on January 26, 1983, in Congress as Senate Joint Resolution 5, which is discussed at length at the end of this essay.

Many Americans believed that the election of fiscal conservatives would restore integrity to the conduct of the nation's fiscal business. They believed that a conservative president, Ronald Reagan, working with a conservative Congress, would gain control over the federal budget process. To their dismay, President Reagan quickly abandoned his goal of a balanced budget by 1984. He has proposed future budgets with all-time record deficits, and he has presided over an overall increase in government spending as a share of GNP. The national debt surpassed $1 trillion in October 1981, and it is now forecast that it will double by the mid- to late 1980s.

175 Years of Fiscal Prudence

The Founding Fathers adopted two explicit constitutional provisions and assumed a third that served to restrain spending and deficits. One reserved powers not expressly delegated to the federal government to the states and to the people. The second provided for per capita distribution among the states of taxes. The third, implicit, assumed that federal spending would not exceed federal revenues except in times of war or recession. All three have been abrogated or eroded by time and events, expecially by the adoption of the Sixteenth Amendment (income tax) in 1913. Indeed, the income tax amendment lies at the root of the current balanced budget amendment movement.

Anyone born in the post-depression era would regard deficit financing as normal practice. Yet until the Great Depression, the balanced budget, save in wartime or recession, was considered part of our "unwritten constitution." Thomas Jefferson warned that "the public debt is the greatest of dangers to be feared by a republican government" and proposed the idea of a balanced budget amendment only one year after the Constitution had been ratified. Alexander Hamilton strongly urged the repayment of national debt. Presidents John Adams, James Madison, James Monroe, John Quincy Adams, and Andrew Jackson all urged avoiding public debt. A balanced budget was synonymous with sound political economy.

Until the Great Depression of the 1930s, budget deficits had occurred only in times of war and recession. The budget surpluses generated in good times were invariably used to reduce the national debt these deficits produced. Historically deficits of large proportions arose during the Revolutionary War, the War of 1812, the Mexican War of 1846, the Civil War, World War I, and during brief recessions in the late 1830s and 1850s. In each instance, the debts were immediately reduced at the onset of peace or prosperity. Between 1795 and 1811, Congress cut the national debt from $84 million to just over $45 million. After the War of 1812, eighteen surpluses between 1815 and 1836 virtually eliminated the national debt. A run of 28 consecutive surpluses following the Civil War lowered the national debt from $2.7 billion to $960 million. Finally, throughout the 1920s, consecutive surpluses reduced the national debt from $24 billion to $16 billion, at the very time that major tax rate reductions were approved.

Sustained deficits first arose during the depression years of the 1930s and the war years of the early 1940s, leaving in their wake a national debt of about $170 billion. These deficits were consistent with the national experience of wartime and recession. When peace returned, deficits again disappeared. Between 1947 and 1960, seven surpluses of $31 billion roughly offset seven deficits of $32 billion. However, for the first time in American history, no effort was made to reduce the national debt.

A Bias Toward Spending

Due to the unwritten norm of a budget balance, the federal government was rarely troubled by deficits through almost 200 years of U.S. history. Indeed, statements of revenues and expenditures were not incorporated into an overall official budget until 1921.

Why then today are federal budgets wildly out of balance?

The answer lies in a political reality—budgetary objectives and the budgetary process are in direct conflict. Congress, as a whole, is concerned with stable prices, low interest rates, and full employment, which require some check on the scope of government spending. As individuals, however, each member of Congress confronts pressures to increase spending. The reality of our system has shown convincingly that the collective need to control spending is no match for the pressures each member faces to increase it.

This bias toward more spending is due, first, to what analysts of government call the phenomenon of "concentrated benefits versus dispersed costs." The benefits of any given spending program normally are concentrated among a small number of persons, while the costs of such a program are dispersed throughout a much larger class, the general taxpayer.

The competition between taxspenders and taxpayers is highly unequal: it is simply not as worthwhile for an individual taxpayer to spend much time and effort to save a few dollars in taxes as it is for the spending interests to secure millions or billions of dollars for themselves. The latter focus intensely on those few spending measures from which they derive benefit; the individual taxpayer, who might normally be concerned about the broader impact, is less likely to organize for the purpose of defeating a particular spending measure. With their organized electoral support or opposition, spending interests are able to reward or punish legislators. Taxpayers find it more difficult to perceive their self-interest in the context of isolated pieces of legislation. Thus, whenever government programs are considered one by one, as they are in our budgetary system, there is a bias toward government growth. The result has been annual budget growth in the neighborhood of $100 billion, with even larger deficits forecast.

The explosion in federal spending is not due to the failure to elect the "right" people, it is an institutional defect. The federal budgetary process is inherently biased toward deficits, higher taxes, and greater government spending. The trends toward bigger government and economic instability reflect the decisions of reasonable men and women in

Congress who, as individuals, cannot successfully resist the pressures they face to increase spending.

A second source of bias toward greater spending and deficits is the separation of benefits, which are short-run, from costs, which are typically more long-run. The benefits of spending programs are immediate, both to the recipients and the sitting legislators who supported them. The costs of spending programs—in the form of potentially higher taxes, higher inflation, higher unemployment, or higher interest rates—will be evident only at some future time, to be borne, perhaps, by future members. Since the electoral time horizon of all representatives and one-third of the senators is never more than a year or two away, short-term benefits invariably take precedence over potentially long-run adverse economic effects due to higher government spending.

A third bias arises within the structure of Congress itself. The committee system, whatever its original intentions, finds members of Congress gravitating to those specific committees that allow them to serve their geographic constituencies by bringing home their "fair share." Farm state members typically serve on the agricultural committees, Western legislators on interior policy committees, urban legislators on urban policy committees, and so on. Re-election rewards those who successfully serve their constituencies; at the same time the actions of Congress as a whole damage the growth rate of the economy. The driving elements in each member's calculation are protecting his or her turf, getting a share of the pork barrel, observing colleagues' committee jurisdiction; in short, concerns about self come first. It is not in the interest of any of the 535 members of Congress to give up those dollars beneficial to constituents since that reduction will have only a modest or even insignificant effect on overall spending. Unless the entire membership can agree to limit spending, no one member or group of members dare risk their constituents' wrath by surrendering benefits that have no appreciable effect on the total size of government spending while their colleagues who do not forgo spending continue to earn the support of their constituents. The only viable solution to this dilemma is to alter the incentives that confront members of Congress. That is, we must change the rules under which Congress operates.

Currently, two major gaps in these rules nourish Congress's spending bias and flout widely recognized customs of fiscal prudence. First, members of Congress enjoy virtually unlimited access to deficit spending. Once the unwritten rule of a budget balance had been discarded, members of Congress could vote to increase spending without a concomitant vote to increase taxes. Spending decisions have become increasingly divorced from the availability of revenues. As a result, members of Congress can satisfy the demands of particular spending interests without either reducing spending for another interest or taking political heat for raising taxes. Rather than choose among alternative spending proposals, members jointly act to increase the deficit. The availability of deficit spending reduces the need for members to make hard political decisions by choosing among spending proposals.

Second, under our present tax system, members of Congress have access to annual, automatic tax increases. Our progressive tax code works to transfer more and more personal income to the government because increases in personal income are taxed at progressively steeper rates. This rising share of national income paid in taxes due to increases in real income or to inflation is known as "bracket creep" and has had the especially pernicious effect of raising tax burdens. In the last decade, government income tax collections rose by about 16 percent for each 10 percent increase in personal income, largely as a result of inflation. Between 1979 and 1982, government receipts outpaced inflation while average weekly earnings in private industry fell in real terms. Resources are increasingly being shifted from private to public hands. By trying to break even through cost-of-living increases, the typical wage earner actually falls behind.

A progressive tax system allows Congress to raise taxes without having to vote an explicit increase either in tax rates or the size of the tax base. Since 1974, federal income tax yields have grown about 75 percent faster than the GNP, which has allowed Congress to collect a growing stream of revenues and enact a sequence of nominal tax cuts. Although Congress passed "tax reform" measures in 1954, 1964, 1969, 1971, 1976, 1977, 1978, 1981, and 1982, taxes have not declined. It is only the rate of increase that has slowed. The accelerating frequency of congressional action reflects the higher rates of inflation throughout the 1970s. In each instance of tax reform, a rising trend of taxation was interrupted, but the long-run trend has been upwards.

Here again, individual members of Congress confront strong incentives to do what is far from the best interests of society. The benefits they must deliver to retain office prompts legislators to support inflationary policies that net them greater spending authority, and hence the ability to meet the demands of special interest groups.

In 1981, Congress voted to correct inflation-generated bracket creep by indexing tax rates to inflation, to take effect in 1985. Under this plan, the progressive tax code would transfer a greater share of personal income to government only when real growth occurs. But many economists and politicians have begun to suggest repeal or postponement of the indexing provision to prevent a drain on Treasury revenues, thus maintaining the automatic increase mechanism.

The Fiscal Experience Since 1960

Since 1960, these biases have led to the current spending habits of Congress; deficits have become the accepted practice of federal budgeting. Apart from a modest surplus of $3 billion in 1969, Congress has imposed a regime of persistent deficits. The national debt rose from $300 billion in fiscal year 1962 to $437 billion in fiscal 1972 and surpassed $1 trillion in October 1981. Eight deficits in the 1970s were $40 billion or greater. Interest payments, which absorbed approximately 6 percent of the national budget twenty years ago, consumed about 12 percent in fiscal 1981. These payments are half as large as spending for national defense and one-third as large as spending for income security programs including Social Security. (Nor does this figure include the growing unfunded liability of social insurance programs and the implicit obligations of loan guarantees.)

The discarding of the balanced budget norm fueled an explosive rise in federal spending. As recently as 1929, federal spending of $3 billion consumed only 3.1 percent of GNP. Since then, the federal sector has demonstrated a continuing propensity for growth, whatever the economic circumstances. In successive decades, federal spending grew to consume 10.0, 15.6, 18.5, and 20.3 percent of GNP, reaching 23.1 percent in 1980. In 1984, federal spending may exceed 25 percent of GNP. In terms of money, federal spending passed the $100 billion mark in 1962. A $200 billion budget was reached only nine years later. In rapid-fire succession came $300 billion (1975), $400 billion (1977), $500 billion (1980), $600 billion (1981), with estimates of $1 trillion by 1985.

The growth of federal spending has carried with it an enormous increase in federal tax burdens, which have risen from 15 percent of GNP in 1949 to nearly 20 percent today. Taxpayers also face much higher marginal rates on income as inflation has pushed them into higher tax brackets. Households in the 70th percentile of taxpayers saw their average top marginal rate rise from 20 percent in 1966 to 28 percent in 1981; for those in the 95th percentile, it rose from 25 to 46 percent. Per capita tax receipts nearly doubled between 1976 and 1981. The number of individual taxpayers paying more than 20 percent of their income to the federal government has nearly tripled since

1966. Rising tax burdens, especially the high marginal rates faced by many taxpayers, have eroded incentives to work, save, and invest.

In sharp contrast to historical experience, the federal government has failed to show fiscal restraint in the post–World War II era. For the better part of 150 years, Americans held the federal government to a limited role. Save for periods of war or recession, revenues from customs and excises were sufficient to fund those activities widely regarded as "proper" federal functions. This consensus has broken down in the past fifty years. The greater part of the current federal budget is devoted to activities not funded fifty years ago.

The Meaning of Deficits

The federal government can finance its deficits in three ways. It can raise taxes. It can borrow in the capital markets. Or, it can print new money. By raising taxes, the government reduces the incentives of individuals and businesses to work, save, and invest. By borrowing, the federal government competes with private borrowers, raises the rate of interest, and ultimately crowds out private borrowing. By printing money, the government fosters inflation, which, in turn, reduces investment by increasing the risk premium on long-term investment.

The conjunction of rising credit demands and lower savings rates in the United States has driven up real interest rates to levels higher than at any period in the nation's history. Deficit financing raises real rates of interest and reduces investment in plant and equipment, leaving fewer tools or machines for our old age and for our children. We consume relatively more today, but we will be poorer and have fewer goods available tomorrow.

The inflation that began in the late 1960s has been associated with large and continuing federal deficits. Apart from Treasury borrowing, the government can also finance deficits by printing new money. This result occurs when the Federal Reserve Board (the Fed) increases its ownership of Treasury debt, which, in turn, effectively increases the amount of money and credit in circulation. This process of "monetizing debt" is largely synonymous with printing money to finance deficits.

Persistently large deficits during a period of economic recovery foster long-run inflationary fears that the Fed might monetize some portion of this debt. In the past decade, purchase of government debt by the Fed has contributed to rising inflation. Inflation, in turn, disrupts savings and investment decisions and decreases the prospects for economic growth. Personal savings rates fell throughout the 1970s.

Americans have increasingly felt the effects of inflation. Between 1958 and 1973, for example, the number of Gallup's respondents naming inflation as the nation's most important problem was always less than 20 percent. Since 1974, the percentage has ranged from a low of 25 to a high of 79. Complaints about taxes and government waste have escalated as taxpayers endured rising rates of inflation and stagnant real income. Indeed, according to Gallup, 80 percent of the American people favor a constitutional amendment to require a balanced budget.

Senate Joint Resolution 5

A Balanced Budget–Tax Limitation Constitutional Amendment

Let us examine each section of the proposed amendment to see how it would redress the present defects of the budgetary process.

Balanced Budget

> *Section 1.* Prior to each fiscal year, the Congress shall adopt a statement of receipts and outlays for that year in which total outlays are no greater than total receipts. The Congress may amend such statement provided revised outlays are no greater than revised receipts. Whenever three-fifths of the whole number of both houses shall deem it necessary, Congress in such statement may provide for a specific excess of outlays over receipts by a vote directed solely to that subject. The Congress and the President shall, pursuant to legislation or through exercise of their powers under the first and second articles, ensure that actual outlays do not exceed the outlays set forth in such statement.

The purpose of Section 1 is twofold. First, Congress would be required to plan to balance its budget every year. It would do so by adopting a "statement," or budget, prior to the start of each fiscal year, in which planned outlays (spending) did not exceed planned receipts (revenue). Congress could violate this rule and plan for a deficit only by a three-fifths vote of the whole number of each house of Congress, not just three-fifths of those present and voting. In contrast, a simple majority could approve a budget surplus. Second, Section 1 also mandates that actual outlays do not exceed the spending levels set forth in the approved statement or budget.

The amendment establishes the basis for a *planned* balanced budget. It does not require that the budget be in *actual* balance during the course of the fiscal year. In some circumstances, actual outlays may exceed actual receipts. For example, a recession might reduce actual receipts below the level of receipts set forth in the planned statement. This is permissible under the amendment, but actual outlays could not exceed outlays anticipated by the statement. Deficits caused by increased spending would not be permitted.

If circumstances warrant, Congress may adopt an amended statement of receipts and outlays for the fiscal year (provided again that outlays do not exceed receipts) at any time during the fiscal year. An amended statement containing a deficit would require a three-fifths vote only if such a deficit were greater than the deficit in the previous statement. Thus the budget could be changed by an explicit vote of Congress in response to changing economic conditions.

An important feature of Section 1 is that it imposes on Congress and the president a mandate to prevent total actual outlays, which include both on- and off-budget items, from exceeding the outlays mentioned in the statement. For example, should the economy perform below expectations, leading to increased spending on entitlements or on debt service due to higher interest rates, Congress would be called on either to increase statement outlays and approve a deficit (by a three-fifths vote) or to postpone spending programs and/or to reduce eligibility for entitlements. To guard against the possibility that actual outlays might exceed anticipated outlays through unintentional and presumably modest error, an obvious remedy would be for Congress to plan a surplus of equivalent size for the next fiscal year.

Congress is expected to adopt the most accurate estimates of receipts and outlays that it can in drafting its budget, but in all cases a congressional majority will be the final arbiter among the choice of estimates. As the fiscal year unfolds, actual receipts may or may not meet expectations. An unexpectedly more robust economy may yield receipts above anticipated receipts; an unexpectedly weaker economy may yield lower receipts. Either result is permissible. The amendment imposes no obligation on Congress to react to the flow of actual receipts during the fiscal year, only to the flow of actual outlays.

In recent years, Congress has failed to adopt a budget by the October 1 date on which a new fiscal year begins. It has funded government operations in such instances by adopting resolutions continuing previous levels of spending. Under the amendment, this practice would be banned. Failure to adopt a statement of receipts and outlays by the October 1 deadline would be construed as an implied adoption of a statement in which both receipts and outlays are zero. In that event, the Congress and the president would be mandated constitutionally to ensure that fiscal year outlays also would be zero. In short, the government would shut down on October 1.

Section 1 proposes to overcome the spending bias of Congress by restoring the linkage between federal spending and taxing decisions. It does not add any specific level of spending or taxing to the Constitution, nor does it intrude on the day-to-day decisions of the government on allocating the federal dollar. It merely restores the balance between taxspenders and taxpayers by constraining spending totals to available revenues.

Under the amendment, if politicians voted new spending programs, they would have to eliminate old programs or vote to raise taxes. Resistance to the elimination of existing programs or to tax increases would discourage many new spending proposals, thereby eliminating the current bias toward overspending. It would end future deficits and reduce the inflationary effect of new money creation, which has in past years both financed a portion of these deficits and raised taxes through bracket creep.

Tax Limitation

> *Section 2.* Total receipts for any fiscal year set forth in the statement adopted pursuant to this article shall not increase by a rate greater than the rate of increase in national income in the year or years ending not less than six months nor more than twelve months before such fiscal year, unless a majority of the whole number of both Houses of Congress shall have passed a bill directed solely to approving specific additional receipts and such bill has become law.

The purpose of Section 2 is to prevent tax receipts from growing more rapidly than the general economy, as occurs with our graduated-rate tax code. Under the amendment, a majority of the membership of both houses would have to vote to permit receipts to outpace general economic growth. In particular, Congress would be required to enact a bill expanding a specified tax base and/or increasing specified tax rates.

Put another way, Section 2 states that the balanced budget required by Section 1 should not occur at levels of receipts and outlays that consume an increasing proportion of the national economy. It attempts to achieve this result by limiting the increase in receipts for a new fiscal year to the percentage increase during a prior congressionally chosen time period. If existing tax laws are likely to yield revenues in excess of this limit, the Congress must modify the revenue laws to reduce anticipated receipts.

The relationship between the growth of national income during the prior period and the growth of receipts during the following fiscal year provides the Congress with reasonably precise guideposts for its budgeting process. Quite accurate estimates of the growth in national income are available by mid-July, well enough before the beginning of the fiscal year to permit adoption of the statement required by Section 1.

In fiscal year 1981, for example, which began October 1, 1980, the rate of increase in receipts would have been limited to the rate of increase of national income for calendar year 1979. Since national income rose 11.4 percent in 1979, receipts anticipated in the statement for fiscal 1981 could not have exceeded fiscal 1980 receipts by more than 11.4 percent. Congress set the planned increase for 1981 with no changes in the current tax law at 14.5 percent. Had the amendment been in effect, the tax law would not have produced this automatic tax increase. Taxes would have been about $16 billion lower. To maintain tax receipts at their actual level, Congress would have had to vote for a tax increase.

Anticipated receipts may also rise by less than the proportionate increase in national income. In that event, the new lower level of receipts would then become the base for receipts in subsequent fiscal years, until the Congress voted a rise in allowable receipts.

To recapitulate how the budget process would work under the amendment, first Congress would determine the increase in national income during a prior period defined in accord with Section 2. That percentage rise, in turn, would determine the maximum increase in receipts the government could collect for the coming fiscal year. If, say, national income rose 10 percent during the prior period, then receipts could rise by no more than 10 percent for the new fiscal year. Since outlays cannot exceed receipts (the budget must be balanced or in surplus), government spending could not rise by more than 10 percent. Sections 1 and 2, in conjunction, establish a *de facto* spending limit. Thus neither taxes nor spending can grow more rapidly than the economy.

The amendment permits federal spending to grow more rapidly

than the economy only if Congress explicitly votes to allow receipts to rise more rapidly than the growth of the economy. It would take a direct vote of a constitutional majority of both houses of Congress to permit the growth of federal spending to outpace the growth of the economy. Or, federal spending may outpace economic growth if Congress approves, by a three-fifths majority vote, a deficit in which outlays from year to year exceed economic growth rates. Thus the federal government is not hamstrung; it can meet what may be regarded as increased genuine needs of the people, if it also is prepared to vote on the record for higher taxes or deficits to finance higher spending.

Wartime Waiver

> Section 3. The Congress may waive the provisions of this article for any fiscal year in which a declaration of war is in effect.

In the event of war, Congress has the discretionary authority to operate outside of the provisions of the amendment. Such a waiver would be on a year-to-year basis by concurrent resolution of Congress, as defined under Article 1, Section 8, of the Constitution. Congress would have to adopt a separate waiver annually for each fiscal year at issue.

Borrowing and Repayment of Debt

> Section 4. Total receipts shall include all receipts of the United States except those derived from borrowing and total outlays shall include all outlays of the United States except those for repayment of debt principal.

The purpose of Section 4 is to exclude the proceeds of debt issuance from receipts. Thus, Treasury notes and bonds would not count as receipts, but as the proceeds of selling debt. Similarly, "outlays" is intended to include all disbursements from the Treasury of the United States, both on- and off-budget, either directly or indirectly through federal or quasi-federal agencies created under the authority of acts of Congress. Section 4 states that funds used to repurchase or retire Federal debt would not count as outlays. Interest accrued or paid in conjunction with the debt obligation would, however, be included in outlays.

The amendment permits Congress to plan for a budgetary surplus. Those surplus receipts, subject to the increase limit of Section 2, used to repay principal—that is, retire the national debt—would not be counted as outlays. Should the government fully retire the national debt, the amendment would still allow the government to plan for an annual surplus and even accumulate reserves. Interest earned on these reserves, however, would be subject to the revenue limit. (Admittedly, it would take generations for this scenario to develop.)

Date of Implementation

> *Section 5.* This article shall take effect for the second fiscal year beginning after its ratification.

Section 5 stipulates when the amendment would take effect. If ratification were completed before September 30, 1984, the amendment would require Congress to adopt its first balanced budget statement before September 30, 1985; if ratification were completed between October 1, 1984, and before September 30, 1985, the first balanced budget adoption would be required by September 30, 1986, and so on.

Enforcement

> *Section 6.* The Congress shall enforce and implement this article by appropriate legislation.

Section 6 gives Congress the responsibility for enforcing the amendment by drafting suitable legislation.

Note on Additional Reading

For a detailed statement on the legislative history of the amendment and definitions of its terms and provisions, see the official committee report: U.S. Senate, Committee on the Judiciary, *Balanced Budget-Tax Limitation Constitutional Amendment: Report*, 97th Cong., 1st sess., Report no. 97-151 (Washington, D.C.: Government Printing Office, 1981).

I have made extensive use in this paper of my earlier thinking and writing on the subject of controlling the federal budget. In chronological order, see "The Balanced Budget Approach," in Phillip N. Truluck, ed., *Balancing the Budget: Should the Constitution Be Amended?* (Washington, D.C.: Heritage Foundation, 1979), pp. 1-5; "Tax and Spending Limits," in Peter Duignan and Alvin Rabushka, eds., *The United*

States in the 1980s (Stanford: Hoover Institution Press, 1980), pp. 85–108; with W. Craig Stubblebine, "A Consensus Balanced Budget–Tax Limitation Amendment," in *The Congressional; Budget Act and Process: How Can They Be Improved?* Proceedings of a Symposium Convened by the Committee for a Responsible Federal Budget and the Joint Educational Consortium, De Gray State Park, Arkadelphia, Arkansas, January 11–12, 1982 (Washington, D.C.: Committee for a Responsible Federal Budget, 1982), pp. 195–205; "Fiscal Responsibility: Will Anything Less Than a Constitutional Amendment Do?" in Michael J. Boskin and Aaron Wildavsky, eds., *The Federal Budget: Economics and Politics* (San Francisco: Institute for Contemporary Studies, 1982), pp. 333–54; *A Compelling Case for a Constitutional Amendment to Balance the Budget and Limit Taxes* (Washington, D.C.: Taxpayers' Foundation, 1982), reprinted in *Balanced Budget, Fiscal Responsibility, and the Constitution* (Washington, D.C.: Cato Institute, 1982); and "A Constitutional Cure for Deficits," in Laurence H. Meyer, ed., *The Economic Consequences of Government Deficits* (Hingham, Mass.: Kluwer-Nijhoff, 1983), pp. 183–99.

12
Congress and the President

Richard T. Burress

Congressional independence is built into the separation of powers system. Given that independence, tension and conflict between the president and Congress are inevitable. When one party controls both the legislative and executive branches, or there is an immensely popular president, differences are minimized. Since 1960, however, the trend has been toward confrontational politics, with Congress attempting to exercise greater control not only in domestic areas but in foreign affairs as well. In the past several years, this reach for power has been exemplified by the dramatic growth in legislative disapproval statutes. Despite a recent Supreme Court decision, which may invalidate such legislative vetoes, this trend will probably continue throughout the 1980s and may become a dominant political factor.

For the eight years of the Eisenhower presidency, the conflict between the president and Congress remained at a relatively low level. Although the Democrats controlled Congress for six of the eight years, cooperation and bipartisanship were the rule. This was especially true in foreign affairs. Politics stopped at the water's edge, and in most domestic matters accommodation was the order of the day. In large part, this was due to Eisenhower's great and continuing popularity. The control and direction of the House of Representatives and the Senate by skilled Southern politicians also had much to do with producing a relatively tension-free era. Then too, despite the absence of a Republican majority in either house during six of his eight years, President Eisenhower normally had a working majority in a coalition of Republicans and Southern conservatives.

With the advent of the Kennedy presidency, Congress was ready to assert its traditional independence. After a brief honeymoon, the Kennedy New Frontier program stalled and for the most part languished in the unsympathetic hands of Southern committee chairmen. The Bay of Pigs fiasco introduced a note of uncertainty in the field of foreign affairs, and only the Cuban missile crisis averted an election disaster for the Democrats in 1962.

The eventual outcome of this period of skirmishing between the president and Congress will never be known, for President Kennedy's assassination and the landslide election of Lyndon B. Johnson in 1964 dramatically changed the political landscape. With overwhelming majorities in both houses of Congress, President Johnson epitomized the activist president. His domination of Congress was so complete that it approved the Great Society domestic program with a whoop and a holler. Nighttime committee sessions were not uncommon. The resulting legislation was replete with errors and omissions. To this day, the cost of these poorly conceived programs is a continuing concern.

In the field of foreign affairs, the country has paid an even greater price for presidential dominance. Congress passed the Gulf of Tonkin Resolution with a minimum of scrutiny, and the ever-escalating involvement in the Vietnam war was officially under way. George Romney's oft-quoted remark that he had been brainwashed may have been naive and may have even cost him the presidential nomination; unfortunately, it was also true—for him and for many others.

The period from 1966 to 1968 became increasingly one of unease and congressional resurgence. In the end, the magic and congressional support slipped completely from President Johnson's grasp. He was a lame-duck president before he announced his decision not to stand for re-election. With the election of Richard M. Nixon, Congress could link its historical reach for independence to its general dislike for the incumbent. The stage was set for a major congressional challenge to the power and authority of the president. All that was needed was a dramatic event that would unite the members and legitimize the action taken. Watergate provided everything needed, and more.

The Battle of the Budget

The first challenge to President Nixon's authority came over the budget. By the early 1970s, there was a growing recognition of the need for budget reform. Federal outlays, which were $118.4 billion in 1965 and $195.6 in 1970, were expanding at an alarming rate. Budgetary power had been centralized in the executive branch, and the authority of Congress had become fragmented. It enacted individual measures with little consideration of overall fiscal or budgetary impact. There was no congressional procedure for taking a comprehensive look at the budget and fiscal policies. Uncontrolled portions of the budget, such as social security, black lung disability payments, and dairy price supports, were fast approaching 75 percent of the budget. Congress all but ignored actual expenditures when budget authority was appropriated. More often than not, it failed to finalize appropriation bills prior to the start of a new fiscal year, and many programs were funded by continuing resolutions.

The increasing use of impoundments by President Nixon was especially galling to Congress, which viewed them as a direct challenge to its constitutional power to determine spending priorities. The lack of a coherent budget process and budgetary expertise, however, placed Congress in a weakened position to contest presidential impoundments. It was in this setting, and on the heels of Watergate, that Congress passed the Congressional Budget and Impoundment Control Act of 1974. This act created separate House and Senate budget committees, the Congressional Budget Office (CBO), and a budget timetable, as well as new rules and related provisions. Separate authorizations and appropriations were still required, however, and there were no changes in committee jurisdictions.[1]

The Budget Act, it was believed, would allow Congress to exercise effective control over the budgetary process and to determine the appropriate level of federal revenue and expenditures each year. It was also believed that there would be impoundment control, that national budgetary priorities could be established, and that the executive would be required to furnish pertinent and detailed fiscal information so that Congress could discharge its duties in a knowledgeable manner.[2]

At the outset, the Budget Act of 1974 appeared to match results with expectations. Timetables were established. The CBO provided expertise and pertinent material never before known at the congressional level. The words *rescission* and *reconciliation* were introduced into the budget process. Deadlines were met, and for the first time, legislative committees faced ceilings and limits on their authorization authority. Power shifted to the budget committees and away from the legislative committees.

Not too surprisingly, with this shift and its profound effect on the legislative process, cries were heard that the authority of the traditional committees were being usurped. At the start of the 1983 congressional session, leaders of the House legislative committees let it be known that they had had enough of Budget Committee bullying. Their views and prerogatives were being ignored, and they wanted to establish their own budget targets. It took the Speaker's personal intervention to avoid a full-scale confrontation, and even then the dispute was merely postponed, not resolved.

In time, the CBO challenged the Office of Management and Budget (OMB) as the authoritative source for budget information and economic data. In the first year of the Reagan administration, however, the OMB projections were instrumental in obtaining the enactment of a Reagan economic program that called for reduced domestic spending, increased defense outlays, and a tax cut. Unfortunately, the OMB projections proved to be less accurate than those of the CBO. Great harm was done to the credibility of the Reagan administration when OMB Director David Stockman related in a feature article that when an OMB computer estimated budget deficits ranging from $82 billion in 1982 to $116 billion in 1984, the computer was changed.[3] As a result, new figures, subsequently proven to be inaccurate, paved the way for congressional cuts in both expenditures and taxes. In the emerging battle of the budget, with a $110.6 billion deficit in fiscal 1982 and an estimated deficit of $210 billion in 1983, the CBO projections tended to dominate. The congressional hand had been strengthened. The CBO's deficit projections of $188 billion for 1984, $208 billion for 1985, $234 billion for 1986, and $248 billion for 1985 set the parameters for the congressional debate.

There is growing concern that the budget process established by the Budget Control Act of 1974 may be collapsing. Many critics now believe that at best the budget is merely an outline for government taxing and spending, with its principal value being that it highlights big spending items and the deficit and sets guidelines. There are those who even feel that the budget has become primarily a political document with little resemblance to reality. In support of this view, they note that the House-approved fiscal 1984 budget plan cut by more than half the president's proposed 10 percent increase in defense spending, raised $30 billion in additional revenues, and still projected a deficit of $174.45 billion because of increased spending for domestic programs. On the Senate side, despite a Republican majority, a budget resolution supported by President Reagan failed to gain enough votes to pass. In its stead, the Senate adopted a resolution that limited the defense-spending increase to 6 percent, raised $9 billion in additional taxes, and added $11 billion in domestic spending, with a projected deficit of $179 billion, as opposed to the administration's budget, with a projected deficit of $185 billion.

While the president cannot veto the budget resolution that emerges from the House and Senate conference and is passed by both houses, he can veto individual spending and tax bills that stem from the resolution's guidelines. This has led some White House officials to comment that they would prefer no budget resolution at all to one that compromised fundamental Reagan positions. This would indicate that they are prepared to fall back to a strategy of vetoing congressional attempts to build a budget piecemeal if the appropriations and tax bills exceed the president's budgetary guidelines.

If the budget process does in fact collapse and Congress is unable to adopt a budget resolution, it could give rise to renewed efforts for a constitutional amendment that would require a balanced budget or one that would give the president a line-item veto. Such a veto would permit the president to strike out specific items without negating a whole appropriations bill and bringing many vital governmental functions to a halt. This would be a dramatic shift from recent budget reforms that tipped the balance of power from the executive branch to Congress.

If Congress reduces defense spending for fiscal 1984 substantially below the 10.7 percent increase requested by Reagan, it would go against his claim that "nothing could bring greater joy to the Kremlin than to see the United States abandon its defense rebuilding program after barely one year."[4] Moreover, a cut in 1984 added to a congressional cut of $17.6 billion in 1983 would emphasize the seriousness of the congressional challenge to the president in the sensitive field of national defense.

Despite the gain of 26 House seats in the 1982 election, the fragile Democratic consensus may, as in times past, break down on the floor of the House. It is there that the presidential advantages and the congressional disadvantages in the battle for fiscal supremacy become evident. House members, with their disparate constituencies, are forced to face political pressures associated with raising taxes and trimming defense spending. Decisions regarding which taxes to raise and which military programs to cut must be resolved in the Ways and Means, Appropriations, and Armed Services committees. Historically, these committees are more conservative and defense-minded.

Congress's attack on the president's defense-spending request is more than a budgetary squabble. While it arises within the context of the budget, it is a challenge to the president's role as commander-in-chief. Having assessed the Soviet challenge and the nation's state of readiness, the president found the former alarming and the latter woefully inadequate.

At the outset of his administration, President Reagan enjoyed broad support for his national defense policies. Much of this was due to the public's reaction to the Carter program, where controlling arms overrode the need for improving and acquiring arms. Thus, a major presidential defeat over defense spending could be more than a legislative setback. It would signal a loss of control in an area where strong leadership may be equatable with the nation's ability to survive.

Congress and Foreign Policy

Despite limited constitutional authority,[5] there has been a continuing effort on the part of Congress to legislate restraints on the presidential conduct of foreign policy. The Vietnam war quickened the pace of this effort and sparked the present-day belief of senators and representatives that Congress and the president are partners in most foreign policy undertakings. This has led to a great deal of confusion and has introduced an element of uncertainty into a field that should be characterized by decisive action. Nevertheless, Congress continues to fashion restrictions and restraints on the president's authority in foreign policy matters.

The War Powers Resolution of 1973 requires the president to notify Congress within 48 hours if U.S. forces are sent into any situation in which they face imminent danger of being involved in combat. Unless Congress approved the mission, the troops must be withdrawn within 60 days. This law severely limited the president's ability to enforce the Vietnam peace agreement and permitted the North Vietnamese to violate the accords with impunity. Its impracticality was further demonstrated when, in a critical situation, President Ford found the "consultation" required by the act impossible because congressional leaders were scattered throughout the world on an Easter recess.

The Jackson-Vanik Amendment of 1974 made a Soviet-U.S. trade agreement conditional on Kremlin pledges to ease restrictions on Jews' leaving the USSR. While the amendment did little to help Soviet Jews, it did have a serious impact on détente.

The Nelson-Bingham Amendments attached to foreign assistance acts beginning in 1974 allowed Congress to veto arms sales negotiated by the administration. This led to dramatic confrontations, most notably in the sale of F-15 fighters and AWACS planes to Saudi Arabia. Although the sales finally went through, much of the benefit to the United States was lost.

The Turkish Arms Embargo Act of 1974 punished Turkey for the invasion of the island of Cyprus. In the process, it demonstrated that Americans of Greek origin had more political clout than Americans of Turkish origin and undermined relations with one of the United States' staunchest allies.

The Clark Amendment of 1976 forbade U.S. aid to military or paramilitary operations in Angola. This law signaled to the Soviets that they could operate many thousands of miles from their homeland, sending in Cuban troops and massive amounts of military equipment, while the United States would not assist a majority of the local people who had requested military equipment in order to defend themselves. In his frustration over this congressional action, President Ford observed, "This abdication of responsibility by a majority of the Senate will have the gravest consequences for the long-term position of the United States and for international order in general."[6]

Although the failed attempt to rescue the hostages in Iran technically violated the War Powers Resolution of 1973, President Carter did not notify Congress of the mission until after it had been launched, had failed, and then been abandoned. In the various postmortems, this aspect of the debacle was overlooked in favor of more substantive questions concerning planning, tactics, and command.

In the classic constitutional areas, President Carter won one and lost one. His all-out drive for Senate ratification of the Panama Canal Treaty was successful, while the Salt II Treaty never reached the floor of the Senate.

The Panama Canal pact was ratified by a 68 to 32 margin—only one vote to spare. Some compared the final Senate vote to the historic showdown on the League of Nations. In that instance, the president was not successful, and some believe that this failure broke the spirit of the presidency of Woodrow Wilson.

Foreign diplomats and many domestic observers pictured the Panama Canal treaties as a decisive test of President Carter's presidency. They believed that victory would strengthen a credibility in foreign affairs that had been battered by the Cuban-Soviet offensive in Ethiopia and the Israeli raid into Lebanon. There was speculation that following ratification, Carter would then move authoritatively in the areas of strategic arms talks, Mideast negotiations, the Horn of Africa, the sagging dollar, and the three-way arms package involving Egypt, Israel, and Saudi Arabia. It was even suggested that his domestic policy record on Capitol Hill, which was mediocre at best, could be saved from further decline by a treaty victory. Events would prove that while losing may have had serious repercussions, winning was not a cure-all for President Carter.

The proposed sale of AWACS radar planes and other military equipment to Saudi Arabia presented President Reagan with his first congressional challenge in the field of foreign affairs. Congressional approval of the sale provided an important early victory. It demonstrated that the president was determined to be an active and successful foreign policy leader.

The power of the presidency in foreign affairs is such that if exercised wisely and forcefully, the odds normally favor the president. Indecisiveness is fatal. Those who want to join the president need to know that they will not be abandoned. Those in opposition must understand that they are challenging the president and a last-minute compromise is not in the cards.

Each new occupant of the White House gives rise to an important question that only time can answer. Every president is a proven campaigner, normally a public figure or skilled politician who has marshaled and led the organizational force required to capture the nomination and win an election. The unknown factor is whether, once in office, the person elected can take and exercise command.

In the AWACS case, the question was posed and the answer was given. President Reagan took command. His meetings with and letter to members of Congress put his personal prestige on the line. His refusal to quit or to compromise turned predicted defeat into victory.

AWACS proved to be only a skirmish in the continuing congressional battle to share presidential authority in the foreign policy field. In December 1982, the Boland Amendment was tacked on to an omnibus government spending bill. This amendment, sponsored by Edward P. Boland, chairman of the House Permanent Select Committee on Intelligence, forbade aid to guerrilla groups "for the purpose of overthrowing the government of Nicaragua or provoking a military exchange between Nicaragua and Honduras."

Soon, there were allegations of CIA and Pentagon support, in violation of the Boland Amendment, for the counterrevolutionary rebel army moving into Nicaragua from Honduras that was seeking to overthrow the Sandinista government. While denouncing Nicaragua as a Marxist government dedicated to overthrowing El Salvador, President Reagan denied attempting to overthrow the Nicaraguan government. In defending his policy, the president expressed his concern that "his powers under the Constitution were unduly restricted by the Boland Amendment."

For both parties, this is a high-risk game. In order to demonstrate that it is not violating the Boland Amendment, the administration may be forced to strip all secrecy from its operations. On the other hand, by supporting the Boland Amendment, Congress may appear to take the side of the anti-American Nicaraguan government.

Recognizing the seriousness of the situation, President Reagan took the unusual step of appearing before a special joint session of Congress. It was only the ninth such occasion since World War II. In his nationally televised address, the president did his best to mobilize public as well as congressional support for his strategy to counter Soviet-Cuban influence in Central America. In his words, "The national security of all the Americas is at stake in Central America. If we cannot defend ourselves there, we cannot expect to prevail elsewhere. Our credibility would collapse, our alliances would crumble and the safety of our homeland would be put in jeopardy."[7]

One of the gravest congressional challenges to President Reagan's authority in foreign affairs has been the nuclear freeze resolution. Although it is largely a symbolic call for a mutual and verifiable halt in the arms race, there is concern that it could undermine the president's ability to negotiate with the Soviet Union. In opposing the proposal, President Reagan claimed that the resolution would hinder, not help, efforts to reduce the risk of nuclear war and that it could be a formula for permanent insecurity.

In August 1982, the House supported President Reagan and adopted, by a 204 to 202 vote, a substitute nuclear freeze resolution that called for negotiated reductions in strategic forces first and then a freeze. In May 1983, with the addition of 26 new Democratic members, the House reversed itself and approved a resolution that called for the president to negotiate a mutual and verifiable freeze and reduction in nuclear weapons with the Soviet Union. The approval came, however, only after adoption of an amendment revoking the freeze if it is not followed by negotiated arms reductions within a reasonable time.

Even with the amendment, the House action may damage the president's bargaining ability. Unless the Senate supports the president, the Soviets may harden their demands at Geneva on the perception that they are dealing with a president whose hand had been seriously weakened at home.

The recent Supreme Court decision that ruled the one-house legislative veto unconstitutional[8] has called into question a device that Congress has used since 1932 in more than 200 laws covering everything from waging war to the running of Amtrak. Many of the laws containing legislative vetoes that have been discussed in this section may be seriously if not fatally impacted by this decision. As the following analysis indicates, only time and congressional, executive, and Court action will provide the answers.

The Supreme Court Enters the Arena

In its landmark decision, *INS v. Chadha*, the Supreme Court ruled by a 7–2 vote that the one-house legislative veto contained in Section 244(c)(2) of the Immigration and Nationality Act is unconstitutional. In its opinion the Court rests on the view that the constitutional mandate for bicameral consideration and presentment to the president for his signature or veto is a universal requirement for all exercises of legislative power. The Court's analysis of Article I of the Constitution may invalidate all legislative vetoes regardless of their form or subject. As a result, this decision could eliminate an instrument of legislative oversight that has been applied for the past fifty years to every field of governmental concern: reorganization, budget, foreign affairs, war powers, and the regulation of trade, safety, energy, the environment, and the economy.

It will be years before all the ramifications of this decision are known. However, some idea of its scope was given by Justice Byron White in his dissent when he observed that the Court's rationale "sounds the death knell for nearly 200 other statutory provisions in which Congress has reserved a legislative veto." Until such time as the questions regarding the application of this decision are definitively answered by the Supreme Court, there will be much speculation as to whether Congress or the executive branch is the real winner. At the outset, commentators and constitutional experts have been divided over this question. Some view the decision as a terrible defeat for Congress with hard-won gains of a decade wiped out and with an enormous increase in presidential power. Others have predicted that the executive branch would lose much of its discretion because Congress would no longer hand over broad grants of power subject only to a legislative veto provision.

A closer reading of history and the ever-continuing struggle between Congress and the executive branch suggests that when the dust settles the net effect of the *Chadha* decision may be zero. In recent years the use of the legislative veto had become excessive and even members of Congress expressed concern. However, no one has argued that congressional oversight is not one of the essential legislative responsibilities and the legislative veto was just one form of expressing that responsibility. If it finally turns out that this particular tool is no longer available, it can be anticipated that Congress will turn to other legislative devices. Such alternatives could include the use of greater precision in the drafting of bills, more careful oversight by congressional committees, and even the expanded use of "sunset" legislation whereby laws are regularly scheduled to terminate.

The battle between Congress and the executive branch dictated by the Constitution will continue. It is the responsibility of the Court to make certain that neither side gains an unfair advantage or distorts the basic system. In the *Chadha* decision, the Supreme Court performed its role as arbitrator well. That there may be confusion, inconvenience, and less administrative efficiency is immaterial. A sidestep toward what might have become a quasi-parliamentary government has been quashed. The bicameral legislative system with a separation of legislative and executive power has been reinforced.

Congressional Staffing

In an effort to be competitive with the greatly expanded executive departments and agencies, Congress has substantially increased the size of its operation. The responsibilities of Congress and its committees have expanded as the magnitude of federal programs and expenditures has grown. Federal expenditures increased from $36.9 billion in fiscal year 1947 to $728.4 billion in fiscal year 1982. During the same period of time, annual appropriations for the legislative branch grew from $62 million to $1.4 billion. Between 1947 and 1981, standing committee staff personnel grew from 167 to 1,843 in the House and from 232 to 1,022 in the Senate. During the same period, personal staffs of representatives grew from 1,440 to 7,487 and of senators from 590 to 3,638.[9] Many in Congress have become concerned at the expansion of congressional staffs and facilities. Some believe that such growth may exceed the members' ability to organize, manage, and utilize the resources available to them.[10] Members have been forced to become administrators rather than legislators. There is the danger that the staff rather than the member may be making the decisions. Members are too busy reading reports, attending hearings, and being briefed to think through a problem. This, plus the legislative activity that a $700 to $800 billion budget requires, has created a situation where both houses of Congress rush from one emergency to another, from one high-pressure situation to another, without the time to think or to reflect. As a result, they are swept along by the breathless pace of television and radio. In many instances, government by press release has been substituted for government by careful analysis and searching debate.

There is yet another side to the problem of staff proliferation that was not apparent at first. As each legislative committee has become larger and as the federal programs that come under its jurisdiction have become more complex, a new bureaucracy has been created. The programs they help to shape and pass become their particular product. Pressure groups become their constituents and the bureaucracy in the executive departments their allies. These alliances cross party and geographic boundaries. The old system that was dominated by party and geographic pressures no longer applies.

A new president and his new department heads, faced with a ballooning budget and escalating demands, look for areas of waste and programs that can be reduced or abolished. The holdover bureaucracy is more than ready to comply. A list is prepared that to the unpracticed eye is both appealing and attainable. Unfortunately, it is filled with politically sensitive programs and services. Unbeknownst to the new appointee, but not to the committee staff that handles the legislation, the cuts and program terminations have been designed to create maximum special interest and constituent protest. The negative reaction of Congress is completely predictable, and when the smoke of battle clears, little if anything has been changed. Interestingly enough, sometimes this procedure works with the wary as well as the unwary. When Lyndon Johnson was president, one of his budgets contained a proposal to close certain veterans' hospitals. The immediate outcry was both embarrassing and effective. There were no closings, and veterans' funds were increased in an effort to make amends for the transgression.

A number of solutions have been suggested to correct the problem created by committee staffs and committee members who have years of seniority and deep ties with special interest groups and departmental bureaucracies. One course of action would be to reduce the number of committee staff personnel. This would retain the core of expertise but limit the manpower available for program enchancement.

Another approach is to divide congressional committee staffs into majority and minority components. This would produce a diversity of thought. Alliances with special interest groups and departmental bureaucracies would vary and in certain cases not exist at all. Historically, the division of committee staffs has presented a number of problems. Recognition of the right of the minority to identifiable staff personnel is a recent innovation. In 1982, House committee staffs, both statutory and investigative, comprised 1,269 majority, 335 minority, and 98 nonpartisan members.[11] The Senate maintains a ratio of one-third to two-thirds in committee staffing.

Taking a cue from the Senate, Republican members of the House advocated that the minority should receive one-third of all funds allocated for staff salaries. This principle has been observed on statutory staffs, but on some investigative staffs a wide disparity exists. For example, in 1982 on the Energy and Commerce Committee, only 10 of 110 investigative staff were allocated to the minority, on the Foreign Affairs Committee 4 of 52, and on the Judiciary Committee 2 of 40.

Another reform would be to increase the staff of the Government Accounting Office (GAO) so that more investigative work could be accomplished by a group of professionals who were not part of a congressional committee and had limited ties to a department or agency. At the present time, the work of the GAO is an invaluable aid to Congress. Its reports have resulted in a number of reforms and cost reductions. Expanding its operations could be a cost-effective and acceptable solution to the problem.

Another suggested solution would be to limit the terms and the seniority of the members. Although the Constitution limits a president to two terms, a senator or a congressman may serve without limit. There is committee seniority as well as overall seniority, and members normally retain committee assignments, especially those on major committees, for as long as they are in Congress. This has placed a premium on length of service and resulted in long-lasting relationships between members and the departments and the special interest groups that regularly appear before their committees. A limit on the number of terms a member could serve, or on the consecutive years of service on a particular committee, would be one method of meeting this problem.

Interestingly enough, the Budget Act of 1974 was the first legislation to limit length of service on a particular committee. No member can serve on the House Budget Committee for more than three full congresses within any ten-year period, the so-called six-year rule.

Congressional Liaison

In earlier times, White House relations with Congress were conducted on a more casual basis. The vice-president spent the bulk of his days in his office just off the Senate floor, dozing and listening to the gentle tinkling of his magnificent chandelier. The president met informally with congressional leaders, and normally their agreements could be carried out by a disciplined and seniority-bound membership. With the advent of World War II, much of this changed. The Pentagon, faced with tremendous problems and an uninformed, if willing, Congress, developed a congressional liaison system that worked with great precision. A key officer in the liaison group was a young man who had served in close relationship with many members of the House of Representatives. Bryce Harlow, an enterprising young man from Oklahoma, was as skilled in the intricacies of Congress as he was in the art of working with often difficult congressmen. General Wilton B. (Jerry) Persons, chief of the Pentagon's Legislative and Liaison Division, put this skill and Harlow's winning personality to good use.

When General Eisenhower became president, he brought into the White House not only the Pentagon's concept of congressional liaison, but the man who had been its chief, as well as his top aide, Bryce Harlow.

For eight years, Bryce Harlow, first as deputy and then as head of the White House liaison group, spread oil on the often troubled waters of Congress. Liaison with Congress became an art form. It provided an important listening post as well as an immediate and knowledgeable conduit into the highest reaches of the Eisenhower administration. It solved the perplexing problem of how to recognize and reward on a day-to-day basis members of Congress who, with a minimum of fuss, complaints, and requests, were always there when needed. Congressional leadership meetings and breakfasts with the president were scheduled on a regular basis. Ongoing contact was maintained with individual members and key committee staff. Legislative surprises and pitfalls were kept to a minimum, and the president's time and prestige were husbanded for critical situations. In the event Speaker Sam Rayburn or Majority Leader Lyndon Johnson needed to get an urgent message to the president, it was known that Harlow could deliver such a message and return immediately with an authoritative reply.

Larry O'Brien, first under President Kennedy and later under President Johnson, carried on a less structured but nevertheless quite effective liaison system. It was generally recognized, however, that Lyndon Johnson provided much of his own congressional liaison. As a shoulder massager, lapel gripper, and one-on-one convincer, Johnson was without peer. His phone was always at the ready, and he was never more than a White House call away from key members, Republican as well as Democrat.

One of Nixon's first moves was to bring Bryce Harlow and his renowned congressional liaison system back to the White House. Under Harlow's tutelage a group was assembled that provided all of the expertise of the Eisenhower years. It was even good enough to overcome the introverted personality of the president and the arrogance of key White House aides. Harlow's loss to private industry after the first two years was compensated in great part by the operation he left behind.

Despite President Ford's amiable style, personal contacts, and long service on Capitol Hill, his relationship with Congress was far from trouble-free. The many vetoes and the fights over Vietnam, Cyprus, and Angola reflected the deep division between a Republican administration and a Democratic Congress. This challenged the ingenuity of a knowledgeable president and an excellent liaison office.

The Carter administration ushered in an era of know-nothingism. Jimmy Carter was an outsider who remained an outsider even after he became president. His congressional liaison office under Frank Moore reflected his style perfectly. It was months before Moore paid a courtesy call on the House minority leader. As far as most members were concerned, he was the ghost who wasn't there. In exasperation over the whole White House operation, Speaker Tip O'Neill referred to Carter's chief of staff as "Hannibal Jerkin." Vice-President Walter Mondale, a former senator, did his best to educate and to coordinate, but it was a losing battle. An offer by Republican congressional leaders John Rhodes and Howard Baker to support a bipartisan foreign policy was greeted with a smile and nothing more. In the end, Jimmy Carter left Washington misunderstood and bereft of understanding.

With the Carter act to follow, the Reagan administration had little trouble demonstrating knowledge and skill in the field of congressional relations. A Harlow lieutenant, Max Friedersdorf, brought back the glory days of congressional liaisoning. This coupled with a sizable electoral mandate and a winning presidential personality produced early budget and tax victories. For the most part, the new administration received good marks from Congress during the first part of its term in office.

With the departure of Friedersdorf and the bitter feuding among top officials in the White House, the congressional liaison office lost much of its effectiveness. After the chief of staff took over the operation, congressional relations were handled on an ad hoc basis. This created difficulties for the president at the very time his dealings with Congress in both the budgetary and foreign policy fields became increasingly strained.

Whatever the form it may take, the congressional liaison office performs an important and essential function in the White House. In many instances, the success or failure of the president's program may depend on the effectiveness of the liaison group.

Is a Fundamental Change Required?

The relationship between any president and any congress will be ever changing and challenging. It will ebb and flow, depending on the personalities involved. One thing remains certain—the congressional reach for executive power will continue, particularly when the president and the congressional majority are from different political parties. The trend that began during the Vietnam war has, if anything, quickened during the Reagan administration.

Understandably, this has led to calls for reform and even a restructuring of the system. Troubled by the overall problems associated with the present relationship, former president Gerald R. Ford observed:

> When I was in the Congress myself, I thought it fulfilled its constitutional obligations in a very responsible way, but after I became President, my perspective changed. It seemed to me that Congress was beginning to disintegrate as an organized legislative body. It wasn't answering the nation's challenges domestically because it was too fragmented. It responded too often to single-issue special interest groups and it therefore wound up dealing with minutiae instead of attacking serious problems in a coherent way. Moreover, Congress was determined to get its oar deeply into the conduct of foreign affairs. This not only undermined the Chief Executive's ability to act but also eroded the separation of powers concept in the Constitution.[12]

President Ford's criticism is doubly important, for he was a man of Congress. From the time of his first election to the House of Representatives in November 1948 until December 6, 1973, when he was sworn in as vice-president, he was a respected member and a talented leader in the House of Representatives. His nomination as vice-president and his subsequent confirmation by an overwhelming majority of both houses of Congress were a tribute to the respect and esteem in which he was held by colleagues on both sides of the aisle. Many times during the confirmation process, the point was made that Congress was confirming more than a vice-president, a soon-to-be president was being born and Congress was the midwife.[13]

There was speculation that Ford's elevation to the presidency might be a political and historical watershed. Chosen by his peers rather than the people, a congressional leader rather than a national figure, some believed it would not be beyond the realm of possibility for him to institute an era of quasi-parliamentary government. A move toward the British system might be in the offing.

During the short term of his vice-presidency (December 6, 1973, to August 9, 1974), there were indications that Ford considered his new post a continuation of his former role as a congressional leader. As vice-president, he enjoyed acting as the president of the Senate. Each day he visited his office just off the Senate floor. He would chair the opening session of the Senate and then return to his office for conferences and to receive visitors. For the first time, a special vice-presidential office near the House Chamber was opened. Thus, in a number of important ways he continued to reflect his earlier background as he carefully retained his congressional contacts.

When Vice-President Ford became President Ford, the early portents of structural change were quickly set aside. The system of checks and balances, division of power, and built-in tension, if not hostility, between the president and Congress took over. In a short time, many in the White House were viewing with dismay those on the Hill who just a short time before were respected and even beloved colleagues. The Founding Fathers must have been relieved, if not pleased, that their work of art had withstood yet another challenge.

Some credit for the change in President Ford's attitude should be given to the House Judiciary Committee. On September 8, 1974, Ford pardoned his predecessor, Richard M. Nixon. There was a storm of protest. Allegations of a secret deal were heard, and Ford's standing in the Gallup poll plummeted from a rating of 71 percent to 49 percent.

Amid rumors and innuendo, a number of privileged resolutions were filed in the House asking that the president respond to certain inquiries. Believing that he had nothing to hide, Ford decided to respond in the most dramatic fashion possible. He would appear in person before the Subcommittee on Criminal Justice of the House Judiciary Committee and answer any and all questions regarding the pardon. Not since the reported but unsubstantiated visit by President Lincoln to deny reports that his wife was a Confederate spy had a chief executive testified before Congress.

For the most part, the committee members were polite. The one exception was Representative Elizabeth Holtzman. Her questions were accusatory in nature and stated in such a manner that there was no time for Ford to answer. After two hours of grilling, the president thanked the committee, convinced that he had accomplished his objective. He left, however, never to return, except in the formalized setting of the State of the Union address. This ended the move, if ever there was one, in the direction of parliamentary government.

Another attempt to reduce the tension and election year animosity between the president and Congress may be found in the quadrennial call for a one-term presidency. Under the pressures of the modern presidency, only two of the first four years are relatively unencumbered by political considerations. All first-term presidents have one thing in common—the all-consuming desire to be re-elected. In its most virulent form, this has spawned a series of misadventures such as Watergate. In milder cases, it has resulted in escalated expenditures, questionable appointments, and a serious drain on the time and attention of the president and his close associates.

Concerned by this problem, a distinguished group of citizens headed by former attorney general Griffin Bell is seeking the enactment of a constitutional amendment limiting a president to one six-year term. Such an amendment, they believe, would permit a longer period of presidential service, help to reduce the level of politics in the White House, and still provide the safeguard of a one-term limitation. Its drawback is that it would change the symmetry of the present system, which places the presidential term in between the two-year terms of representatives and the six-year terms of senators, and would mean that the president is a lame duck from his first day in office. It would also mean an additional two years before a generally shared desire for change could be implemented. This could result in a period of great public dissatisfaction—the safety value of a timely election served well, for example, in 1932 and 1980.

An amendment of this type also might lead to a broader consideration of the whole elective process, especially the two-year term for representatives. At present, every other year is an election year for House members. As a result, they are perpetually either running or getting ready to run for office. There is a minimum period of time for considering serious legislative matters. Moreover, as in the case of President Eisenhower, a president may lose his majority in one or both houses of Congress after only two years. To correct these defects, it has been suggested that the term for House members should be changed from two to four years. The hope is that a majority of House members elected for four years and at the same time as the president would be more responsive to his leadership for a longer period of time before the pressures of partisanship and the next election eroded their spirit of gratitude and cooperation. Based on past performance, few believe this would happen. In addition, such a change would mean that the American people would be deprived of their present right to have an input and to make a course correction every two years. The importance of this vote was demonstrated in 1966 and 1974.

Without a radical constitutional change that would substitute parliamentary government for the present separation of powers system, the tension and conflict between the president and Congress will continue. Unless both Houses of Congress are controlled by the same party as that of the president, the split between the two can be deep and occasionally irreconcilable. At times, this may be true even though the president and a majority in both Houses share the same party and the same political beliefs. This is the price that is paid for a checks and balances system with its attendant safeguards against a monolithic government that could have unbridled power to move too far, too fast.

As long as the president is the leader of his party as well as the operating head of the government, he must be an active and important participant in the political process. It is impossible for him to be otherwise. Without tight party discipline and a system that would ensure the election of a president as well as a majority in both Houses from the same party, a four-year term for House members or one six-year presidential term is not a definitive answer.

What if anything, then, can be done to improve the present system with its conflicts, confusion, and possible stalemate between the president and Congress? First, as to the president, in his relations with Congress, it is extremely important to maintain close relations and to be skilled in the art of compromise. It also helps to have a substantial electoral mandate. Congress takes a keen interest in election results and is responsive to a president who commands broad public support. Whenever possible, there should be a conscious effort on the part of the president to keep clearly perceived presidential activity separate from partisan political maneuvering. President Eisenhower was a master at this. Ike carefully cultivated his presidential role while keeping the political side and partisan activity mostly hidden from public view.[14]

For most Americans, the president, once elected, becomes the leader of all the people. Acting in this capacity he can normally draw on a reservoir of public trust and support, especially in the area of foreign affairs. As a result, the power and prestige of the presidency should be reserved for only the most important issues. But once a decision has been made, it must be pursued with a singleness of purpose and great intensity. Then and only then should the president join the battle as advocate, communicator, and leader.

In the continuing contest between Congress and the president, Congress may have the greater burden. A growing number of Americans have come to believe that Congress is ineffective, if not inoperative, in fiscal and budgetary matters and overly intrusive in foreign affairs. With a $200 billion deficit and a national debt well on its way to $2 trillion, the congressional budget process is viewed with suspicion and perceived to be in danger of collapse. With its legislative vetoes (which have now been called into question), restrictions on military aid and arms sales, and curbs on covert action, Congress is seen by many as deliberately trying to obstruct the president on foreign policy matters.

In this context, it is significant that following President Reagan's speech on Central America, House Democratic leader Jim Wright called for a bipartisan foreign policy. "We've got one president. We haven't got a Democratic president and a Republican president who take turns at bat in making foreign policy. That's not the way it works. It never will work that way."[15]

This could signal a return to a less partisan approach to foreign policy by the opposition party. Once again, politics would stop at the water's edge. Such a redirection would be in the tradition of Sam Rayburn and other great Speakers of the House of Representatives. It would recognize that the Speaker is a national leader, third in the chain of succession, and not just a partisan politician. Under this approach, the Senate could resume its role in foreign affairs as a thoughtful, deliberative body. Following the example of Senators Walter George and Arthur Vandenberg, in time of international crisis it would seek to provide bipartisan support for the president's foreign policy initiatives.

Given the frustration of the American public, Congress and the president must address the deepening fiscal crisis more responsibly. A protracted stalemate with growing deficits, higher unemployment, and an end to the economic recovery is totally unacceptable and poses serious political risks. Unfortunately, despite a rising tide of red ink and a collapsing budget process, Congress appears to be institutionally incapable of rationally allocating government resources. The president, on the other hand, appears to have accepted the political and fiscal consequences of $200 billion deficits rather than seeking a compromise with Congress that would reduce defense and domestic spending and increase taxes.

In the present situation, there are no easy answers, magic solutions, or shortcuts. The Supreme Court had made this painfully clear in its legislative veto decision. Therefore, in spite of historical differences, ever-present tension and conflict, and a less than perfect system, Congress and the president must find a way to surmount these difficulties and work together. There is no other choice.

Notes

1. *Manual on Legislative Procedure in the U.S. House of Representatives* (Washington, D.C., 1982), p. 234.

2. *The Congressional Budget Process: A General Explanation*, 11–8460 (Washington, D.C.: Government Printing Office, 1982).
3. *Atlantic Monthly*, December 1981.
4. Televised address, March 23, 1983.
5. Constitution, Art. I, sect. 8, and Art. II, sect. 2.
6. Gerald R. Ford, *A Time to Heal* (New York: Harper & Row, 1979), p. 150.
7. Televised address, April 27, 1983.
8. *Immigration and Naturalization Service v. Chadha et al.*, Supreme Court of the United States, June 23, 1983, no. 80-1832.
9. American Enterprise Institute, *Vital Statistics on Congress, 1982*, Studies in Political and Social Processes (Washington, D.C., 1982).
10. *Studies Dealing with Budgetary, Staffing and Administration Activities of the U.S. House of Representatives, 1946–1978*, 32–983 (Washington, D.C.: Government Printing Office, 1978).
11. *Congressional Record*, March 22, 1983, p. H1487.
12. Ford, *Time to Heal*, p. 150.
13. Robert T. Hartman, *Palace Politics* (New York: McGraw-Hill, 1980), p. 73.
14. F. I. Greenstein, *Hidden Hand Presidency: Eisenhower as Leader* (New York: Basic Books, 1982).
15. Statement, April 29, 1983.

13
Reagan's Regulatory Record

Thomas Gale Moore

In January 1981, President Ronald Reagan's new administration came into office with three economic goals: cutting taxes, reducing spending, and reforming the regulatory system. Because of its great initial success in lowering tax rates, the administration has become preoccupied with shaving domestic spending to keep the budget deficit within tolerable limits. As a consequence, the government has done little to implement long-term reforms of regulation, and many improvements are administrative and can be overturned by the next administration. The sad fact is that the Reagan administration has followed the traditional Republican role of cleaning up and making workable policies introduced by the previous administrations.

One major handicap faced by the administration in its efforts to reform regulation has been the predilection of the courts to second-guess administrative actions. In fact, the federal courts have become regulatory bodies, imposing huge roadblocks to reform of government controls over the private sector. For example, the Supreme Court prohibited the use of cost-benefit analysis for new Occupational Safety and Health Administration (OSHA) regulations relating to toxic substances, and it also blocked an attempt to rescind the air-bag requirements for autos; another court annulled a new administrative rule on the grounds that it changed another administrative rule in effect for fifty years; and the Fifth Circuit Court of Appeals held that the Interstate Commerce Commission had gone too far in relaxing entry standards.

Like its predecessors, the Reagan administration has had both successes and failures. Undoubtedly, its greatest success has been the decontrol of crude oil pricing and allocation. This single act contributed to a weakening of the Organization of Petroleum Exporting Countries and to a great reduction in oil imports. While the president does deserve credit for speeding this decontrol effort, the Carter administration had already scheduled the elimination of federal regulation for some eight months later. Some cynics have attributed the Reagan acceleration to a desire to gain additional revenues from the "windfall profits" tax.

Perhaps a more uniquely Reagan reform was the dropping of antitrust cases against International Business Machines (IBM) and cereal manufacturers and the settlement of the American Telephone & Telegraph (AT&T) case. These cases had dragged on for years under dubious theories of antitrust. Their settlement and the promulgation of new and more soundly based merger guidelines were highly desirable steps.

Both the antitrust reforms and the decontrol of crude oil were administrative reforms. The White House has made other significant administrative improvements in regulation, but its greatest failure is the lack of legislative reform. For the first two years, with the possible exception of legislation dealing with the banking industry, it failed to propose or to push any major legislation to reduce the burden of government regulation. Except where existing legislation mandated deregulation, for example, in the oil and airline industries, almost all of the reforms of the Reagan administration can be revoked by a new president. Moreover, existing statutes have built-in limitations; in the regulatory area new legislation is vitally important for the deregulation of such sectors as natural gas, banking, trucking, railroads, and pharmaceuticals, as well as in the areas of air and water pollution rules. Moreover, with the courts' taking such an active role in the regulatory process, legislation is necessary if any significant changes are to be made.

In fairness, after two years in office Reagan finally did propose legislation to deregulate the natural gas industry. Unfortunately, this complex proposal would (1) impose limits on pipelines passing through price increases until 1986, at which time all controls would be lifted; and (2) authorize gas pipelines to renounce some long-term supplier contracts. Under this plan, gas now exempt from regulation will in effect be brought under temporary price controls. The hope is that with pipelines able to abrogate contracts, new, lower-priced gas will be substituted for higher-price gas; and by the time the new controls expire, market-clearing gas prices will actually be lower than those required by law. But if controlled prices are well below free-market levels, will controls be extended again?

Probably the single most significant move of the administration, outside of oil price decontrol, was President Reagan's immediate creation, in February 1981, of a high-level administrative program for regulatory reform, embodied in Executive Order 12291. This executive order required all executive agencies to use a cost-benefit test for any proposed major regulation. However, the administration's appointments to the independent agencies, with some notable exceptions, have been from disappointing to poor. Consequently, reforms in these agencies have been slowed or in part reversed.

These themes of court interference, lack of legislative action, smoother regulatory processes in lieu of deregulation, and inadequate agency appointments are visible in many regulatory reforms and agencies. Under the Office of Management and Budget (OMB), which is charged with overseeing regulatory reform under the executive order, progress (or the lack of progress) can be seen in such executive agencies as the Environmental Protection Agency (EPA) and the Department of Labor and in such independent agencies as the Interstate Commerce Commission (ICC), the Civil Aeronautics Board (CAB), and the Federal Communications Commission (FCC). While far from exhausting all of the major regulatory areas, these programs demonstrate the major problems, successes, and failures of regulatory reform under President Reagan.

The Executive Agencies

The agencies of the executive branch are more immediately controlled by the administration and therefore more accurately reflect its philosophy. They are subject directly to the procedures outlined in Executive Order 12291. With the exception of the first year of the EPA, under administrator Anne Gorsuch (Burford), the regulatory record has been modestly better in these agencies than in the independent agencies.

Executive Order 12291

With Executive Order (EO) 12291, President Reagan established the Presidential Task Force on Regulatory Relief, chaired by Vice-President George Bush. The EO built on preceding administrations' experiences with the necessity to control eager bureaucrats who often ignore costs and conflicting goals in their single-minded devotion to pursuing specific regulatory objectives. The administrations of Presidents Nixon, Ford, and Carter had each delegated to a central agency the authority to oversee new regulations and to ensure that they were consistent with good cost-benefit analysis. For instance, under the Republicans the Council on Wage and Price Stability included a section to regulate other regulatory agencies. Jimmy Carter established a White House task force to monitor new regulation, with representatives from the various regulatory agencies. The Reagan plan expanded and systematized these previous efforts. It also extended the review to existing regulations, whereas earlier efforts had been confined to simply stemming the flow of costly and poorly conceived new rules.

EO 12291 requires that all regulatory proposals of executive branch agencies be submitted to the OMB, together with an analysis of the costs and benefits. While the EO does not require that all benefits be quantified, it does order that they be identified. The EO also requires agencies to examine alternative methods of achieving the same aim and to choose the most cost-effective plan. The OMB is authorized to oversee this effort and to send back to the agency proposed rules that fail to meet the guidelines. In addition, each agency is required to review existing regulations systematically to ensure that they meet a cost-benefit test and are cost-effective. The presidential task force was given the job of supervising this effort and reconciling differences between the OMB and the particular regulatory agency.

In August 1982, the Presidential Task Force on Regulatory Relief issued a report on its major accomplishments. In an update to this report, the OMB reported on March 10, 1983, that of the 119 major regulatory programs that the task force had identified as high-priority candidates for review, 66 (up from 51 in August) had been revised or rescinded, 31 had proposed revisions, and 22 (down from 25 in August) were still under review.[1] Further, the August report claimed that the administration had made 22 other major regulatory relief decisions. The task force report took credit for savings of at least $6.0–6.2 billion annually and a savings of capital costs of $9–11 billion. The administration also maintained that during 1981 the OMB had reviewed a total of 2,803 regulations proposed by federal agencies and returned some 13 percent to the agencies for revision or withdrawal. During the first seven months of 1982, the OMB asserted it had reviewed 1,506 regulations and again returned about 13 percent for revision or withdrawal. The Reagan administration has been issuing final regulations at a rate 22 percent less than that of the Carter administration during its last year in office. Moreover, the number of proposed rules per month is down 34 percent from the last year of the Carter period.

The number of rules rescinded or prevented does not indicate whether the reforms are trivial or major. The OMB's estimated dollar savings give a measure of the significance of these changes. Of the $6 billion annual savings from these reforms, two changes account for $2 billion, or a third of the total. Most important, and one of the most controversial, was the proposed rescision of the passive restraints standard, which the OMB estimated would save $1 billion. The rescission was promptly challenged in court. The U.S. Court of Appeals for the District of Columbia held that the Department of Transportation (DOT) had acted arbitrarily and capriciously and ruled that the requirement for passive restraints be reimposed. The court's primary objection to the rescission was that a "sudden and profound alteration in an agency's policy constitutes 'danger signals' that the will of Congress is being ignored."[2] Nevertheless, there is nothing in the statute or in its legislative history to conclude that Congress ever intended the DOT to impose a passive restraint standard. In a unanimous decision, however, the Supreme Court upheld the Court of Appeals and found that the DOT had not justified its action.

This case is one of the most striking examples of the substitution of a judge's views for that of the administration. It becomes very difficult for an administration to change a proposed rule. By the reasoning of the court, any government policy started by one administration cannot or should not be reversed by another, even if the new president ran on the platform of overturning that policy. This is a strange position for a court to take.

In a related case that was a setback to the Reagan administration's deregulation efforts, a U.S. district court judge ruled that the Treasury Department had ignored Congress's will by repealing a 1980 regulation that required makers of alcoholic beverages to disclose the ingredients of their products. The department had found that the rule failed a cost-benefit test, but the judge struck down the use of costs and benefits because the costs and benefits had "already been articulated by Congress."[3] The judge also asserted that the repeal effort deserved close scrutiny because it reversed a year-old policy. This case strikes at the heart of EO 12291 by ruling out cost-benefit tests; further, it increases the difficulty of overturning existing regulations.

The second major reform that the OMB estimated will save the country over $1 billion a year is a simplification and streamlining of the Army Corps of Engineers' permit program. This reform will streamline the process of securing a permit for dredging and construction activities in navigable waters, saving considerable time. It also will lead to a quicker resolution of disputes between the corps, the EPA, and the Interior and Commerce departments. The new permit process also will allow the use of nationwide permits.

While highly worthwhile, the streamlining of this water-permit policy does not constitute deregulation. It simply makes the regulatory process less cumbersome. Had the reform moved toward marketable permits for particular watersheds, it would have been more significant.

However, the reform of the corps' permit program does reflect an ongoing theme in the Reagan administration: an attempt to make regulation work better. Traditionally, the Republicans have played the role of reforming *how* the government works, while the Democrats have played the role of changing *what* the government does. Here again, rather than eliminating regulation, the administration is simply facilitating its implementation.

Unfortunately, the administration's commitment to deregulation is waning. In August 1983, it was quietly announced that the Presidential Task Force on Regulatory Relief, chaired by Vice President Bush, had completed its task of identifying all existing regulations requiring regulatory relief! Apparently it was easier to declare victory than to defeat the special interest groups that support specific regulations. The little deregulation that was proposed offended too many supporters of the president.

Environmental Protection Agency

The EPA has had a stormy career under President Reagan. Ann Gorsuch (Burford) came to the agency as a protégée of Secretary of Interior James Watt. Her law background did not prepare her for the many economic issues that she faced in office.

Probably the most serious regulatory problem facing the country, and certainly the environmental area, comes from the requirements laid down by the Clean Air Act and its amendments. This act, while purporting to protect the air, also protects certain industries, jobs, and regions at the expense of other industries, jobs, and regions and, unfortunately, at the expense of the environment.

The act and its amendments prohibit the degradation of the air of any region whose air is better than the national standard. It becomes difficult for new plants, especially those of heavy industries, to be built in these regions, most of which happen to lie in the Sun Belt. In addition, the act requires that for any new facility the "best available technology" (BAT) be used to control air pollution. In practice, building a new facility is very expensive. Again, the impact of this provision is to protect aging and increasingly inefficient steel plants, oil refineries, and power plants from needed new and more efficient installations. Part of the difficulties that the United States' auto and steel industries are having in competing with foreign producers may be attributable to the bias against new modern plants. Another provision of the act makes it virtually impossible and very costly to use low-sulfur coal in place of locally mined coal in the Middle West. This provision protects the jobs of coal miners in Illinois and Ohio but contributes to acid rain and air pollution.

No one knows the exact cost of the Clean Air Act, but it is large. The Business Roundtable retained Arthur Andersen & Company to conduct a study of the cost of various regulations to American industry. This study found that for the 48 companies analyzed, the EPA accounts for more than 77 percent of the total cost involved, and 60 percent of the cost of EPA programs is attributable to the air pollution program.[4] In other words, the clean air program is responsible for nearly half of all regulatory costs imposed on American industry. These costs do not include the retardation in economic growth and productivity due to the bias against new facilities, which incidentally would be less polluting than the older plants.

Despite the high priority that should be assigned to amending the Clean Air Act, the administration has failed even to introduce a bill to do so. Early in the administration, a proposed set of amendments was prepared within the executive office of the president, but Gorsuch rejected them. Although individuals within the administration admit that the act inhibits economic growth and productivity, they claim that there is no possibility of securing passage of any amendments that would improve matters.

This is a pessimistic view. Since parts of the act actually lead to more air pollution, environmentalists, properly approached, should be willing to support change. Undoubtedly there is considerable opposition to removing the regional protection aspects of the act, but with the population of the Sun Belt growing, change should be possible. In any case, the current high costs should make worthwhile a serious attempt to amend the act.

Initially, Gorsuch opposed using economic incentives to improve the environment. She forced out aides who worked for such policies as the bubble concept, which allows a firm or group of firms to trade off reductions in emissions from one source for greater emissions from another. However, there has been a major change for the better since early in 1982. The EPA is now embracing the use of economic incentives. The bubble concept was approved in 25 cases up to November 1982. Over an eight-month period, there were over 2,000 trades, 90 percent of which were between branches of an individual firm. For example, the concept was applied to two boilers of the Central Illinois Public Service Company by permitting a scrubber on one to be operated at a very stringent level and leaving the other boiler free from controls. The EPA estimates this will save the utility some $200 million in capital costs since the company will have to install scrubbers on only one boiler; operating expenses will be shaved by about $15 million to $20 million annually. The EPA hopes to expand the area within which trading is permitted, for additional significant gains.

Unfortunately, the courts have blocked regulatory reform and improvements in efficiency here as well. In one case, *National Resources Defense Council v. Gorsuch*, handed down in August 1982, the D.C. Court of Appeals ruled that a change in the definition of "new source" was an abuse of discretion and an unjustified change in earlier policy. During the 1970s, the EPA had two definitions of "new source."[5] In "attainment" areas—that is, portions of the country that met the national ambient air standards—a whole plant was considered a "source." Consequently, only new plants were subject to the large procedural and costly hurdles required for new sources. However, for nonattainment areas, any emission point was subject to new-source review. The Carter administration had considered changing this dual attainment standard. Shortly after Reagan took office, the acting administrator promulgated a unified definition that made a whole plant a single source. By considering a whole plant, a company could modernize a portion of its operation to reduce emissions in part of the plant and trade this off against increases elsewhere, for large cost savings. The OMB estimated that this bubble concept would save $1.3 billion in California alone. The court, however, held that the bubble concept cannot be used in nonattainment areas. The administration is appealing this decision.

When questioned about the most important success that the Republicans have had at EPA, the administration has expressed much pride in a new agency management system that allows for systematic review of proposed regulations before they are made public or submitted to the OMB. In addition, the EPA has moved to integrate the various aspects of environmental regulation to identify the trade-offs. For the steel industry, the subject of the EPA's first attempt at integration for a single industry, air pollution, water pollution, and soil wastes will be considered together. Thus if more constraints are put on air quality, the policy will allow the EPA to see how this impacts on water quality and on solid wastes.

Like other agencies, the major reform involves making the regulations work better, not changing the rules. Despite the benefits that can come from an improvement in administration, changes in the laws, as pointed out above, are of crucial importance. Unless the Supreme Court overturns the appeals court, and there is no guarantee that it even will hear the case, legislation will be necessary to clarify the definition of "source."

Labor Regulation

The courts have played a major role in shaping and limiting regulatory reform for labor. Three precedent-setting court decisions, the Cotton Dust decision, Castle & Cooke, and the Davis-Bacon ruling, are important not only to labor but to the whole deregulatory movement. The Cotton Dust decision may limit significantly the use of cost-benefit analysis in regulatory areas.[6] The Castle & Cooke decision authorizes, at least under certain circumstances, the application of cost-effectiveness analysis.[7] The Davis-Bacon ruling requires extensive justification of any proposed changes in an administrative rule.[8]

In the Cotton Dust decision, handed down by the Supreme Court on June 17, 1981, the industry had sued the Carter OSHA to require the agency to use a cost-benefit standard in determining permissible levels of cotton dust. Upon taking office, the Reagan administration requested the court to vacate the decision of the lower court upholding the Carter Labor Department's refusal to use a cost-benefit standard. The Supreme Court refused, striking down cost-benefit on the grounds that the act requires that the standard "assures, to the extent feasible . . . that no employee will suffer material impairment of health." The operative word in this case is "feasible," which the Court interpreted to rule out any weighing of costs against benefits.

This decision is limited to new OSHA standards regarding toxic materials and harmful physical agents. While it is unfortunate that sensible procedures cannot be utilized openly in making certain OSHA rules, a careful interpretation of the word "feasible" may partly remedy the problem. Congress should amend this act, although again most

Washington observers doubt that any change could be made at this time.

The Castle & Cooke case involved a suit brought by this pineapple producer in a noise case. Castle & Cooke wished to use earmuffs to meet the noise standard; the Carter Labor Department insisted on engineering changes. The Ninth Circuit Court upheld the company since earmuffs meet the legal decibel levels and are considerably cheaper. In this case, therefore, the court upheld a cost-effectiveness approach to regulation.

The Davis-Bacon case was brought by the construction workers' union against a Reagan administration proposal to modify regulations issued to implement the Davis-Bacon Act. This act and related laws require the payment of "prevailing wages" on government-assisted projects. The secretary of labor sets the level of prevailing wages.

In May 1982, the Department of Labor issued a revised set of regulations interpreting the Davis-Bacon Act. These new rules (1) changed the means of calculating the prevailing wage from rates paid to as few as the top 30 percent of workers to a test of over 50 percent; (2) prohibited the use of urban wages in calculating prevailing wages in rural areas; (3) prohibited the use of previously calculated prevailing wages when calculating the current prevailing wage; and (4) permitted an expanded use of "helpers" (who can be paid less than the prevailing wage) on federally financed projects. In July 1982, the U.S. District Court for the District of Columbia issued a preliminary injunction, which was made permanent in December, barring all the proposed changes except the first. The judge ruled against the government in part because of

> the long and consistent administrative practice prior to the issuance of the new regulations . . . the fact is that the Secretary has given no reasoned explanation for the new regulations, which departs from a rule adopted by the Department of Labor on the very day the 1935 Act became effective . . . For forty-seven years thereafter, through the administrations of eight Presidents and fifteen Secretaries of Labor of many political and ideological persuasions, those interpretations and those regulations stood without substantive alteration. During that period none of the administrators effected the kinds of fundamental changes that are brought about by the regulations adopted two months ago . . . when an agency abruptly changes a long-standing administrative position, regardless of the context, it may be expected at a minimum to show that the earlier understanding of the statute was wrong or that experience has proved it to be defective.[9]

In other words, if the public votes into office a new administration that has run on a platform of changing certain government regulations, it cannot do so without significant justification. The administration is going to appeal this decision. Unless the appeal is successful, this decision could make administrative changes in government regulation much more difficult.

Even in the absence of court roadblocks, progress in regulatory reform is slow. By the end of 1984, the Department of Labor expects to have issued thirteen health and sixteen safety regulations, which would be considerably more than were made final in a similar period under Carter. Most of these changes will involve relaxation of rules or proposed rules. For example, the carcinogenic policy proposed under the Carter administration would have required the department to list any substance that any study, no matter how flawed, found produced cancer or indications of cancer. The proposed new standard will require that regulators consider the quality of studies that have *failed* to find any carcinogenic effects as well as those that have detected an effect. This seems like a much more sensible policy.

In addition, the department has exempted from accident record-keeping many industries that have very safe records. For example, there seems little sense in requiring legal firms to maintain health and accident records for their employees. OSHA has estimated that this change alone has reduced record-keeping by 60,000 work-hours, for a $0.5 billion saving during the first year alone.

In summary, given the law and court decisions, the Department of Labor appears to be making progress, although the OMB has criticized it for lagging far behind other agencies in implementing reforms.[10] For example, the OMB complained about the lack of progress on workplace rules on carcinogens and the use of personal protection devices instead of expensive technology controls.

Fundamentally, it may be necessary to go to Congress at some time to lower the burden of regulation. The administration is seeking a lower minimum wage for youths doing summer work, which is a start in changing the law. Although the president did promise during the campaign not to seek repeal of Davis-Bacon, it might be time for him to propose changes in the act.

Independent Agencies

Government regulation of transportation and communication has been carried out mainly by agencies statutorily independent of presidential control. The president can only indirectly influence the behavior of these agencies through the appointment process and through the administration's control of their budgets. As is clear from the Carter years, the appointment of deregulatory-minded individuals can have a major impact on the behavior of the agencies and, in turn, on congressional action.

Unfortunately, Reagan's appointments to the independent agencies have not been good. In both the ICC and the CAB, the strong free-market approach of the regulatory agencies under the Carter presidency has been muted.

Surface Transportation

Unwisely, at the ICC many of the strongest advocates of deregulation have been forced out or have left the commission. Immediately after Reagan took office, Darius Gaskins, the incumbent ICC chairman under Carter, was asked to resign and Reese H. Taylor, Jr., was appointed as his replacement. Taylor, a former regulatory commissioner from Nevada, has never been an enthusiast for free markets. Since his appointment, he has slowed the movement toward deregulation.

In fairness to the Reagan administration, three of the other four appointments, Malcolm M. B. Sterrett, Frederic N. Andre, and Heather S. Gradison, have increasingly formed a majority in favor of less regulation. In fact, Andre and Sterrett have been strong advocates of abolishing regulation of trucking and reducing it for railroads. Reagan's fourth appointment, J. J. Simmons, was disappointing but he has left the commission.

Chairman Taylor has attempted to lead the ICC to construe the Motor Carrier Act of 1980 as narrowly as possible. Applications for new licenses have been granted to serve only those points and to carry only those products for which a shipper had indicated specifically that the service was needed. For example, one carrier, Hagen Inc. of Sioux City, Iowa, applied for general authority to haul nationwide. The Review Board of the ICC granted authority only for "transporting essentially the traffic of those shippers at the points or facilities where shippers demonstrate a need for service."[11] Hagen was granted very limited service.

Concern with rate cutting has preoccupied Reese Taylor. He has called tariffs that give lower rates to specific shippers "discriminatory" and "illegal." He voted to suspend a discount tariff proposed by Roadway Express on the grounds that the lower rates might be predatory. In October 1982, a majority of the commission led by the chairman held a hearing on rate discounts, which Taylor felt were a major problem. *Traffic World* reported that the chairman was concerned that something must be done to curb pricing practices that are designed to 'drive out the efficient carriers who simply don't have as big a bankroll as the others. It is irresponsible to ignore the pricing area.' "[12]

In 1982, the commission split on a Conrail request to cancel some joint rates for the movement of grain and grain products. Chairman Taylor voted against the Conrail request on the grounds that some of the smaller railroads would be endangered financially. This contravenes the intent of the 1980 act, which was intended to promote deregulation in order to prevent regulatory agencies from protecting one carrier from the actions of others.

By the start of 1982, the chairman was claiming that he favored deregulation and had acted solely to carry out the law. In February 1982, the commission sent a bill to Congress to abolish the needs test for the granting of new certificates. Taylor, however, wants a more stringent fitness test that includes "financial fitness, operational fitness and safety fitness." As Commissioner Robert Gresham wrote: "Unless this proposal is revised substantially, it easily could be used to retreat to the less competitive oriented regulatory environment which predated the Motor Carrier Act of 1980 and lead to a greater degree of regulatory control over the motor carrier industry."[13]

In this area as in others, the courts have played an active role in limiting deregulation. In October 1981, the Fifth Circuit Court of Appeals struck down the practice of the Carter commission of granting wide authority to applicants.[14] It contended that inadequate consideration had been given to the fitness of the carrier and the willingness and ability of the carrier to provide the service. The commission split, with the chairman voting against appealing the decision. After the Appeals Court ordered the ICC to enforce its ruling, the commission voted to appeal both that order and the original order, although under normal procedure the appeal was too late.

Many observers believe that the Motor Carrier Act dismantled entry barriers almost completely. While the barriers have been much reduced, the attempts by some ICC commissioners to restrict new authority as much as possible indicates that there are still limits on entry. Moreover, apparently several bulk carriers have told firms applying for new authority that they will protest any application for bulk authority, which would add significantly to the cost of securing the new rights. Strengthening the position of these protesters has been the attitude of the chairman, who opposes the granting of any bulk authority if not requested. For example, an ICC board granted a trucker, C.D.B.,

Inc., new authority without restriction.[15] After this grant was protested, C.D.B. told the commission it would be willing to forgo the bulk authority if that would satisfy the protestants.[16] The commission voted three to two, with the chairman in the minority, to grant the commodity authority with no restrictions on bulk carriage.

Several contract carriers and the contract carrier conference of the American Trucking Association have requested that the commission exempt contract carriers from the obligation to file rates. Under the Motor Carrier Act, common carriers are free to form subsidiaries that are contract carriers. Moreover, limits on what a contract carrier can do have been relaxed. If the ICC grants a general exemption for filing of rates, the commission's control over rates will largely disappear. Truckers avoid ICC control simply by offering low rates through their contract subsidiaries. Reportedly, the chairman is opposed to any blanket exemption or to extending the exemption beyond the few contract carriers already exempted.

All is not bad news in the surface transportation sector. The ICC has moved to exempt from rail regulation boxcars and coal for export. These decisions were carried over the objection of the chairman, who was outvoted by three other Reagan appointees. The commission has proposed a moderately liberal lid on rates for what is called "captive traffic" (freight from shippers with no good alternative method of moving their goods except for a given railroad).[17] Under this rule, railroads could raise rates 15 percent a year above inflation up to the cost of constructing new rail facilities. Commissioner Fred Andre wanted to set the limit at only the new-construction costs. In addition the commission has abolished restrictions on ownership of trucks by railroads.

During 1982, the Department of Transportation prepared a bill to totally abolish economic regulation of trucking, water carriers, and freight forwarders. Elizabeth Dole, who became secretary of transportation in 1983, endorsed this proposed legislation and sent it to the Office of Management and Budget. The OBM strengthened the bill by tacking on a provision to abolish the ICC. However, when the proposed bill was due to be presented to the president, Secretary of Labor Raymond Donovan relayed the Teamsters Union's strong opposition to deregulating trucking. The Teamsters, one of the few unions that supported Reagan in 1980, threatened to withdraw its political support of the president if the bill was submitted to the Congress. As a consequence, the proposed bill was withdrawn from cabinet consideration and as of September 1983 remained in limbo. Once again the Reagan White House has revealed the superficiality of its commitment to deregulation.

Airline Regulation

Reagan's appointees at the CAB, while not as controversial as ICC's Reese Taylor, have failed to be strong deregulators. Fortunately, airline deregulation has gone so far that there seems little chance of turning back the clock. There has been talk of bringing back regulation, but there is little support for such a move. Ironically, World Airways, which led the movement toward lower fares, asked the CAB to end the "disastrous and completely irrational" fare wars. The CAB denied the request.

Nevertheless, Reagan's appointment as CAB chairman, Dan McKinnon, has failed to support a strongly pro-competitive position. Under the Carter administration, the CAB had proposed eliminating the antitrust immunity of U.S. airlines participating in the international aviation cartel, IATA. Early in the Reagan administration, the CAB announced that it would lift antitrust immunity for rate making on the North Atlantic run. Faced with protests from foreign governments, the president asked the CAB to postpone its order. Subsequently, the administration worked out with the CAB and European governments an agreement to permit participation in IATA rate making in return for authorizing a range in which carriers could price freely. Since the bottom of the range, however, was above the lowest fares then charged, the impact was to eliminate the lowest fares. Apparently the change in chairmen led the board to back off from its strong pro-competitive position.

Chairman McKinnon also was less willing to support the majority in the Competitive Marketing Investigation, which in December 1982 proposed to eliminate government rules for selling airline tickets. Essentially this rule, if implemented, would permit the airlines to market tickets as they wish. Thus, travel agents could no longer be sure of receiving a fixed commission; other types of outlets, such as Ticketron, could be given the right to sell airline seats as they sell theater seats.

Communications

During the first two years of the Reagan administration, the most significant development in the communications sector was the Justice Department's settlement of the AT&T case. This decision, which is leading to the divestiture of local phone companies by AT&T, will leave a stripped-down company that faces competition in all its markets. This provides an opportunity for a significant reduction in regulation. With the AT&T decision making competition possible in long-distance phone service, there is a major opportunity to let the market set rates and services.

Unfortunately, in its regulation of common carriers, the FCC is continuing to cling to power. The commission apparently will continue to regulate the Bell System's long-distance charges and service quality. Inevitably, the commission will have to control minimum rates, the rates of the new competitors, and eventually entry. This is unnecessary and undesirable. Although AT&T currently has over 90 percent of the market, if the commission deregulates the long-distance market and AT&T attempts to raise rates to take advantage of its dominant position, the phone company will quickly lose its market share. On the other hand, if AT&T cuts rates below cost, it will suffer huge losses. Once its rates are raised to profitable levels, new competition will develop rapidly unless there exists a cost advantage over other firms.

Presidential appointees to the FCC have been less concerned with promoting free markets than would be desirable. Mark S. Fowler, Reagan's appointee as chairman, came to the FCC with an industry background in broadcasting. He had been a lobbyist for the Virginia Association of Broadcasters, and the industry welcomed his selection. He was quoted as saying shortly before he took office:

> If introducing 30 more radio stations into a particular market erodes the broadcasters' economic base so they can't afford to produce news and public shows anymore, is that in the public interest? In some places, it's hard for broadcasters to do well. It's been very tough to survive, you know, because there are already too many of them.[18]

The Carter FCC had unanimously endorsed shrinking the channel spacing for AM broadcasting from ten kilohertz to nine, which would have made possible a large number of new stations and would have made the U.S. spacing identical to that in Europe. The industry opposed this change strongly, charging that it would be very costly for both broadcasters and home receivers. On the basis that the costs outweighed the benefits, Fowler managed to engineer a reversal of this decision after several Carter appointees had left the commission.

The commission under Fowler has moved slowly in a number of areas. The proposal to roughly double the number of orbital slots for communications satellites by decreasing the spacing from four degrees to two may not pass. Again, the cost of making the change, it is argued, makes it undesirable. Of course, the cost estimates come mainly from the industry, which prefers the status quo to new competitors.

The FCC also has failed to act on the Multi-point Distribution System (MDS), which potentially could provide significant benefits for consumers while providing competition among cable systems. Under the current frequency allocation, no more than two MDS channels, which can broadcast pay video to properly equipped receivers, can operate in any community. For about three years, the commission has been considering a proposal to reallocate some unused spectra from instructional use to MDS. If it did so, in many markets there could be as many as eight to twelve channels. These channels could then offer pay TV in direct competition with cable.

A plan to increase the number of VHF stations by "dropping in" new stations has been under consideration since mid-1980. The Carter FCC had identified 100 areas where new VHF stations could be dropped in without causing interference.

The commission has been reluctant to use lotteries or other devices to allocate frequencies. Because Congress essentially instructed the FCC to use lotteries for allocation of new low-powered TV stations, the FCC will probably use some such arrangement. But in other allocative sectors, such as satellite slots, VHF drop-ins, and the new cellular mobile communications system, the commission prefers to decide on the "merits" of each competing application. For the cellular mobile, which is rapidly moving ahead, the FCC has given local telephone companies one of the two allocations of spectra and then will decide among other applicants who is to receive the competing allocation. In practice, this means that telephone companies will have systems operating several years before competitors are licensed.

More significantly, the FCC ruled that RCA's use of an auction to sell space on its communications satellite was discriminatory. This decision reflects the bias against using the marketplace, even under a Republican-dominated commission.

On the positive side, the Fowler FCC has moved to eliminate the remaining restrictions on subscription TV. The commission has granted eight construction permits for direct satellite-to-home broadcasting.

Virtually all content controls over radio broadcasting have been eliminated, including the obligation to survey the community and to provide public interest broadcasting. Nevertheless, the commission did inexplicably withdraw the license of one small FM station that was devoted almost entirely to classical music; the commission decided the station had failed to broadcast enough news, interviews, and educational material.

The commission appears unlikely to repeal the "access rule," which prohibits the major networks from broadcasting between 7:30 and 8:00 P.M. As a result of this rule, local stations must provide their own material, which is often of significantly lower quality. Apparently the networks have agreed not to seek a repeal of this rule, provided the FCC moves to abolish restrictions on network program origination, syndication rights, and financial interest in programs. Current regulations limit the number of programs networks can originate and own. In addition, the networks cannot secure a portion of the earnings from syndication rights for programs that they show. The networks are anxious to have these restrictions removed, while independent program producers are arguing strongly for their retention. A free-market approach would be to repeal these rules as well as the access rule, but the commission will probably bow to the dictates of pressure groups and maintain some or all of these restrictions. Moreover, any change by the FCC in these rules is almost certain to be challenged in the courts.

No academic observer of the real world is ever satisfied. The private sector is always flawed; the government always makes mistakes. The government should have done this or that. In the case of the Reagan administration, many hoped that it would do more and feared that it would do less. However, the abolition of the Presidential Task Force on Regulatory Relief is a dismal sign. Claiming that the task force had accomplished its job is equivalent to declaring victory in Vietnam prior to withdrawal of troops.

The administration has not been aggressive in making substantive changes in the law. Given the predilection of the courts to force strict standards, new legislation may be the only way to achieve long-term reform. Had the administration moved promptly during the first year, much might have been accomplished. On the other hand, given its priorities of tax and budget reforms and Congress's ability to deal with only a limited amount of legislation, it was probably impossible to do more. Nevertheless, legislation to abolish trucking regulation is long overdue. The political costs are so modest that only the absence of commitment to free-market principles explains the lack of concern.

The administration, however, should consider its appointments to the independent commissions more carefully. Loyalty to Ronald Reagan is not enough. A dedication to the twin goals of moving toward free markets and less regulation should be a prime criterion. The lower priority given regulatory reform probably accounts for the lack of detailed attention given to the appointment of competent (de)regulators.

On the positive side, the administration is attempting to secure a youth differential for the minimum wage and to make some significant changes in natural gas regulation, which may result in total deregulation. Much has been accomplished in administrative reform of the regulatory process that no new administration is likely to overturn.

A major problem is the power of the courts. As previously noted, in a number of cases the courts have cited past practices in voiding administrative changes in rules. In the passive restraint case, the court held that a rule that had not even gone into effect could not be changed. In the new-sources case, a simple modification that would have made the definition of "new source" consistent was thrown out. The court clearly ruled against change in the Davis-Bacon case because the regulations had been in effect for years, even though the law gave discretion to the secretary of labor. The effect of these decisions is to limit significantly what can be done to change past practices, notwithstanding the voters' desire for change.

This administration has been a genuine disappointment to those who considered regulatory reform an important goal. Let us hope that the Reagan administration and future ones will pay more attention to regulatory issues. More progress will come only when regulatory reform is moved from the back to the front burner.

Notes

1. Presidential Task Force on Regulatory Relief, *Reagan Administration Achievements in Regulatory Relief: A Progress Report* (Washington, D.C., August 1982); and *Inside the Administration*, March 25, 1983, p. 9.
2. 680 F. 2d 206, 221 (1982).
3. *Center for Science in the Public Interest, et al., v. Department of the Treasury, et al.*, U.S. District Court for the District of Columbia, civil action no. 82-610, February 9, 1982, p. 12.
4. Arthur Andersen & Co., *Cost of Government Regulation*, Study for the Business Roundtable, Executive Summary (March 1979), pp. 22, 24.
5. 685 F. 2d 718 (1982).
6. *American Textile Manufacturers Institute v. Donovan*, 452 U.S. 490.
7. 692 F. 2d 641 (1982).
8. *Building and Construction Trades Department, AFL-CIO, et al., v. Raymond J. Donovan, et al.*, 533 F. Supp. 352 (1982).
9. Ibid.

10. *Inside the Administration*, March 25, 1983, p. 9.
11. MC-127042, cited in *Traffic World*, September 14, 1981, p. 42.
12. Ibid., January 24, 1983, p. 44.
13. Ibid., February 22, 1982, pp. 30–32.
14. *American Trucking Associations, Inc., et al., v. Interstate Commerce Commission and the United States of America*, 673 F. 2d 82 (1982).
15. MC-143776, Sub. 34, C.D.B., Inc., Extension-Texas.
16. *Traffic World*, March 7, 1982, p. 58.
17. Ibid., February 28, 1983, p. 7.
18. *Wall Street Journal*, June 9, 1981.

14
The Future of Bank Regulation

Kenneth Scott

For the past decade, the primary issue in bank regulation has been whether a business that by law has been fragmented and narrowly limited in both its geographical and product markets would be allowed to become an integral part of a larger and more competitive financial services industry. Resistance has at times been fierce, both from rival industries and from those banking institutions benefiting from protected geographical markets. But although the battles are not all over, the outcome seems ordained. Driven by technological advances and high rates of inflation, competitive forces have thoroughly undermined the old regulatory structure, to the point where its maintenance intact is no longer viable. Removal of all barriers to nationwide banking and more convenient financial service packages may take years, but the trend now seems firmly established.

The central issue for bank regulation in the coming decade may well be quite different: how to adapt the system of federal deposit insurance to a broader and more competitive banking industry. At present, all banks or all savings and loans are charged the same premium for federal insurance of deposits, no matter how risky their operating policy or how poor their financial condition. In a largely deregulated environment, that allows a bank or a thrift to buy funds on a national market at close to the rate for risk-free U.S. government debt, given the federal insurance, and invest them at whatever level of risk it desires. If that course is successful, the institution (and its owners) reap the gains; if not, the Federal Deposit Insurance Corporation (FDIC) or Federal Savings and Loan Insurance Corporation (FSLIC) takes most of the loss in the event of insolvency. The risk-subsidy issue has always been inherent in a uniform premium system, but its potential adverse consequences are greatly enlarged in a less regulated world. In April 1983, at Congress's request, the FDIC and FSLIC released reports of their views of the problem.[1]

These issues are interrelated because of the possibility that a perceived need to protect the deposit insurance system might be used to thwart or even reverse the trend toward a less protected and more competitive banking industry. If that happened, it would be a most regrettable outcome for banking customers and consumers generally.

Regulation

The past few years have seen the financial services industry, and its regulatory constraints, in a period of remarkable flux. There have been significant shifts in the structure of the industry, as firms have made acquisitions across traditional institutional and geographical lines and broadened their own product offerings. There have also been major, although laggard, changes in the regulatory rules.

Recent Developments

To recapitulate some of the highlights of recent acquisition developments, in 1982 Citicorp successfully acquired Fidelity Savings and Loan of San Francisco, marking the first entry by a major bank holding company into the savings and loan business. BankAmerica Corporation received a favorable ruling from the Fed on its acquisition of Charles Schwab & Co., a discount brokerage firm. Dreyfus Corp., a mutual fund management company, obtained approval to acquire a state bank and establish a national bank, both in the nonbank format (requiring them to forgo either demand deposits or commercial lending). Earlier, American Express acquired Shearson Loeb Rhodes, a major stockbroker, while Prudential Insurance Co. took over Bache, and Sears Roebuck and Co. bought both Dean Witter Reynolds and the real estate brokerage firm of Coldwell Banker. Clearly, new financial service packages are being assembled at a rapid rate.

That same process is evidenced by the product innovations being introduced by leading firms. Merrill Lynch led the way in 1977 with its Cash Management Account, adding credit card, checking account, and interest payment features to the traditional brokerage account; other brokerage houses have followed. Banks such as Crocker, Security Pacific, and Chemical are entering the discount brokerage business through subsidiaries or contractual arrangements with independent firms. Money market funds are being offered not only by brokerage firms but more recently by Sears, by the MasterCard bank credit card network, and (subject to litigation) by the Boston Five Cents Savings Bank.

The movement of financial intermediaries like banks and savings and loans from local to regional or national firms is also accelerating. The acquisition of a California savings and loan by New York's Citicorp has already been mentioned. Subsequently, the Fed allowed California-based BankAmerica Corporation to acquire the troubled Seattle–First National Bank. Since 1981 the Federal Home Loan Bank Board (FHLBB) has approved more than a dozen interstate mergers of troubled savings and loans, beginning with the formation of First Nationwide Savings (California, New York, and Florida) in 1981. Major banks have started positioning themselves for interstate operations by acquiring small (under 5 percent) or nonvoting equity interests and future options (short of present control) in out-of-state banks. Increasing use is being made of nonbank banks to escape the Bank Holding Company Act restrictions on interstate expansion and product line combinations, a process that the Federal Reserve Board is now opposing and will no doubt end up in court. Dimension Financial Corporation was formed to apply for 31 such national bank charters in 25 states, after which the comptroller of the currency in April 1983 announced a moratorium on further nonbank applications.

The regulatory pattern has also been changing at what is for banking a dramatic pace. The deposit interest rate ceilings imposed by the Federal Reserve's Regulation Q were eroded throughout the 1970s by developments such as NOW (negotiable order of withdrawal) accounts, automatic funds transfer services, and share drafts, and by the rise of new intermediaries like money market funds. As a result, the Depository Institutions Deregulation and Monetary Control Act of 1980 officially decreed that deposit ceilings were to be terminated by 1986. The phaseout process was put in the hands of the Depository Institutions Deregulation Committee (DIDC), consisting of the relevant agency heads, which became a federal czar over savings competition by banks and savings and loans throughout the country. As part of the Garn-St Germain Depository Institutions Act of 1982, the banking business obtained an instruction to the DIDC to establish a new account without any rate ceiling or lengthy maturity, in order to do battle with the money funds; the DIDC accordingly authorized money market deposit accounts in December 1982, with immediate and dramatic impact on savings competition.

The FHLBB, faced with a thrift industry in near collapse, has aggressively tried to expand that industry's scope of operations, in both product and geographical terms. The FHLBB authorized entry into brokerage services (through a new Savings Association Investment Securities firm) and approved interstate supervisory mergers; it proposed (but withdrew) major liberalization of rules on service corporation activities and interstate branching.

Causes of Change

What have been the driving forces behind this industry and regulatory ferment? Among a number of interacting developments, three stand out as pre-eminent. First, there has been a rapid and continuing growth in computer and communications technology. Second, over the past decade and a half, the nation has experienced generally rising levels of inflation and correspondingly high interest rates. Third, interest rates have become more volatile as well as higher, exhibiting wide fluctuations over relatively short periods of time.

The computer and communications technology involved in storing, processing, and transmitting information has advanced at a truly impressive pace in the postwar period, generating dramatically declining costs for keeping records and handling transactions. For financial service markets, this progress has had two main consequences. First, to operate at the least cost scale requires transactions networks of considerable size; by one estimate, an efficient electronic funds transfer (EFT) network should have about 50,000 terminals, processing at least $2 billion a year in payments.[2] Both the technology and the economies of scale that characterize it imply a significant expansion of the geographical market for bank services. Second, product lines are being redefined and broadened. In part, this seems to be the result of efficiencies of joint production, making use of a more comprehensive household data base and adding credit lines to the asset holdings of a securities account and checking account. In even larger part, from the consumer's standpoint, it reflects delivery efficiencies; it is more convenient and economical for the consumer to have access to a number of services through a single card or office. As per capita income has risen over the postwar period, so has the value of the customer's time saved by making fewer trips or waiting less in line.

The high levels of inflation and high interest rates that were experienced in the 1970s and especially in the early 1980s increased not only the costs to the customer of idle balances and rate ceilings but also the profitability to the financial institution, at least initially, of obtaining those account balances. Hence competition for deposit customers heated up, and new products and new intermediaries, outside the regulatory web, were devised at an accelerated pace. Ultimately, innovation will so undermine the traditional regulation that it must be either abandoned or greatly extended.

Interest rates in the recent period have not only been high, they have also been extremely volatile. The average investment yield on 90-day banker's acceptances went from 4.9 percent in 1967 to 7.9 percent in 1969, back down to 4.6 percent in 1972, up to 10.3 percent in 1974, down to 5.3 percent in 1976, up to 11.5 percent in 1979, on to 16.2 percent in 1981, then down to 8.4 percent by January 1983; this record contrasts sharply with the preceding decades of stability in money market rates. Such rate fluctuations increase risks for both creditors and debtors and produce a variety of responses. One is to induce the development of market instruments for hedging and shifting the fluctuation risk. New forms of options and future contracts arise; variable-rate loan agreements come into use. Another response is to try to counter the increase in bankruptcy risk and collection costs by combining production of different financial services in a single firm, which may be better able to utilize information about customers and to offset fully credit extensions against their asset holdings.

Future Prospects

Against this background, how may we expect the regulatory environment to change over the coming decade? To begin with, although the trend is now toward less restriction, a revolutionary breakthrough in deregulation and radical restructuring of the financial services industry seem unlikely. Each trade group skillfully fights a rearguard, delaying action to protect its regulatory advantages vis-à-vis potential competitors. Significant changes are still to come, but they will be piecemeal and incremental and thus considerably slowed; this puts banks in the position of generally trying to catch up with the innovations introduced by nonbank competitors. For similar reasons, Congress may seriously consider consolidation of the various federal regulatory and supervisory agencies into a single banking or financial institutions commission, but it is unlikely anything sweeping will be achieved; the progress of deregulation would not be advanced if it were.

The development of EFT technology and networks will press ever harder on the geographical barriers created by regulation to the service of customers throughout natural market areas. This process has been under way for some time, as banks have pursued commercial customers across state lines through loan production offices and Edge Act corporations;[3] the one-bank holding company became a means of pursuing retail customers through finance company or mortgage banking subsidiaries. But court rulings that their automatic teller machines (ATMs) were branches confined banks, in offering deposit and withdrawal services to retail customers, to whatever areas were permitted by state branching laws. The costs to consumers of maintaining these restrictions, and the profitability to banks of evading them, are becoming ever more apparent and larger over time. The remaining barriers to intrastate and interstate banking, such as the McFadden Act[4] and the Douglas amendment[5] to the Bank Holding Company Act, are prime candidates for extinction.

As local market protection crumbles and banking moves nationwide, the scale economies of the new technology will force substantial consolidation on an industry that now contains almost 15,000 banks, 4,000 savings and loans, and over 20,000 credit unions, with an excessive number of offices as well. To some, this raises the specter, at the opposite pole, of the creation of a highly concentrated industry extracting monopoly profits and dominating the political system. This specter represents the main political argument for retention of geographical restrictions in banking, but in the end it probably will not prevail. There is very little empirical basis for the supposition that banking is a natural monopoly or an industry in which scale economies are so strong as to leave room for only a handful of efficient firms; available studies suggest instead a picture more like that of retail merchandising, with the market divided among a few national giants, some regional chains, and numerous specialized local stores, none of them in a position to obtain significant monopoly profits. Creating an artificial monopoly in banking by mergers or agreements among competitors would run into the same trouble under the Sherman and Clayton acts as it would in other industries, to say nothing of the added hurdle posed by the requirement for supervisory agency approval under the Bank Merger Act of 1960. The argument about concentrated political power has considerable emotional appeal, however, whatever its accuracy, and may delay or even limit the acceptance of nationwide banking in its most explicit and overt forms.

Progress in information and communications technology also presses against the activity barriers that limit the product packages that may be offered by individual financial institutions. Banks are confined, by state or federal law, to carrying on the "business of banking," whatever that may be; Comptroller of the Currency James J. Saxon tried in the 1960s to define it broadly for national banks and was reined in by the courts to an essentially historical perspective, which, of course, largely excludes what new technology may make possible or economical. The bank holding company became a way around such narrow attitudes, until it was confined by the 1970 amendments to activities "so closely related to banking . . . as to be a proper incident thereto"; this more liberal but opaque language has been interpreted, on the whole conservatively, by the Fed to permit entry into the band of related activities set forth in its Regulation Y. Not included are the securities-underwriting functions specifically prohibited to banks by the Glass-Steagall Act of 1933.

Without this complex set of activity constraints, where would the new technology logically carry banks? That is hard to discern precisely; it depends on joint production and joint consumption economies that are only now being explored and ascertained. It appears likely that banks, with their familiarity with account record-keeping and payments-processing systems, would be inclined to expand more into other routine processing services, such as securities transactions, than into areas that are personnel intensive, such as life insurance sales. But the outcome will also be determined by consumer convenience in having access to and consuming service packages. From the public standpoint, the outcome should be tested and determined in the marketplace, not by regulatory preconceptions, but that may not be fully allowed.

Geographical market protection is clearly crumbling rapidly already, through the use of nonbank devices, and seems most likely to be under continuing pressure. It has been under assault by academic economists and lawyers and finds few supporters beyond obviously self-interested ones like the Independent Bankers Association. It is probable not only that restrictions on market extension by existing firms will fall, but also that the supervisory approval requirements will become simpler and more perfunctory.

Rate ceilings in competitive industries are thoroughly discredited intellectually and become untenable politically whenever the gap between ceiling and market rates becomes large enough to make evident their perverse effects. Regulation Q is scheduled to disappear by 1986, but the DIDC's initially dilatory progress toward that goal has been speeded up by the money market account and differential elimination sections of the 1982 act. If interest rates come down and stay down, what is left of the existing rules might get something of a reprieve. But essentially there has already developed something close to a free market for deposit funds, as the opposition continues to unravel. A free market for deposit funds, bearing federal deposit insurance up to the $100,000 limit per account, may greatly accentuate the problem that has always inhered in the current uniform-premium structure of the FDIC and FSLIC.

Deposit Insurance

To begin, it is necessary to return to a concept of the basic purpose of the federal deposit insurance statute. Why should not bank deposits, like practically every other form of investment, be subject to the risk of uncertain returns and insolvency? That risk is inherent in the economic world, exists in varying degree in all investments, and is compensated for by a promised or expected return commensurate with the risk.

Various rationales for deposit insurance can be offered, and it makes a difference which we accept. The one that seems soundest is that deposit insurance is justified in order to protect the safety of the payments mechanism and money supply and avoid the transactions costs of inquiry into the condition of the drawee bank, followed by appropriate discounting. Given the volume of payments transactions reached in the U.S. economy, those costs could be quite high compared with the costs of the insurance system.

A payments rationale, however, justifies insurance coverage only for what have come to be called "transactions accounts." It does not extend to investment accounts, such as passbook savings or certificates of deposit or money market deposit accounts. Perhaps at one time it may have been thought that there was a social need to create a risk-free investment for small savers, but that need is now met in other, quite adequate ways; U.S. government debt constitutes a riskless investment, and intermediaries such as money funds deliver it efficiently to small savers. Higher returns can be obtained if there is a willingness to accept higher risk, and the choice should be left up to individual investors in the light of their own circumstances.

Thus the limit on deposit insurance should be one of function, not amount. Distinguishing an insured payments account from an uninsured investment account could be accomplished in various ways, such as a below-market rate ceiling or restrictions on withdrawal flexibility. The consequences would include a major reduction in insurance exposure for the FDIC and FSLIC and the ability, even with present methods, to handle much larger failures through insurance payouts.

The argument for limiting insurance to the payments mechanism and not treating investments in banks or savings and loans differently from investments in other firms will be put to one side in the balance of this essay. The coverage of savings accounts at risky banks or savings and loans is, or so it would be asserted, now politically irreversible. If the industry lobbies can make customers think they have a big stake in preventing interest withholding and make an overwhelming majority of Congress toe the line on that issue, what couldn't they do with an effort at repeal of insurance coverage on savings accounts? The problems to be discussed below have been aggravated by the attempt to convert risky investments into risk-free accounts, however, and that original error should at least not be extended by increasing the insurance coverage on investment deposits.

The incentives that the insurance scheme places on bank management are troublesome, as already noted. The insurance premium is uniform across all banks, ignoring risk differences and inviting management to game against the insurer. Banks can buy deposit funds, since they are federally insured, at something near the government debt or risk-free rate, invest them in a risky loan and investment portfolio, and keep practically all the risk premium for themselves even though the risk is largely borne by the FDIC. This problem has always existed, but its extent was limited under the old below-market Regulation Q ceilings to local service area funds that could be purchased with convenience. Now, with Regulation Q about defunct, most any bank can raise large funds through brokers on the strength of the insurance guarantee at near risk-free rates. The risk arbitrage game may be about to explode to unprecedented dimensions.

The problem is exacerbated if all liabilities of large banks are *de facto* insured because the FDIC and FSLIC have no practical method of coping with the failures of large institutions except through merger or "purchase-and-assumption" arrangements, which pay off all general creditors in full. Otherwise, large depositors and lenders to a bank have an incentive to assess the riskiness of the bank's asset portfolio and operating policies and charge accordingly; that both imposes a cost disincentive on risk acceptance and acts as an objective signal of the bank's condition. But although it works in the right direction, the cost disincentive that can be imposed by even uninsured creditors is inadequate in amount; for the banking industry as a whole, about 90 percent of assets are financed by deposits of which around 70 percent are insured and about 7 percent of assets are financed by equity capital (at book values). In short, no more than 30 percent of assets are financed by creditors who are sensitive to risk and rate of return, while 63 percent are financed by depositors whom the FDIC insures *de jure,* for a premium not based on risk. The market discipline that, in principle, large depositors and creditors could exert on bank operating policies is helpful, but the premium structure would still constitute a powerful subsidy to risk acceptance by insured banks.

That is not an argument for disregarding the market discipline imposed on banks by creditors who estimate and charge for risk; it is an argument for bolstering that influence. There are several ways that could be done (all of which would be simpler or more effective if the insurance system were confined to payments accounts).

Variable Premium

One approach would be to abandon the statutory fixed, uniform insurance premium for all banks and charge a premium based on institutional risk. In principle, that could end the risk subsidy that currently underlies about two-thirds of bank liabilities and confront bank management with a much more appropriate set of operating incentives. The problems, political enactment aside, lie in the implementation. How is the correct premium to be calculated? It is a function of asset portfolio risk (in both credit and interest rate terms), of debt/equity leverage, and of management of asset and liability maturity structures, among other factors. Calculation of the appropriate premium by a governmental agency is bound to be judgmental and disputable. That may not be sufficient reason for giving up the endeavor, and the FSLIC (though not the FDIC) seems willing to pursue it, but it is a good reason to search for a market solution if possible.

To create a market assessment of an institution's risk of default, there would have to be a requirement that at least part of the insurance coverage be purchased in a private market—from insurance companies or other financial institutions (which could include other banks). It seems probable that the capital base for such private insurance would not be sufficient (particularly if investment accounts in banks are to continue to be insured), and the FDIC or FSLIC would continue to be essential in a reinsurance capacity or to cover the prospect of a correlated wave of failures produced by errors in the conduct of national macroeconomic policy by the government. But if the insurance premium is set in the first instance in a competitive private insurance market, the high-risk institution would be deprived of running to Congress with a complaint of arbitrary discrimination by government bureaucrats.

There is another aspect of deposit insurance and the determination of the appropriate insurance premium that differs from customary insurance underwriting. Default and the triggering of insurance payment are not natural and largely indisputable events like fires or accidental deaths. A bank "fails" when a supervisor decides, under some statutory delegation of authority, to close it; a discretionary judgment is involved. If the discretion is exercised while the institution still has sufficient assets to cover liabilities, only the equity owners may be losers. The risk of the insurer, therefore, may be redefined as the risk that the supervisor will not end the game before the institution's net worth becomes negative; an assessment of the amount of that risk depends on an assessment of how large the negative net worth will become before the supervisor can act or chooses to act. That involves passing judgment on the state or federal supervisory agency rather than on the individual bank by itself and no doubt could be politically even more sensitive—an additional reason for trying to invoke the impersonal operation of a competitive market to set the premium. Alternatively, the private insurers might become involved by contract in the closure decision itself.

Claim Priority

Another approach would be to reduce the riskiness of insured deposits by giving them priority over all other creditors in claims against the assets of the failed institution. Carried to its ultimate, and assuming enough junior claims or sufficient alacrity in closing the bank, insured deposits would all in fact be risk-free debt; a low and uniform insurance premium would be appropriate, and incentives for bank management would not be distorted by a risk subsidy.

The consequence of an automatic priority for insured deposits would be an increase in risk for all other creditors, giving them more reason to monitor bank performances and to charge for the degree of risk assumed. The increased charge for risk would no doubt lead most of the banking industry to oppose such a move politically, but it would not be easy to claim that the opposition was on behalf of the interests of insured depositors.

To the extent there is a thick layer of debt claims, as well as equity, that are junior to the insured deposits, the insurer's risk is less sensitive to the accuracy of the supervisory determination to close the bank. There might also be less reason to have a special receivership process for that purpose, outside the more familiar and better developed procedures of the general bankruptcy laws.

Disclosure

Any reliance on private market discipline is enhanced by increased disclosure of the information about a bank's condition and performance that is already being reported or obtained through examination. The argument that bankers will be less forthcoming to examiners if the information is to be revealed to the world is really an assertion of the lack of efficacy of the supervisory process; the premise is that bankers will tend to withhold information that might cost them some penalty, but that consequence is much less to be feared from the examiners and supervisors than from the marketplace.

Added disclosure requirements on a current basis would also increase the reliability of the signals contained in a private-market-based insurance premium or the interest rate on junior debt. Those rates would change more rapidly than could a classification scheme based on examination reports obtained at intervals of a year or more and could be taken advantage of in a supervisory agency's early warning system.

The Final Period Problem

When the equity of a bank has been largely wiped out by losses, from whatever source, and the owners are nearing the point where closure is to be expected, their incentives shift to taking high risks even at unfavorable odds. If the gamble fails, the cost is borne almost entirely by the creditors or insurance corporation; if the gamble succeeds, the owners reap a large part of the gain. Longer-run considerations count for little, if the equity is gone and the game is about to terminate.

The problem is not unique to insured banks or savings and loans but is likely to be more acute in this setting because such a large proportion of their debt capital comes from creditors with no incentive to protect themselves through covenants in debt indentures or loan agreements. In the typical long-term loan covenant, failure to maintain liquidity and net worth ratios well in excess of insolvency will trigger default (and acceleration and possibly bankruptcy). If recent experience is the guide, on the other hand, receivership for a bank or savings and loan is not imminent until book net worth is nearly exhausted (and market net worth is substantially negative).

Regulation seems no answer to the final period problem. Blocking off bank management from all avenues that might lead to high risk would severely constrict the functions of banks as intermediaries. Nor would a variable premium do much for this problem. Rate setting lags behind events, and a huge premium would simply add to management's desperation; insurers would refuse coverage if they saw a final period in the offing, a process that would tend to work back and force earlier closure. Claim priority might be of real assistance, however, both by decreasing the insurer's exposure and by increasing other creditors' use of protective covenants in advance of insolvency.

Large Failures

There are difficulties for a limited insurance fund in covering the failures of large institutions. For smaller banks or thrifts, insurance payout and liquidation are feasible courses to pursue, and uninsured creditors bear a share of the loss. But for larger institutions, the insurance corporations have made capital contributions to permit mergers or purchase-and-assumption transactions, avoiding insurance payout and asset liquidation and thus also avoiding stress on their liquidity and staff capacity. In theory, the avoided expenses result in a net saving to the insurance fund, even though uninsured creditors are made whole and bear none of the loss; thus they are also deprived of a reason to exert market discipline on management.

Realistically, how can an insurance fund cope with the failure of a bank or savings and loan that is a large fraction of the size of the entire fund, or even larger? Several observations may be made. (1) The fund's liquidity is a separate issue from its adequacy to absorb losses. There is no reason for the fund to provide all conceivably necessary liquidity; that can be obtained by borrowing through an appropriate statutory line of credit at the Treasury or Federal Reserve System. (2) The problem would be reduced by the claim priority approach already mentioned. The insurance corporation would be legally obligated in a purchase-and-assumption operation to protect fully only the priority claimants, so losses could still fall on general creditors who were uninsured. At the same time, the insurance corporation's level of expected loss would be lower. (3) For the very large banks, other reorganization techniques could be devised. For example, a public offering could be employed. Suppose a $30 billion bank, with $20 billion in insured deposits, $8 billion in other general claims, and $2 billion in book net worth fails (that is, its assets are estimated to have a market value of only, say, $26 billion), under present law with no claim priority for insured deposits. Assume that the law gave the FDIC as receiver and insurer the authority to recapitalize the bank at what it judged to be an adequate level (perhaps in this instance by putting in $4 billion of new funds), replace management to the extent deemed advisable, and have an underwritten public offering of all the stock of the new bank. To the extent the offering produced less than $4 billion, the proceeds would all go to the FDIC, and the shortfall could be shared *pro rata* with all general creditors; to the extent that the public offering brought in more than $4 billion, the excess (over expenses) would go to junior claimants and old stockholders. The institution and its going-concern value would be preserved, without the problems of merger with another giant bank; asset liquidation would be conducted, in effect, by the successor management; all insured deposits and the bulk of other claims could be currently met; supervisory loss estimates would be subject to a second guess in the market, as a protection to junior claimants. The insurance fund would recoup the bulk of its outlays quite promptly and would be left with only its share of the ultimate loss, as presently estimated by the market. Even for a very large bank, that could be a manageable sum.

The foregoing comments are intended to explore some of the basic issues in recent and future bank regulation. The unifying theme has been how to make more effective use, wherever possible, of market forces rather than regulation and how to give bank management the proper set of incentives. The risk subsidy in the present insurance scheme creates problems that are likely, however, to get progressively more acute unless addressed now.

Notes

1. FDIC, *Deposit Insurance in a Changing Environment* (1983); FHLBB, *Agenda for Reform* (1983).
2. W. Baxter, P. Cootner, and K. Scott, *Retail Banking in the Electronic Age: The Law and Economics of Electronic Funds Transfer* (Montclair, N.J.: Allanheld, Osmun & Co., 1977), p. 102.
3. Edge Act (12 U.S.C. §§611–31) corporations are bank subsidiaries formed under a special law for the limited purpose of financing international trade.

4. The McFadden Act of 1927, 12 U.S.C. §36, prohibits interstate branching by national banks and limits their in-state branches to those permitted state banks by state law.
5. The Douglas amendment to the Bank Holding Company Act of 1956, 12 U.S.C. §1842(d), bars bank holding companies from acquiring an out-of-state bank unless its state law gives express permission.

15
Transportation: Policy, Goals, Accomplishments

Darrell M. Trent

Underlying Principles

The Reagan administration's transportation policy reflects the same economic principles that underpin the president's economic approach and is an integral part of the commitment to limited government. Over the years, the federal government's role in transportation decisions, programs, and funding had expanded and intruded on the private sector. Reagan is committed to reducing this role and placing greater reliance on the private sector marketplace to distribute services efficiently. The administration's transportation policy is based on the belief that state and local governments should play a greater role in the delivery of transportation services to their citizens. It accepts that overriding national concerns may require federal involvement in raising and distributing funds and managing programs, but the programs must be efficient and not unduly burdensome on governments or citizens.

Early on, the administration translated these general principles into three specific objectives, which it then used to guide the development of the budget and legislative initiatives of the Department of Transportation (DOT):

1. To finance federal transportation outlays, whenever possible, through charges levied directly on the user of a federal transportation service or facility;
2. To reduce unnecessary federal intrusion by proceeding with economic deregulation of all forms of transportation to the extent practical and feasible in order to encourage greater reliance on the for-profit motivations of private operators;
3. To reform existing regulations to eliminate unduly burdensome, cost-ineffective, and duplicative requirements in the operation of federal oversight and funding.

Based on these objectives the DOT has begun an extensive reform of its broad range of programs.

Transportation Programs

User Fees

The user-fee policy is based on the premise that rather than levying general taxes on the population as a whole, it is preferable to have the immediate beneficiaries of a transportation service or facility pay as much of their share of the cost as is practicable. The DOT has applied this approach to all modes of transport, but especially to freight shipping, where the users are typically commercial companies. It judged that exceptions to this policy should be made only when there are overriding national considerations. In essence, the administration's transportation user-charge policy is based on twin considerations:

1. *Equity.* Those who obtain valuable services from the government or use government-funded facilities should pay for them; nonusers should not be asked to share the cost with users.

2. *Efficiency.* For the market to operate as an efficient allocator of resources, the prices of goods and services must reflect full costs. When government relieves one mode of transportation of the costs of government-supplied services or facilities, the price of that mode's services can be artificially lowered, diverting traffic from more efficient modes and encouraging uneconomic investment in the subsidized mode.

There is also a powerful philosophical reason for emphasizing a user-charge approach to recovering the costs of federal transportation programs. Society and the economy will benefit if spending decisions are based on a clear understanding of program costs. When a public good or service is free, the user is more likely to ignore waste, redundancy, and inefficiency. Users who are paying the full cost for such goods or services will have strong incentives to insist on efficient and economical operations and will evaluate proposed public investments more critically.

Highways and Transit. The most visible and successful of the initiatives to apply the user-fee policy was passage of a five cent per gallon increase in the federal gasoline tax, to be used to reconstruct and rehabilitate highways and bridges.

The highway program has been self-supporting through gasoline taxes since its inception. Unfortunately, much of the system is now more than twenty years old and badly in need of capital improvement. The ten percent of the system yet to be constructed is located in or around urban areas and will be extraordinarily expensive. Increased revenues in the highway fund were essential in order to protect and expand the national investment in highways. Also, over 23,000 bridges need to be replaced or rehabilitated (40 percent are more than forty years old). The magnitude of this problem and the inability of the states to finance reconstruction have made federally raised funds essential for this pressing national requirement.

A matter of considerable controversy was the administration's decision to permit one of the five cents raised, or approximately $1 billion per year, to be used for transit purposes. Transit is, in fact, a local concern, and pressures should be applied to local governments and operating authorities to raise revenues through increased fares and taxation. Only the adoption of this policy will encourage operating entities to keep costs down and increase efficiency. However, over the past two decades, it has become clear that existing transit systems are unable to support themselves solely with local revenues. Recognizing this reality, the Reagan administration set as its priorities the elimination of the federal operating subsidy, which works against efficiency and cost cutting, and the continuation of a healthy, although budget-constrained, capital replacement program. Unfortunately, despite the administration's aggressive pursuit of these goals, Congress continues to insist on increasing federal funding levels for *both* capital and operating subsidies. Thus, one cent of the gasoline tax will be devoted to transit, and operating subsidies at the federal level will persist.

Airways and Airport Development. The U.S. aviation system is the best in the world in terms of safety and efficiency of operation. When the Reagan administration evaluated this system, it was apparent that several challenges needed to be addressed immediately. The first was that the air traffic control system must be modernized even to continue at its current level of operation. This had been apparent for some years; however, no consensus had developed on implementing or funding the modernization. Second, as air traffic levels grow, the system must be expanded. Third, this modernization and growth must be accomplished in a manner that will assure the existing high safety standards. These efforts toward upgrading, expansion, and safety assurances must be carried out in a constrained budget environment.

In order to accomplish these goals, the administration proposed early in 1981 to "defederalize" the largest airports, which are capable of financing their own development projects, and instead to provide them with greater flexibility to levy "user fees" by removing the federal prohibition against airport passenger "head taxes." The proposal would have raised user charges on aviation gas and jet fuel so as to recover the full costs to the federal government of providing air traffic control services. It would also have permitted the states to administer funds for deserving projects at smaller airports, which typically do not have the resources for their own development projects. The administration's judgment that the major airports could be self-supporting did not prevail even though the airports supported the proposition, but Congress raised user fees considerably and increased funding for the airway redevelopment program, which had been well defined and was proceeding on plan. Because airlines and consumer groups balked at the prospect of head taxes, Congress decreed that the DOT re-examine defederalization. While the resulting legislation did not accomplish all of the administration's goals, it was consistent with continued movement in the desired direction and was considered a legislative victory in the face of many conflicting interests.

Railroads. Amtrak was established in 1970 as a passenger railway network. The dream was that it would become a profitable corporation, needing federal assistance only for a transition period. Since then, it has become clear that Amtrak may never earn a profit because the capital and operating expenses of passenger railroads probably cannot be lowered sufficiently to permit full cost recovery at fare levels that attract passengers away from other modes of transportation.

However, the demand for passenger rail services in high-density corridors is substantial. The public benefits are debatable but deemed by a vast segment of the population to warrant continued federal support. The Reagan administration recognized the popular support of the program but moved to reduce Amtrak subsidies and require the company to cover at least half of its noncapital costs from fares and state and local contributions. The objective was to contain Amtrak's federally financed deficit at a level that compared more reasonably with the public benefits received. This pressure on Amtrak through legislative changes and diligent program management was intended to reduce the company's deficit through improved pricing policies, route changes, discontinuation of "worst-case" services, and improved labor and management productivity.

The administration's principal policy objective in the rail freight sector was to minimize federal involvement and to rely on private enterprise and the freest possible regulatory environment to ensure efficient rail service to the shipping public. Conrail was already benefiting from early reform of economic regulation that gave management greater flexibility in pricing Conrail services and managing its operations. The Northeast Rail Service Act of 1981 continued this thrust toward unfettered private sector operation by introducing additional labor protection reforms and permitting the transfer of commuter rail responsibilities to states and localities. In 1983, Conrail turned a profit on its freight operations, and the administration was seeking a buyer for the entire system in order to return it, intact, to the private sector.

Waterways. Since the beginning of the republic, the federal government has financed directly the bulk of the improvements and the maintenance of domestic navigable waterways. This includes the shallow-draft inland waterway system, the Great Lakes/St. Lawrence Seaway System, and the deep-draft channels of the Great Lakes and coastal ports. Over much of this period, the federal government aggressively pursued waterway development and expansion as a means of stimulating economic growth.

Today, circumstances have changed. Most of the readily exploitable waterways have been developed, and as in all transportation modes, the emphasis has shifted from developing new capacity to maintaining and making the best use of existing capacity. The federal financial role in water transport is also changing, as it is in all transportation modes. Federal budgetary concerns have become paramount, and equity demands that the general taxpayer not be required to assume a significant share of the costs of profit-making transportation enterprises. It has become clear that continuing subsidies to any freight-carrying mode causes competitive distortions and efficiency losses to the economy as a whole, as well as misallocation of the nation's investment resources.

In the case of the St. Lawrence Seaway System, which is operated jointly with Canadian transport authorities, users have long been paying almost all of the seaway's operational and improvement costs through user fees. The Seaway competes with the inland waterway system, which has been heavily subsidized at the federal level. As a result, during inflationary periods, the St. Lawrence Seaway has had difficulty attracting cargoes, and revenues have suffered.

The administration developed legislation for increased cost recovery of federal outlays from commercial users of the inland waters and deep-draft channels. The original proposal called for 100 percent recovery of costs of operation, maintenance, and capital improvements for the commercial inland navigation system and of channel dredging in deep-draft ports. User opposition to the legislation was immediate and unrelenting. The administration then worked to develop a more gradual proposal. The prospects for such legislation are good, and the administration intends to pursue it vigorously in order to place these waterways on an equal footing with competing modes while maintaining efficient access to inland and coastal ports.

Coast Guard User Fees. The Reagan administration sought congressional approval of a program of user fees that would shift some of the costs of Coast Guard services to the maritime community and away from the general taxpayer. The proposed legislation provided authority to collect 100 percent of the costs to those Coast Guard operations that serve specific, identifiable users. The proposal covered operations in marine search and rescue activities dealing with non-life-threatening situations, short-range aids to navigation such as buoys and lighthouses, marine radio-navigation systems, commercial vessel safety programs, and recreational boating safety services. The proposal did not affect many program elements because they were not directly of service to an identifiable, discrete group of users or were considered to be in the general public interest. These services included acquisition, construction, and improvement of facilities and equipment; enforcement of laws and treaties; marine science activities; polar ice-breaking operations; and military readiness efforts.

Despite continuous efforts by the administration, the proposed legislation enjoyed little success. The administration will pursue its proposals, with the revised objective of recovering approximately one-third of all Coast Guard operating costs and one-quarter of the total Coast Guard budget from the direct beneficiaries of the services.

Economic Deregulation

Consistent with its interest in returning economic decision making to the private sector, the Reagan administration has supported the continued deregulation of the nation's transportation system. It has become increasingly clear that the original justifications for economic regulatory authority at the federal level are no longer valid since the added costs and elaborate structures necessary to administer programs provide only marginal benefits. In the case of railroads, the fear was that powerful monopolies would abuse their privileges and charge discriminatory or unreasonable fees for services. The regulatory schemes ultimately protected railroads from competition from other emerging modes of transportation, which were, in turn, regulated.

During the Depression, the public concern over fly-by-night operations was reflected in safety-oriented regulatory authority. Today, mature transportation modes are ready and anxious to subject themselves to the rigors of the free marketplace and have been seeking increased freedom from federal intervention in their business decisions. Deregulation of the railroad, trucking, and airline industries is delivering the benefits foreseen by its proponents. It is providing greater flexibility in operations and marketing choices, fulfilling the objective of the Reagan administration.

Bus Deregulation. In late 1982, after considerable effort on the part of the administration, Congress passed a bill providing for the deregulation of interstate busing. This bill allows companies greater freedom to enter the market, to discontinue unprofitable operations, and to set prices. The removal of these regulatory restrictions will increase the efficiency of bus operations, enabling the industry to exploit its inherent energy efficiency to the maximum extent, to improve overall profitability, and to provide better service to the traveling public. Like other deregulatory schemes, this initiative contains reasonable assurances that small communities will be given all due consideration in the provision of services and continues to impose necessary safety assurance requirements on intercity bus operators.

Maritime Reform. With the transfer of the Maritime Administration from the Department of Commerce to the Department of Transportation in August 1981, the Transportation Department gained responsibility for nearly all federal activities in all the various modes of transportation for the first time. This transfer facilitates the development of unified policies and programs in maritime safety and security, regulation, and promotion. It encouraged the administration's primary objectives—the development of a healthy and efficient United States Merchant Marine and a more competitive international ocean shipping system.

Ocean shipping presently occurs within a complex international regulatory regime dominated by restrictive treaties and ocean-liner conferences (rate-making cartels). The United States has long favored a more free-market, open-seas approach, and this has been manifested in a regulatory approach to its foreign ocean trade that differs from other nations and that, unfortunately, has placed U.S. carriers at a competitive disadvantage and become a major source of irritation to the United States' trading partners.

To improve U.S. carriers' competitiveness and to foster comity in international shipping, the administration has supported changes in the existing U.S. maritime economic regulatory scheme. Primary among these changes has been an effort to provide greater certainty to the antitrust immunity extended to conference activities by the Federal Maritime Commission. In the past, insecurity regarding the scope of this immunity has hampered the ability of carriers to price their services without undue fear of federal intervention and penalties.

Without question, certain activities of an antitrust nature should be prohibited, and the penalty for engaging in such activities should be swift and certain. Therefore, the administration has sought to clarify the definition of both the penalties and the available authorities to correct acts specifically prohibited by the Shipping Act.

The Demise of the Civil Aeronautics Board. The Civil Aeronautics Board (CAB) is scheduled to terminate on January 1, 1985. This would be the first disbandment of any federal independent economic regulatory agency and will rid the domestic airline industry of the last vestiges of economic regulation. In fact, with the exception of assuring the provision of service to small communities, the CAB no longer engages in domestic regulation.

Unfortunately, vested interests again threaten to change the law so as to provide for the continuation of this agency despite industry support of its demise. Congress seems to be rethinking its decision to abolish the agency. Board members are reluctant to see their jobs disappear, even though the action has been scheduled for five years. CAB staff are fearful of losing their jobs or do not like the prospect of transferring to the Department of Transportation with the remaining international aviation and small-community service programs.

The administration proposed legislation in early 1981 to disband the CAB earlier than scheduled. By mid-1983, it appeared that such efforts were doomed, and the administration devoted itself to accomplishing the task within the original timeframe. If the public is to be assured that an outdated and inefficient style of regulation will not creep back into existence, this must remain a priority of the administration.

Support for Interstate Commerce Commission Decisions. As indicated, provisions that permit the economic deregulation of trucks, railroads, and buses have been provided for in law. The implementation of these deregulatory initiatives is largely the responsibility of the Interstate Commerce Commission (ICC). Although the ICC is an independent regulatory body, the DOT is able to intervene in its deliberations in order to present the administration's position. Without exception, the department has argued for the most deregulatory of positions and for the most part has prevailed with the majority of the commissioners. In order to move away from this cumbersome procedure, the administration will propose legislation to deregulate completely the modes of transportation under the jurisdiction of the ICC. The ultimate goal is, again, to abolish the agency in order to assure the public that federal intervention in the efficient working of the marketplace will cease.

International Aviation Pricing Flexibility. International aviation pricing has historically been regulated by bilateral agreements between the United States and foreign countries. For the most part, fares are jointly established by the carriers under the auspices of the International Air Transport Association (IATA) with a grant of antitrust immunity from the Civil Aeronautics Board. The Carter administration had proposed withdrawing this grant of immunity from the U.S. carriers who were flying the North Atlantic routes while continuing to grant the immunity to foreign operators.

The Reagan administration considered the proposal harmful to U.S. interests since foreign governments could retaliate by various means against U.S. carriers and would certainly force U.S. carriers to charge the fares the foreign national carriers wanted. Since U.S. carriers had typically pressed for low and innovative fares within the IATA forum, it was highly likely that the consumer would pay in the form of higher fares.

Instead, the United States began negotiations in 1981 to develop a multilateral aviation regime and tabled an extremely innovative proposal that would have eased the regulatory burden associated with obtaining approval of fares, in return for the grant of immunity for participation in IATA. The interim understanding, which will be refined in expectation of a permanent agreement, essentially stipulates zones of pricing flexibility within which fares will be accorded automatic approval by signatory governments. The hope is that this agreement, which was signed by fifteen European countries and the United States, will be the framework for further multilateral regulatory reform of international aviation practices.

Regulatory Reform

Consistent with the principle of returning powers and functions to state and local governments and placing greater reliance on private market forces, the DOT reviewed and reformed the entire body of federal transportation regulations in order to eliminate or modify requirements that were out-of-date, not cost-effective, unduly burdensome, or duplicative of other requirements. To the extent possible under statutory constraints, it eliminated existing regulations unless (1) they were essential to accomplishing national goals, and (2) the benefits outweighed the costs. These same rigorous tests were applied to all rules and regulations promulgated by the administration.

The department's regulatory review program consisted of three parts:

1. *Priority Review Program.* Under this program, the department identified the most costly and controversial rules for priority review immediately after President Reagan assumed office.

2. *Regulatory Flexibility Act Reviews.* In accordance with the Regulatory Flexibility Act, the DOT examined the regulations affected to determine whether they could be changed to minimize any significant economic impact on a substantial number of small entities.

3. *General Reviews.* In accordance with the department's regulatory policies and procedures, it constantly reviewed other regulations in response to such criteria as complaints, difficulty in enforcement, and changed circumstances.

The administration's reform efforts at the DOT have resulted in significant benefits. Cost reductions are associated primarily with the elimination of unnecessary burdens, but revisions in regulations have also resulted in savings. For example, changes in DOT rule on the provision of services to handicapped people should result in a one-time savings to transit operators of at least $2.2 billion. The record-keeping burden within the DOT has been streamlined, resulting in a reduction of the paperwork burden of over 41 percent between 1980 and 1983. Where practical, mandatory regulations have been converted to guidelines, thereby permitting regulated parties to determine for themselves specific methods for meeting the requirements. An example is the Federal Highway Administration's decision to rely on state procedures for conducting environmental reviews under the National Environmental Policy Act rather than imposing specific federal requirements.

While these benefits may seem routine, in the past they were never the basic foundation for the development or implementation of regulatory authority. This initiative fulfills one of President Reagan's primary campaign pledges—to remove the burden of federal authority from the backs of the American citizen.

The following are but a few of the outstanding examples of reform of transportation regulations undertaken by the Reagan team.

Documentation of Vessels. These regulations implement several very old vessel documentation laws that stipulate commercial vessel owners must obtain documentation on their vessels from the Coast Guard. The existing regulations were extremely burdensome because of heavy paperwork requirements. The final rule, which was published in June 1982, reduced the paperwork requirements by an estimated 250,000 hours per year and will save about $5 million annually.

Drivers' Logs. The "driver's log" is a record-keeping requirement used to enforce the Federal Highway Administration's hours-of-service safety rules for bus and truck drivers. The department studied this requirement in detail because of the tremendous burdens it imposed while accomplishing its desirable safety objectives. Based on the analysis, the department revised and simplified the rule, saving an estimated 11 million hours per year by reducing unnecessary record keeping.

Advanced Design Bus (ADB) Specification. The ADB specification was a binding, detailed set of construction requirements applicable to the ADB, one of the two principal bus models manufactured in the United States. Any ADB purchased by a transit authority with DOT financial assistance had to comply with this specification. The specification had received considerable criticism from transit authorities for a number of reasons, including increased costs, lack of flexibility in bus design, and constraint on innovation. In October 1982, the department revised the specification to provide for optional requirements except for the safety-related features.

Automatic Occupant Protection for Automobiles. Since the scheduled requirement for automatic restraints in automobiles (air bags or passive seatbelts) promised to entail capital and recurring costs to the automobile industry and to consumers of approximately $1 billion per year, a review of this regulation was conducted early in the administration. On the basis of this review, the regulation was rescinded in October 1981. Based on procedural considerations, the Supreme Court subsequently overturned this action, and the administration is making every effort to find ways of mitigating the adverse impact of a mandatory standard consistent with the court's guidance. In the meantime, the administration has moved aggressively on a campaign to convince the public of the advantages of seatbelts.

The transportation policies and objectives of the administration are an integral part of President Reagan's overall commitment to accomplish a historic and necessary change in the nation's long-term national economic policy. This is as it should be because the transportation system is an integral part of the economy, not an independent enterprise. The success of the system depends on the overall well-being of the national economy; conversely, the well-being of the economy depends on a healthy and efficient transportation network.

Fulfilling these principles requires a new and firmer attitude from managers, both in the private sector and in state and local government. As the federal government eliminates subsidies and regulations and institutes user fees, private sector managers must become more realistic in labor negotiations and efficient in using resources. Managers in state and local government will bear similar responsibilities, plus increased responsibility for political leadership in program areas formerly and inappropriately administered by the federal government.

The results of these changes, both in the economy as a whole and in the transportation sector in particular, will not be painless. A gradual transition to new policies and programs will be needed in some cases in order to prevent undesired disruption. But with continued national resolve, it will be possible a few years from now to look back on these changes as the groundwork for a much healthier and more efficient transportation system operating within a sound and growing economy.

16
The Agenda for Corporate Reform

Robert Hessen

Within the next two to four years, Congress will be urged to enact a new law to restructure America's 800 largest corporations. The goal of the proposed legislation will be to "reform corporate governance"; that is, to strip executives of their discretionary authority. According to the advocates of reform legislation, the chief executive officers of large corporations currently wield untrammeled power and are answerable to no one except themselves. Critics accuse them of shortchanging shareholders on dividends, injuring consumers by selling defectively designed products, exposing workers to health and safety hazards, polluting the environment, crushing smaller competitors, evading taxes, and destroying local communities by suddenly closing unprofitable factories.[1]

The advocates of the reform legislation want executives to be restrained by corporate boards of directors. Nominally, directors already choose and control the executives, monitor their activities, and prevent them from causing harm to others or violating any laws. But the boards' power is illusory, say the critics, because most boards are dominated by "insiders"—members of management, commercial and investment bankers, and attorneys from firms representing the corporation. These insiders give the executives a free hand in running the corporation. Therefore, the critics argue, executives must be subordinated to a reconstituted board, one that represents *all* groups in society affected by corporate actions. Two specific remedies are proposed. One would bar all insiders from the boardroom, even the chief executive officer. The second has a more modest objective: to require that a *majority* of every board be "outsiders"—individuals who are independent because they have no direct or indirect economic ties to the corporation.[2]

Advocates of Reform

The idea of restructuring corporate boards is not a new one. As far back as the 1930s, Professor William O. Douglas of Yale Law School wrote a sharp attack on insider domination of boards and urged appointment of outside directors. But nothing changed, even after he became chairman of the Securities and Exchange Commission and, later, an associate justice of the Supreme Court. Instead, a new trend began after 1945, when the same suggestion was made by Gerard Swope, chairman of General Electric.[3] Coming from a prestigious leader of big business, the idea did not seem heretical, and a number of companies began to add one or two outsiders to their board. But the newcomers—clergymen, college presidents, and executives from unaffiliated firms—were never intended to exercise any independent power or to constitute a majority of the board; instead, their function was ornamental, to lend the prestige and dignity of their positions to boardrooms.

In response to growing criticism that corporate boards fail to represent other "constituencies" (such as workers or consumers), the number of outside directors has risen substantially during the past two decades. Nearly all major corporations have added economists and educators or former ambassadors and Cabinet officers to their boards. But the selection of these outsiders has not silenced corporate critics, chiefly because they still regard the new directors as being mere tokens—ceremonial figures who lack any decision-making power. The goal of reform legislation is to assure not only that outsiders will form at least a majority of the board, but also that they will be truly independent.

The most vocal advocates of reform are Ralph Nader and Mark Green. Since 1971, they have repeatedly testified and written about ways to change the present system of selecting directors.[4] In 1976, they tried (unsuccessfully) to persuade the platform committee of the Democratic Party to endorse federal chartering of corporations. Four years later, they led a broad-based coalition working for enactment of a bill called the Corporate Democracy Act of 1980, but their efforts failed to create a ground swell in Congress. Nonetheless, they attracted (and retain) the support of other leading critics of big business, including Tom Hayden (Campaign for Economic Democracy), Richard J. Barnet (Institute for Policy Studies), Gar Alperovitz (National Center for Economic Alternatives), and Alice Tepper Marlin (Council on Economic Priorities). They won endorsements from economists (John Kenneth Galbraith, Robert Heilbroner, and Robert Lekachman), from union leaders (Douglas Fraser, Jerry Wurf, and William Winpisinger), and from leaders in the ecology movement (David Brower and Barry Commoner). But their most important support came from members of Congress, especially Senator Howard Metzenbaum, chairman of the Subcommittee on Shareholders' and Citizens' Rights of the Senate Judiciary Committee, as well as from Harold Williams, then the chairman of the Securities and Exchange Commission.

The advocates of reform are not a monolithic group. They agree on the necessity of ending "insider" control of the boards of large corporations, but they do not agree on how to achieve this goal. John Kenneth Galbraith offered the most daring solution. He suggested making the federal government the *only* shareholder in large corporations, thus enabling it to elect all the directors. To overcome the obvious obstacle—the fact that millions of Americans are corporate shareholders—he recommends that their shares be revoked and replaced with interest-bearing bonds.[5]

Other corporate critics favor a less radical method of altering the composition of boards. They supported various bills introduced in Congress in 1980, all of which were sidetracked by Ronald Reagan's election. Presumably when the bills are next introduced, they will bear a strong resemblance to these recent prototypes; a look at them provides a preview of the coming political agenda.

Blueprint for Reform

In Nader's draft bill, the Corporate Democracy Act of 1980, a person would qualify to serve as an independent director only if he or she "is not, and was not within the past five years, an officer or an employee of the firm or any of its parents, subsidiaries or affiliates." Nor could an independent director be a relative of a corporate officer, either by marriage, blood, or adoption; or own stock in the company; or be connected with any investment or commercial banking firm that did business with the company; or be involved in any capacity with any supplier or customer whose business derived more than 1 percent of its revenues from the company.[6]

In April 1980, two bills similar to Nader's were introduced in Congress. The first, sponsored in the House by the late Benjamin M. Rosenthal and eight other members, bore the same title, "The Corporate Democracy Act of 1980." The second, submitted by Senator Howard Metzenbaum, was entitled the "Protection of Shareholders' Rights Act of 1980."[7]

In all of these bills, the outside or independent directors are intended to be *adversaries* of the corporate officers. Their role would be to discover and expose—to the whole board and to government agencies—any improprieties or illegal activities within the corporation. Nader urges that at least nine directors be given the special responsibility to oversee and investigate such areas as consumer protection, environmental protection, community relations, compliance with the law, and antitrust violations. The Rosenthal and Metzenbaum bills would create the same watchdog or whistle-blower role for independent directors, but they reject the idea of assigning special areas of responsibility to individual directors. Instead, these bills would fulfill the same functions by creating two new committees within a board. Both the "supervisory committee" and the "public policy committee" would consist of a majority of independent directors, who would be on constant vigil to detect and publicize any wrongdoings of officers.

Another difference between these bills is their scope. The Nader and Rosenthal bills would apply only to corporations whose annual sales or total assets exceed $250 million, or whose employees number more than 5,000. The Metzenbaum bill would apply to corporations whose sales exceed $100 million or whose assets exceed $1 billion, but it makes no mention at all of the number of employees. The provision requiring a majority of the board to be independent would not apply to corporations with less than 25 shareholders (the Nader and Rosenthal versions) or less than 500 shareholders (the Metzenbaum bill)—whatever their sales or assets. Based on these criteria, at least 800 corporations would be subject to this legislation.

None of these bills (nor any supporting material) contains any explanation of how these figures were chosen. This omission serves a dual purpose. First, it permits the sponsors to be open to bargaining and compromise on the criteria; second, if Congress enacts any version of the proposed law, there will be no way to argue effectively against extending it to the next hundred or the next thousand smaller corporations.

Nor is there any explanation of why the proposed legislation applies only to industrial, retail, and transportation corporations, but excludes—regardless of size—banks, insurance companies, and public utilities. It is also unclear whether the legislation will apply only to publicly traded corporations, or also to privately held giants, such as Cargill (grain), Mocatta Metals, Koch Industries (oil), United Parcel Service, Mars (candy), Reader's Digest, Hallmark Cards, Gallo, the Hearst and Newhouse publishing empires, and the five largest accounting firms. And it is unclear why giant cooperatives (such as Sunkist and Ocean Spray) are excluded, even though their sales and assets far exceed the minimum criteria for corporations subject to this legislation.

Instead of justifying their choice of criteria and categories, the critics stress the urgency of the proposed reforms. Large corporations, they charge, are chronic lawbreakers. A "corporate crime wave" is sweeping the United States. They never respond to the objection that the "crimes" in question—pollution, for example—are already punishable under federal and state laws, and that increasing the penalties might be a more direct and effective deterrent than forcing large corporations to adopt a complex new system of independent directors. They also fail to acknowledge that the offenses commonly called "corporate crimes" are not unique to corporations, and they offer no evidence that these crimes are committed disproportionately by large corporations or with increasing frequency as companies grow larger. If such evidence did exist, one can be certain that corporate critics would publicize it. Instead, they propound a theory of "original sin" based on size, implying that *all* large companies share the guilt for violations of law by *some* companies. Their goal in equating size and crime is to persuade Congress that large corporations have forfeited any right to internal autonomy, and that chief executive officers should be forced to relinquish authority to a board controlled by outsiders.

Private Companies or Private Governments

The proposed legislation is designed to institutionalize the principle that corporations cease to be private if they grow beyond a certain size. The validity of this idea depends on the meaning of "private." Corporations are undeniably private, rather than public, if private means "apart from the state," that is, not a branch of government, like armies, courts, or prisons. But those who deny that large corporations are private have something quite different in mind. By private, they mean "limited in effect to an individual or a small group." By this usage, nearly everything is public, and private would refer only to a hermit, a recluse, or a sole proprietorship with a small clientele.

What conclusion follows from the critics' claim that corporations are public rather than private? Clearly, they say, groups affected by corporate actions should be granted seats on the board of directors. Nader and Green offer the most comprehensive list of those entitled to be represented: "shareholders, workers, consumers, local communities, taxpayers, small businesses, future generations."[8] It is hardly self-evident how representatives would be selected for all of the groups on this list—by what process, for example, would members of "future generations" indicate their needs and preferences?

But, more important, it is not self-evident that outside groups are *entitled* to representation in every organization whose activities affect them. If this were a valid general principle, it hardly would apply to corporations only. *Every* organization, regardless of size or purpose, would be required to grant representation to outside groups affected by its activities. The possibilities are intriguing: seats on the College of Cardinals for non-Catholics, seats on labor union boards for employers and competing nonunion workers. The fact that such changes stand no chance of being enacted is irrelevant. Logical consistency would require advocacy of such changes.

How, then, can critics justify imposing changes only on large corporations? The answer, they say, is that these companies are unique in one respect: unlike any other organizations, they are "private governments." The premise of the critics is that if corporations wield the power of government, then their structure should be democratic, and voting rights should be accorded to all who live under their jurisdiction.[9] But what does it mean to say that corporations are "private governments"? It means, according to Ralph Nader, that they "have a direct and decisive impact on the social, economic, and political life of the nation." Mark Green agrees: "Our largest firms exercise extraordinary influence over the citizens of our country and other countries."[10] But neither description is unique to large corporations; both equally well fit the major religious groups, the largest universities, the leading foundations, and the biggest labor unions. Yet critics are not proposing that outside groups be represented on the governing bodies of these organizations.

Nader and Green offer a second definition, also designed to fit large corporations only. These firms "are tantamount to private governments" if government is defined as "an entity that can tax, coerce or even take life."[11] To sustain the analogy between business and government, Nader and Green equate taxing and price-fixing; they classify pollution as coercion because it leads to involuntary consumption of industrial waste products; and, as an analogy to government's taking of life, they cite the marketing of dangerous or defective products whose use could cause death.

Clearly, the analogy is contrived. One cannot, for example, equate the *intentional* taking of a life by government—the death penalty lawfully imposed on a convicted murderer—and a negligent, *unintentional* death that might result from marketing a dangerous product, which then subjects the company to civil liability. Moreover, fixing prices, polluting, and selling hazardous products are acts that can be committed by smaller corporations (not merely the 800 largest) and also by noncorporate businesses (such as partnerships). Therefore, reserving the term "private government" for large corporations is unjustified. More important, although the companies that commit these offenses are breaking the law, they do not thereby become governments, unless that concept is to be robbed of all precision and analytical value.

Another approach used by critics to equate corporations and governments is to relabel every role. Shareholders are renamed "citizens"; the board of directors the "legislature"; and the officers the "executive branch." They also call the articles of incorporation a "constitution," the bylaws "private statutes," and merger agreements "treaties."[12] But no matter how ingeniously anyone may extend the analogy, it is defective. First, it cannot encompass all the major groups within the corporation. For example, if shareholders are called citizens or voters, what would one call other suppliers of capital? Are bondholders "resident aliens" because they cannot vote? And are the buyers of convertible debentures "citizens in training" until they acquire voting rights? Clearly, a belabored analogy cannot justify equating business and government.

Second, and more important, to justify calling corporations "private governments," the powers of a business and a government would have to be parallel. A government can compel obedience to its laws, can conscript capital or manpower, and can impose taxes, including charging people for services they may not want or actually consume. By contrast, no business firm, however large, can ever exert that kind of power. A business can only exercise *economic* power, which means it can offer something of value to potential customers, workers, and investors, who are free to reject the offer. No business can force anyone to purchase its stocks or bonds, or work for it, or buy its products, or pay for services they have never sought or used. The difference between political power and economic power is qualitatively different, not just a matter of degree. Therefore, any claim that businesses are "private governments," either because they are large or because they are corporations, is indefensible.[13]

Excluding Executives

If the Nader-Green blueprint for reform is enacted into law, executives will be excluded from corporate boardrooms. They will be barred by law from serving as directors or playing any role in selecting directors. Nader calls this process "the complete preclusion [exclusion] of operating management from corporate suffrage." The alternative favored by Harold Williams, former head of the Securities and Exchange Commission, is only slightly less draconian: he would allow the chief executive officer to be the only insider on the board, but not to serve as its chairman.[14]

Other proposed changes would foster internal factionalism and introduce costly, time-consuming changes in procedure. For example, Nader and Senator Metzenbaum propose to give the board of directors its own staff of lawyers, accountants, economists, labor experts, and consumer advisers.[15] This change would create two competing groups of specialists within each corporation. The draft legislation also facilitates direct nomination of board candidates by shareholders, and Nader's version requires all "fundamental transactions" to be authorized by the shareholders, obtained by conducting special plebiscites, with balloting by mail.

All of these changes, and numerous others, simply overlook one fact: a large business cannot be managed successfully as a debating society, with on-the-job training for independent directors, especially if their primary qualification for serving is the absence of firsthand knowledge of the company. The advocates of these schemes do not even pretend to demonstrate that the proposed changes would increase (or, at least, not reduce) the profitability of companies subject to the new restrictions, or provide a higher return to shareholders, or enable a company to meet more successfully the challenges of its domestic and foreign competitors. Instead, all they do is demand restrictions on companies that have grown beyond a certain size. But companies that were less competently managed, that failed to grow, that could not attract capital from investors, that could not arrange mergers because they had little to offer to a prospective merger partner—these companies are exempt from the proposed legislation. In effect, large companies are to be punished for their successes.

Directors and the Legal Model

The advocates of reform legislation say their goal is to force large corporations to obey the law. State law *requires* directors to be independent of executives, they claim, but the states fail to enforce this provision. Consequently, federal legislation is needed.

What model of authority is prescribed by state law? According to Nader, shareholders are supposed to elect the directors, who, in turn, "are expected to select and dismiss corporate officers." The authority of the officers should be "limited to those responsibilities which the directors delegate to them." He adds: "In reality, this legal image is virtually a myth. In nearly every large American corporation, there exists a management autocracy. One man—variously titled the President, or the Chairman of the Board, or the Chief Executive Officer—or a small coterie of men rule the corporation. Far from being chosen by the directors to run the corporation, this chief executive or executive clique chooses the board of directors and, with the acquiescence of the board, controls the corporation."[16]

It is true that every corporation must have a board of directors, but this does not imply that shareholders, directors, and officers must be three distinct groups of individuals. In fact, in the so-called one-man corporation, the same person is the owner, director, and president. Some states specify two or three directors to meet the statutory requirement for incorporation, but the usual procedure—which is completely legal—is for the owner to select others, such as a spouse, friend, or attorney, who can be trusted not to dilute the owner's authority to make decisions. Similarly, in the so-called family or closely held corporation, the owners first elect themselves to be its directors and then, acting as directors, they elect themselves the corporate officers. The structure of one-man and closely held corporations proves that state laws do *not* require directors and executives to be independent, let alone adversaries.

Where does the large, publicly traded corporation fit in? Initially, these firms are small—they do not suddenly spring into existence full-grown—and typically they are the creation of one person or a handful of founders. When such a corporation is first created, its officers, directors, and shareholders are the same individuals serving simultaneously in three roles. The founders elect themselves directors, and then, acting as directors, they name themselves the corporate officers. Subsequently, the founders' seats on the board are filled by executives groomed to succeed the founders in running the company. As the company continues to grow, seats on the board continue to be filled by this process of co-optation.[17]

Once the capital requirements of a company exceed the assets of its owners or their willingness to reinvest their profits, the company may "go public" by selling equity shares to outside investors. The occasion of going public is usually the first time that anyone other than the original owners is elected to the board. The newcomers are likely to be investment bankers, representatives of insurance companies, or wealthy private investors whose condition for making a large investment is a seat on the board so they can monitor the company's activities more easily.

At the time a company goes public, most of the stock is likely to be bought by small-scale investors, but it is unlikely that they will exercise their right to vote for directors. The opportunity to participate in corporate elections is not what interests them; they are seeking profits and dividends and are willing to leave the selection of directors to those who have more time and knowledge to devote to the business and a larger investment at stake. Small-scale investors rarely intend to get involved in choosing directors, and they know in advance that the board will be composed of insiders, but this does not dissuade them from buying shares. On the contrary, they freely defer to the insiders because the company's performance record is what attracted them to buying its shares. The new shareholders do not want to interfere with or dismantle the existing managerial system; instead, they willingly entrust their savings to it.[18]

Accountability to Shareholders

Insider control of the board does not mean that shareholders are exploited or victimized. Shareholders know that the best safeguard for their investments, if they grow dissatisfied with the performance of the company, is their ability to sell their shares. They know there is a simple gauge to test the progress of their investment. The daily price of the stock and the earnings reports and dividend rate announced each quarter enable them to assess their situation easily.

Professor F. A. Hayek once identified the existence of money prices as a major virtue of the marketplace. He noted:

> ... how little the individual participants need know in order to be able to take the right action. In abbreviated form, by a kind of symbol, only the most essential information is passed on and

passed on only to those concerned. It is more than a metaphor to describe the price system as a kind of machinery for registering change, or a system of telecommunications which enables individual producers to watch merely the movements of a few pointers, as an engineer might watch the hands of a few dials, in order to adjust their activities to changes.[19]

Through the mechanism of the stock market, each investor obtains a barometer for business in general and for any particular company. Instead of devoting hundreds of hours to studying the credentials of competing candidates for the board of directors, or to comparing the prospectuses, balance sheets, and annual reports of dozens of different companies, the small-scale investor has to monitor only a few basic indicators.

Those who say that shareholders are being denied control over corporate affairs or that shareholders are being shortchanged on dividends overlook the fact that millions of people freely choose to invest their savings in the shares of publicly traded corporations. If they were being denied dividends or otherwise defrauded, it would be impossible for corporations to raise additional capital through new stock offerings. And if existing shareholders sold their shares, they would take a loss so they could liquidate a diminished resource. Clearly, the best way to judge the expectations and preferences of shareholders is through their actions, not by the reforms proposed by corporate critics who claim to be speaking in their name.[20]

Future Options

A point often overlooked is that large companies are not required to be operated as corporations. The legal form in which a firm is organized is not dictated by its size. The choice of form is optional, not mandatory, and any form can be modified to suit the needs of any company, regardless of its size.[21]

A giant enterprise, for example, can be operated as a partnership, as Baldwin Locomotive and Gimbel Brothers once were. But in a partnership, there is no board to supervise or monitor the executives. The partners have a choice: either they share power among themselves, each with an equal voice and vote; or, if they prefer, one of them, usually the pre-eminent founding partner, can be designated as the managing partner, with exclusive authority to run the firm and select a successor. Similarly, large companies can be organized as limited partnerships.

The executives are the general partners, and the investors are limited partners who, by law, cannot vote or exercise a voice in management. Consequently, the general partners possess undivided authority within the enterprise, with no independent board to monitor them.

A third option is to organize a large firm as a business trust. Like limited partners, investors who buy trust certificates acquire freely transferable shares with limited liability and no voting rights or voice in management. The investors—the trust beneficiaries—are entitled to the profits, but legal title and exclusive power of control over the trust's assets are vested in the trustees.

In each of the three major unincorporated forms of business, the executives are not subject to supervision by an independent board of directors. Consequently, large corporations that chose to resist turning over control to independent directors could be reorganized and operated in one of the unincorporated forms.

However, it is unlikely that they will choose to exercise this option. In fact, the idea that a majority of directors must be independent has aroused very little opposition from the major corporations that would be affected. The Business Roundtable—an organization composed of the chief executives of the 200 largest corporations—actually endorsed the idea. They merely oppose any law *imposing* this requirement on them. A law is not needed, these business leaders say, because companies already are engaged in voluntary self-reform.[22] In effect, they are saying to Congress, and to their critics: "Don't rush us. We will make the changes you demand, though perhaps more slowly than you would like."

This conciliatory response was rejected by Senator Metzenbaum, who declared: "We can't rely on voluntary self-reform." He added: "Reform is in the air and it will come. History is full of examples where those in power failed to recognize and embrace some moderate changes, only to be confronted later with more drastic measures, which they could not resist."[23] At the moment, corporate leaders seem committed to slowing down their loss of autonomy, rather than resisting it. If the only choice is voluntary self-reform or legally mandated changes, then the debate on restructuring large corporations is really a monologue.

Perhaps corporate leaders feel they have no choice except acquiescence—because they think they cannot enlist any allies in a struggle to preserve their autonomy. If so, then one recent event might cause them to re-evaluate their strategy. In the face of the most overwhelming odds, the banks in 1983 organized a campaign to force Congress to repeal a law it already had enacted. The banks succeeded, by enlisting the energies of millions of their depositors, in forcing repeal of the withholding tax on dividends.[24] The lessons of that episode have not been fully appreciated by either side. Perhaps a similar campaign by large corporations, directed to their shareholders, might preserve their autonomy and their profits. The possibility of provoking such a campaign might make corporate critics more cautious in issuing their demands, because they do not want to appear to be launching a frontal attack on corporate profits and shareholder dividends. And the victory of the banks might embolden corporate leaders to resist those demands. If so, the outcome of the struggle to restructure large corporations is anything but inevitable.

Notes

1. See, for example, Morton Mintz and Jerry S. Cohen, *America, Inc.* (New York: Dial Press, 1971); David W. Ewing, "The Corporation as Public Enemy No. 1," *Saturday Review*, January 21, 1978, p. 12; Arthur S. Miller and Lewis D. Solomon, "Constitutional Chains for the Corporate Beast," *Business and Society Review*, Fall 1978, pp. 15–19; Fred Branfman, *Public Control of Corporate Managers: Focal Point for the 1980s* (Los Angeles: California Public Policy Center, 1979); Tom Hayden, *The American Future: New Visions Beyond Old Frontiers* (Boston: South End Press, 1980), pp. 153–221; Mark Green and Robert Massie, Jr., eds., *The Big Business Reader: Essays on Corporate America* (New York: Pilgrim Press, 1980); and Mark Green, *Winning Back America* (New York: Bantam Books, 1982), pp. 43–55.

2. To trace the "corporate governance" debate in the popular press, see Jethro K. Lieberman, "New Fire in the Drive to Reform Corporation Law," *Business Week*, November 21, 1977, p. 98; Thomas E. Mullaney, "Governance of U.S. Companies: Proposals on Reform Likely Soon," *New York Times*, February 24, 1978, p. D3; Shirley Scheibla, "Bossing the Boss? Management's Right to Manage Has Come Under Mounting Attack," *Barron's*, July 17, 1978, p. 4ff; Editorial, "The Adversarial Board," *Wall Street Journal*, October 20, 1978, p. 18; Tom Goldstein, "Who Governs Corporations?" *New York Times*, December 22, 1978, p. D4; Judith Miller, "At Odds over Corporate Governance," *New York Times*, Business and Financial Section, December 24, 1978, p. 1; James W. Singer, "Trying to Make Corporations Answer to the Public," *National Journal*, July 14, 1979, pp. 1159–1161; Thomas C. Hayes, "Board 'Outsiders' Win Favor," *New York Times*, March 30, 1980, p. D1; and Deborah A. DeMott, ed., *Corporations at the Crossroads: Governance and Reform* (New York: McGraw-Hill, 1980).

3. Morrell Heald, *The Social Responsibilities of Business: Company and Community, 1900-1960* (Cleveland, Ohio: Case Western Reserve University Press, 1970), pp. 192, 310; William O. Douglas, "Directors Who Do Not Direct," *Harvard Law Review* 47 (1934): 1305, reprinted in his *Democracy and Finance* (New Haven: Yale University Press, 1940); and Gerard Swope, "Some Aspects of Corporate Management," *Harvard Business Review* 23 (1945): 314.
4. See, for example, Nader, "Chartering Corporations," *New Republic*, March 11, 1972, p. 9; Nader and Green, eds., *Corporate Power in America* (New York: Grossman Publishers, 1973); Nader and Green, "The Case for Federal Charters," *Nation*, February 5, 1973, p. 173; Nader and Green, "Is the 'Worldcorp' Above the Law? Time for the U.N. to Move," *War/Peace Report*, September/October 1973, p. 7; testimony of Ralph Nader, U.S. Congress, Senate, Committee on Commerce, *Corporate Rights and Responsibilities: Hearings*, 94th Cong., 2d sess., June 17, 1976, pp. 197-218; Nader, Green, and Joel Seligman, *Taming the Giant Corporation* (New York: W. W. Norton & Co., 1976); Nader, Green, and Seligman, "The Myth of Corporate Democracy," *Washington Monthly*, July/August 1976, p. 54; interview with Mark Green, "Federal Chartering of Corporations: The Idea You Love to Hate," *MBA*, July/August 1976, p. 24; Nader and Green, "Corporate Democracy," *New York Times*, December 28, 1979, p. A27; Mark Green, *The Case for a Corporate Democracy Act of 1980* (Washington, D.C.: Public Citizens Congress Watch, 1980); and Green, *Winning Back America*.
5. Galbraith, "What Comes After General Motors," *New Republic*, November 2, 1974, p. 16.
6. Green, *Corporate Democracy Act of 1980*, p. 9.
7. H.R. 7010, 96th Cong., 2d sess., April 2, 1980; and S. 2567, as reprinted in *Congressional Record: Senate*, April 16, 1980, pp. S3751-757.
8. Nader and Green, "Corporate Democracy."
9. David Vogel, *Lobbying the Corporation: Citizen Challenges to Business Authority* (New York: Basic Books, 1978), pp. 6, 8.
10. Nader et al., *Taming*, p. 17; and Green, *Winning Back America*, p. 44.
11. Nader and Green, "Corporate Democracy"; and Green, *Winning Back America*, p. 44.
12. Nader et al., "Myth of Corporate Democracy," p. 54.
13. Professor Arthur S. Miller claims that corporations and governments are indistinguishable. "Calling corporations private governments," he writes, "may be misleading in one respect, for they are not really private. Their function is public." (*The Modern Corporate State: Private Governments and the American Constitution* [Westport, Conn.: Greenwood Press, 1975], p. 132.) Similarly, Professor Charles Lindblom claims that all business executives are really government functionaries—because they are performing activities that would have to be carried out by government if money and

markets were outlawed. (*Politics and Markets* [New York: Basic Books, 1977], p. 172.) For a rebuttal, see Robert Hessen, ed., *Does Big Business Rule America?* (Washington, D.C.: Ethics and Public Policy Center, 1981), pp. 1–5 and *passim*.

14. Nader, Green, and Seligman, *Constitutionalizing the Corporation: The Case for the Federal Chartering of Giant Corporations* (Washington, D.C.: Corporate Accountability Research Group, 1976), p. 204; and Harold Williams, "Corporate Accountability," in Donald E. Schwartz, ed., *Commentaries on Corporate Structure and Governance* (Philadelphia: American Law Institute, 1979), p. 520.

15. Nader et al., *Taming*, p. 121; and Metzenbaum, "Reform Is in the Air," in Schwartz, *Commentaries*, p. 511.

16. Nader et al., *Taming*, p. 75–76.

17. For an elaboration of this argument, see Robert Hessen, *In Defense of the Corporation* (Stanford: Hoover Institution Press, 1979), pp. 49–59.

18. Ibid., pp. 42–46, 79–83.

19. F. A. Hayek, *Individualism and the Economic Order* (Chicago: University of Chicago Press, 1948), p. 86–87.

20. Interestingly, many critics who say their goal is to protect shareholders also advocate changes that would sharply reduce corporate profits. Ralph Nader, for example, wants to dismantle large corporations because they are "monopolistic" and "anti-competitive." He recommends that an antitrust dissolution suit automatically be initiated whenever "four or fewer corporations account for 50 percent or more of the sales in any line of commerce in any section of the country in any consecutive two-year period within the most recent five years." Similarly Mark Green criticizes the requirement under the Sherman Act that the government must prove that a company "intended" to obtain a monopoly. He writes: "Instead of this subjective and difficult search for motive, a new prospective standard would be a 'no fault' oligopoly law—whenever a firm, or up to four firms, controls 50 percent of a market, it would have to be decentralized into smaller units unless they could argue by a preponderance of the evidence that economics [*sic*] of scale required their size." Neither Nader nor Green mentions how stockholders would be indemnified for the decline in profits, stock prices, and dividends that would result from enactment of the antitrust policies they advocate. (Nader et al., *Constitutionalizing*, p. 385; Nader et al., *Taming*, p. 233; and Green, *Winning Back America*, p. 49.)

21. Robert Hessen, "The Modern Corporation and Private Property: A Reappraisal," *Journal of Law and Economics* 26 (June 1983): 273–89.

22. Statement of the Business Roundtable, *The Role and Composition of the Board of Directors of the Large Publicly Owned Corporation*, reprinted in *Business Lawyer* 33 (1978): 2083; and Kenneth R. Andrews, "The Roundtable Statement on Boards of Directors," *Harvard Business Review*, September–October 1978, pp. 24–38. For a similar stance by the National

Association of Manufacturers, see Alexander B. Trowbridge, "Self-Reform: The Way of the Modern Corporation," *Enterprise*, April 1980, pp. 4–7.
23. Metzenbaum, "Reform Is in the Air," p. 512.
24. See "Behind the Banks' Victory," *Newsweek*, May 2, 1983, p. 28; Timothy B. Clark, "Banks' Opposition to Withholding May Leave a Bitter Legislative Aftertaste," *National Journal*, April 2, 1983, pp. 700–3; Steven Pressman, "Bankers' Massive Lobbying Effort Pays Off," *Congressional Quarterly*, April 23, 1983, p. 771.

17

Corporate Income Tax: Restoration, Integration, or Elimination?

Charles E. McLure, Jr.

In off-the-cuff remarks in early 1983, President Reagan described the corporate income tax as "hard to justify." This view, which Reagan did not further explain, could be interpreted in at least two ways: that the corporate tax should be *eliminated* or that it should be *integrated* with the personal income tax. Although few tax specialists hold the corporate tax in high regard, it is unlikely that many tax economists think that it should simply be eliminated. On the other hand, many did favor integration of the two taxes during the late 1970s when integration was being actively debated in public policy circles.

A different view of the corporate tax, most commonly heard from the liberal end of the political spectrum, holds that the corporate tax should be *restored* to its pre-1981 vitality through repeal of more of the tax-reducing provisions contained in that year's Economic Recovery Tax Act (ERTA).

The traditional case for integration of the corporate and personal

---

The author wishes to acknowledge valuable comments on an earlier draft of this paper by Larry Dildine, George Mundstock, and Emil Sunley. He is solely responsible for the views expressed.

income taxes rests largely on neutrality arguments; an integrated system is said to distort economic choices less than one that includes a separate unintegrated tax on corporate income as well as a tax on dividends. (These neutrality arguments are explained in the next section.) Some advocates of integration suggest that it would increase capital formation. Proponents of a separate corporate tax, however, see it as necessary to protect the individual income tax; in the absence of a corporate tax, a large fraction of economic activity would be channeled through sham corporations to avoid tax. Members of this group may or may not accept the neutrality arguments for integration, but they argue that integration is a very expensive—and potentially counterproductive—way to stimulate capital formation. And they definitely do not like the reduction in progressivity many forms of integration would involve. Of course, on distributional grounds they would find elimination of the corporate tax even more objectionable than integration.

Much has changed since late 1977, when integration was most recently considered to be a viable policy option. Most obviously, ERTA, even as modified by the Tax Equity and Fiscal Responsibility Act of 1982 (TEFRA), substantially reduced the taxation of income resulting from new investment in depreciable assets. Income produced by some types of new assets is actually taxed at rates that are now very near—or even below—zero. But the effective rates of tax differ widely among types of assets—especially between machinery and equipment on the one hand and structures on the other—and therefore across industries. In such a world, the case for integrating the income taxes is weaker than, or at least very different from, the case before ERTA. During the brief period when ERTA was in effect, outright elimination of the tax began to look attractive. Advocates of a separate corporate income tax argue that even more of the ERTA provisions that reduced the corporate tax base should be rescinded.

Economists' perceptions of the likely effects of even a pre-ERTA-style income tax have also changed significantly over the past half-dozen years. Because of this, the traditional analysis underlying the case for integration is said to be largely irrelevant to corporate investment, much of which is financed from retained earnings. This new view of the economic effects of the corporate tax is also relevant for analysis of the post-ERTA-TEFRA tax.

This essay examines the proper course of policy in this field from a microeconomic perspective—that is, leaving aside the effects higher or lower corporate taxes would have on prospects for balancing the federal budget and the likelihood of maintaining more nearly stable prices and high employment. In a nutshell, should the corporate tax be restored, integrated, or eliminated? It begins with a brief description of the traditional case for and against integration. Modifications to this line of reasoning based on recent analytical insights and on changes in the taxation of corporate income resulting from ERTA-TEFRA are then discussed. The upshot of the analysis is that none of the options under consideration—restoration, integration, or elimination—is fully satisfactory by itself. Taxation should be made more neutral, at whatever average effective rate is deemed appropriate, and it should be insulated from inflation. If that were done, integration would be attractive, but not as attractive as in the days before ERTA, when effective rates were higher. And the problems of how to treat tax preferences in an integrated system would become vital, given their magnitude under present law or under a more neutral law that, on average, retained the present favorable treatment of investment.

The Traditional Arguments

The case for integration has usually been presented by comparing the taxation of a given before-tax return from investment in corporate equities and in a fully taxed noncorporate investment.[1] Although the preferential tax treatment of capital gains plays a potentially important part in the story, attention usually focuses on the double taxation of corporate equity income that is distributed to shareholders. The first two columns of Table 17.1 present an example that illustrates the problems (note that the second line should be ignored at this point).

In the traditional view, double taxation of dividends has a number of adverse allocative effects, all based on distortions of the decisions of investors, businessmen, and consumers. Such taxation makes debt financing more attractive to the corporation than equity financing; the presumed result is increased vulnerability to bankruptcy, especially in times of recession. Corporations favor retained earnings over the issuance of new shares as the source of equity finance. This gives established firms an advantage over new ones and unfairly favors shareholders who do not need dividends to meet current expenses. Finally, the overtaxation of the return to equity capital in the corporate sector inhibits capital formation, induces corporations to rely too little on capital-intensive means of production, and accentuates distortions of consumers' preferences in favor of output of the noncorporate sector.

Appraisal of the equity effects of a separate tax on corporate income is tricky because it depends on how the problem is approached.

Table 17.1

Comparison of Taxation of Returns to Alternative Assets

	Funds Originally in Investor's Hands, Invested in		Funds Originally in Corporate Solution	
	Noncorporate assets	Newly issued corporate shares	Distributed and invested in noncorporate assets	Retained in corporate solution
Gross funds available	1,000	1,000	1,000	1,000
Personal tax on dividends (50%)	*	*	500	*
Net funds invested	1,000	1,000	500	1,000
Gross earnings (at 10%)	100	100	50	100
Corporate income tax (50%)	*	50	*	50
Net corporate income	*	50	*	50
Dividends	*	50	*	50
Personal tax base:	100	50	50	50
Personal income tax (50%)	50	25	25	25
Net personal income	50	25	25	25

Double taxation of dividends increases tax burdens, in relative terms, more for taxpayers subject to low marginal personal tax rates than for those who pay high rates. But ownership of corporate equity is concentrated in high-income groups; as a result, the existence of a separate corporate income tax does add significantly to the progressivity of the tax system. Moreover, the tax prevents the possibility of accumulating income free of current taxation in the form of retained corporate earnings.

All those distortions (except the disincentive to save, which would be reduced) and inequities would be eliminated by completely integrating the income taxes, that is, by treating corporations for tax purposes like partnerships with a multitude of members. Under complete integration, all corporate income would be included in the taxable income of shareholders, whether distributed or retained. But complete integration would entail severe administrative problems. These involve primarily the attribution of retained earnings to shareholders. Thus policy discussion generally focuses on eliminating part or all of the double taxation of dividends, leaving the corporate tax intact as a final levy on retained income. Foreign experience, especially in Europe, demonstrates that dividend relief is administratively feasible.

Dividend relief can be provided in two ways: the corporation can be allowed a deduction for dividends paid, or shareholders can be allowed a credit for corporate taxes paid on income resulting in dividends. European countries that provide dividend relief commonly employ the latter approach; West Germany combines the two. (Actually, West Germany applies different rates to retained income and distributed income; this is equivalent to allowing a deduction for part of dividends.) Dividend relief, while not totally neutral, has many of the allocative advantages of integration. But it would encourage firms to distribute earnings since such relief is available only when dividends are paid; thus its effects on capital formation are unclear. It would, of course, substantially reduce the progressivity of the income tax system since individual recipients of dividends are predominantly in high-income classes.

Tax preferences—deductions, credits, and special rates that reduce taxation relative to what it would be if a standard rate of tax were applied to economic income—pose two interrelated questions that must be addressed in designing a system of dividend relief. First, should preferences be passed to shareholders when preference income is distributed, or should they be available only on income retained by the corporation? Second, in what order should it be assumed that preference income and fully taxed income are distributed? Common European practice is to allow preferences only on retained income, but to treat preference income as the last to be distributed. Preferences are nullified by imposing a compensating tax on distributions of preference income equal to the credit that will be taken by the shareholder who receives the dividend. Because of the order in which dividends are assumed to be paid—from taxed income before preference income—most preferences are preserved, as long as they are modest in total.

Simply eliminating the corporate income tax would not have attractive allocative or equity effects. To the extent that income on corporate equity was distributed, the effects would be exactly those of integration—taxation at the marginal rates of shareholders. But elimination of the corporate tax would produce powerful incentives to distribute as little income as possible, to leave it in corporate solution to grow tax-free and eventually be taken out as preferentially taxed capital gains. Besides the obvious equity implications of such an approach, there would be a massive distortion in favor of equity financing, capital-intensive production in the corporate sector, and consumption of goods and services produced in the corporate sector.

Another View of Integration[2]

The traditional view of the undesirable effects of an unintegrated corporate tax implicitly assumes that a would-be investor compares the tax treatment of the return to various types of investment, including newly issued corporate shares. In fact, most equity investment in U.S. corporations comes from retained earnings, not from new issues. For this flow of investable funds, it makes no sense to focus on the double taxation of dividends, as does the traditional analysis of the case for integration. This is true because retained earnings currently in corporate solution are, in a sense, trapped there; they will be subject to personal tax when distributed, whether distribution occurs now or later.[3] Another way of saying this is that retained earnings are a reinvestment of pretax rather than aftertax dollars by the individual investor. This stands in marked contrast to the situation analyzed in the traditional case for integration, where the tax on dividends must be paid only if aftertax funds are newly invested in the corporate sector and generate income. (Of course, the alternative noncorporate investment also derives from aftertax income.)

This reasoning has two important implications. First, a given amount of retained profits in corporate solution is worth less to an investor than an equal amount of funds held in other ways. This would occur if share values were reduced enough that shares would be an attractive investment, despite the personal tax on dividends. A corollary of this is that any form of integration or dividend relief—and, of course, elimination of the corporate tax—would result in large windfall gains to present owners of corporate equities. Second, for purposes of determining the allocative effects of a separate tax on corporate income, the relevant tax to compare with the personal tax on noncorporate income is simply the corporate tax, not the combination of the corporate tax and the personal tax on dividends, as under the traditional analysis.

These points, which are crucial to the argument that follows, are illustrated by the example presented in the last two columns of Table 17.1. In this example, unlike that in the first two columns, it is assumed that $1,000 is in corporate solution, rather than in the hands of investors. Income earned on funds retained and reinvested in the corporate sector (column 4) is taxed to the corporation and, if distributed, to the individual investor. In this sense, the result is the same as that for investment in newly issued corporate equity (column 2). But if the corporate and personal tax rate are the same, exactly the same result occurs if funds originally in corporate solution are distributed and then invested in noncorporate assets. This occurs because personal tax is collected when the previously retained earnings are distributed, as well as when the funds invested in noncorporate assets yield a return to the individual. The second line of column 3 shows more clearly why the personal tax is capitalized in lower share prices. The $1,000 in corporate solution is worth only $500, due to the 50 percent personal tax that must be paid when the funds are distributed. Although it does not appear so clearly, the same is true in column 4; aftertax earnings on the $1,000 retained in corporate solution cannot be withdrawn without paying the personal tax.

The efficiency arguments for integration are much weaker under this view of the situation than under the traditional view. For one thing, the personal tax on dividends does not distort the choice of whether to pay dividends or retain earnings in the corporation in any given year; the personal tax will eventually be paid in any case. The only issue is whether the personal tax on noncorporate income exceeds the corporate tax. If the corporate tax is higher, there is an incentive to distribution; if it is lower, retention is favored. Beyond that, there is no distortion in the debt-equity ratio. Investors subject to marginal personal tax rates above the corporate rate would prefer to hold corporate equities, and those subject to lower rates would prefer to hold other securities, including corporate debt. But as far as tax considerations are concerned, corporations would be indifferent between debt and equity financing. Finally, distortions of production techniques (factor intensities) and consumer choices would be far less worrisome than under the traditional view.

The upshot of this view of the corporate tax is that while integration is desirable for income attributable to newly issued shares, it is not needed for returns attributable to retained earnings and, indeed, would have adverse allocative and distributional effects if extended to them. There would be windfall gains to owners of existing shares, and the relatively neutral constellation of personal and corporate taxes described in the previous paragraph would be upset. In order to avoid these allocative effects and windfall gains, members of an American Law Institute (ALI) project have suggested, in effect, that corporations be allowed to deduct dividends paid only on new shares. (In late 1974, President Ford proposed similar treatment of dividends on newly issued preferred stock of public utilities.) Of course, crucial to the economic attraction of such a proposal, compared to relief for all dividends, is the extent to which share prices currently reflect the existing dividend tax, as posited by the new view of the corporate tax.

Advocates of a separate corporate tax naturally draw comfort from this new view of the tax. As noted, it substantially weakens the case for integration and dividend relief. Moreover, if the adverse effects of the corporate tax are not as bad as commonly believed, they would say, it made no sense to reduce the tax through ERTA, and TEFRA was a step back in the right direction.

The discussion to this point is summarized in the first line of Table 17.2. As indicated, eliminating the corporate tax was not attractive in the pre-ERTA world, whether one took the classical or the integrationist view of the corporate tax. Integration was favored under the traditional view of the corporate tax, but under the new view the prevalence of financing through retained earnings made the case for integration weak. Those who adopted the new view preferred to see dividend relief limited to new shares (the ALI proposal).

Effective Tax Rates Under ERTA and TEFRA

Most of the discussion thus far in this essay, like the earlier literature on integration, implicitly assumes that the corporate income tax is actually levied on most economic income originating in that sector. If that state of affairs actually prevailed, advocates of integration would need to be concerned, at most, with how to treat preference

Table 17.2
Summary of Appraisals of the Corporate Tax

Policy Period	"Classical" Viewpoint	Integrationist Viewpoints	
		Traditional	*New*
1. Pre-ERTA	Classical	Integration	ALI
2. ERTA	Restore pre-ERTA	Eliminate tax	Eliminate tax
		Unify treatment of investment	Unify treatment of investment
		Inflation-proof capital consumption allowances	Inflation-proof capital consumption allowances
3. TEFRA	Restore pre-ERTA	Integration	ALI
		Concern with preferences	Concern with preferences

income—by assumption a quantitatively minor problem. In fact, since 1981 most equity income resulting from new corporate investment has not been subject to full taxation because of the extremely rapid depreciation allowances and the investment tax credits (ITCs) provided under ERTA and only partially eliminated by TEFRA. On some such income, the effective corporate tax rate has actually been negative. Preferences of this magnitude are not merely a footnote to the discussion of integration and dividend relief; they change the entire nature of the debate.

A fundamental theorem of the economics of taxation states that immediate expensing of equity-financed investment is equivalent to exempting from taxation the income from the privately financed portion of such investment. (To see this, consider the investment of $100. If the tax rate is 46 percent, immediate expensing implies that the private investor actually puts up only $54; the government provides the remainder through the tax saving resulting from expensing. The government will take 46 percent of the net before-tax income produced by the asset. But this is best seen as the government's return on its 46 percent of the initial investment rather than as a tax. The investor is allowed to keep the full 54 percent of net income resulting from the 54 percent of the investment that is privately financed. Thus the income attributable to the privately financed part of the investment is taxed at a zero effective rate.) Besides being independent of the nominal rate of tax and the before-tax rate of return on investment, this equivalence holds regardless of the rate of inflation; since expensing occurs in current-year dollars, its value cannot be eroded by inflation. This equivalence makes expensing a useful benchmark against which to appraise the post-ERTA-TEFRA corporate income tax.

In a time of stable prices, if depreciation allowed for tax purposes reflects economic depreciation and there are no other tax preferences, the tax base for business taxation will be economic income and the statutory and effective tax rates will be the same. If, however, depreciation for tax purposes is more rapid than economic depreciation and prices are stable, the tax base will be less than economic income and the effective tax rate will be lower than the statutory rate. Conversely, if tax depreciation is based on economic depreciation of historical asset values but there is inflation, the effective tax rate will exceed the statutory rate. Finally, one rough way of offsetting the erosion of the value of depreciation allowances that results from inflation is to grant tax depreciation that is more rapid than economic depreciation based on historical costs. This has been given as one justification for the Accelerated Cost Recovery System (ACRS) of capital consumption allowances and the ITCs provided under ERTA.

The depreciation allowances provided under ERTA, when combined with the investment tax credit of 10 percent, were much more generous than economic depreciation. Indeed, for rates of inflation within the range of recent experience, they were even more generous than outright expensing for some kinds of assets. This implies, of course, that effective tax rates on income from some equity-financed investments were very low; in some instances, effective rates were actually negative. The president's Council of Economic Advisers, in its *Annual Report* for 1982, estimated that once ERTA was fully phased in, a pretax rate of return of only some 2.9 to 3.2 percent on construction machinery, general industrial equipment, and trucks, buses, and trailers would result in an aftertax rate of return of 4 percent, given an inflation rate of 8 percent.[4] In other words, for income from assets of this type the corporate income tax would involve a subsidy of 25 to 38 percent rather than the apparent tax of 46 percent implied by the statutory rates. For higher or lower rates of inflation, the subsidy rate would be lower or higher, respectively, but even with 12 percent inflation the subsidy would be roughly 8 percent for income from these kinds of assets. By comparison, income from industrial and commercial buildings would be taxed at rates of 38 to 42 percent if the inflation rate were 8 percent, and at 34 to 38 percent with an inflation rate of 5 percent. These differentials in rates across types of assets would naturally distort corporate investment decisions toward the more lightly taxed—or more heavily subsidized—assets. Moreover, it would favor some industries, such as transportation, over others, including utilities, services, and trade.

The perceived inequity and inefficiency of this policy, which was accented by the spectacle of safe-harbor leasing (the selling of depreciation allowances and ITCs by firms that could not use them to firms that could) helps explain the backtracking that occurred in TEFRA. Besides effectively eliminating safe-harbor leasing, that law required that the depreciable basis of assets be reduced by one-half the amount of ITCs and eliminated the acceleration in depreciation scheduled for 1985 to 1986. Even with these reforms, some types of investment are still treated roughly as favorably as under expensing, at least for relatively modest rates of inflation. Table 17.3 indicates the effective tax rates applied to income from five types of assets under TEFRA, for alternative assumptions about the rate of inflation.[5]

Expensing—for all or part of investment—would have been a far more neutral way of achieving what ERTA and TEFRA accomplished. As noted earlier, the benefits of expensing do not depend on the rate of inflation, as do those of ACRS. Moreover, expensing is neutral be-

Table 17.3

Effective Tax Rates Under TEFRA, by Asset Class, for Alternative Rates of Inflation

ACRS Category	Rate of Inflation (percentage)		
	2	6	10
Machinery and equipment			
3 year	−48.5	−3.9	18.3
5 year	−32.6	−0.3	17.2
10 year	6.6	22.0	30.9
15 year	21.9	36.3	43.8
Structures (15 year)	28.8	36.6	41.2

NOTE: Assumes 4 percent real aftertax rate of return.
SOURCE: U.S. Treasury, Office of Tax Analysis.

tween assets of different useful life. By comparison, there are wide discrepancies in the treatment of machinery and equipment (basically expensing, at a 6 percent rate of inflation) and of structures under ERTA-TEFRA. These are reflected in the differences in effective tax rates applied to different industries, depending on the composition of their asset structure.

Integration Under ERTA and TEFRA

The traditional case for integration had little force in the brief world of ERTA. This can be seen most easily by considering the tax treatment of income from new investment financed by the issue of new shares, for which the case for integration is strongest, even under the new view of the corporation. If the effective corporate income tax on such income is low, or even negative, there is little need for relief from double taxation of dividends. In the extreme case, the only corporate tax that would be collected under the shareholder credit approach would be the compensating tax required to nullify preferences upon the distribution of preference income.[6] Under these conditions, the compensating tax would be merely a withholding tax on dividends, and dividend relief would be largely a charade. Of course, withholding on dividends is a good idea, but it could be implemented without the complex trappings of integration. Under the new view of the corporation, the corporate tax on income to be distributed is the only one that matters. But under ERTA this tax was near zero, on average, for income from new investment.[7] Again, the case for integration was not strong.

A much more sensible approach, at least for income from new investments, under either view of the corporate tax would be to eliminate it, rather than retain it in its post-ERTA form. In many respects, ERTA combined the worst aspects of taxation. The tax would yield little revenue beyond that from income produced by prior investments and the return to the government-financed portion of new investment. And yet, despite the inframarginal failure to raise revenue on income from new investment, the tax might actually involve serious disincentive effects at the margin, where decisions are made. (For example, ACRS and ITCs might reduce tax liability to near zero, but any additional income not connected with new investment would be taxed at 46 percent.) Finally, as noted above, ERTA created undesirable distortions in the choice among assets of various types and among industries—distortions that depended crucially on the rate of inflation. Eliminating the tax would at least have combined the desirable characteristic of neutrality—toward investment decisions and with respect to the rate of inflation—with zero revenue yield.

The second line of Table 17.2 describes differing opinions of ERTA. Those who had earlier favored integration, in either its traditional form or that proposed by the ALI project (only for new issues) would presumably have found eliminating the tax preferable to the post-ERTA tax—at least for income from new investment. But those who had earlier favored a classical system were more likely to prefer repeal of the liberalized treatment of investment under ERTA. The latter group was ultimately partially successful, as evidenced by the passage of TEFRA.

TEFRA raised effective tax rates on income from new investment substantially; according to U.S. Treasury estimates, for an inflation rate of 6 percent, TEFRA roughly doubled the weighted average effective rate of tax, from about 13–14 percent (with ERTA fully phased in) to 28 percent. It also narrowed somewhat the range of effective tax rates applied to income from various types of new investment (machinery and equipment, compared to structures). But the range is still too great, and effective rates still depend too much on the rate of inflation.

One way to gain greater uniformity of effective rates would be simply to lower the statutory rate. But this approach reduces the spread of effective rates only by having them converge toward zero. Moreover, it provides windfall gains on the income from prior investments.

A more sensible approach to reducing business taxation would have been to allow expensing for part of investment and economic depreciation for the rest.[8] Since both are neutral toward investment choices, at a zero rate of inflation, their combination is neutral. Such an approach would be vulnerable to the erosion of the depreciation allowances in times of inflation. But this could be overcome by implementing the imaginative system of first-year capital recovery proposed by Alan Auerbach and Dale Jorgenson.[9] Under this proposal, firms would be allowed to deduct, in the first year, the present value of economic depreciation.[10] Like expensing, this deduction would be inflation-proof, but if used exclusively, it would equalize the effective and statutory tax rates. Any effective tax rate between zero and the statutory rate could be implemented for income from new investment by varying the mix of expensing and first-year recovery. Whatever the mix chosen, the effective tax rate would be independent of the rate of inflation, and it would be uniform across assets and industries.

Even if TEFRA were replaced by a more neutral means of taxing corporate income, say by choosing a mix of expensing and first-year recovery that approximated the existing average effective tax rate (currently roughly 28 percent on fully taxable income resulting from new investment, at an inflation rate of 6 percent), the question of whether to integrate the tax, eliminate it, or restore it to its pre-ERTA level would remain.[11] The relevant arguments are similar to those outlined in the second and third sections, but the relative emphasis is somewhat changed.

Conceptually, the traditional case for integration is the same as before ERTA; but as a practical matter, it is weakened by the reduction in effective rates, as well as by the new view of the tax. (Indeed, the taxation of income resulting from reinvestment of corporate retained earnings is now low enough that investment decisions may not be seriously skewed against the corporate sector even under the traditional view.) Of course, the reduction in effective rates underlies the position of those who favor a classical system and would like to see the corporate tax restored to roughly its pre-ERTA shape. These views are reflected in the third line of Table 17.2

A final word must be said about the role of tax preferences in a world in which dividend relief is enacted in the context of an effective tax rate of roughly 28 percent achieved through partial expensing rather than rate reduction.[12] (If the rate were simply cut to 28 percent, but applied to economic income, the issue of preferences would not arise.) It is one thing to discuss dividend relief when preferences cause minor deviations between statutory and effective rates. It is something else when partial expensing reduces the effective rate on income from new equipment from 46 percent to 28 percent. Considerable effort has been devoted to the complex technical problems of how to treat preferences under various approaches to dividend relief. More attention probably needs to be paid to identifying and resolving the economic issues, under either traditional dividend relief or the ALI proposal.

Notes

1. For a presentation of the traditional case for (and against) integration, see Charles E. McLure, Jr., *Must Corporate Income Be Taxed Twice?* (Washington, D.C.: Brookings Institution, 1979), especially chap. 2; and idem, "A Status Report on Tax Integration in the United States," *National Tax Journal* 31 (December 1978): 313–28 and literature cited there.
2. The next two sections draw heavily on Alan J. Auerbach, "Tax Integration and the 'New View' of the Corporate Tax: A 1980's Perspective," in *Proceedings of the Seventy-Fourth Annual Conference on Taxation* (Columbus, Ohio: National Tax Association–Tax Institute of America, 1982). pp. 21–27.
3. It might appear that the preferential treatment of long-term capital gains would allow shareholders to avoid paying the full tax on dividends by selling stock at appreciated prices that reflect retained earnings. This is not the case since the price that can be realized on the sale of stock reflects the obligation of the purchaser to pay personal tax when he or she receives dividends. But the dividend tax can be avoided by a carefully designed plan to use retained earnings to repurchase shares from shareholders. Double taxation of dividends also vanishes under this approach.
4. See the discussion in *Economic Report of the President* (Washington, D.C.: Government Printing Office, 1982), pp. 122–26.
5. These comparisons cover only taxation of income from investment in depreciable assets. Expenditures on research and development are expensed, and some even carry additional credits. To the extent that firms use first-in, first-out methods to account for inventories, income is overstated during inflationary periods.
6. Under expensing, if the firm is growing fast enough, it never has to pay the government its 46 percent share of net profits. In particular, if a firm's growth rate of investment exceeds its before-tax rate of return, its deductions for the expensing of investment will perpetually offset its entire before-tax income. If, contrary to the example in the fourth section, the firm is partially

debt-financed, its capital stock need grow only by a fraction of the rate of return (before deduction for interest) equal to the fraction of capital financed by equity in order to avoid taxes. Similar principles apply in the worlds of ERTA and TEFRA.

7. One technical feature of ERTA needs to be mentioned. Under U.S. law, distributions are treated as dividends that are taxable to recipients, up to the limits of "earnings and profits." Additional distributions are tax-free return of capital, up to the investors' basis in shares. Beyond that, distributions are taxed as capital gains. Thus it is in the interest of shareholders to have earnings and profits be as small as possible. If ACRS were employed in the calculation of earnings and profits, personal tax on distributed corporate income, as well as the corporate tax, would be largely eliminated. However, ERTA does not allow ACRS to be employed in calculating earnings and profits.

8. The idea of combining these two neutral ways of taxing business income is commonly attributed to Arnold C. Harberger. See, for example, his "Tax Neutrality in Investment Incentives," in Henry J. Aaron and Michael J. Boskin, eds., *The Economics of Taxation* (Washington, D.C.: Brookings Institution, 1980), pp. 299–313. The fraction of investment to be expensed could be chosen to produce any effective tax rate between zero and the statutory rate. Since the relevant neutrality theorems apply only to equity-financed investment, it may be desirable to provide further adjustments based on reliance on debt finance.

9. See Alan J. Auerbach and Dale W. Jorgenson, "The First-Year Capital Recovery System," *Tax Notes*, April 14, 1980; and "Inflation-Proof Depreciation of Assets," *Harvard Business Review*, September–October 1980, pp. 113–18.

10. Consider the following simple example: an asset costing $100 that depreciates to zero in two years, on a straight-line basis; thus depreciation is $50 each year. The present value of the first year's depreciation allowance is $50, but that of the second year's is only $45.45, if a discount rate of 10 percent is employed. Thus the investor would be allowed first-year capital recovery of $95.45, the sum of the present values of depreciation in the two years. By comparison, under expensing the full $100 would be deducted in the year of acquisition.

11. See Auerbach, "Tax Integration and the 'New View,' " for a more ambitious approach that involves conversion of the personal income tax to a levy on consumption.

12. A further question that must be addressed if dividend relief is considered is the treatment of capital income flowing internationally to or from the United States. For more on this, see McLure, *Must Corporate Income Be Taxed Twice?*, chap. 6. Eliminating the corporate tax would entail a large loss of revenue now received from foreign firms.

18
Pursuit of Excellence? The Income and the Outcome of Education

Roger A. Freeman

American education at all levels is in deep trouble.

Some may react to that statement with: "So what else is new? The schools always seem to be in some sort of trouble, but in the end they come out on top most of the time." There is a kernel of truth in that flippant response. The schools appeared to face their worst crisis at midcentury when the postwar baby boom threatened to engulf them in a tidal wave of students. To hire the teachers and build the classrooms that a doubled enrollment would require seemed beyond the financial capacity of the existing support system. Administrators and friends of the schools mounted a national campaign for a rescue operation by the massive infusion of federal funds. But they were never able to convince Congress, which year after year refused to authorize such a program. In consequence, the federal share of educational financing barely rose, from 6 percent in the early 1950s to a stable 10 percent since the mid-1960s. How then did schools and colleges weather the "tidal wave"? Surprisingly well—state and local governments and private sources managed to lift total educational support from $11 billion in 1951–52 to $200 billion in 1981–82, far exceeding even the fondest hopes.

Expressed in *constant* (inflation-adjusted) dollars, education funds increased by 400 percent over that 30-year period, while the number of students rose 75 percent, the number of teachers 157 percent, cutting class sizes substantially during a time of unprecedented attendance growth.[1] Instead of building 600,000 classrooms to meet the public schools' essential needs of the decade of the 1960s, a task that President Kennedy told Congress was beyond the capacity of state and local governments and could be accomplished only through a huge federal program, the schools built 700,000 classrooms on their own—without federal aid.

Quantity and Quality in Education

In magnitude and resources, our educational structure is truly remarkable. Education has long been one of the country's largest industries and is, in terms of the number of participants, the biggest of them all. It occupies, mostly on a full-time basis, nearly 30 percent of the resident U.S. population: 59 million as students, almost 8 million as employees. Education has also been one of our most ebullient growth industries in economic terms: its share of GNP doubled over the past three decades—from 3.4 percent of GNP in 1951 to 6.8 percent in 1981—though enrollment expansion of 75 percent only moderately exceeded the simultaneous rate of general population growth of 48 percent. Growth in education came to a halt a few years ago, as it did in some other big industries, and was followed by a gradual decline. There is no prospect of a sizable enrollment increase for the balance of this century and beyond.

This does not mean that schools and colleges have solved their worst difficulties and can look forward to an easier future. Quite the contrary. The problems ahead may prove to be more intractable than those of the past because they are politically tougher. Public controversies over education are likely to grow fiercer as decisions will have to be made on divisive policy issues. Meanwhile the nature of education's problems is changing drastically.

In the third quarter of the twentieth century the issue was largely one of numbers: of students, teachers and their salaries, and, above all, dollars. The quantity of human, physical, and financial resources drew most of the attention. But for some years now it has become painfully apparent that the paramount problem of American education is and will increasingly continue to be not quantity but quality.

Until about the midcentury, Americans had good reason to take pride in the excellence of their educational institutions, which were envied in much of the rest of the world. Education could claim much of the credit for the country's spectacular and rapid advance from a primitive area, most of it primeval wilderness, to recognized leadership of the free world as its most prosperous, powerful, and respected nation.

In the first ten or fifteen years after World War II a few keen observers of the education scene—including George Iddings Bell, Arthur Bestor, Hyman G. Rickover, Mortimer Smith, James D. Koerner, and Rudolf Flesch—voiced concern over a decline of learning in the schools and warned of ominous consequences. In the 1960s and more widely in the 1970s parents, employers, and educators watched with dismay as the skills and knowledge of the younger generation kept sliding to ever lower levels. Gradually the American public lost confidence in the methods, competence, and effectiveness of its schools.

Speaking about available information, Secretary of Health, Education and Welfare Wilber Cohen complained in 1967 that "practically none of it measures the output of our educational system in terms that really matter—that is in terms of what students have learned." He added that it was an "incredible fact that the nation has, year after year, been spending billions of dollars on an enterprise without a realistic accounting of that investment." But evidence multiplied from many sources: steadily falling SAT scores; the decline (except in the lowest grades) in scores on tests of the National Assessment of Educational Quality (established by the states in 1969 because the schools would not disclose evidence that might ill reflect on their product); the need for colleges to run remedial "bonehead" classes for freshmen; and the inability of high school graduates to qualify for or cope with job requirements. Hundreds of articles and books appeared in recent years that documented and enlarged on what more and more people sensed from their own observations: the educational attainments of American school graduates are on the downgrade.

Cross-national comparisons in the twelve-volume series of studies by the International Association for the Evaluation of Educational Achievement (IEA) were well summarized by Barbara Lerner in 1982:

> In the late 1960s and in the 1970s, American students did not perform as well as most of their peers in other developed nations . . . American secondary school students were in the bottom half of the distribution on seven out of eight tests and at the very bottom of the distribution of developed nations on six of them . . . The evidence pointing to a decline in the cognitive achievements of American high school students in the last two decades is conclusive.[2]

This is made even more astounding by these facts: more young Americans are attending school for more years than their counterparts abroad, class sizes in the United States are generally smaller, teachers have more years of postsecondary education, and they are better paid. Expenditures for education, whether measured on a per-student basis or as a percentage of GNP, are much higher in the United States than in other Western countries or in the Soviet Union.

In *The Literary Hoax* Paul Copperman expressed the situation concisely: "For the first time in the history of our country, the education skills of one generation will not surpass, will not equal, will not even approach those of their parents."

Copperman's statement was quoted by the National Commission on Excellence in Education in a scathing indictment, in almost apocalyptic terms, of the deterioration in American education and especially the decay of the high school. In its April 1983 report, *A Nation at Risk*,[3] the commission listed as "Indicators of the Risk" (pp. 8–11) ample evidence to support its charges.

Commenting on the report, *Newsweek* (May 9, 1983) wrote: "How we got into this mess is less important than how to get out of it, and the commission recommends a host of reforms." However, without full knowledge of why education in the United States sank to its sad status, there is little hope of being able to devise an adequate strategy to correct the faults and resurrect educational quality. The commission's charges repeat what many others have said over the preceding thirty years, and it offers often-heard recommendations that have not halted or reversed the downward trend. If the report helps to awaken the nation to its "clear and present danger" and leads to further, preferably nongovernmental, studies to identify the cause of the fall of American education from its former status of eminence, it will have done a worthwhile job.

The American people are now getting less education for a great deal more money—whether compared with earlier times or with other nations. There seems to be an inverse ratio between the income and the outcome of education (see Table 18.1).

The per-student cost in public education, in constant dollars, multiplied nearly three times over the past 30 years. We may ask: If a tripling of expenditure did not raise the quality of education, or even maintain it, what reason do we have to accept the claim that more money would solve the quality problem in education?

In a recent major study, James S. Coleman showed that the students in an average private school score higher on standard achievement tests than students in public schools, although the typical

Table 18.1
Enrollment and Expenditures of Public Schools and Colleges, 1951–52 and 1981–82

	1951–52	1981–82	Percentage Increase	Percentage Increase (in constant dollars)
Governmental expenditures for education	$9.0 billion	$161.2 billion	1698	402
Enrollment in public educational institutions	27.9 million	50.2 million	80	
Cost per student	$322	$3,218	899	179

nongovernmental school has larger classes, lower-paid teachers, most of whom are not "certificated," and substantially lower resources and expenditures on a per-student basis.[4]

In his monumental study of American schools in 1966, Coleman had found—to his surprise—that "the evidence revealed that within broad geographic regions, and for each racial and ethnic group, the physical and economic resources going into a school have very little relationship to the achievements coming out of it."[5] Christopher Jencks, in summarizing the ensuing national debate, concluded: "Variations in schools' fiscal and human resources have very little effect on student achievement—probably even less than the Coleman report implied."[6]

These statistics prove without doubt that the existence of a positive cost-quality relationship in the schools is a myth, created and maintained by groups trying—quite successfully—to generate more jobs for their members at higher wages. The fact is that differences in achievement are far wider within schools than among schools and thus not related to financial support. Analysis of New York City data shows that schools with the highest per-pupil spending score quite low on tests of cognitive achievement.[7] Those discrepancies persist and have shown no sign of disappearing or even narrowing.

That reduction of the teacher-pupil ratio and of class sizes does not raise pupil achievement has long been known. A third of a century ago the *Encyclopedia of Educational Research* (1950 edition), summarized several hundred research studies:

On the whole, the statistical findings definitely favor large classes at every level of instruction except the kindergarten. The general trend of evidence places the burden of proof squarely upon the proponents of small classes.

Numerous subsequent studies have confirmed this. A 1979 report by a committee of the National Academy of Education found "that there is no consistent relationship between cognitive achievement and class size. In fact, more often than not, any effect of class size or teacher-student ratio is found to be absent."[8]

But research findings did not keep school authorities from hiring more and more teachers and other staff (see Table 18.2). The number of employees per 100 students doubled between 1952 and 1982; in 1982, 57 percent of the employees were teachers; two-thirds of the staff in colleges and one-third in the elementary schools were noninstructional.

Approximately three-fourths of the school budget is allocated to salaries and wages. It is therefore easy to understand that the disproportionate staff increases resulted in an extraordinary spending growth that nearly tripled per student costs in the past three decades. If more

Table 18.2

Students and Staff in Public Education, 1951–52 and 1981–82

	1951–52	1981–82	Percentage Increase
Student enrollment	27,900,000	50,100,000	80
Full-time and part-time employees	1,850,000	6,920,000	274
Full-time equivalent employees	1,655,000	5,414,000	227
Employees per 100 students full-time and part-time	6.6	13.6	106
Full-time equivalent	5.9	10.8	83

SOURCES: Student enrollment: U.S. Office of Education, *Statistical Summary of Education, 1951–52*; and U.S. Department of Education, *Digest of Education Statistics, 1982*; 1981–82 data are for fall 1981, the latest available. Employment: U.S. Department of Commerce, *The National Income and Product Accounts of the United States, 1929–76*; and U.S. Department of Commerce, *Survey of Current Business, July 1983.*

money and more teachers and supporting staff are not the magic keys to improvements in educational quality, what is? The most frequent suggestions by observers of the educational scene, whether trained professionals and scholars or laymen, are for a more rigorous curriculum in the basic "hard" subjects, tight discipline and ample homework, a rise in the standards of grading, promotion, graduation, and, at the postsecondary level, higher requirements for admission. These, in essence, were the recommendations of the Commission on Excellence in Education in April 1983.

A substantial upgrading of curriculum and standards would appear to be the most obvious and direct method to bring about educational improvement. But whenever such plans are proposed or attempted, they run into strong opposition. Charges of elitism, of favoritism for the naturally endowed or the children of the rich and the upper middle class, and of unfairness and discrimination against the disadvantaged, the children of the poor and ethnic minorities, have soon ended local attempts to carry out such plans.

Who could or would be able to establish higher standards in the public schools and maintain them? If state and local boards of education and administrators were in favor of higher standards and more rigorous curricula, why did they move in the opposite direction for the past thirty or more years? Why have they reduced requirements to take "tough" subjects and virtually abandoned standards of promotion? Why do they give high school diplomas to students who perform at an eighth-grade level or lower? The forces opposed to raising educational standards in the public schools are nationally well organized and have been able to nip such local endeavors in the bud or kill them soon after they started. Nothing but a national movement for higher standards that is sufficiently strong and effectively organized can change that.

Should the federal government intervene in favor of higher standards? Should it impose them by mandate or by conditioning financial aid on the adoption of such reforms by the recipient governments? That would run counter to a firmly rooted American tradition of state and local control of education. The U.S. Constitution never mentions education—and not because of an oversight—while all state constitutions declare education to be a foremost state responsibility.

We all know that federal influence on educational policies and procedures has grown enormously in recent decades. The number of aid programs expanded to over 70 by 1980, with each program imposing its own rules. Federal influence was generally not aimed at the pursuit of excellence but at using education as the Great Leveler to adjust everyone to the lowest common denominator. Could federal influence be used *for* rather than *against* higher standards? To employ federal power to force state and local authorities would be wrong. But there would be nothing wrong with the president and other high federal state and local officials and political, business, and civic leaders taking the lead in a drive to resurrect American education from the low status to which it has fallen, stressing the nation's imperative need for a better educated citizenry.

The Reagan administration, in its first two years, aimed to reduce the federal role in education, in terms of central control and regulation as well as finances. It recognized that too many federal education programs had proved effective only as a means to distribute large sums of money but had not raised the academic achievements of the students. The president proposed to abolish the U.S. Department of Education, which had been established at the insistence of President Carter as a payoff for the help he had received from the National Education Association in the 1976 election campaign. Mr. Reagan was successful in getting congressional approval for combining several federal categorical programs into one educational block grant, though the extent of the merger was cut to 30 minor programs, which in the aggregate equalled only 5 percent of the department's funds. The block grant is part of the administration's attempt to strengthen the decision-making power of states and communities and to widen the freedom of choice of parents and students.

The Reagan administration has made no proposals to reform education, a program to lift its quality, because it regards this as a state-local, not a federal responsibility. Nor did the 97th Congress consider measures to raise educational quality, and none likely to be effective seem in prospect in the 98th Congress.

A presidential appeal to improve education probably would have to be addressed more to state and local authorities and to the American people than to the Congress. Most of the action would have to be taken at nonfederal levels.

Elementary-Secondary Education

For most of the past two centuries education did not play a major role in the agenda of Congress, but moved to the forefront of legislative interest only on rare occasions. Congress gave intense and lengthy consideration to a series of general school support bills during the post–Civil War reconstruction period of the 1870s and the 1880s, but it did not pass them. The post–World War II baby boom brought about extensive hearings and floor debates on a sequence of classroom construction plans in the 1950s and early 1960s. But when proponents were unable to prove their case to the satisfaction of a reluctant Congress, and when school-building volume soared to unprecedented heights in the 1960s, interest in federal action faded.

Education was conspicuously absent in the long list of social programs that President Roosevelt sent to Congress to form the New Deal edifice that became his lasting monument. But his disciple Lyndon Johnson, thirty years later, made aid to "educationally deprived" children a focal part of his War on Poverty and railroaded a bill through Congress. At an annual cost of over $3 billion, it still is the only large federal school aid program. Close to six dozen other programs, ranging from vocational, bilingual, and Indian education to school lunches and "impacted" areas were passed and were in existence in 1981 when 30 of them, mostly small, were combined into a block grant.

The annual setting of appropriations and the periodic renewal of expiring programs rekindle basic arguments over their justification, effectiveness, or optimum magnitude. Some wonder why vocational education—started to meet the need for mechanics in World War I—should continue as a permanent federal function; some doubt that bilingual education speeds up the process of assimilating children from a foreign language background and fear that it may serve as a crutch, thus slowing down their acquisition of proficiency in English; others wonder why the national government should take from millions of parents the duty to feed their children just because a school lunch program at some time seemed an effective method to dispose of surplus agricultural commodities accumulating in government warehouses. While the rapid expansion of the military establishment in World War II and the Korean War justified payment to schools in the affected areas—because the properties involved could not be taxed by local government—it is highly questionable whether the communities that were successful in the fierce competition for the location of federal installations deserve permanent rewards in the form of "impact" payments.

In eighteen years of operation the program for "educationally deprived" children has proved that it can distribute several billion dollars a year among 80 or 90 percent of the country's school districts and thereby provide employment for more than 100,000 teachers who otherwise might have to look for nonschool jobs—because teachers' colleges have for many years been turning out far more graduates than the declining school enrollment required. Numerous reports have shown that "compensatory education" proved an abject failure in terms of its purpose: to raise the basic skills of children lagging one or several years behind their peers in the three R's. That lag is as big as it was at the outset of the program, if not bigger, especially in the middle and upper grades. The program itself, however, like other federal handouts, continues to enjoy great popularity among its recipients.

Many federal school programs have benefited a majority of students only marginally or not at all and contributed little if anything to solving the primary problem in American education: falling quality. It is truly amazing that after a more than century-long intensive campaign by teacher associations and their allies for a broad federal school aid program, the aggregate of all federal outlays for education accounts for a mere 2 percent of the U.S. budget. That may not express as much the extent of congressional interest as a conviction that education basically is not a federal responsibility. It also seems to suggest that there are greener pastures than the halls of Congress in which to seek solutions to the major problems of education, financial or qualitative.

Education is the biggest item in most state budgets, accounting for nearly 40 percent of aggregate state and local government general expenditures. School funding and the taxes needed to finance it often dominate state legislative sessions. Substantive issues such as curriculum, standards, testing, teacher qualifications, and salaries rank as high as finances—if not higher—among the disputes that occupy state legislators, boards of education, and communities. That is not surprising. State and local governments are the arenas in which, under our constitutional and traditional system, educational problems and differences are to be fought out and resolved.

To be sure, the federal government has sharply increased its control of educational affairs in recent decades mostly through conditions attached to granting aid and through voluminous regulations. Federal influence has generally not been employed toward a more rigorous curriculum or the imposition of higher standards. Nor have state and local authorities done better. The deterioration in discipline, the growth of easy electives as substitutes for hard subjects, the grade creep, and the resulting fall in the level of skills and knowledge could not have occurred without their explicit or implicit approval of relaxation or abandonment of standards and requirements.

Why did state legislatures, boards of education, and administrators at all levels of government allow this downward slide of education and teaching? Why did they not mandate that schools maintain—or raise—standards? Because they know—as many critics of current school practices apparently do not—that, given the present structure and organization of our public school system, the imposition of higher standards would create chaos and make the outcome for many students even worse than it now is.

If all pupils were required to meet grade standards before being permitted to advance to a higher grade, many millions would fail. Retention in grade cannot solve that problem. To hold a student back for one year may sometimes help him catch up. But retention for several years creates more problems than it solves. Looking for a way out, the schools a few decades ago discovered the secret of perpetual promotion: very few pupils are now held back and most are promoted annually until, after twelve years of residence, they are handed a diploma that some of them cannot read. "Social promotion" faces the teacher with an insoluble problem: basic skill levels within a classroom may be four, six, or more years apart. The lag tends to grow. A pupil who is six months behind on entering first grade may be four years behind when he reaches the top grades.

No teacher, no matter how dedicated, no matter how small the class, can do justice to pupils in, for example, a sixth-grade class when some read and write at a third-grade level and others at an eighth-grade level. Neither gifted nor poorly endowed children will progress as well as they could if each child were faced with a learning task appropriate to his individual capacity. We know that it would be nonsense to have all people jump hurdles of the same height. Whatever uniform height we choose would be too high for some, too low for others. Why do we expect that what does not work in an athletic pursuit will work in an intellectual pursuit?

Some schools try to cope with the wide range of human capacities by offering several curricula, from vocational to academic, by operating two or more parallel "tracks" and assigning pupils according to their individual ability and aspirations. But the egalitarian forces that have dominated school policies for many decades frown on tracking. Some courts have held tracking to be unconstitutional. That is why tracking, where practiced, is usually underdeveloped, kept under cover, and treated as if it were an illegitimate offspring. Nor is such informal tracking adequate to meet the problem.

How do schools outside the United States deal with widely differing abilities? No other country tries to keep all children up to age eighteen in the same type of school, promotes all or almost all of them every year, or gives all of them, or almost all, a diploma of graduation whether or not they have acquired the proper levels of skills and knowledge. In most European countries, for example, all children attend a primary school for about four or five years and then apply or are assigned to an appropriate secondary school. Between 15 and 25 percent of the pupils enter one of several types of academic school, usually after passing an examination. The majority enroll for four to five years at a school at which students improve their mastery of the basic skills and essential knowledge. Then they begin an apprenticeship, sometimes combined with another year or two of part-time school attendance, leading to a journeyman's standing in a trade.

As a result, the graduates of a European secondary academic school are about two years ahead of U.S. high school graduates and ready to enter a university—which in Europe means a graduate or professional school. Thus they are ready to complete studies and practice their chosen profession several years earlier than their American counterparts. Upon finishing a basic or vocational school, Europe's young people usually are more firmly grounded in what they need to qualify for and succeed in a routine job. Too many American youngsters with a high school diploma lack a marketable skill and remain chronically unemployed or underemployed. That is why we have various federal programs to train adults or near-adults belatedly in minimal occupational subjects or even the three R's that they should have learned earlier.

A division of children by capacity and aspiration was for all practical purposes in effect in America some decades ago when only one-fourth or one-half of the primary school pupils progressed to or graduated from high school. But high schools have since debased their curricula and abandoned standards so they could graduate more than three-fourths of all young people. Many of those graduates each year learn the hard way that a high school diploma is no substitute for the possession of essential skills and knowledge.

To institutionalize tracking in American public high schools will prove to be a highly controversial issue. It seems to violate the egalitarian principle that has so long dominated public policy in education and is largely responsible for the decline of educational quality in recent decades. Education cannot be turned into a pursuit of excellence by toughening curricula and lifting standards until the public schools differentiate between students who can meet them and those who cannot.

Several related problems will have to be resolved if educational quality is to be improved. A major reason for the failure of learning is the frightful lack of discipline that school administrators have allowed to grow into a blackboard jungle—sometimes because of restraints imposed by federal judges or bureaucrats. The quality of the teacher corps has been declining, partly because so many teacher candidates come from the lower half, in academic terms, of the college population, partially because their education has been misdirected toward mediocrity. Some would blame low teacher salaries for low teacher quality. Actually teachers' pay has risen at least parallel to the general trend in wages—although productivity in the schools declined (see Table 18.2) while it improved in the private economy. Teachers' salaries are substantially higher in the United States than in virtually all other countries.

Outstanding teachers may not be adequately compensated. But this cannot be corrected under union-enforced contracts that dictate uniform pay scales governed by college-earned credits and length of service. Instructional pay in higher education is not based on the credits the professors earned or the number of years they have taught. Professors are usually rated according to individual merit and salaries set commensurately, considering the earnings potential in each market. For example, salaries in law, medicine, and engineering are higher than in history and literature. In government and throughout the private economy, professional workers are graded and paid according to performance and the scarcity or surplus of qualified persons in each field. Public schools probably underpay outstanding and above-average teachers under the current system. But the American people will never be willing to pay *all* teachers as much as *good* teachers are worth. Merit pay for teachers may become a growing issue in the years ahead. This is particularly true with respect to science and mathematics teachers, whose numbers now are inadequate—because the teacher unions will not permit the schools to pay science teachers wages attuned to market levels rather than uniform teacher pay scales.

While quality is and will remain the crucial problem in American education, there are many other ongoing controversies that show no promise of being resolved. The division of school support between the states and their local school districts as well as state efforts toward equalization of local fiscal capacity and support were significantly affected by the *Serrano* case, which mandated equal per-pupil expenditures throughout the state of California, and by the passage of Proposition 13, which halved property taxes. Though both applied only to California, reverberations were felt in many other states. It appears that state governments may enlarge their financial as well as command role in the schools, but that the absolute equality of per-pupil revenues envisaged by the *Serrano* decision will not be generally accepted.

Although efforts at the federal level to shift from categorical grants to block grants may continue, prospects for broad success seem poor. Proposals to abolish the U.S. Department of Education appear to be more cosmetic than substantive. The name of the administrative unit—whether department, office, foundation, or some other term—is less important than the programs the unit administers and the powers it exercises. Debates over some of the programs will undoubtedly go on, but major changes do not now seem likely.

The fiercest battles have been fought and will continue to be waged over compulsory busing that attempts to achieve a racial balance in every public school. Opposing sides are about as far apart as they ever were, and there is little indication that either party is ready to make far-reaching concessions or to compromise its basic position.

Mandatory busing has evidently succeeded in desegregating many or most schools in the South that were formerly segregated by law. The center of controversy has shifted to the North. Whether northern schools are now less or more segregated than they were, can be and is being argued. Many figures are bandied about that are less than conclusive. The fact remains that at the time of the *Brown* decision in 1954 all but one of the nation's largest cities had a white majority in the public schools. Seventeen of the top twenty now have nonwhite majorities. A flight from the cities or from the public schools to escape busing probably was the major factor in that shift.

Some hold that the transfers have improved education while others contest that sharply. The response of millions of parents, white or black, to mandatory busing has been negative, and their actions speak louder than words. Busing has substantially lowered the quality of public education in most of the nation's major cities. The resulting population and economic shifts severely jeopardize the future prospects of many of the cities themselves. Many people believe that no effort and no sacrifice are too great to accomplish the aim of mixing white and black children in the schools in the proper statistical proportion and that those efforts must continue at an undiminished pace. Others regard the action to be unfair because well-to-do parents are able to avoid having their children bused while poor families have no choice but to obey the orders.

Numerous polls have shown consistently that about three-fourths of the U.S. population are opposed to compulsory busing and that a majority of both black and white people are. The Supreme Court has painted itself into a corner from which it may have difficulty extricating itself. It spelled the aim of its action in *Brown* II (1955): ". . . to achieve a system of determining admission to the public schools on a nonracial basis . . . ." Sixteen years later in *Swann* the high court upheld the assignment of children to schools on a racial basis and their mandatory busing when it turned out that few black parents and almost no white parents exercised the right to enroll their children at a school with an enrollment predominantly of the other race. From a *right* not to be denied access to a school mostly of the other race ("freedom of choice") it had been turned into a constitutional *obligation* to attend such a school.

The busing controversy will undoubtedly continue for a long time to come. But the chances are that the right of people to be regarded as individuals on their own merits rather than as members of an ethnic group, and to be treated "without regard to race, color or national origin" will gain ground, not in big steps but by slow progress toward the principle of color-blind policies.

Some believe that the quality of education is low because of the virtual monopoly position of the public schools: there is almost no competition that would offer a higher-quality education. Most parents simply cannot afford to send their children to a private school and to pay twice for education—through school taxes and tuitions. If the penalty for attending a private school were lowered, public schools would have to compete for pupils by offering a higher-quality education.

Spokesmen for the public schools like competition no better than most people do in their businesses. They hold that all children should attend common schools to be taught values, concepts, and skills essential to the success of a democratic society where they must mix and get along with members of other social, ethnic, and economic groups. Attempts to force all children to attend public schools were declared unconstitutional by the Supreme Court more than half a century ago, and the issue is unlikely to be raised again. But the public school forces demand that nonpublic schools at least not be aided by the government, financially or otherwise.

Substantial direct governmental support for private schools is unlikely to materialize because the majority of those schools are church-connected. In 1947 the Supreme Court ruled in *Everson* (by a vote of 5–4) that "no tax in any amount, large or small, can be levied to support any religious activities or institutions." Some regard this to be an erroneous interpretation of the words and intent of the First Amendment. But it is not likely to be overruled.

However, tax deductions for contributions to churches and other religious institutions have long been recognized and have not been questioned. Thus the idea arose of permitting a tax deduction or credit for tuition payments to schools, regardless of their affiliation. It can hardly be held that tuition payments to church-connected schools "advance religion" while donations to those schools or to churches do not. Why should the former be unconstitutional while the latter are not? The Supreme Court has never adjudicated the constitutionality of federal income tax credits for tuitions because Congress has never enacted such credits, though it debated them on several occasions. In July 1983, however, it upheld, by a 5–4 vote, the constitutionality of tuition tax credits on the state income tax in Minnesota. President Reagan has repeatedly and strongly proposed tuition tax credits—at all levels of education—but Congress has so far not acted on them. Public school forces and their allies are strongly opposed to such a measure. The budget's heavy deficit condition in the 1980s may make such a measure difficult to pass. But the issue is likely to continue on the agenda, and educational credits may some day be enacted. It could turn out to be a major force in improving education in public as well as in private schools, because "tracking" would be a likely result of public versus private school competition.

Higher Education

Enrollment expanded even more rapidly in institutions of higher learning (IHLs) than it had, a few years earlier, in the secondary schools. This was caused only in part by the postwar baby boom, which nearly doubled college-age population (18 to 24 years) over the past thirty years. Technical, scientific, economic, and social developments created a need for more highly educated people; many youths attended college who but a generation earlier would not have thought of it; and an unprecedented number of women flocked to academe, until, by the late 1970s, men had become a minority on the nation's campuses. The enrollment ratio jumped from one person in five in the college-age group to one in two. That multiplied the number of students more than five times, from 2.3 million in 1951–52 to 12.3 million in 1981–82.

Not all of those who enrolled as freshmen made it through to graduation, as a growing number fell by the wayside. Even so, the number of degrees conferred by IHLs multiplied 3.5 times over the past three decades. That far exceeded the absorptive capacity of the college-level job market and created problems that will haunt us through the 1980s and beyond.

IHLs absorbed the tidal wave with amazing ease as they succeeded in boosting their revenues from all sources, governmental and private, from $2 billion in 1951–52 to $73 billion in 1981–82, thus multiplying their funds ten times in constant dollars. The soaring cost of attending college did not seem to deter the new masses or their parents until in the 1970s enrollment growth began to flatten out. Though tuition averaged $2,653 at public (governmental) and $6,190 at private IHLs, in 1981–82 it contributed less than half the cost of running the enterprise at most private and less than a fourth at state and city institutions. Adding room and board, books, and other expenses to fees and tuitions, the bill for four years of college attendance now runs from $25,000 to well over $50,000, not counting four years of forgone wages.

What explains that frantic rush for college despite high costs? For some it manifests a thirst for more knowledge. But most people view a college degree above all as a passport to a well-paid and secure job. Some statistics seem to back them up: in 1980 a man with four years of college averaged $4,842 more in annual income than a high school graduate; if he had completed five or more years of study he added another $3,379 for a total of $8,221 more. A 1983 Census Bureau study of lifetime earnings (P-60 #139) estimated that a man with four years of college earned during his working life an average $329,000 more than a high school graduate. Media reports and commentators—and their audience—interpreted that as meaning that a young person after finishing high school could add $329,000 to his lifetime earnings by going to college for four years.

That, of course, is unmitigated nonsense. The statistics do not prove that the higher income is the *result* of the additional years of schooling. More likely both the college attendance and the level of income reflect the intelligence, aspirations, persistence, and personal drive of the individual. Most young people quit when they feel that they have reached the upper level of their absorptive or learning capacity and/or energy for academic study.

The monetary value of higher education has in all likelihood been oversold. A November 1982 study of the National Center for Education Statistics concluded: "Over the long run for both men and women, the financial return of a college education may repay the actual costs of schooling, as well as the wages lost by not working during the college years."[9] This suggests that the individual may—with emphasis on the "may"—be able to recover the money spent on higher education, not that it turned out to be a profitable investment.

Tuition at state or municipal IHLs, which enroll more than three-fourths of all students, may run as low as 10 or 20 percent of the instructional cost, with the taxpayer picking up the tab. The taxpayer of course also foots the bill for federal, state, and municipal student aid programs.

Is higher education a profitable investment? It usually is—for individuals with adequate talent and stamina to succeed in their studies and chosen profession. It may be a losing proposition for the naturally less endowed who—or whose parents—exhausted their savings and assumed heavy obligations they may be years in repaying. Many students would have been better off pursuing occupational goals within their potential reach. Too big a share of the $20 billion in annual public student aid programs and uncounted billions in voluntary contributions to the same purpose is now going to students whose lack of capacity or self-discipline to cope with an academic curriculum should have been apparent in the upper high school grades. Contrary to a widespread belief, education is not the "great equalizer." It may widen the difference between those who are capable of utilizing to the fullest what an academic education has to offer and others who may derive little from it besides, possibly, a sheepskin.

How can so many American families bear such a heavy burden, from $25,000 to over $50,000, for one or several of their offspring? To the rich this presents no problem, and to the poor it means that college depends on finding someone else to pay for it. But to a middle-class family, whence most students come, it often calls for a sacrifice. At least half the students need and get financial aid from private institutions or governmental programs, of which the federal have become the biggest.

The federal government got into the business of student aid in a small way in 1958 when Sputnik and national defense were hitched to the sled to pull or push the bill through Congress. That was only a modest beginning. In the mid-1960s Lyndon Johnson's superb political skills maneuvered direct loans and loan guarantees (with interest subsidies), grants (scholarships and fellowships), and work-study through Congress.

Student financial assistance now accounts for about 90 percent of all federal aid to higher education. The great controversy now—and probably for many years into the future—is whether federal student aid programs should be expanded or whittled down. The Reagan administration in 1982 tried for cutbacks but lost when pressure by the well-organized higher education community on and through Congress succeeded in restoring higher authorizations. The question is: Where do we go from here?

From some quarters the answer comes loud and clear: there can be no more worthy cause for allocating public funds than the development of the new generation's talents. What could bring higher returns to the nation and more richly benefit its future? Unfortunately, the issue is not so simple. We are told of large numbers of young people who would like to go to college but lack the necessary money. What we must not forget is that lack of money is a far more comfortable explanation for not devoting years to demanding study than to admit lack of talent, drive, and the willingness to work hard and defer receipt of the harvest for some years. That is why the alibi of "no money" cannot always be taken at face value.

The paramount question in regard to expanding or restricting student aid programs is: Does the United States need more college students and graduates than it now has and is producing? The answer, from all available evidence, must be in the negative. Unemployment was minimal among educated persons until a few years ago, when overproduction in the 1960s and 1970s created a glut in the market. Large numbers of graduates are now looking for jobs that do not exist or are unlikely to come into being for a long time. The Bureau of Labor Statistics estimated that in the current decade the United States will graduate over one-fourth more people than there will be college-level jobs. Small wonder that graduates become frustrated and bitter when after months of intensive and fruitless search they are faced with the alternative of remaining in the army of the unemployed or trying to find jobs at a lower level that they could have obtained four or five years earlier, *before* they entered college. Many will regard it as a cruel hoax that they were shown a mirage of well-paid jobs that financial aid through college would help them secure. We ought to remember that several revolutions within the past century were started and led by an "educated proletariat," young people who despaired of finding the jobs they had been led to believe were rightfully theirs. We ought not to raise hopes beyond possible fulfillment.

The number of degrees conferred by IHLs rose 250 percent over the past 30 years while population grew 48 percent, the labor force 73 percent. That was too great a discrepancy despite growing job sophistication. According to a 1977 U.N. study, the latest of its kind, enrollment in higher education equals 5.2 percent of population in the United States, 1.3 percent in Great Britain, 1.7 percent in Germany, 2.1 percent in France, and 2.0 percent in the Soviet Union. The percentage of our college-age population entering IHLs is two to four times as high as it is in other industrial nations.

There is no reason to believe that we need or can absorb several times as high a ratio of college-trained workers as comparable countries. It would be absurd to assume that the United States has three times as great a talent pool in proportion to population than other developed countries. Our trouble is not just that so many college graduates are unemployed but that so many of them are unemployable in college-level jobs.

The fact is that many of the entrants into and graduates from our IHLs are years behind their counterparts in European and other advanced countries. In our eagerness to make everybody fit for college we have made college fit everybody. More than one-fourth of the average freshman class needs and gets remedial instruction in subjects the students should have mastered before being awarded a high school diploma. Why should taxpayers be called upon to support in college young people who do not even possess a high school level of skills and knowledge? A university is not the best place to acquire a high school education.

It has been long and firmly established that talented but impecunious young people should be aided in developing their ability to the fullest. Students with a demonstrated potential can be helped by loans that they can pay back from their higher earnings over a lifetime. United Student Aid Funds, a private organization, provided loan guarantees nationwide for many years until in the mid-1960s it was overshadowed by federal intervention. Young people with a limited potential are less able to pay back loans. That is why in the 1960s the emphasis of federal student aid was shifted from loans to grants.

The basic shortcoming in federal student aid—and in many nonfederal programs—is that they are totally unrelated to the applicant's academic achievements and prospects. By conditioning student aid on demonstrated ability, many young people could be saved the excruciating experience of failure; they could be trained in subjects within their capacity and begin their working career several years sooner. SATs may not be perfect, but they still are the best predictors of academic success and should be used in decisions on student aid applications. That would sharply reduce the number of unqualified or marginally qualified students and eliminate from the process those most likely to fail. It would also cut the need for federal student aid, which would gradually diminish and might eventually vanish.

College attendance now imposes the heaviest burden on the middle class, as mentioned before. The impact could be alleviated by tuition tax credits, which have long been under consideration and were approved a half-dozen times by the Senate but have never been passed by both houses. An additional result of tax credits might be a halt and possible reversal of the shift from private to public institutions. Historically, until about midcentury, enrollment was about evenly split between public and private IHLs. A wide and growing tuition gap between public and private institutions gradually changed that to a 78–22 split in favor of state and municipal IHLs. Tax credits could widen the choice of institution for many families that currently cannot afford a private college. In the process, it could lighten the load on taxpayers by reducing the financial needs of state and municipal institutions.

A reduction in federal programs could be instrumental in helping to deregulate education, which has become one of the most heavily regulated industries, generally for the purpose of social engineering. Top officials of IHLs have long complained about the extent of federal control, but with little success. Federal rules and supervision now govern most actions with regard to faculty and staff, construction, admission, advancement, and disciplining and graduation of students. As in other industries, efforts to deregulate education will be a highly controversial issue, cutting across political party lines. Decentralization of decision-making powers could help advance the general status of education, although it may upset some special interests.

Conclusion

The magnitude of school and college financial needs and of federal, state, and local appropriations to meet them will play a major role in public disputes over education in the years ahead, as they always have. But money alone offers no solution to education's most crucial problem: declining quality. Pouring greater resources into educational institutions was the principal thrust of the past three decades. In an attempt to find an egalitarian solution, educational policymakers avoided having to face up to the root of the problem: the wide discrepancies in human capacities. Former U.S. Commissioner of Education Sterling McMurrin identified the leading causes for the deterioration of educational quality as "the doctrinaire egalitarianism that is the popular expression of our national ideal of equality" and "the anti-intellectualistic attitude that has in considerable degree been a pervasive quality of our culture over the past half century."[10]

An appalling decline in the skills and knowledge of the schools' products suggests that a return to pursuit of excellence may be the only way to restore the high academic level, effectiveness, and reputation of American education. A rigorous curriculum in the major subjects, objective and strictly enforced standards of grading, promotion, graduation, and, in higher education, admission are the sine qua nons of raising education from the lows to which it has fallen. This probably cannot be done unless the schools use several curricula at differing levels of academic difficulty, matching the wide range in individual capacities. It means that students must be grouped according to ability as they are nearly everywhere outside the United States. This enables every student, whether highly talented or poorly endowed, to advance in the shortest time to the upper limit of his individual capacity.

Progress in lifting the quality of education may be accompanied by a shrinking of the federal role in education and the return of decision-making power to state, local, and private authorities, boards, and administrators. Political-ideological controversies over these goals and the policies to achieve them will be fierce in the years to come.

The federal government has an important role to play in education, not as a maker of decisions to be obeyed by educational institutions but as a source of information that can assist educational authorities to carry out their mandate. Comparable data from all areas and schools on a nationally uniform basis are important and can best be gathered by federal instrumentalities such as the Bureau of the Census, the National Center for Education Statistics, and the National Institute of Education. Above all, we need nationally recognized yardsticks to measure educational achievements objectively and consistently in every state, school, and class and for every student. This does not mean that national standards should be established that all students are expected to meet. To sponsor, conduct, and coordinate research in education may also be regarded as a proper activity for the national government—though not through a Department of Education, which is a goal-oriented policy agency that is not in a good position to pass objective and impartial judgments on its own activities. There is really no need for a Department of Education in a constitutional system under which education is a state responsibility.

Notes

1. These and most subsequent statistical data are taken from *Digest of Education Statistics, 1982, The Condition of Education, 1982 edition*, and *Projections of Education Statistics to 1990-91*, all three publications by National Center for Education Statistics, U.S. Department of Education, 1982; and U.S. Department of Health, Education and Welfare, Office of Education, *Statistical Summary of Education, 1951–52* (Washington, D.C., 1955).
2. Barbara Lerner, "American Education: How Are We Doing?" *Public Interest*, Fall 1982.
3. Superintendent of Documents, Government Printing Office, Washington, D.C.

4. James S. Coleman, Thomas Hoffer, and Sally Kilgore, *High School Achievement: Public, Catholic and Private Schools Compared* (New York: Basic Books, 1982).
5. James S. Coleman, "Toward Open Schools," *Public Interest*, Fall 1967.
6. Christopher Jencks, "A Reappraisal of the Most Controversial Educational Document of Our Time," *New York Times Magazine*, August 10, 1969.
7. Marilyn Gittel, ed., *New York School Fact Book* (Institute for Community Studies, Queens College of the City of New York, 1968).
8. Douglas M. Windham, ed., *Economic Dimensions of Education*, Report of a Committee of the National Academy of Education (May 1979), p. 41.
9. National Center for Education Statistics, *Does College Pay? Wage Rates Before and After Leaving School*, Bulletin (November 1982).
10. In his introduction to James D. Koerner's book, *The Miseducation of American Teachers* (Boston: Houghton Mifflin Co., 1963), pp. ix–x.

19
The Politicization of the University

Sidney Hook

The development of modern society, particularly post-industrial society in which the role of complex technology is pervasive, has made universities, research centers, and other institutions of higher education of greater importance than in any other period. Not only do the level of productivity and the opening of a new frontier of exploration and discovery depend on the effective functioning of the university, but in an age of universal access to some form of higher education, the value system of the community is profoundly affected by what is taught there and how. The churches no longer have dominant sway over the population; the public media undoubtedly exercise a far greater influence on the mores and practices of their communicants than do traditional religious teachings. But the media are not self-sufficient mechanisms. They are instrumentalities operated and controlled by the men and women who constitute the personnel of the newspapers, periodicals, radio and television stations, and the other organs of public opinion.

The universities are the reservoir of the personnel that ultimately engage in all the forms of communication and education in society. At any given moment in time, they probably have no more impact on the moods and value judgments of the masses than do the churches. But over the long stretch, they count for more than the churches and all other social agencies, especially in our age of instant access to higher education. It is to them we must now look to fashion the standards and critical ideals that, one may hope, will enlighten and elevate popular sensitivity, appreciation, and judgment in all areas of experience, not excluding citizenship and politics. Whether universities succeed in this task depends on many things unrelated to their own intellectual activities in the pursuit of academic goals or to dedication to their academic mission. There will always be other determinants of culture—economic, historical, and physical—much more powerful than the influence of the quality of university life. Nonetheless, the quality of that life will affect to some degree the traditions, class interests, and group ambitions that enter into the patterns of history.

It is fidelity to the academic mission of the university that is imperiled by politicization. By its very nature in the marketplace of public opinion, a political decision must have a partisan character no matter how enlightened such a decision may appear to those who support it. When the university as an institution or corporate body, as distinct from individual faculty members exercising their duties as citizens, takes an official stand on any policy in dispute, it abandons its academic mission. It becomes an instrument of ends and purposes extrinsic to its own. Although this view would have been considered commonplace during the years in which John Dewey and Arthur O. Lovejoy founded the American Association of University Professors, since the 1960s it has come under continuous criticism and challenge.

Three generic lines of criticism have developed of the view that the academic mission of the university requires a position of principled neutrality or nonpartisanship. The first is that such political neutrality is impossible; therefore the requirement is impossible and its pursuit unwise. The second criticism is that universities have in the past always taken political positions and that the demand or even expectation that they eschew taking political decisions in the present is naive or hypocritical. The third criticism charges inconsistency in the thinking and action of those who conceive the academic mission as incompatible with political partisanship. The incompatibility, it is alleged, results from the advocacy of official public stands by the university on matters affecting academic freedom. If the university can take an official stand on a matter as important as academic freedom, it is justified in taking an official stand on other matters equally or more important in human affairs.

The argument that unpolitical or depoliticized higher education is impossible is based on the premise that all education, regardless of its professions, is political. The attempt to purify education of political bias would result in the abolition of liberal education, for it would mean that the curriculum would have to forgo the study of the state, political thought, and political behavior. Every institution has a political dimension—the school no less than the church and the family. The fact that the source of support of universities is either public or private, through tax-exempt subsidies, is proof that a political commitment is involved. To the extent that the church and family are protected by a complex body of legislative statutes, they, too, have a political complexion. "No politics in the university" is itself a political cry. Those who defend the university against demands that it be "radicalized" are taking a position just as overtly political as those whom they are criticizing. Let us therefore have done with the pretense that the mission of the university is not political but scholarship of a politically neutral kind. Those who speak of the mission of the university in this way are either intellectually dishonest or intellectually incompetent. The question is not whether the university should be political—for the upshot of this analysis is that it must be—but what kind of politics it should espouse. So runs the argument.

What shall we make of it? This argument in many variations was advanced not only by radical students during the 1960s but by some professors as well. At first blush it seems to be based on a violent abuse of language. It defines the term "political" in such a way that the exercise of a value judgment in every field is political. As applied to human affairs, the term "political" would then have no intelligible opposite, so that by definition, all human institutions, the university, the church, professional associations, even the family and kindergarten, would be political. As well say, "To be is to be political."

All of a piece with this mode of argument is the contention that there is really no difference between teaching and indoctrination since they are both goal directed. This ignores the crucial difference between teaching that aims to induce belief by argument and evidence and teaching that resorts to nonrational or irrational means of persuasion. Some of the bolder spirits in this descent into absurdity often deny that there is any such thing as objective truth, meaning not that its achievement is difficult or that it is unwarranted to claim to know the whole truth about anything but that the very concepts of objectivity and truth are vacuous, question-begging, and therefore unintelligible expressions.

Those who oppose the politicization of the university certainly do not mean that the study of politics be eschewed or that the political rights of the faculty as citizens of the community be in any way curtailed. They contend that the university as an institution should not espouse any particular brand of politics and that the academic freedom of the individual faculty member bestows no right to violate accepted standards of professional ethics in inquiry and teaching or corresponding immunities from disciplinary action when these standards have been violated.

The second argument for politicization of the university takes its point of departure from historical truth and uses it to justify a questionable policy. The truth is that for many centuries the university as an institution did have a specific political character and often took positions on controversial current political issues. It is therefore argued that such politicization is natural and, where the politics is right, desirable. As it stands the argument is an obvious non sequitur. The historical facts are that for many centuries the universities of the Western world were committed to religious dogmas and that membership or belief in certain religious confessions was a requirement for membership in the academic community as teacher or student. But the vast majority of those who advocate or even tolerate the politicization of the university would certainly not wish to restore religious belief or faith as a pillar of the university today. The truths of history, whatever they are, cannot be decisive in formulating satisfactory policy in any field in the present.

Actually, the history to which resort is made is highly selective and truncated. It omits the significant historical fact that uncertain progress of academic freedom in the Western world is largely the history of university secularization and depoliticization. This is especially true of American colleges and universities. The recognition of, and struggle for, academic freedom in the United States was based on the realization that the meaning of academic freedom for scholars and teachers required the emancipation of institutions of higher education from the religious and political commitments of university boards of governance. This was vividly brought home to me when I served on the Council of the American Association of University Professors (AAUP) in the 1930s—a period in which the principles of academic freedom were formulated. The gist of these principles, expressed in different ways by John Dewey and Arthur Lovejoy, was that academic freedom was the freedom of professionally qualified persons to seek, teach, and publish the truth as they saw it in the field of their inquiry, subject to no restrictions or limitations except those flowing from the standards of professional ethics. The acceptance of this principle of academic freedom raised in some minds the question of the very legitimacy of religiously oriented colleges and universities. A special statement was drawn up by the AAUP in which the right of such colleges and universities to regard themselves as institutions of higher education was grudgingly acknowledged, subject to their willingness to define clearly in advance the narrow area in which doctrinal orthodoxy would be expected. It is not necessary to deny that some great works of scholarship were achieved in periods in which academic freedom was absent any more than that great works of art were painted when artists lacked artistic freedom. The evidence is overwhelming, however, that in areas in which academic freedom prevails, especially in the sciences, far greater fruitfulness results whenever respect for the dignity of the uncoerced mind and will flourishes.

The relevant American history for our purpose is the emergence and widespread recognition, in the first half of the twentieth century, of the validity of the principles of academic freedom in university life and their gross violation during the 1960s, when attempts were made to capture the university for purposes of social reconstruction.

The third argument for politicization stems from the willingness of the defenders of academic freedom not merely to countenance but to urge universities, as corporate bodies, to endorse measures to further academic freedom, to protest when violations of academic freedom take place, and to engage in a whole cluster of other activities in this direction. It is asked: If such practices are legitimate, why can't the university endorse other political positions and take overt political stands?

The simple but adequate answer is that the university's stand for academic freedom falls within the pursuit of its academic missions in a way in which its support for or against free enterprise, for or against political democracy, does not. Individual members of the academic community are free to approve or oppose economic freedom or political democracy both in their scholarly judgments and in their civic capacities. That is what is meant by academic freedom—an individual's qualifications and tenure as a teacher do not depend on anything except scholarly and professional behavior. An individual's judgment does not commit the university. On the other hand, when the university as a corporate body takes a particular stand on anything, it commits all of its teachers, some of whom may be in strong opposition to that stand.

There are some difficult cases in which the exact bearing and scope of the university's concern for academic freedom may be hard to determine. It is clear that the abridgment of freedom of inquiry and teaching and the expulsion or imprisonment of dissident or heretical scholars in communist and fascist universities are legitimately subject to rebuke by universities as corporate bodies. But it does not follow from this that the university, as integral to its academic mission, is warranted in condemning communism or fascism as forms of social organization. The university may rightfully protest discrimination against students and teaching staff on racial or religious grounds, but this does not necessarily require that it *officially* condemn churches and governments as such. To the extent that the university officially condemns the absence of academic freedom in any university, it is implicitly condemning any form of society that requires the suppression of academic freedom.

A few years ago, the question of defense-related research in its bearings on academic freedom agitated the campuses of the nation. There has been a curious confusion about this subject. One can only call bizarre the spectacle of individuals demanding that the university commit itself to explicitly political positions on questions of war and peace and at the same time protesting the presence of voluntarily accepted defense research projects as a violation of the principles of academic freedom. The blatant disregard of the academic freedom of scholars to pursue such research is not the only inconsistency in this attitude. It ignores the well-attested fact that defense-related research projects on the campuses of our major universities during the war against fascism had no adverse effects on the practices of academic freedom in those or other areas.

The argument in justification of such research is a simple but compelling one. Academic freedom, as understood in the United States or as defined by all professional organizations, can survive only in a free society. Consequently, those who wish to defend academic freedom have a moral responsibility to defend free society within the limits of their power. Research on defense projects may be necessary to defend free society in an age when the sudden death of cultures is possible. But is not the presence of classified or secret research incompatible with the practice of academic freedom? Not necessarily, as the experience of World War II demonstrates. The alarm over the aspects of secrecy involved in such research is largely a red herring. To be sure, the campus is not the best locus for classified research; it can be pursued elsewhere. Except in situations of national emergency, there is no need to conduct classified research on campuses. And the university is always free to decline grants if accompanying conditions do not suit it. Incidentally, it has not been unknown for members of a department on the eve of important breakthroughs in an area unrelated to defense or national security to pursue policies of strict secrecy without consequences adverse to the practice of academic freedom—or even without provoking criticism by their colleagues.

When we look at the academic scene today, from what quarters do threats of politicization emanate? To some extent from the fallout of the 1960s and early 1970s, when both administrations and faculties of many of our most prestigious universities capitulated to the demands of politically motivated student rebels and threw the corporate weight of their institutions into the political battles of the day. In October 1969 some went so far as to suspend classes and officially endorsed the "moratorium" against the Vietnam involvement. At the time of the entry of American troops into Cambodia, many more not only officially suspended classes but canceled examinations and commencements. Few took disciplinary measures to prevent the disruption of speeches of those whose views were uncongenial to student rebels.

The memory of this period is still alive. It becomes fresh whenever proposals are made for academic communities as a body to take a position on the "nuclear freeze" or similar issues.

Perhaps the most palpable evidence of the politicization of higher education is the transformation of the program of affirmative action from a principled commitment to *refrain* from invidious discrimination on the basis of race, sex, and national origin into a program of social action and change. Whereas the original executive orders for affirmative action prescribed the use of one standard of judgment in appraising the merit of all applicants for admission or promotion, the current interpretation in academe explicitly takes into consideration racial, ethnic, and sexual factors. Where there is marked disparity in the numerical composition of successful candidates as measured by the proportions in the general population or in the pool of the potentially qualified, it is assumed that practices of invidious discrimination have been followed. The underlying motive in this perversion of the civil service principle of fairness to the individual, which was the gist of affirmative action as originally conceived, is to reform or modify the social structure so that both sexes and all minorities share proportionately to their numbers in the distribution of offices and rewards at every level. Whatever may be said in justification of this Procrustean project and newly minted quota system, it certainly is not entailed by dedication to the academic mission of the university. On the contrary, with respect to cases in which the best qualified are passed over, it is in flat conflict with it.

An even more flagrant illustration of the politicization of the university is observable today on many campuses in which women's studies, black studies, Chicano studies, and the like have been integrated into the curriculum. These are legitimate studies and when properly taught relevant to the educational needs of some students. But almost universally, the selection of the personnel to teach these studies is determined by ideological considerations. One will not find a scholar who is opposed to the perversion of affirmative action programs into quota systems or to preferential hiring or reverse discrimination selected to teach black studies. Nor will any woman, however well qualified, be appointed to teach in women's studies who is opposed to the Equal Rights Amendment.

The pursuit of objective truth is integral to the academic mission; although truth is not always attainable, honest inquiry in the quest for it always is or should be the goal. For some strange reason some have contended that the denial of the fact/value distinction makes this description of the academic mission otiose. However, the denial of the distinction itself presupposes a fact that is not affected by any value judgment, unless a judgment of fact is *identified* with a judgment of value. Even those who maintain that the distinction between fact and value cannot be sustained themselves argue that better grounds exist for advocating one policy or judgment of value—their own—rather than for others. The validity of the *grounds* is deemed an objective fact, independent of the value being appraised. The university curriculum does not and should not regard judgments of policy, value, or worth as beyond the purview of rational inquiry. That is why it cannot make adherence to any dogma beyond challenge. That is why no university faithful to its academic mission can declare that it accepts as a final unchallengeable truth the moral validity of free enterprise or collectivist economy. That is why the university should not proscribe the political beliefs of any individual teacher, whether they be fascist or communist or what not, provided they are independently arrived at, not dictated by an outside group, and honestly presented together with their alternatives.

There is no objection to the existence of different schools of thought in the universities. They have always been there in various disciplines, especially psychology and the social sciences. Normally they do not constitute a threat to academic freedom or the mission of the university, for there is nothing in their doctrines that requires them to engage in practices that violate the principles of academic freedom. In the light of this analysis, there can be no objection to Marxists on the teaching staffs of universities, that is to say, to scholars whose point of view in research, publication, and teaching is based on the open acceptance of the validity of key Marxist doctrines. The difficulty arises from the variety of conceptions and practices embraced by some avowed Marxists who interpret and apply Marx's doctrines in such a way, falsely on my view, as to justify violations of academic freedom. The nub of that difficulty is to be found in conceptions of Marxism that require its adherents to engage in what they call "revolutionary praxis," by which is meant efforts to transform the capitalist world by actions such as mass strikes, political organization of the workplace (in this case departments and classrooms), and other strategies on the road to power. When Marx spoke of revolutionary praxis, he was addressing himself to the working classes, urging them to direct their activities to the overthrow of the wage system. He was not addressing himself to the professoriate, whom he certainly did not regard as part of the proletariat.

When Marxists believe that their acceptance of Marxism commits them to a program of revolutionary activity, not merely in the sphere of citizenship and the marketplace, but in the academy, they may become involved in activities incompatible with principles of academic freedom, such as preparing the way for new accessions to the department primarily on the basis of ideological loyalty, barring the way of potential colleagues who are non-Marxist or anti-Marxist, proselytizing students to adopt their doctrinal positions, and converting their classrooms into propaganda sessions for the party line, whatever it may be at the moment. This strategy, recommended by Marxists like Mao Zedong in Asia and Gramsci in Europe, has sometimes been called "the long march through the institutions of bourgeois society." The point is that the practices to which it leads would be wrong and intolerable from the point of view of the academic mission of the university, no matter what the ideology in whose name it was being justified. At the present time, however, I know of no other ideological tendency, with the possible exception of those who wish to Christianize the university, that professes this view. It has an echo in this country among some Marxists. The most notable instance is the case of Bertram Ollman, a Marxist professor at New York University, who in discussing the questions of objective teaching and indoctrination wrote:

> If non-Marxists see my concern with such questions as an admission that the purpose of my course is to convert students to socialism, I can only answer that in my view—a view which denies the fact/value distinction—a correct understanding of Marxism (as indeed of any body of scientific truths) leads automatically to its acceptance.[1]

The plain implication of this passage is that if students are not converted to Marxism by Ollman, they have given proof positive that despite his labors they have not understood it, and presumably must be judged accordingly. This shocking statement, among other things, reveals a scandalously perverse misconception of the nature of the scientific method. The understanding of a statement in science does *not* lead to such assent to its truth. One can understand an assertion in science or any discipline perfectly and yet reject it in the light of the evidence as false. One can easily understand what it means to say that X is innocent (or guilty), and yet reject the statement as false. If Ollman was right, we would have no need of experiment in science to test the validity of any assertion. We could not even experiment without begging the question. Nor does it follow that the denial of the fact/value distinction requires one to believe the absurd proposition that meaning and truth are logically equivalent and the still more absurd consequences that flow from it.

Ollman's behavior is of a piece with his thought. It is significant that even before he was recommended, by a questionably competent search committee, to be head of the political science department at the University of Maryland and before the recommendation had been submitted to the president of the institution for approval, he had invited another avowed Marxist professor to come to Maryland for interviews so that he might be considered for hiring as a member of the faculty.[2]

It bears repeating that professors holding *any* views who interpreted and acted on them as Ollman is prepared to do with respect to his Marxism would have rendered themselves *ipso facto* unfit to exercise their professional obligations properly. They would be violating the principles of academic freedom. In justice to other Marxist scholars, it should be pointed out that not all of them hold their views as Ollman does his.

How can the politicization of the university be prevented? Certainly not by state intervention, even when universities are dependent on state subsidies. It is the faculties themselves that must take the responsibility for enforcing the standards of professional integrity. In the past they have shown courage in withstanding onslaughts against academic freedom from without. But they have been notoriously weak in resisting violations of their academic mission from within. The growth of academic self-governance has not been accompanied by a heightened consciousness of the necessity of self-discipline in preserving the integrity of the educational process. There has been an insufficient recognition of the academic obligations and duties correlative to the rights guaranteed by academic freedom.

Notes

1. "On Teaching Marxism," *The Insurgent Socialist* 6, no. 4 (Summer 1976): 37–50.
2. Cf. the opinion of Justice Alexander Harvey in the case of *Ollman v. Toll*, July 21, 1981, in the United States District Court for the District of Maryland, Case No. H-78-1402, p. 26.

20
Civil Rights: The Reagan Record

John H. Bunzel

It would be an understatement to say that the Reagan administration's civil rights policies have received critical reviews. Civil rights leaders have bitterly attacked the president for undermining and reversing the civil rights policies of his predecessors and for dismantling the federal affirmative action machinery set up during the 1970s to enforce the rights of women and minority groups. They charge that actions taken by the administration to relax the rules and regulations—for example, reducing the number of companies required to conform to affirmative action quotas—have lessened the pressure to investigate and prosecute civil rights violations, thereby narrowing the campaign against discrimination started years ago. When President Reagan took office, the civil rights leadership (in the words of the *New York Times*) "had all but disappeared," and popular support for an activist civil rights agenda was in decline. Furthermore, civil rights leaders did not want to run the risk of isolating themselves politi-

---

In the course of preparing this essay, I interviewed more than a dozen people, some in the White House and others working in or closely identified with the administration, on the general subject of civil rights since 1981. In exchange for their candid comments, their names have not been used.

cally by attacking in his first year a president who had been elected by a landslide. Today there is no such reluctance. In every available forum, they now denounce the president for "retreating from civil rights" and abandoning the struggle against racism and injustice.

The administration's response has been to have the president reiterate as often as possible his determination to "root out any case of government discrimination . . . we will not retreat on the Nation's commitment to equal treatment of all citizens," and to make public what the White House believes is a solid but neglected record of accomplishment in the area of civil rights, including special attention to long-standing problems of mismanagement and inefficiency in the compliance, investigation, and enforcement efforts of the federal government. In its first year the administration became convinced that there was substantial duplication in the activities of agencies charged with eliminating discrimination and that "their collective effectiveness in doing so was diminished as resources were squandered in fruitless competition for jurisdiction."[1]

The administration has consistently argued that simply spending money on civil rights does not guarantee that they will be secured. It insists that it has judged civil rights programs on their merits and not treated them as the budgetary equivalents of "sacred cows," to be increased or maintained on a quota basis (only to be ignored during the remainder of the year). The administration has increased expenditures for some civil rights programs, including federal efforts to assure protection of each person's fundamental rights, nondiscrimination in federally assisted programs and activities, equal employment opportunity, fair housing, and equal credit, as well as civil rights–related research activities.[2] Other civil-rights expenditures have been decreased; many others have been maintained at the same level.

The achievements especially emphasized by the administration in the area of constitutional and civil rights reflect its particular interests and concerns. The following is a partial listing:[3]

- During 1982, the FBI completed 7,983 investigations of alleged violations of the fundamental rights of institutionalized persons. It expects to perform in excess of 10,000 such investigations per year through 1984. Other components of the Department of Justice completed 3,600 investigations of such violations in 1982, and the department expects this number to increase to 3,800 in 1984.
- The Criminal Section of the department's Civil Rights Division is responsible for prosecuting criminal civil rights violations.

During 1982, the section reviewed approximately 3,200 matters investigated by the FBI and approximately 7,100 other inquiries and complaints and presented the results of 81 investigations to federal grand juries. As a result, 50 indictments were returned and six informations were filed charging a total of 98 defendants. Trials were conducted in 43 cases, resulting in the conviction of 23 defendants. Another 25 defendants tendered guilty pleas.

- To assure that statutory protections of the right to vote are maintained and strengthened, the president signed the Voting Rights Amendments of 1982 into law. Partly as a result of the administration's efforts, the act did not include language, found in earlier versions of the legislation, that could have been interpreted as requiring proportional representation based on race or national origin.

- During 1982, the Department of Justice was particularly active in enforcing the Voting Rights Act and similar statutes. Further, the president's budget provides for a substantial increase in resources devoted to assuring that the presidential election of 1984 is conducted in full compliance with the Voting Rights Act and other federal guarantees of the right to vote. In addition, the Office of Personnel Management (OPM) provides observers to monitor compliance with the Voting Rights Act. During 1982, the OPM assigned 937 observers to two elections. During 1984, the OPM expects to assign 1,350 observers to ten elections in furtherance of the President's commitment to assure that the "crown jewel of America's liberties" is not withheld from any American on the basis of race, color, or membership in a linguistic minority group.

- In 1982, when the "Infant Doe" case revealed that an untold number of infants with disabilities were being denied the care and treatment necessary to sustain life,[4] the president instructed the attorney general and the secretary of the Department of Health and Human Services (HHS) to take immediate steps to notify hospitals receiving federal funds that the statutory prohibitions against discrimination in the provision of services most definitely applied to those services necessary to save and sustain lives.

- The Department of Education's Office for Civil Rights (OCR) undertook a wide range of reforms designed to improve methods for allocating work and measuring performance, reduce the amount of resources wasted on duplicative or otherwise unnecessary paperwork, and eliminate unnecessary levels of management review. The OCR also moved to streamline compliance procedures by implementing the Early Complaint Resolution procedure. As a result of these and other management improvements, the OCR reduced its workload of pending complaints by 27 percent and (in a marked departure from past years) kept abreast of its incoming workload and made progress in eliminating the backlog of complaints from previous years. In addition, in 1982 the office initiated 36 percent more compliance reviews, and completed 16 percent more than in 1981.

- During 1982, the Department of Justice continued to implement its new policy for remedying *de jure* segregation. In past administrations, the department concentrated on simply substituting new patterns of discriminatory assignment of students for old ones, through forced busing. Based solely on race or national origin, such mandates not only excluded many students from the schools they wished to attend but also frequently reassigned students to schools that were no better than those they had previously attended. The department is now securing remedies that assure not only equal access to education, regardless of race or national origin, but also access to education of equal quality.

- In 1981, the Justice Department implemented an approach to remedying employment discrimination different from that of past administrations. (Joseph Califano, former secretary of HHS, reports that he was instructed by President Jimmy Carter to "review the work of our subordinates, and 'get rid of all those who are incompetent, except minorities and women.' "[5]) In place of the employment quotas of the past, the department is requiring employers found to have discriminated to institute specific programs that assure that members of groups previously excluded are considered for future employment opportunities. The department will also assure that genuinely nondiscriminatory procedures are used in selecting from the resulting pool of eligibles.

- During 1982, the Department of Housing and Urban Development (HUD) continued its efforts to expand involvement of state and local agencies in assuring fair housing. HUD obligated over $5 million for direct grants and technical assistance to help state and local agencies develop procedures, train staff, and implement other measures necessary to develop the capacity to process fair housing complaints. As a result, the number of state and local agencies processing complaints grew by 60 percent. Through 1984, HUD expects to increase the number of participating state and local agencies to 90, almost tripling the number in the program at the beginning of 1981. The number of complaints processed at the state and local rather than the federal level will further increase in 1984. The costs of the program, however, will decrease (to $3.7 million a year, mostly for grants to defray the costs of complaint processing) because the initial high outlays for start-up costs will no longer be necessary.

- The administration has continued and expanded the improvements secured during the 1970s in implementing the complaint-processing and enforcement responsibilities of the Equal Employment Opportunity Commission (EEOC). However, the administration found that many endemic management problems remained to be addressed. The General Accounting Office (GAO) and the Office of Personnel Management were asked to assist in the effort to define those problems so that they might be corrected. The GAO found that many of the same record-keeping and financial management problems it had identified in 1976 continued to exist in 1981. For example, the EEOC had no accurate records of the money owed it, and the personnel responsible for handling its funds were poorly supervised and trained and their duties not adequately separated to preclude fraud and waste. Compounding these difficulties, necessary financial management audits were not being performed because the agency's internal audit staff was too small. After reviewing the deficiencies discovered by the GAO and the administration's efforts to correct them, the chairman of the Senate committee responsible for oversight of the EEOC's activities observed:

This administration and this committee have been criticized for lack of commitment to civil rights, yet . . . our goal has been that of increasing our efforts at pursuing those goals. Because we ask critical questions and take the studies of GAO seriously, we are accused of being anti–civil rights. I must question whether those who criticize are also the same as those who would allow the conditions which the GAO reviewed at EEOC to continue and thereby deny the services to the people who need the assistance for which the agency was created?[6]

Other civil rights initiatives by the administration include the shielding of minority businesses from budget cuts, President Reagan's explicit support of historically black colleges and universities,[7] and the appointment of Sandra Day O'Connor to the Supreme Court.[8] The president's plan for urban enterprise zones provides significant tax relief for businesses that relocate in impoverished areas and create new jobs for the poor and disadvantaged, especially blacks and Hispanics. As President Reagan said, "It's time for us to find out if the two most dynamic and constructive forces known to man—free enterprise and the profit motive—can be brought to play where government bureaucracy and social programs have failed."

One might assume that many segments of the liberal and minority communities would unanimously condemn the concept as another feeble attempt at further tax giveaways to corporations already reaping the benefits of huge tax reductions that would do nothing to solve urban poverty. But as Norman Hill, president of the A. Philip Randolph Institute, has observed, this is not the case. The president's private sector approach has won the support of both Republicans and Democrats. Moreover, similar enterprise zone legislation introduced in Congress by conservative Republican Jack Kemp and liberal Democrat Robert Garcia is backed by two Democrats in the Senate (Quentin Burdick and Daniel Inouye) and seventeen Democrats in the House. At a time of massive cutbacks in social spending, says Hill, "some liberals apparently are willing to grasp at straws in the wind."

Those who are skeptical of the president's plan will revise their thinking only if there are unanticipated and surprising answers—meaning solid results—to some of the questions they have raised. For example, will new jobs actually be created, or will those corporations that find enterprise zones attractive enough to relocate simply transfer their facilities? Is there any assurance that the minority poor will be trained in the skills necessary to survive in today's increasingly complex economy? Will the enterprise zone program provide "up-front" money to enable marginal businesses to take advantage of the plan's big tax breaks? Or will only prosperous businesses with sufficient capital to move into an enterprise zone derive significant tax reductions?

In spite of rising criticism of the administration's record in the area of programs for the poor, Mr. Reagan has never wavered in his belief that the disadvantaged "would be appreciably better off today" if the Great Society had never been inaugurated. He has repeatedly stated that the economic health of the 1950s was destroyed by the Great Society of President Lyndon Johnson because "government began eating away at the underpinnings of the private enterprise system." This is vintage Reagan. He has believed for years that "the big taxers and big spenders in the Congress" started a binge that slowly changed the nature of our society "and, even worse, threatened the character of our people." The "wonderful intentions of costly liberal programs" did not create social mobility for black Americans or help the needy but instead "fostered a state of dependency." The way to break this "degrading cycle" is to put a stop to "runaway Government spending that has broken the backs of working people, destroyed incentive and siphoned off resources needed in the private sector to provide new jobs and opportunity."[9]

Although it acknowledges that there are differences over how to achieve equality for all Americans, the Reagan administration has been persistent in claiming that its involvement in assuring civil rights reflects a national commitment to implement the country's highest ideals. It believes its accomplishments in restoring substance to this involvement are significant when judged by traditional measures: resources devoted to civil rights enforcement, management improvements, cases and charges handled, actions brought, settlements reached, and compensation and opportunities restored to wronged individuals. In the president's own words, "sometimes, amidst all the overblown rhetoric, the differences tend to seem bigger than they are. But actions speak louder than words."[10]

The president is surely right. But there have been times when the actions of the White House spoke so loudly of incompetent bungling that all the words of explanation that later followed could not erase the political harm done. The announcement that the administration would revoke the twelve-year-old government policy of denying tax exemptions to private schools that discriminate against blacks created such an instant and powerful protest that President Reagan was forced to backtrack within a matter of days. He explained that he personally favored the policy and would ask Congress for legislation forbidding exemptions for schools that discriminate, something the Internal Revenue Service had been doing since 1969 under a body of law, policy, and precedent. Congress ignored the president's request on the ground that the law was already clear. It was a monumental mistake (the president publicly acknowledged that the whole matter had been badly handled), among other reasons because it reinforced the perception that the Reagan administration was totally insensitive to the vital interests of the black community.

The whole controversy over private-school tax exemptions spilled over into the debate on the details of the bill to extend the Voting Rights Act, which came to the Senate in late January 1982. The administration had always favored extending the law but opposed Section 2 of the House version, which, in the opinion of the Justice Department (and other witnesses called to testify), changed the standard of having to show discriminatory intent to a new demand that the ballot box, although "equally open" to everyone, must yield equal results for certain racial minorities. The principal concern was that such a radically new electoral process would further proportional representation based on race. In addition to failing to make its position clear on this complex issue when it was before the House, the White House quickly discovered, in the words of a key administration supporter in the Senate, that "the IRS tragedy mucked up the government's ability to have any influence at all on the Voting Rights debate. They had been so badly wounded by the fiasco over the tax-exempt status of discriminatory schools that they had no political leverage." Put very simply, the administration had lost its credibility.

But the Reagan White House has a more fundamental problem in the area of civil rights. There has been a considerable gap between rhetoric and action in the approach of the White House to affirmative action—specifically, with respect to what policies to pursue and actions to take in light of Mr. Reagan's frequently expressed view that race, sex, and color are inappropriate tests of an individual's worth and his belief in the color-blind concept of nondiscrimination embodied in the Civil Rights Act of 1964. It is as if there were a certain schizophrenia running through the administration's whole posture, leading many observers to wonder if this might help explain why the White House appears to have found it difficult to decide whether race- and sex-conscious employment practices (mandated by the federal government for more than a dozen years) are "an issue of principle or a problem of paperwork."[11] It is not clear from the record whether the White House is committed by deep conviction to implementing a return to the basic principle that all government contractors should take affirmative action to eliminate all forms of discrimination based on race, color, religion, sex, or national origin, or feels it should direct its primary efforts merely to trying to reform an overly intrusive federal civil rights bureaucracy that has increasingly arrogated to itself the authority to set broad policies by regulatory fiat. The vacillation about what it should do and how it should proceed reveals, at the very least, the way that principle, pragmatism, and compromise are combined in the Reagan presidency.

Generally speaking, under the leadership of William Bradford Reynolds, assistant attorney general for civil rights, the Justice Department has been the most persistent advocate within the administration of reversing the tide of affirmative action policies that have led to governmental race-consciousness, the remedial use of class-based preferences, and the blurring of the concept of racial neutrality into the concept of racial balance. The department's principal effort has been to bring about some positive changes in the area of civil rights law, in the belief that "the acceptance of race as a valid selection criterion can only delay, rather than hasten, arrival of the day when race is rendered irrelevant and the ideal of a color-blind society is realized."[12] Thus, in two important reverse discrimination cases in December 1982 and January 1983, it intervened on the side of whites in a Boston racial layoff quota case and sought to overturn a court ruling in New Orleans under which the city promised to promote black and white police officers on a one-to-one quota basis. Both decisions represented significant departures from the policies of previous administrations.

The Justice Department has also taken action in cases involving mandatory busing. In the Nashville, Tennessee, case, it filed an *amicus* brief with the Supreme Court, arguing that the Court of Appeals erred in reversing a district court's ruling that mandatory busing in grades one through four has yielded a decade of unsatisfactory results and ought to be replaced with other desegregation measures. Although the Supreme Court declined to review the case, the filing demonstrated the department's determination to seek reversal of what it regards as the ill-advised path that the law of school desegregation has followed for over a decade. It also filed briefs with the Supreme Court supporting statewide initiatives in California and Washington that sought to outlaw mandatory busing by school districts to correct *de facto* racial segregation in public schools (that is, racial segregation brought about by phenomena—demographic shifts—unconnected with any type of government coercion). It won the California case, but lost the Washington one. In the Chicago school desegregation case, the department supported a school plan that relied wholly on voluntary desegregation methods; mandatory busing was not even a backup component of the plan. The district court accepted the all-voluntary plan, remarking that it was the approach most likely to bring meaningful and stable desegregation to Chicago's public school system.

Although the Justice Department has consistently decried race-conscious affirmative action policies and practices, the position of the White House has been far more cautious and often ambivalent. When

Assistant Attorney General Reynolds pledged that the administration "will no longer insist upon, or in any respect support, the use of quotas or any other numerical or statistical formulae designed to provide nonvictims of discrimination preferential treatment based on race, sex, national origin, or religion,"[13] he was speaking more for his own Civil Rights Division than for those in the White House who work closely with the president. *Fortune* magazine's Daniel Seligman put it very simply: "If you view reverse discrimination as the main issue—which is the way it has been cast in much Reaganite rhetoric—then clearly the main issue is not to be tackled. The Administration plans to leave in place the goals and timetables that have hitherto constituted an irresistible pressure for preference."[14] While advisers to the president insist that color-blind hiring is still the "ultimate goal," it is also true that the White House has arrived at policy decisions about affirmative action not by consulting some moral touchstone but by calculating the political costs.

The president's chief of staff, James Baker, describes the process by which policy positions are reached as one of "tension or competition among alternative judgments about policies or tactics." When Mr. Reagan came into office, he wanted "ideologically rooted policy analysts, tested in their loyalty to his principles, and he wanted practically oriented implementers, tested by their experience. I think he got both," says Baker, adding that "properly managed, it is a formula for success in advancing an ideology, while adapting as necessary to the practical dictates of a less than fully accommodating reality."[15] It is the same formula that Ronald Reagan has used ever since he became governor of California; namely, to say clearly and unambiguously what he believes and wants in speeches, radio broadcasts, and the like—and then settle politically for as much as he can get. Those who have said (correctly) that President Reagan is one of the most ideological presidents ever to occupy the White House have frequently failed to observe that he is also a skilled compromiser.

It is this very system of what Baker calls "multiple advocacy with multiple honest brokers," as applied in the area of civil rights, that has angered and saddened many of the president's strongest supporters. They do not believe that the quota-ridden machinery of affirmative action implemented in the 1970s, which the 1980 Republican platform explicitly opposed and the president campaigned against, should be met with irresolution or compromise. They go further. "It isn't that the White House doesn't know what to do," one high official in the administration remarked privately. "It just hasn't had the courage to do it for fear of the political fallout." Another influential colleague said that White House policymakers are "filled with uncertainty about how to deal with affirmative action because they have not been willing to address the basic principles. The color-blind standard which President Reagan believes in has never been elevated to a recognizable priority position. Why? Because to this day the principle is not settled."

He cited as an example of the continuing vacillation in the White House the Department of Labor's plans to issue new regulations that would ease affirmative action requirements for businesses doing work for the federal government. "All the proposed new rules would do is relax the paperwork burdens on employers, make it easier to do compliance reviews, and institutionalize flexible quotas," he said. "They make changes on the periphery, but they skirt the issues many of us maintain are matters of principle—whether, for example, employment hiring is to be race-conscious. That's one of the basic tenets of affirmative action that this administration is clearly opposed to—as it turns out, I'm afraid, only in words. Those in the White House on the other side believe that half a loaf is better than none. I understand that. But some of us don't think you can have half a principle."

Another person who wants the White House to "reassess the fundamentals" is even blunter. "At no time has the debate on civil rights policy been redefined. It's the bureaucracy that has framed the options. No one has yet presented to the president a set of distinct policy choices," he says. "The discussions that have taken place have been episodic and idiosyncratic. All we've really done since we've been in office is take the Democrats' affirmative action programs, knock 'em down three notches, underfund them, and call them ours."

In the early months of the Reagan administration in 1981, the troubled economy and the nation's defense posture were the principal concerns of the White House and occupied most of the attention of the Cabinet. In addition, work was immediately begun on the 1982 budget. "No one wanted to deal with civil rights as a priority issue early on," another high-ranking official commented. "A few attempts were made to stress its importance and there was some polite listening, but that's all. The economy was the critical worry. We were always told there wasn't enough time to deal with civil rights. Unfortunately," he added, "a lot of people concluded—and there was some truth to it—that the new administration really wasn't that interested. That's always been something of a problem for Republicans, especially conservative Republicans. I don't think the policymakers in the White House really knew what they *should* do even if they had felt they had the time. Anyway, no one was thinking much about a new approach or set of ideas in the area of civil rights."

In early 1983, a senior White House aide confirmed that the administration had been preoccupied with the economy and defense. "This did not mean that we weren't interested in taking a fresh look at the whole domain of civil rights," he said. "But sometimes the urgent has to take precedence over the important."

He was asked if any consideration was ever given to having President Reagan seize the initiative in his first days in office and issue a new executive order to all departments—in particular, the Department of Labor—banning racially preferential treatment, goals, and timetables and, with a stroke of the pen, return to a color-blind system of antidiscrimination.

"I don't think the idea was ever even discussed," he said. "Besides, we always had to keep in mind that too bold or strident a change would feed the attack of minority groups. These things are always politically symbolic, and we didn't want to create the wrong symbols. You have to remember that the politics of this is an inhibitor of taking action. Even simply to raise some issues," he added, "is fraught with risks downwind. The political costs can be heavy."

He knew that public opinion polls have regularly shown that the American people—by wide margins—are opposed not only to quotas but any form of absolute preference and do not support affirmative action when it is carried to the point of reverse discrimination. "But we have a real political dilemma," he said. "There is no natural constituency working against the civil rights groups, which are well organized. Maybe the president should have tried to reach and appeal to public opinion. The truth is," he conceded, "we never really defined for ourselves which route we were going to take in dealing with civil rights."

Many observers believe that the key to the initial successes of the White House in getting Congress to pass a big tax cut and make substantial spending reductions was the president's capacity to deal with his ideological convictions in a strategic manner. Part of this strategy has been for Mr. Reagan to distance himself as much as possible from politically costly social issues. Daniel Seligman may be right in saying that nobody in the highest levels of the administration "now has the heart to throw on the table any large initiatives in the civil rights area."[16] It is a good bet that some of the persistent demands of the self-styled "truly committed" affirmative actionists—among them, that governmental race-consciousness, quotas, and preferential treatment are necessary "to get beyond racism" in American society—will be ratified, not overturned, by Ronald Reagan's presidency.

Notes

1. U.S. Office of Management and Budget, "Special Analysis J: Civil Rights Activities," *Special Analyses: Budget of the United States Government, Fiscal Year 1984.* (Washington, D.C., 1983), p. J-2. This document presents an excellent overview of the president's budget proposal for each federal agency as well as analyses highlighting different program areas.
2. Ibid., p. J-3.
3. I have cited examples and used the language in "Special Analysis J" because this report is the best summary of many of the administration's major concerns regarding civil rights problems and policies.
4. The "Infant Doe" case was a well-publicized incident in which a child with disabilities born in Bloomington, Indiana, died as the result of the denial of lifesaving care.
5. Joseph A. Califano, *Governing America: An Insider's Report from the White House and the Cabinet* (New York: Simon & Schuster, 1981), p. 341.
6. Quoted in "Special Analysis J," p. J-21.
7. The president signed an executive order strengthening the federal commitment to these institutions, and the administration has provided $9.6 million in additional Title III funding (an 8 percent increase). The administration also moved quickly to save Meharry Medical College (which has trained more than 40 percent of all black physicians) not only by providing several million dollars in assistance to the medical school but also by acting to expand the Veterans Administration's affiliation with it. Such expanded affiliation had been sought by Meharry, without success, through several previous administrations.
8. The White House hoped that the appointment of the first woman to the U.S. Supreme Court would signal the proper message—namely, that the new administration was sensitive to the concerns of women. But since 1981 there has been a sharp decline in support for President Reagan among women, which, as the 1984 election approaches, is a major worry of the White House. One reason is that, until recently, few women were considered or selected for high-level positions in the government. As one knowledgeable official in the Reagan administration put it, "I hate to admit it, but there was a lot of implicit sexism—there is no other word for it—in the early days when the administrative team was being put together. Many of the men around Reagan, older and quite set in their ways, just didn't feel comfortable working with women. They never really did. The thought that women might be just as competent as they were never occurred to them. It was pretty much a men's club, and they liked it that way." It was a perception that took root (and has remained) in the minds of many women—and in politics, as every one who knows the stakes fully understands, perception is what must be constantly dealt with. There are, of course, other causes of the "gender gap" now worrying the administration.

9. From an address by President Reagan to the National Black Republican Council on September 15, 1982. More recently, the president has also called for increased jobs spending and education to help prepare young workers for meaningful jobs in growing industries.
10. "Special Analysis J," p. J-32.
11. Chester E. Finn, Jr., " 'Affirmative Action' Under Reagan," *Commentary*, April 1982, p. 27.
12. *Ibid.*, p. 22.
13. Quoted in an address by Charles J. Cooper, deputy assistant attorney general, Civil Rights Division, Department of Justice, to the Equal Employment Advisory Council Seminar, February 10, 1983, p. 13.
14. Daniel Seligman, "Affirmative Action Is Here to Stay," *Fortune*, April 19, 1983, p. 144. The statement by Mr. Reynolds appears on the same page.
15. From remarks by James Baker during a panel discussion at Princeton University as reported in the *Princeton Alumni Weekly*, March 23, 1983, p. 15.
16. Seligman, "Affirmative Action Is Here to Stay," p. 162.

21
Demographic Dilemmas in the Mid-1980s

Kingsley Davis

The United States has never had an explicit domestic population policy. It has had such a policy for American aid to Third World countries, but at home—despite the urging of the Commission on Population Growth and the American Future (appointed by President Nixon) and *The Global 2000 Report to the President* (initiated by President Carter)[1]—it has had only policies that, incidentally and often unintentionally, affected the size, growth, and composition of the population.

Although I think the formulation of an overall national population policy would be desirable, my purpose in the present essay is not to argue that point but rather to outline some of the major demographic dilemmas that now, in one way or another, challenge national policy.

The dilemmas can be phrased in terms of questions: Will the country continue to increase its population by large numbers each year? Will it continue to accept more immigrants, legal and illegal, than any other in the world? Will it continue to be satisfied with a very low birthrate? How will it adjust to a rapid aging of the population? How will the United States cope with continued world population growth and the wide disparity in growth between Third World and advanced countries?

Discussion of these questions will involve many aspects of American policy. Let us start with the central question, the overall size of the nation's population.

How Many People Do We Want?

In the media there is currently some confusion about our population growth. After pointing out that the birthrate is below replacement, commentators often draw the conclusion that the population is either stagnant or declining and that there is thus no need to worry. Also, commentators often cite rates without mentioning absolute figures.

Actually, the intercensal increase in the American population between 1970 and 1980—23.92 million—was the second highest on record. The highest increase, 27.67 million, occurred between 1950 and 1960, and the third highest, 23.91 million (almost as high as in 1970–1980), occurred between 1960 and 1970. All told, the increase in the nation's population from 1950 to 1980 was 76.5 million, slightly more than the entire population of the nation in 1900. After the first census in 1790, it took 113 years for the United States to add as many people as it added in 30 years after 1950.

With such numbers being added, why the widespread impression of stabilization? One reason is the tendency to look at rates rather than absolute numbers. The rate of increase in the U.S. population has been around 1 percent per annum since 1970, whereas from 1940 to 1970 it was almost 1.5 percent. Even at 1 percent, however, a population will double in 69 years; and since the base gets larger, the 1 percent yields an ever greater absolute number.

Another source of confusion is that demographers use abstract concepts such as "total fertility rate" (TFR) and the "gross reproduction rate" (GRR) that are easily misunderstood. The TFR is the number of births 1,000 women *would* have *if* they *all* lived through the reproductive age and *if,* at each age, they had the rate of childbearing that the actual population had at the given time. The utility of this index is that unlike the crude birthrate—births per 1,000 population—it is independent of the age structure. *If* the age-specific rates of a given date were to continue indefinitely, and *if* the TRF were less than 2,000, the population would not replace itself. This is the current situation in most industrial countries, including the United States. The TFR in the United States fell below 2,000 in 1973 and stayed below, averaging 1,803 during the eight years of 1973 through 1980.

But notice the "if's" in this index. We know that the age-specific rates at any particular time will *not* remain fixed and that, in fact, the actual output of births depends in part on the age structure. Despite its nonreplacement TFR, the United States has, and will long continue to have, an excess of births over deaths. During the twelve years, 1970 through 1981, there were 40.6 million births and 22.5 million deaths, yielding an excess of 18.1 million births. The reason for the excess is that, due to the postwar baby boom, the population has a bulge in the young adult ages (when the probability of pregnancy is high and the probability of death low).

Still more confusion about the nation's population growth arises from forgetting immigration. Unfortunately, we do not know the number of immigrants because many of them are illegal, but we can estimate from censuses and vital statistics that during the twelve years from 1970 through 1981, counting both the migrants and their births, immigration added about 9.9 million to our population, or about 37 percent of the total increase. This, together with the increase of the native population, gave us a total of 27.2 million added during the twelve years.

Does the nation want to keep on adding 20 to 30 million to its population each decade? Would it be better off in terms of air, water, energy, and other resources if it had only half the present population? It is difficult to justify added population but easy to argue against it. For this reason, many people welcome the low fertility now characterizing the United States. But even if the natural increase eventually turns negative, the population will continue to grow unless immigration is stopped. It makes little sense for Americans to deny themselves the number of children they want only to have immigrants fill the vacuum.

The Low Birthrate

There can be no doubt that U.S. fertility is low. The baby boom reached its peak in 1957 (see Table 21.1), after which the birthrate declined swiftly until 1976. After 1976 it recovered slightly, but on average during the late 1970s and 1980s the rate was so low that, on a steady-state basis, 1,000 American women would replace themselves by only some 850 women.

One expects fertility to remain low because that is what young women themselves expect. In 1976–1981, women aged 18–24 anticipated a lifetime average of only 2.03 births.[2]

Table 21.1
High and Low Fertility Rates in the United States

Point in cycle	Date	Births per 1,000 women aged 15–44
Low	1936	75.8
High	1947	113.3
Low	1950	106.2
High	1957	122.7
Low	1976	65.8
?	1982	67.8

Sources: National Center for Health Statistics, *Vital Statistics of the United States, 1978*, vol. 1, *Natality* (Washington, D.C.: Government Printing Office, 1972), p. 5; idem, "Advanced Report of Final Natality Statistics, 1980," *Monthly Vital Statistics Report* 31, no. 8, supplement (November 30, 1982): 9; and idem, "Births, Marriages, Divorces, and Deaths for November 1982," *Monthly Vital Statistics Report* 31, no. 11 (February 11, 1983): 1.

Even if they met their expectations, these women would not replace themselves. But on average they will not meet their expectations because a sizable portion, mostly due to involuntary factors, will have no child or only one. In 1981, among women aged 40–59, the proportion childless was 10.7 percent and the proportion having only one child was 10.3 percent.[3] If this many women cannot meet their expectations or their desires, the rest would have to exceed theirs by a wide margin to attain the overall average expected childbearing rate, but this they will not do.

Why the Low Fertility?

Whatever the explanation of the low birthrate, it cannot be in terms idiosyncratic to the United States because low fertility characterizes virtually all industrial societies. These societies have evidently weakened family incentives while strengthening individual interests apart from the family. In the absence of normative support, the family lacks a strong basis for cohesion. Its members are of different age and different sex, and hence of different interests. Unless external controls are reasonably strong, as in traditional village societies, the family tends to fall apart.

Indeed, norms favoring the family have changed in many ways. The special approval of marriage as a sexual and reproductive relationship has been diluted by widespread acceptance of cohabitation, illegitimacy, and homosexuality. The stability of marriage has been undermined by easier divorce, culminating in no-fault divorce. The complementarity of sex roles has been upset by married women's entry into the labor force. But what lies behind these normative changes? In my view, it is the conditions of life in urban-industrial societies. The surveillance and stability of the village are gone. The division of labor has become extremely complex, in units far larger than the family. Specialized agencies have taken over many services the family once performed for children, reducing parental control and authority. People participate in the economy as individuals rather than as members of families, and the role of the family as a welfare unit has been partially displaced by impersonal agencies.

Some of the major changes can be documented:

1. *The increasing work of married women outside the home.* In 1970, 39.3 percent of married women (husband present) were employed; by 1981, the figure had risen to 47.9 percent.[4]

2. *The rising education of women.* In 1960, women accounted for 34.5 percent of college enrollment; in 1981, for 49.9 percent.[5]

3. *The rise in the divorce rate.* In 1960, there were 35 divorced persons per 1,000 married persons with spouse present; by 1981, there were 109.[6]

4. *The postponement of marriage.* In 1970, only 10.5 percent of women aged 25–29 had never married; by 1981, the proportion had risen to 21.8 percent.[7] Among men, the rise was from 19.1 to 33.8 percent.

5. *The rise in the ratio of illegitimate to legitimate births.* In 1950, only 4 percent of births were to unmarried mothers; by 1980, the ratio reached 18.4 percent.[8]

Some of these trends may be at or near their zenith. For example, the number of first marriages ending in divorce, now about 50 percent, may not climb higher. The postponement of marriage, if people marry at all, has a limit, and the labor force participation of married women, if it continues to rise, will soon rival the participation of men. But the whole package of developments taken together shows little sign of reversing itself, particularly since some of the changes are mutually reinforcing. Postponement of marriage raises the ratio of illegitimate to legitimate births; more education gives women greater career opportunities, which in turn encourage female financial independence and more divorce.

One can look at the changes from children's point of view. Children are now biologically better off than in the past because they are healthier, less likely to die, and more likely to have parents surviving until their adulthood. Socially, however, their situation is more debatable. Their parents may not be married to each other or, if married, may get divorced or else may have been married to others. Children must therefore reckon with the possibility of living in a single-parent household,[9] of having "siblings" who are either half-siblings or unrelated wife's, husband's, or paramour's children. They face the possibility that a parent will have a succession of lovers or that he or she will become sexually deviant. Naturally, children do not accurately perceive these possibilities, but they gain a vague sense of them as they more frequently encounter peers who have experienced family difficulties.

As children reach puberty, their parents may be too preoccupied to give guidance, and other agencies—school, health, police, and church authorities—deal with them without much reference to their family. In planning their own future, children therefore often receive mixed signals. They are not strongly motivated to get married and found a family. To enjoy sexual relations, they do not need to marry, and if they do, they find that it is easy to escape because most states now have "no-fault" divorce by request of either party.

A man does not count on getting traditional services from a wife because she will probably be working. Although her income may be valuable, the extent to which it is for joint use, compared with his income, is uncertain, as is the question of whose job shall determine where the couple will live. Also, the taxes he must pay in a welfare state to support those who are not working and his inability to pay for suitable housing militate against his forming a family. So he postpones marriage or gives it only a halfhearted try.

Similarly, the young woman is not impelled by financial need to look for a husband. She knows that after marriage she will probably continue to work and that marriage *per se* provides little security, emotional or financial. If she has children, she will have a longer period of life after they have left home than she did while they were young. She, like the young man, tends to postpone marriage and, if she does marry, to give it a halfhearted try.

Under these circumstances, the commitment and work involved in having children seem barely worthwhile. A divorced father may have to pay for his children's upkeep and never, or only rarely, be allowed to see them. A divorced mother may receive no help from her ex-husband and thus may have to bring up her children in poverty. Although most Americans value children, they expect to have only two or three. As we have seen, this will not replace the population.

In such terms, one can understand not only the low birthrate, but also the grounds for not expecting it to rise much. Weddings and offspring may return to fashion, but not without major changes in the society. The pronatalist policies usually adopted in welfare states—subsidies for housing, child allowances, maternity leaves—alter the fundamentals too little to succeed. At the moment, Czechoslovakia probably has the most thoroughgoing policy of this sort, but it has not prevented the birthrate from reaching one of the lowest levels in Eastern Europe.[10] Similarly, Sweden, famous as a welfare state, had in 1982 a birthrate only two-thirds as high as that of the United States.

Will Immigration Be Controlled?

If fertility were the sole cause of changes in population, the United States could look forward to a gradual cessation of population growth. Immigration, however, may keep that from happening. Officially, in the three years 1977–1979, the United States admitted an average of 508,000 immigrants per year. Except for three brief periods—1881–1884, 1902–1914, and 1921–1924—this was the largest legal immigration in U.S. history.[11] If data on illegal entrants were available, it might show that immigration has been greater in recent years than in any comparable period; but, unfortunately, there are no precise estimates of illegal immigration. We know only that the net illegal immigration in the 1970s was in the millions.[12]

What is the evidence that this migration, most of it from Third World countries such as Mexico, El Salvador, Jamaica, South Korea, Colombia, Nigeria, Haiti, Hong Kong, and Vietnam serves the long-run interest of the United States? The usual justification is short-run—namely, that immigrants "take jobs that nobody else wants." If true, there must be something wrong with native motivation for work because the nation's unemployment rate, especially among the young and unskilled, is running at high levels. It seems likely that, to a considerable extent, immigrants compete directly with the very groups in the native population whom we most wish to see employed. In 1981, among youths aged 16–24, there were 1.4 million Hispanics employed and 0.9 million blacks *un*employed. Although in the general population black youths outnumbered Hispanic youths nearly two to one, they barely outnumbered them in absolute employment. The rate of black unemployment was 33.1 percent, while that of Hispanic youths was 15.5 percent.[13] Presumably, the competitive success of immigrants rests on their acceptance of low, often illegally low, wages and docility, traits that endear them to employers.

The boon to employers is short-lived, however, because soon the migrants and their children spurn the jobs they first obtained. Also, many immigrants, such as those from Hungary, India, and Cuba, do not start at the bottom of the social ladder but compete for clerical and professional jobs.

The "dirty-work" argument for continued immigration seems weak compared to the long-run consequences. One of these consequences, added population growth, has already been mentioned. With 235 million in 1983, the United States hardly needs more people. Immigrants add to the total population not only directly but also indirectly through births after they arrive. The fertility of recent immigrants is not known, but indications that it is very high—at least for those from less developed countries—are convincing. (For the reproductive performance and expectations of women aged 30–34 in 1981, see Table 21.2.) Although the Hispanic population includes not only immigrants but natives whose ancestors were born in the United States, the fertility of this group by age 30–34 is 32 percent higher than that of the white group and slightly higher than that of the black population. The differences in lifetime births expected are much the same. Among the states with 6 percent or more Hispanic inhabitants, there is a correlation of .62 between the percentage Hispanic and the crude birthrate. Excluding states with a high proportion of Mormons (such as Utah and Idaho) or a very young population (Alaska), New Mexico has the highest proportion Hispanic and the highest crude birthrate.

Since Latin American immigrants not only enter in large numbers and have high birthrates, but also concentrate in the Sunbelt states along the southern border (in 1980 eight states with 35 percent of the nation's people had 81 percent of the Hispanic population), they are difficult to assimilate. Indeed, assimilation is now taboo in Hispanic intellectual circles, where cultural separateness is the goal. There is a possibility, then, that the United States will create, through its migration policy, an American Quebec. This would not be what the American public wants, and it would be out of proportion to the short-run advantage of supplying low-paid workers to employers.

Table 21.2
Actual and Expected Fertility of Women Aged 30–34 by Race

	Births per 1,000 women to date	Lifetime births expected per 1,000 women
White	1,797	2,044
Black	2,323	2,531
Hispanic	2,378	2,638

SOURCE: U.S. Bureau of the Census, "Fertility of American Women: June 1981," *Current Population Reports*, series p-20, no. 378 (April 1983): 7.

Congressional proposals to control immigration are so replete with compromises that they appear to be ineffective. It seems likely that any legislation will fail to reduce illegal immigration to the extent that it—

1. Gives amnesty to illegal immigrants who were in the United States prior to some cutoff date. By rewarding foreigners for violating U.S. immigration laws, this encourages more violations in the future.
2. Fails to enact penalties for employers who hire illegal workers. Immigrants come mainly for jobs; if the jobs are not there, they will not come.
3. Fails to enact an identity system for foreigners. Anyone seeking a job should be prepared to offer proof of citizenship or, if not a citizen, a work permit.
4. Gives welfare, health, and educational benefits to aliens in this country illegally. These benefits often exceed wages in the country of origin.
5. Forgoes the right to select immigrants on a merit basis, case by case, instead of on a group basis. The criteria should have to do with whether, on the basis of his skills, the prospective immigrant will contribute substantially more to the United States than what he will cost.

The magnitude of the immigration problem is often underestimated. If Central America and the Caribbean get the natural increase predicted for them by the United Nations, they will add 77.2 million to their population in twenty years (1980–2000). Already in 1980 the population density in this region was 89 percent greater than in the United States. By the year 2000, according to the projections, it will be 166 percent greater. If the migration to the United States were to remove all the increase from this area, it would have to take 3.86 million per year. In addition, Africa, Asia, and the Pacific would contribute many more. With all the Third World taken into account, the United States is a potential haven for at least 30 million immigrants per year.[14]

Throughout the world, restriction of immigration is the rule. Japan excludes virtually all immigration; Australia selects carefully the immigrants it will receive; Mexico does not allow foreigners to own real estate or to work without a permit; Israel admits non-Jews only under special circumstances. Canada has recently made immigration much more difficult.[15] In my opinion, failure to stem immigration into the United States is due more to lack of will than to the difficulty of the task. Insofar as immigration is harmful, the harm is spread over the population at large; it affects each individual only to a minor degree, hardly enough to arouse him to political protest. The benefit, however, is concentrated in employer circles, and it can be big enough to arouse employers to intense lobbying against restrictive laws.[16]

This interpretation helps explain why, in democratic industrial countries, government officials generally favor immigration despite public opinion to the contrary. For instance, in 1980 a Gallup survey found that 56 percent of American respondents opposed the immigration of Cubans and only 35 percent favored it. A Harris poll in the same year found a three-to-one agreement that "it is wrong for us to let so many Cuban and other refugees into this country." Sixty percent wanted to get rid of as many Cuban refugees as possible. According to Gallup, opposition was greater among nonwhite than among white Americans, but equal as between the two major political parties. The main reason given by opponents was fear of unemployment. No less than 66 percent of Gallup respondents agreed, and only 26 percent disagreed, that the government should halt all immigration until the unemployment rate falls below 5 percent. Similarly, public opinion in Canada was 63 percent against, and only 29 percent for, the admission of more than 50,000 Indochinese refugees.[17]

A view sometimes heard is that immigration is desirable as a means of keeping the U.S. population young. An influx of young foreigners with high fertility will keep elementary schools occupied and minimize the aging of the population. As we have seen, however, it is precisely the young who are experiencing the greatest unemployment. Large immigration exacerbates the problem of youthful unemployment. If a young population *per se* had economic advantages, Mexico, El Salvador, Jamaica, Bangladesh, Zaïre, and Syria would all be prosperous.

It is frequently assumed that migration from Third World countries is caused by lack of development and that, to stem the influx, the United States should provide generous foreign aid. The evidence, however, casts doubt on this assumption. Massive emigration more usually occurs when countries are in the rapid phase of development. For instance, the movement of Japanese into North and South America did not occur during medieval times in Japan but in the post-Meiji period when development was rapid. The United States receives more immigrants from South Korea and Nigeria than from less progressive countries in these regions. Turkey, a major recipient of U.S. aid, has had a high rate of postwar emigration. Giving abundant aid to a backward country generally lowers the death rate and causes the population to surge. But most of the surging population is unskilled, and much of it is unemployed and hence not involved in the process of development. This rising surplus of people seeks opportunities abroad. If Mexico were to receive more economic aid, Mexican immigration into the United States might increase rather than decrease. It is doubtful that any amount of economic aid would be so worthwhile to Mexico as to remove a million of its inhabitants each year.

An Aging Population

Like other industrial nations, the United States pays a price for its low fertility. One part of the price is personal: people have fewer children, on average, than they would like to have. Another part is demographic: the population is aging. In 1890 only 3.9 percent were aged 65 and over, but by 1980 the figure had climbed to 11.3 percent. In the year 2000, it will be, according to projections based on medium assumptions, 13.1 percent. This aging is retarded significantly by immigration because immigrants come primarily in the young adult ages, but immigrants eventually grow old themselves and thus, unless new immigrants keep coming, eventually contribute to the old-age contingent.

What effect does an aging population have? Does it cause political opinion to turn conservative? Does it cause the economy to slow down? These questions permit no definitive answer. It is only the advanced industrial nations that have aging populations. Although they have, in general, not only more political stability than the less developed countries but also more welfare and liberal-democratic policies, one cannot attribute such traits to the elderly population. In poor and largely illiterate countries, high school and college students often dominate the political scene with their schemes, either strongly left (as in Nicaragua) or strongly right (as in Iran). The elderly, in seeking their own advantage, have also hatched some radical schemes, one of which was the Depression-born Townsend Plan in California, which would have given $200 each month to every elderly person. It is difficult to prove that an aging population thrusts the political outlook either left or right.

A Graying Labor Force?

Although many observers infer that an aging population has meant a "graying" of the labor force, the opposite has occurred in the United States. In 1960, in the labor force age 20 and over, 57.6 percent were between 20 and 44 years of age; by 1980, 66.7 percent were between those ages.

The reasons for this younger labor force are twofold. First, employment has been greatly augmented in recent years by an influx of young women. Second, the elderly have increasingly retired from the labor force. As Table 21.3 shows, between 1960 and 1980 the labor force aged 20 and over increased by 30.7 million. Of this, 19.2 million (or 63 percent) was an increase in the *female* labor force, and 15.5 million of that (or 81 percent) were aged 20–44. The male labor force aged 45-plus showed almost no growth because males of advanced age were leaving the labor force in droves.

In the future, however, an aging of the labor force may occur. If female participation grows equal to that of men, if the normal age at retirement is raised, and if immigration is controlled, the labor force will grow older. However, it is one thing to produce this aging by increasing the participation of the elderly, and another to do it by reducing the participation of the young. So far, the participation rate among young males has held up while that among males 45-plus has plummeted. Among women there has been a gain at all ages except 65-plus, but most of the gain has come among women under 45. Insofar as the labor force is kept young by reducing the number of workers over 45,

Table 21.3
Increase in the U.S. Labor Force, 1960–1980, by Age and Sex

Age	Increase in labor force (millions)		
	Total	Male	Female
20+	30.7	11.5	19.2
20–44	26.3	10.8	15.5
45+	4.3	0.8	3.5

SOURCE: Calculated from *Statistical Abstract of the United States, 1981* (Washington, D.C.: Government Printing Office, 1981), p. 381. (Columns do not necessarily add to total because of rounding in the source.)

there is a loss of overall production; if it is done by stepping up participation at young ages, there is a gain in production.

Labor-force participation rates are somewhat deceptive, however, because unemployment varies by age. If we look at the employed population separately, we find it is older than the labor force as a whole. By reducing unemployment, the nation could make its working population younger than it is now.

The Source of the Old-Age Burden

In addition to the graying of the labor force, another misconception is that the "problem of the aged" is due to an aging population. While the proportion of the aged has certainly risen, the root issue is not how many aged there are but how they are handled. Up to now, as I see it, they have been handled in the wrong way. As just noted, they have been leaving the labor force en masse. Having left the labor force, the elderly are now living on savings, pensions, Social Security, and welfare. They have become consumers rather than producers, and the resulting economic burden has grown at a rapid rate. In only eleven years, from 1971 to 1982, federal benefits for the elderly multiplied nearly 4.5 times, going from $44 billion to $195.1 billion.[18] By 1982, on average, each person aged 65 or more received $7,271 in federal benefits alone, to say nothing of benefits received

Table 21.4

Percentage Age 65+ in Labor Force

	Males	Females
1890	68.3	7.6
1950	45.8	9.7
1981	18.4	8.0

SOURCES: U.S. Bureau of the Census, *Historical Statistics of the United States, Colonial Times to 1970* (Washington, D.C.: Government Printing Office, 1975), p. 132; and *Statistical Abstract of the United States, 1982–83* (Washington, D.C.: Government Printing Office, 1983), p. 377.

from local governments, private pensions, savings, and other sources of unearned income. The burden on the working population has become very heavy. In 1950, there were 25 nonworkers above age 60 for each 100 workers 20–59 years old; by 1981, the ratio had climbed to 31 per 100.[19]

The working population under age 45 bears a double burden. In addition to the indirect support of the nonworking elderly through Social Security and pensions, it provides direct support for its own children as well. Since this second obligation is direct, it is clearly realized, and there is a remedy—keeping fertility low. The support of the elderly, on the other hand, is not so clearly recognized as such, and the individual as a taxpayer has no way of avoiding it. Formerly, it was only the disabled elderly who needed transfer income; now it is nearly all the elderly. The current assumption is that each worker reaches a moment in life when a *rite de passage* called "retirement" occurs, after which, no matter how capable he may be, he does no more work. This is not a natural or a necessary idea, but a peculiar one. If the world had unlimited resources, automatic retirement might be feasible, but in the actual world it is inappropriate. In past times, the old-age burden was slight, not only because there were few old people, but also because they worked as much as they could. The disabled elderly were not cared for by impersonal agencies such as pension funds and Social Security, but by family members. Their cost was thus limited by the means available to family members. Now the aged are more numerous, nearly all are nonworking, and nearly all are being supported by impersonal agencies.

Future Changes and the Old-Age Problem

In the future, as far as demographic forces are concerned, the old-age burden will expand for two reasons: First, as noted already, the proportion of the elderly in the population will increase, and second, the rate of disability among the aged will rise, both because the elderly population itself is aging and because its increased longevity is not fully matched by health improvements.

Table 21.5 shows that, among persons aged 65-plus, the proportion over 75 has been gaining at the expense of those under 75. In 1950, only 31.5 percent were over 75; by the year 2000, according to the medium projection, 49.5 percent will be over that age. Insofar as advanced old age is associated with chronic disorders and failing health, this aging of the elderly population will tend, in itself, to create more disability. This effect could of course be mitigated or eliminated if, along with gains in longevity, corresponding improvements in health were also made. The evidence, however, suggests that the rather remarkable gains in longevity have not been accompanied by commensurate gains in health.

Only a few years ago many observers thought that gains in total life expectancy were diminishing because, since almost everybody was living through the young ages, further gains would have to be made in

Table 21.5
Age Composition of the Elderly Population

Date	Total 65+	65–69	70–74	75–79	80+
1950	100.0	40.8	27.8	17.3	14.1
1980	100.0	34.4	26.6	18.8	20.3
2000	100.0	26.0	24.5	20.7	28.8

NOTE: Each age group as percentage of those age 65+
SOURCES: U.S. Bureau of the Census, "Estimates of the Population of the United States, by Age, Color, and Sex: July 1, 1950 to 1962," *Current Population Reports*, series P-25, no. 265 (May 21, 1963); idem, "Age, Sex, Race, and Spanish Origin of the Population by Regions, Divisions, and States: 1980," *1980 Census of Population, Supplementary Reports*, PC80-S1-1 (May 1981); and idem, "Projections of the Population of the United States: 1982–2050 (Advance Report)," *Population Estimates and Projections*, series P-25, no. 922 (October 1982).

older ages where improvements were slow and hard to make. Yet, beginning in the 1950s for females and in the 1970s for males, a remarkable increase in life expectancy at older ages occurred. The improvement started at ages 60–75 and soon spread to ages 75 to 85. According to the white mortality rate of 1980, the average woman aged 65 would live 18.5 more years, and the average man 14.1 years, compared with 15.0 and 12.8 years in 1950.

As a result of this unanticipated extension of life in the older ages, the projections of the elderly population for Social Security purposes have been too low. Relying on cause-of-death changes during 1968 to 1977, Eileen Crimmins has estimated the population 65-plus for the year 2000 at 35.7 million, instead of the 31.9 million officially projected.[20]

Unfortunately, this success in keeping the elderly alive does not seem to have been achieved by making them correspondingly more youthful and vigorous. In 1969–1970, 42.3 percent of persons aged 65-plus had a chronic limitation on their activity; by 1980, 45.2 percent had such a limitation.[21] Patients in nursing homes rose from 756,000 in 1967 to 1.24 million in 1978. The number of beds in such institutions per 1,000 persons aged 65-plus rose from 33.6 in 1964 to 59.7 in 1977.[22]

The unanticipated size and cost of the elderly population have created a crisis in the nation's Social Security and health care systems, a crisis that promises to occupy attention throughout the 1980s. The situation suggests that the wholesale removal of the elderly from the labor force is a mistake. If a higher proportion of them are now disabled by chronic disease and old age than was formerly the case, this underscores the advisability of keeping the ablebodied, who are still a majority, at work and receiving a wage consonant with their abilities. As things stand, the overwhelming majority of the aged are not in the labor force and yet, on the average, they are drawing a substantial amount from the economy. In 1980, the per capita income of families headed by a person age 65 and over exceeded that of all other families except those headed by persons 45–64.[23]

Sex-Role Changes

What kind of a society is it that has a consistently low birthrate, a helpless immigration policy, an aging population, a high level of consumption, and a sizable rate of transfer payments? The name for it is not utopia or the affluent society, but rather the welfare state, and perhaps its chief feature is that, through ever more intervention by an impersonal government, it fundamentally alters the traditional system of rights and obligations. We have just seen how the traditional system of relations between the generations has been altered. Now let us see how another system—relations between the sexes—has been changed as well. In doing so, we should keep in mind that it is not government alone that makes social changes; rather, it is the interplay between demographic and economic changes on the one hand and political responses on the other that provides the results actually seen.

A demographic change that has basically affected sex roles is the marvelous gain in life expectancy in general and of female life expectancy in particular. Under the mortality conditions of 1980, the average white woman in the United States would live 78.1 years, the average white man 70.5 years, a difference of 7.6 years. This gives women a clear majority in the population, but owing to the fact that more males are born than females (1,058 male babies per 1,000 female babies in 1980), a female majority is not reached until after age 45. Once that age is reached, however, the feminization is rapid, as Table 21.6 shows.

The sheer shortage of males at ages over 45 means that a high proportion of women cannot be married. In addition, as is well known, when men remarry, they tend to marry women younger than themselves by a wider margin than when they first married. This circumstance greatly reduces the chances of older women in the marriage market, as Table 21.7 shows. These ratios account for the fact that a high percentage of women beyond age 55 are unmarried. At ages 55–64, the percentage is 29.6 percent; at ages 65–74, it is 49.6 percent; and at ages 75 and over, 76.5 percent. In present-day society, therefore, if a woman does marry, she cannot count on having a husband when she gets beyond 60 years of age; yet at 60 she still has 22.4 years of life remaining. Nor can she count on having children in the home, because her last child leaves home when she is around 48 years of age, at which time she still has 33.7 years to live, a substantially longer period of life than the approximately 28 years she spends with children.

In the past, a woman who married could count on spending her entire life with children in the home because she bore her last child later in life and had a short life expectancy. The new situation thus represents a revolutionary change. Women are being forced to plan their lives on an individual basis, not just in terms of marriage and children. They are not entering the labor force in large numbers solely

Table 21.6
Sex Ratios, 1980

Age	Males per 100 females
0–19	104.8
20–34	100.2
35–49	97.4
50–64	90.4
65–79	73.7
80+	48.2

SOURCE: U.S. Bureau of the Census, *Census of Population, Supplementary Reports,* PC80-S1-1 (May 1981), p. 3. The figures are for the white population, used here because the blacks are both more under-enumerated and less modernized than the white population.

Table 21.7
Unmarried Males per 100 Unmarried Females

Age	Number
20–29	124.0
30–39	99.9
40–54	71.0
55–64	46.7
65–74	25.5
75+	21.6

NOTE: "Unmarried" includes single, divorced, separated, and widowed.
SOURCE: U.S. Bureau of the Census, "Marital Status and Living Arrangements: March 1981," *Current Population Reports,* series P-20, no. 372 (June 1982): 8.

to supplement the family income, but also to take care of themselves as individuals with their own careers.

Obviously, the division of labor between the sexes—a division that centered on the family—is breaking down. Women are becoming more like men in their activities, and vice versa. Once such confusion of sex roles sets in, the development of new guidelines for the two sexes with respect to each other becomes highly problematic. No one knows what to expect and hence expects too much or too little. In the uncertainty, marriage is postponed or forgone altogether, the divorce rate rises, sexual behavior becomes more promiscuous, and fertility is reduced.

In a democratic welfare state, there seems little chance of establishing a new set of firm guidelines because guidelines require authority and sanctions, both of which are eroded by liberal individualism. If so, then the fate of such a society is eventual replacement. Some would say that the massive migration coming from Third World countries represents such replacement. In any case, the situation of the United States cannot be assessed solely in domestic terms, for the nation exists not only in interaction with the rest of the world, but as a leader of that world as well. Let us turn, therefore, to the field of international demography.

Facing World Population

In the 1950s and 1960s, projections of what the world's population would be in the 1980s had an eerie ring to them. Could the world's people really multiply that fast? Now, unfortunately, those projections have come true. In 1957, for example, when the world's population stood at 2.9 billion, the United Nations, in its "medium variant," predicted the population in 1980 would be 4.2 billion.[24] This would be an increase of 1.37 billion in 23 years, almost half the existing population, which seemed to stagger the imagination. How could we possibly feed all those extra people? The actual population in 1980, according to the United Nations' *Demographic Yearbook* of that date, turned out to be 4.43 billion, 200 million higher than the 1957 forecast. By 1983, the world total had climbed to about 4.68 billion, nearly 2 billion more than it was in 1957. Evidently, we were able to feed all those people.

Although the rapid world population growth proves that the necessities for existence have expanded commensurately, the cost has been enormous. Human beings do not live for necessities alone. They live for the amenities as well, and the population surge in the world has been achieved at frightful cost. Water and air pollution, extinction of species, malnutrition and undernourishment, crowding and congestion, poverty and disenchantment—all indicate that success with the necessities has dehumanized hundreds of millions of people in the world. They have enough to keep alive and multiply, but not enough to enjoy living.

The world is currently adding about 80 million to its population each year, nearly twice the number that were being added during 1950–1955. During the entire decade of the 1980s, the number to be added to the earth's population is 810 million.[25]

In the 1980s, then, the United States finds itself in a world with unprecedented population increase. Usually, in its international policies, it overlooks this fact. It assumes that the problems are political, economic, or medical, and that they can be solved in those terms. It forgets that the problems may also be demographic.

The world demographic situation, however, is more complex than the global figures indicate. For well-known reasons, nearly all the world's excess of births over deaths in the 1980s will be concentrated in the poorest countries; 91 percent of the next generation will be born in the three-fourths of the world regarded as less developed. These are, of course, the countries least equipped to train children to use today's advanced technology, which is now necessary to support the swollen world population.

The difference in population growth is widening the economic and social gap between industrial and nonindustrial nations. Between 1960 and 1979, for example, commercial energy consumption per capita increased in the industrial market economies 34 times as much as it did in the low-income economies and more than 5 times as much as it did in the middle-income economies. Had there been no disparity in population growth, the differences would have been smaller. Effectively priced out of the market for commercial energy, the less developed countries have been forced to scramble for noncommercial sources. They have, for instance, been rapidly depleting their forests for firewood.[26]

They have also been borrowing heavily. During the 1970–1980 decade, their foreign public debt, as a percentage of GNP, increased significantly (see Table 21.9). They are incurring foreign debt to meet interest payments on debts already outstanding. In 1980 Zaïre's external public debt was 78.5 percent of its GNP; the figure for Mauritania was 139.7; for Nicaragua, 83.0; for Jamaica, 54.1; and for Panama, 70.1 percent. The chance that Third World countries will repay these loans is slight. To assume that "development" can be brought to the less developed countries without controlling something as important as population growth, or in general without exercising the social discipline that a modern economy requires, is to invite a communist take-

Table 21.8
Increased Energy Consumption in Countries by Economic Level, 1960–1979
(in kilograms of coal equivalent per capita)

Low-income economies	90
Middle-income economies	547
Industrial market economies	3,036
Nonmarket industrial economies	2,909

SOURCE: World Bank, *World Development Report, 1982* (New York: Oxford University Press, 1982), pp. 122–23.

Table 21.9
Foreign Debt of Less Developed Countries
(as percentage of GNP)

	1970	1980
All low-income economies	15.6	19.2
Low-income economies except India and China	16.5	31.4
Middle-income economies	11.8	17.4

SOURCE: World Bank, *World Development Report, 1982* (New York: Oxford University Press, 1982), p. 138.

over. The revolutionaries of the Left capitalize on the problems created by pursuing traditional free-world development—that is, economic growth—without regard to demographic and social consequences. The revolutionaries, promising instant relief, are irreversibly hoisted to power. Soon they, too, are plagued by the underlying maladies that the capitalists encountered, but their power is already consolidated.

On the surface, the United States has taken cognizance of the population question in the Third World. Mainly through the Agency for International Development but also through U.S. support of international organizations such as the United Nations Fund for Population Activities and the Population Division of the United Nations, it has invested hundreds of millions of dollars in "population programs" in developing countries. Private American foundations—for instance, the

Ford Foundation, Rockefeller Foundation, and Population Council—have also given millions to such programs. As the statistics on population growth show, however, the results have been disappointing. To understand why, we need to recall that virtually all the effort has gone into "family planning"—that is, the furnishing of contraceptives, abortion, and sterilization, along with propaganda concerning the desirability of small families. As the sole approach to population control, family planning is inadequate because it deals only with means. It does not deal with the incentives for having children in agrarian societies. Unless the incentives are changed, people in developing countries will continue to want four or more children. But changing the incentives means going against cherished values and traditional institutional arrangements. It is more difficult and more politically risky than simply furnishing technological gadgets to couples and letting everything else alone.

The only agrarian country that has developed an effective population control policy in advance and in behalf of economic development is Communist China, and it is significant that it has done so without aid from the United States and to the surprise of the so-called experts—the family planners—in Western countries. The essence of the Chinese policy is to use state control of the conditions of existence to provide incentives for late marriage and low fertility (one or two children per couple) and disincentives for high fertility (more than two children).[27] To turn the world's most familistic society on its head in this way, the communist dictatorship must have viewed the country's demographic situation as desperate. Characteristically, however, instead of praising China for leadership in developing effective fertility control in an agrarian economy, American commentators have tended to condemn the policy as involving compulsion. Unfortunately, there have been some excesses, but one must recall the painful compulsions and tragedies that China is trying to solve by its population policies.

It is hard to avoid the conclusion that with respect to population in the Third World, the United States has been a source of misguidance. It has been a leader in the good work of reducing mortality, but it has also led countries down the false trail of thinking family planning would be adequate to arrest the resulting unprecedented population growth. It has tended to reject alternative policies as being authoritarian. There is thus poetic justice not only in the Third World's hostility but also, ironically, in its unrelenting pressure on the United States to absorb immigrants and provide economic aid. Somehow, if the United States is to protect its still fairly high level of living and its amenities as a nation, it must come to grips in the 1980s with the world's population problem. The industrial nations are now islands of prosperity in an ocean of poverty. Contributing only 8 percent to the next generation, their prosperity will inevitably be diluted by the rest of the world—perhaps not so much by Third World countries directly as by their playing off one group of industrial nations against the other.

Notes

1. See *Population and the American Future: The Report of the Commission on Population Growth and the American Future* (Washington, D.C.: Government Printing Office, 1972); and Council on Environmental Quality and U.S. Department of State, *The Global 2000 Report to the President: Entering the Twenty-First Century*, vol. 1 (New York: Penguin Books, 1982).
2. U.S. Bureau of the Census, "Fertility of American Women: June 1981," *Current Population Reports*, series P-20, no. 376 (April 1983): 7.
3. Ibid., p. 28.
4. *Statistical Abstract of the United States, 1982-83* (Washington, D.C.: Government Printing Office, 1983), pp. 41, 50.
5. Ibid., p. 160.
6. U.S. Bureau of the Census, "Marital Status and Living Arrangements: March 1981," *Current Population Reports*, series P-20, no. 372 (June 1982): 3.
7. Ibid., p. 2.
8. *Statistical Abstract of the United States, 1982-83*, p. 66; and National Center for Health Statistics, "Advance Report of Final Natality Statistics, 1980," *Monthly Vital Statistics Report* 31, supplement (November 30, 1982): 25.
9. U.S. Bureau of the Census, "Marital Status and Living Arrangements," p. 3.
10. See Tomas Frejka, "Fertility Trends and Policies: Czechoslovakia in the 1970s," *Population and Development Review* 6, no. 1 (March 1980): 65-93.
11. U.S. Bureau of the Census, *Historical Statistics of the United States, Colonial Times to 1970*, part 1 (Washington, D.C.: Government Printing Office, 1975), p. 105.
12. "The 1980 census enumerated about 5.5 million more persons than were previously estimated for April 1, 1980" (National Center for Health Statistics, "Advance Report of Final Natality Statistics," 1980, p. 3). Since the estimates had been made by taking the 1970 census, adding births and legal net immigration and subtracting deaths, this difference could be interpreted as representing illegal net immigration of about 550,000 per year.

    However, if the 1980 census achieved a more complete overall enumeration than the 1970 census, not all of the 5.5 million surplus could be attributed to illegal immigration. On the other hand, if there was greater underenumeration of illegals in 1980 than in 1970—as might be the case due to the agitation over illegal migration during the 1970s—then the 5.5 million could be an underestimate of illicit aliens.

13. *Statistical Abstract of the United States, 1982–83*, p. 381.
14. See Kingsley Davis, "Emerging Issues in International Migration," in *Solicited Papers of the International Population Conference (Manila, 1981)* (Liege, Belgium: International Union for the Scientific Study of Population, 1981), 1:419–30.
15. Roderic Beaujot and Kevin McQuillan, *Growth and Dualism: The Demographic Development of Canadian Society* (Toronto: Gage Publishing, 1982), pp. 100–101.
16. "Hired Hands: California Growers Rail Against Efforts to Stem Flow of Illegal Aliens," *Wall Street Journal*, August 4, 1983, pp. 1, 13.
17. *Gallup Report*, no. 177 (April–May 1980), no. 197 (February 1982); and *World Opinion Update*, no. 3 (May–June 1980): 79.
18. *Statistical Abstract of the United States, 1982–83*, p. 318.
19. Ibid., p. 324; and ibid., *1981*, p. 327.
20. Eileen M. Crimmins, "The Changing Pattern of American Mortality Decline, 1940–77, and Its Implications for the Future," *Population and Development Review* 7, no. 2 (June 1981): 250–51. For official projections, see Jacob S. Siegel, "Prospective Trends in the Size and Structure of the Elderly Population, Impact of Mortality Trend, and Some Implications," *Current Population Reports*, series P-23, no. 78 (Washington, D.C.: Government Printing Office, 1978).
21. *Statistical Abstract of the United States, 1982–83*, p. 121.
22. Ibid., p. 116.
23. Ibid., p. 435.
24. United Nations, *World Population Prospects as Assessed in 1963* (New York: United Nations, 1966), p. 15.
25. United Nations, *World Population Prospects as Assessed in 1980* (New York: United Nations, 1981), p. 5.
26. See World Bank, *World Development Report, 1981* (New York: Oxford University Press, 1981), pp. 40–41.
27. See Nick Eberstadt, ed., *Fertility Decline in the Less Developed Countries* (New York: Praeger, 1980), especially the chapters by John S. Aird, "Fertility Decline in China," and William Petersen, "American Efforts to Reduce the Fertility of Less Developed Countries." See also John Aird, "Population Studies and Population Policy in China," *Population and Development Review* 8, no. 2 (June 1982): 267–97.

22
The Economy, Elections, and Public Opinion

Seymour Martin Lipset

Both practitioners and students of politics increasingly recognize that electorally determined shifts in government in Western countries, particularly in the United States, are heavily determined by changing economic conditions.[1] Seemingly voters are disposed to credit or blame incumbent administrations for the state of the economy. Recent alternations between the Left and Right, therefore, generally do not reflect an ideological change in the view of the electorate.

The 1980 Election

In line with this generalization, it seems evident that the Reagan and the GOP congressional victories in 1980 did not represent the beginning of a new conservative trend, but rather involved a rejection of an incumbent party that had presided over a declining economy and a reduction in the United States' international power and prestige. The election coincided with an increasing disenchantment with the ability of the state to control the economy and a growing belief that governmental intervention was an ineffective, inefficient, and wasteful way to deal with domestic problems.² In line with these views, Americans favored cutting taxes and reducing government spending. But the same polls also reported that substantial majorities continued to support most of the specific programs that constitute the welfare state and to oppose curtailing them. In a real sense, Americans have become ideological conservatives, while remaining operationally or programmatically liberal on economic and welfare issues.³ As Everett Carll Ladd and I noted in a 1980 review of public opinion and public policy, "people in all social classes, in all regions of the country, and of all political persuasions now consistently endorse high levels of public expenditures for most social services," although they also endorsed a reduction in the scope of government.⁴

These conclusions are reinforced by the analyses of Reagan's principal pollster, Richard Wirthlin, who found during the 1980 campaign that the great majority of Republicans as well as Democrats disagreed with most of Reagan's specific policies:

> Survey research conducted in the primary states showed that Ronald Reagan was winning among Republicans, not because his ideological positions were congruent with the electorate, but rather, in spite of a substantial ideological gap between himself and the average Republican. The extent of that gap was remarkable . . . Ronald Reagan was further from the average individual's ideological position than even Congressman John Anderson.⁵

Based on his survey analysis, Wirthlin concluded that to win the general election, "issues and themes had to be developed to override ideology as a vote determinant." Specifically, the Reagan campaign had to find ways to attract the traditional constituencies of the Democrats—"the somewhat less affluent and less educated voters, union members, blue-collar voters."⁶ And given the minority status of the Republican party, Wirthlin told his candidate 21 days before the election:

> We must shed every overt Republican symbol . . . bring the focus of the campaign back to the economic issues . . . The thrust of speeches must be directed toward:
> - inflation
> - jobs
> - economic growth, and
> - a more responsible and more efficient federal government.⁷

The "Misery Index"

The electoral success of the Reagan campaign followed a pattern common to the Western democracies in the past decade. With a few exceptions, whenever the sum of the inflation and unemployment rates, the so-called misery index, stood at 10 percent or more, the incumbent party or governing coalition was defeated.[8] Since 1979 such parties lost in seventeen out of the twenty elections in which an alternation was possible and the misery index was above 10 percent, while governments were re-elected with an increase in the popular vote in four countries that had a misery index below 10 percent.[9] In 1983, the sitting conservative parties were turned out of office in Australia and Portugal, while in Austria, the Social Democrats lost their parliamentary majority, although they remained in office by forming a coalition with a small third party. The French Socialists suffered a sharp loss in local elections in 1983, much as the Republicans did in the off-year congressional and state elections in November 1982. All five countries had a misery index above 10 percent at the time of the elections. In Britain, however, the Conservative administration was returned to office, in spite of a misery index of 17 percent. (This deviation from the pattern is discussed in detail below.)

The international pattern is striking and supports the argument that the volatile sector of the electorate largely responds to the performance of the economy, not to the ideological or policy alternatives offered by the parties. In the fourteen national elections between 1979 and 1983 in countries in which an alternation between left- and right-wing governments was possible and the incumbent lost (other than the three held in Ireland, which are hard to classify in left to right terms), socialists and liberals replaced more conservative rivals in seven, while more right-wing parties defeated left-of-center incumbents in seven.

Given the lack of any ideological pattern in the responses of democratic electorates to economic conditions, it is not surprising that the findings of various public opinion surveys do not indicate that electoral turnovers reflect significant shifts in the thinking of voters on major policy matters. In the United States in 1980, Republicans and conservatives won control; in France in 1981, Socialists replaced conservatives in the presidency and the Chamber of Deputies. It can be argued that Americans did not reject the welfare state in favor of a free-market economy, the French did not vote for socialism over capitalism.[10] In both countries, voters facing similarly high misery indices (18–19 percent) chose to replace the incumbents with the opposition. And two years later in congressional and local elections, the electorates, faced with a sharp increase in unemployment in each country, reversed themselves in favor of the Democrats in the United States and the conservatives in France. Concurrently, the approval ratings of both Presidents Reagan and Mitterrand changed in tandem with economic indicators.[11]

Every macroscopic generalization is susceptible to modification by the introduction of other factors. The economic analysis of electoral outcomes is no exception. The variables with the greatest potential to upset and reverse the relationship between economic trends and the popularity of incumbents have been divisions within the opposition and the tendency of the public to rally around an administration when the peace and security of the nation are threatened.[12] Recent political developments in Britain illustrate the way a political leader and party that successfully managed such an event, the Falklands war, can regain support and be re-elected even though presiding over a depressed economy.

Margaret Thatcher and her Conservative government were re-elected in June 1983, despite a misery index of 17 percent (13 percent unemployment and 4 percent inflation). The British victors, however, suffered a decline in popular support, from 44 percent in 1979 to 42 percent in 1983. The proportion of the electorate expressing satisfaction with the government in the polls taken during the three-week election period was 44 percent. The Tories' major rivals, both clearly to the left of Thatcher on domestic and foreign policy issues, Labour and the Social Democratic–Liberal Alliance, received 53 percent between them, 28 for the former and 25 for the latter. As the *London Sunday Times* editorialized:

> No General Election result since universal suffrage has been so flagrantly unfair. The Prime Minister sits in triumph in Downing Street not on a surge of popular support but as a result of unjust electoral arrangements. Her Parliamentary majority tripled; yet her share of the popular vote has actually diminished. For the Alliance, on the other hand, one in four of the votes cast has been rewarded with one in 28 of the Seats.[13]

Yet Thatcher was able to improve her political position, after a sharp decline in the opinion polls during the winter of 1981–82, a period of rising unemployment and massive inflation. She was saved by her international and domestic opponents. As Andrew Neil emphasized, she "was swept back into power by the war in the Falklands, and the war in the Labor Party."[14]

Although the British election results run counter to the assumption that governments and political leaders lose support during periods of economic adversity, until the spring of 1982 Britain conformed to the relationship between economics and public opinion. As unemployment continued to grow and inflation stood at a record height, the opinion polls revealed that the Conservatives had fallen to third place, behind both Labour and the Alliance. But with the Falklands war, Thatcher and her party literally leaped up in public support. The *Economist* (London) summed up the developments:

> The winter of 1981–2 showed every sign that the government was in trouble. Mrs. Thatcher's poll rating in January was the worst of any prime minister since the war. Only 25% expressed satisfaction with her performance. Industrial production was falling, both interest rates and unemployment were rising . . .
> Then came the Falklands. The impact of the Falklands war on Mrs. Thatcher and the course of her government cannot be overstated . . .
> The Falklands war transformed Mrs. Thatcher from an electoral liability into an indispensable asset. Pre-Falklands, the Tories had been in a humiliating third place in the polls for almost a year. Post-Falklands, their lead was a stunning 20% and has remained seemingly impregnable ever since.
> For this turnround there was little domestic justification, except the sharp fall in inflation. The anticipated recovery in economic growth and employment had not materialized . . . Yet these factors, which had seemed so overwhelming a year earlier, no longer rated in the opinion polls. True, unemployment was the dominant issue of the day [according to the polls], but the issue seemed to have no effect on Mrs. Thatcher's reputation.
> The conundrum . . . remains the Falklands. It unlocked an admiration in the public, a willingness to take her on trust, and gave her a wholly new self-confidence in her handling of public issues.[15]

The intra-election surveys of how people would vote if the election were held today tell the story. In May 1979, the Conservatives were elected with 44 percent of the vote. By November 1981, Tory support had fallen to a pitiful 27 percent, rising a scant 4 percentage points to 31 by the first quarter of 1982. But the spring brought the Falklands war and a jump in Conservative strength to 42 percent, which placed the party well ahead of its two opponents. And the Tories remained in that position, around the mid-40 percentiles, until the election. They were usually about 15 percentage points ahead of the second-place Labour party, despite a growing unemployment rate.[16]

Governments, of course, do not always benefit from international crises or wars. Harry Truman and Lyndon Johnson lost support during the Korean and Vietnamese wars, and the Iranian hostage crisis played a role in Jimmy Carter's defeat in 1980. Studies of reactions to international tensions indicate strengthened support for incumbents under conditions parallel to the situation in Britain at the time of the Falklands, "when the administration has a virtual monopoly of information about the situation, [and] opposition political leadership tends to refrain from comment or to make cautiously supportive statements." This leads the media as well "to carry an unusually uncritical mix of news about . . . [governmental] performance . . ."[17] And, it should be added, a quick and decisive victory helps.

Although the Falklands effect was clearly the most important factor overcoming the negative impact of the economy on the behavior of the British electorate, the opposition parties were unable to recover during the following year in large part because their leaders and policies proved to furnish a weak alternative to the new perception of Thatcher as a strong, effective leader. The main opposition party, Labour, had shifted sharply to the left, taking a number of positions unpopular with most British voters, particularly support for unilateral nuclear disarmament and "a blueprint for extending state control and union power over the economy and industry."[18] It also suffered from the weak image of its left-wing leader, Michael Foot, who came across as ineffectual. His approval ratings in the polls hovered around 20 percent. The move to the left led a considerable segment of Labour's moderate and right wings to split off and form the Social Democratic party, which joined in an electoral alliance with the Liberal party. The Alliance, which initially did well in the polls, declined subsequently, in part because, like Labour, it selected a leader, Roy Jenkins, who the polls indicated was personally unpopular. The Alliance also was unable to create an image of where it stood on issues, other than occupying a center position. In any case, the resultant division of the opposition made it impossible for either party to appear as a realistic alternative to the Tories, as having a leader as able as Thatcher, or as being capable of forming a majority government.

The significance of the ideological and personal image of party leaders in Britain can be seen in the results of a Marketing and Opinion Research International (MORI) poll taken four weeks before the election, which pitted the Conservatives under Thatcher against Labour led by Denis Healey, the chief moderate leader in the party. Under these conditions, the two major parties were even, 42 percent each, with the Alliance losing votes to Labour. Hence, it may be argued that the Tories might even have been defeated in a predominantly two-party race, in which its principal opponent took a moderate left position.

Economic Conditions and Presidential Popularity

The changes in the U.S. economy, a deepening recession beginning in the fall of 1981 that seemingly bottomed out at the start of 1983, were paralleled by shifts in the public's evaluation of the impact of the economy. Americans who had initially been optimistic about the impact of President Reagan's economic program, began to tell pollsters that administration policies would have an adverse effect on them. According to the Gallup Poll, more people were positive than negative about their prospective economic position until the fall of 1981. From then on, pessimism took over as the dominant response, until by March 1982, a majority anticipated a worsening. But as the economy showed signs of improving in the spring of 1983, the proportion expressing the belief that their financial position would get better increased, up from 25 percent in January to 34 percent in March.

The ABC News/*Washington Post* poll also found that negative evaluations of the effect of the president's policies also bottomed out in January 1983 when 58 percent responded "worse" and 20 percent said "better" to the question: "Thinking of Reagan, would you say his presidency has made things better for people where you live, made things worse, or what?" By mid-May, the percentage saying "worse" had declined to 50 percent, with 31 percent replying "better."

Questions dealing with the state of the economy revealed a comparable pattern. The president's pollster, Richard Wirthlin, reported from his own surveys that as of January 1983, "only 19 percent... thought the economy was better off than a year earlier while the number increased to 39 percent by mid-March. By the end of April the figure had risen to 57 percent."[19] The *Los Angeles Times* found that the proportion who described "the nation's economy" as in a recession or major depression fell off from 49 percent in November 1982 to 28 percent in May 1983 and down further to 22 percent in September. The ABC News/*Washington Post* also reported a steady increase in those saying "the economy is getting better" from 18 percent in January to 50 percent at the beginning of August.

Not surprisingly, reactions to President Reagan and to his program moved in tandem with respondents' judgments of the state of the economy and their own financial position. The parallel movement of evaluations of the president and rises and declines in economic indicators is evident in all opinion polls. The Gallup Poll, for example, has repeatedly inquired: "Do you approve or disapprove of the way Ronald Reagan is handling his job as President?" During his first seven months in office, Americans approved of his performance by roughly two to one, 60 percent to 30 percent. As unemployment rates began to increase in the fall of 1981, the percentage of favorable ratings dropped into the middle or low fifties, while disapproval climbed to the mid-thirties. And as the recession deepened, the public turned against the president. From December 1981 to June 1982, support stood in the middle to high forties, but from April on, negative judgments outweighed favorable ones. By the end of 1982, 50 percent of those polled disapproved of Reagan's handling of his job, while 41 percent approved. In January 1982, 56 percent expressed disapproval, and 35 percent approved. Using the same question, the ABC News/*Washington Post* poll reported a similar pattern, a steady decline from 61 percent approval in October 1981 to 54 percent disapproval in January 1983.

The spring 1983 opinion surveys, taken at a time when various economic indicators and the behavior of the stock market suggested that the recession was ending, showed increased support for Ronald Reagan. Reagan's approval rating in the ABC News/*Washington Post* survey improved from 41 percent in January to 45 in March to 49 in mid-April to 53 in mid-June. Positive evaluations of the president in the Gallup Poll rose from 35 percent in January to 41 in March to 43 at the end of April to 46 in late May to 47 in late June. The May survey was the first taken by Gallup since March 1982 in which the approvers outnumbered the disapprovers. In commenting on these results, George Gallup noted that the "upturn in President Reagan's job performance ratings—which undoubtedly reflects, at least in part, the strengthening of the economy—runs counter to the historical pattern observed for his elected predecessors during the third year of their tenure. Presidents Carter, Nixon, and Kennedy suffered significant declines during this period, while President Eisenhower in May, 1955, stood about where he began the year."[20]

A factor analysis by Stephen Cole, the director of the *Newsday* poll, of the reactions by respondents to 28 possible reasons for judging Ronald Reagan, found that "economic conditions are seen by the voters themselves as being the most important influence on their evaluation. The strongest factor . . . was made up of four economic items."[21]

Although the economy continued to improve in summer 1983,

foreign policy issues appeared to take over as the main determinant of changes in the public's evaluation of the president. His actions in Central America and Lebanon, perceived and opposed by most Americans as overly hawkish, sent his approval ratings down in the first two summer months, while his reaction to the Soviet downing of a Korean airliner, seen as exhibiting restraint, led to a sizable increase in positive judgments of his job performance.

The decline in Reagan's approval ratings in the summer of 1983 may be explained by increased public concern over his defense and foreign policies, particularly the growing fear that he might lead the nation into a shooting war. (The polls on these issues are discussed in a later section.) The Gallup Poll reported that 41 percent approved of his job performance at the end of July, down from 47 percent a month earlier. The ABC News/*Washington Post* survey also found that the positive trend for Reagan, reported above, halted in August, although the difference between the mid-June and early August polls was insignificant, a drop of one percentage point. In interpreting his July results, George Gallup suggested that reaction to Reagan's Central American policy was responsible, noting that "on the day the . . . survey began, Reagan unveiled his administration's plan for a substantial increase in U.S. military involvement" in the region.[22] Commenting on the mid-summer ABC/*Washington Post* survey, the *Post* noted that the "new poll strongly suggests that concern over the direction of foreign affairs is having a dampening effect for Reagan. Overall, 42 percent of those interviewed rate him favorably for his handling of foreign affairs and 49 percent unfavorably, his worst score in any of 17 surveys by the *Post* and ABC."[23] But when the president showed that he could be moderate and calm in the face of a major Soviet provocation at the end of August, his job rating moved up in most polls, e.g., from 46 percent in August to 56 percent in September in the Harris Survey, his largest gain since he took office.

Respondents also exhibited great volatility when asked to choose between Ronald Reagan and a given Democratic candidate. In early 1981 trial heats pitting the president against Walter Mondale, Ronald Reagan led decisively in all the polls. By late 1982, the former vice-president had taken the lead. But by spring 1983, as the economy showed signs of improving, both Mondale and Senator John Glenn had either fallen behind or were tied with Ronald Reagan (see Table 22.1). Surprisingly, however, the Gallup and the ABC News/*Washington Post* polls found a Democratic upsurge in June with both Mondale and Glenn gaining a strong lead over the president, one that fell off slightly in both polls at the beginning of August and remained at the same level in late September.

Table 22.1
Trial Heats for the Presidency
(percentages)

"If the 1984 presidential election were being held today and the candidates were Ronald Reagan, the Republican, and Walter Mondale (John Glenn), the Democrat, for whom would you vote?" (ABC News/*Washington Post* poll)

	Mondale	Reagan	Other	Undecided
April 22, 1981	27	65	—	5
September 13, 1982	38	45	2	11
January 22, 1983	44	42	2	6
April 12, 1983	45	45	2	5
May 15, 1983	42	45	2	6
June 19, 1983	50	42	1	4
August 1, 1983	49	46	1	3
September 26, 1983	48	46	1	5

	Glenn	Reagan	Other	Undecided
January 22, 1983	44	41	1	9
April 12, 1983	42	44	2	9
May 15, 1983	45	42	1	9
June 19, 1983	52	39	1	6
August 1, 1983	50	43	1	6
September 26, 1983	52	42	1	5

The results of the *Los Angeles Times* poll exhibited a similar pattern, an initial upswing for the president, from 3 percentage points behind Mondale (47–44) in April to an 8-point lead (48–40) in May, then down to second place (47–43 percent) at the end of June, and back in the lead in mid-September (46–43 percent).

The State of the Parties

The serious downswing in the economy, followed in time by the passage of the Reagan first-year program of cuts in taxes and spending for various entitlements, also had a strong impact on the attitudes of Americans toward the two major parties, one that hurt the GOP more than the president. The CBS News/*New York Times* poll reported striking shifts between the summer and fall of 1980 and January 1982 in the party named by interviewees as best able to handle the problem they felt was the most important one facing the country, as well as in the party they identified with.[24] In the 1980-1981 polls, the Republican party was repeatedly chosen—generally by a margin of about ten points. In the January 1982 poll, for the first time, the Democratic party led, by 36 to 32 percent, a sharp reversal from the 46 to 31 percent advantage held by the GOP in September 1981. By late October 1982, the Democratic plurality had widened to 41 to 34 percent. In response to the same question, the Gallup Poll found the Democratic lead had increased to 21 percentage points by late April 1983 (41 to 20 percent), but it declined somewhat with the improvement in the economy to 38 to 24 percent in July.

The Democrats also held a large advantage in the electorate's preferences in congressional elections by the summer of 1983. In August, Harris asked, "In the race for Congress in your district in 1984, if you had to choose right now, would you vote for the Republican or Democratic candidate for Congress?" Fifty-three percent replied Democratic; only 37 percent said Republican. This response may be compared to the 54 to 44 percent vote in favor of the Democrats in November 1982, and the 51 percent Democratic and 46 percent Republican vote in the 1980 House elections.

Party allegiance followed a similar pattern, changing from a move in partisan identification toward the GOP in 1980-81 to a shift back in 1982-83 to the pre-election level of Democratic dominance. As Martin Plissner, the political director of CBS News, noted in 1982:

> Shortly after the 1980 election, poll-takers throughout America found a remarkable shift in the proportion of Americans who identified themselves as Republicans and Democrats respectively. For several decades the margin of Democrats over Republicans had ranged about 20 percentage points in favor of the Democrats. In 1981 polls by CBS and *The New York Times*, that margin dropped to 10 points. In mid-summer the Republican National Committee actually claimed from a privately commissioned poll that the parties had drawn even in public identification. There was heady talk about a potential "realignment" of popular support for the parties that could shape history. The Republican National Committee has been relatively silent on this subject lately,

and the latest CBS News/*New York Times* poll suggests that the current trend may be back towards the old pre-election alignment.[25]

The Gallup Poll reported comparable trends. During 1981, the gap between identified Democrats and Republicans averaged 14 percentage points. The mean difference in the levels of party identification among the electorate increased to 20 percentage points through 1982. In averaging the results of five surveys conducted in July and August 1983, Gallup found that it remained at that level, 45 percent Democrats to 25 percent Republicans. The recession led many voters to return to the Democrats, whom they perceived as the party that could best deal with unemployment. After 30 months of the Reagan presidency, the GOP was once more in the situation that had led Richard Wirthlin to advise his candidate in October 1980 that to win the election, "we must shed every overt Republican symbol."

A comparable though less dramatic trend with respect to ideological identification was reported by the Harris Survey, which regularly inquired: "How would you describe your own personal philosophy—conservative, middle of the road, or liberal?" As Louis Harris notes, the drift under Reagan has been away from conservatism:

> Since early 1981 when Ronald Reagan entered the White House, the country has grown politically less conservative and more moderate. In the first five months of 1981, a 57-39 percent majority of Americans was either moderate or liberal, rather than conservative. Now, in a comparable period of 1983, from January to May, a more substantial 60-35 percent majority of the public views itself as not having a conservative political philosophy.
>
> While the number who classify themselves as conservatives has dropped four points since 1981, from 39-35 percent, the number who view themselves as middle of the road has gone up marginally from 40 to 41 percent, and the percentage of self-identified liberals has increased from 17 to 19.[26]

Survey evidence from a variety of polling organizations clearly continues to support the generalization that changing economic conditions play a major, if not dominant, role in the shifting political fortunes of presidential contenders and the two political parties. Support for Ronald Reagan and his party fell off sharply as unemployment rates moved up and interest rates remained high. But as the economy improved, the president's chances for re-election improved as well. The upswing in approval of and support for Reagan, however, was not accompanied by an increase in identification with or endorsement of his party. The

GOP continued to lose ground to its major party rival through the spring of 1983, back to its pre-Reagan state of being favored by only a fifth of the electorate. Seemingly, high rates of unemployment revived the Depression-born linkage in the public mind between joblessness and Republican control of government, an association that the slight decrease in the unemployment rate did not change.

Given Americans' ideological conservatism and programmatic liberalism, changing economic conditions also affected the public's spending priorities. Specifically, support for domestic spending increased, particularly for the poor, the disadvantaged, and minorities, while backing for defense spending declined. Moreover, the public's perceptions of the fairness of the Reagan program also changed over time.

Domestic Issues

By the end of the 1970s, the dominant mood of the public was *ideologically* conservative—in favor of reducing government regulations, taxes, and spending—but *programmatically* liberal—opposed to eliminating most specific regulations and favorable to spending the same amount or more for most social programs designed to benefit the underprivileged. This dichotomy may result from the way the regulatory-welfare state is conceptualized and discussed—spending for the disadvantaged is called an "entitlement," a right, and it is difficult to cut someone's rights. Similarly, collective goods such as regulations are perceived as public or collective rights. These "rights" are hard to oppose in the concrete, but easy to reject in the abstract. In 1980, Americans voted for Republicans and conservatives to secure a more efficient, less wasteful government, which they hoped would reduce unemployment and inflation rates, but not by reducing the role of most regulatory agencies or by cutting back on social programs for the underprivileged.

The contradiction between the general commitment to reducing the role and cost of government and the desire to see government intervene to accomplish various specific social objectives is strikingly apparent in attitudes toward government regulations.[27] According to a *Los Angeles Times* national poll, 53 percent of the public voiced approval in November 1982 "of President Reagan's proposals to remove many government regulations," while only 28 percent disapproved. But when asked about individual regulatory targets, respondents reversed their opinions strikingly (see Table 22.2).

Table 22.2
Attitudes to Specific Regulations
(percentages)

"President Reagan wants to remove a number of government regulations that he says are holding back American free enterprise. How do you feel about some of them? For example, would you be in favor of keeping present regulations on [specific item] or would you favor easing those regulations—or haven't you heard enough about them to say?" (*Los Angeles Times* poll, November 1982)

Regulations	Registered Democrats		Registered Republicans		All Respondents	
	Keep	*Ease*	*Keep*	*Ease*	*Keep*	*Ease*
Gas and oil prices	38	32	31	33	34	34
The environment	52	26	47	33	49	28
Industrial safety	69	16	65	21	66	18
Minimum wage for teenagers	62	26	54	35	58	29
Auto emission and safety standards	61	26	51	38	59	29
Federal lands	44	25	41	27	43	27
Offshore oil drilling	50	28	40	34	46	29

Thus, even when the question was posed in terms of encouraging free enterprise, most of those responding approved of continuing regulations affecting the environment, industrial safety, the minimum wage for teenagers, auto emission and safety standards, federal lands, and offshore oil drilling. The only regulation not endorsed was control of gas and oil prices, but even here there was as much support as opposition. Republicans were less likely to approve than Democrats, but surprisingly the partisan differences were not great. The various regulations had more supporters than opponents even among registered Republicans.

The *Los Angeles Times* poll returned to the subject of regulation with a different set of questions in April 1983, asking about various controls, whether "they are stricter than they need to be, . . . adequate, or . . . aren't strong enough." Averaging the reactions to thirteen different regulatory policies, the poll found 5 percent of the respondents answering "too strict," 35 percent "adequate," and 42 percent "not strong enough."

Public support for regulation increased during the Reagan years. The CBS News/*New York Times* poll, for example, found a steady growth in approval for the extreme proposition that "protecting the environment is so important that requirements and standards cannot be too high, and continuing environmental improvements must be made regardless of cost," from 45 percent in September 1981 to 52 percent in September 1982 and to 58 percent in April 1983.

The polls reported a similar response to questions dealing with the Reagan programs of cuts in taxation and spending as a means to improve the economy. Consistently large, though declining, majorities approved of them when they were presented in general terms, but at the same time, increasing numbers opposed most specific proposals for reductions in social entitlements or transfer payments to the poor. And by midyear 1983, a majority favored eliminating or postponing the third-year reduction in income taxes. When asked by Harris whether they favored "postponing the 10% federal income tax cut due in July," opposition to postponement led by 49 to 44 percent in March, but by June 49 percent of the respondents supported postponement compared to 42 percent opposed.

Backing for programmatic liberalism, of course, predated Reagan's election and continued through the 1980 election year. National surveys conducted by NORC in the spring of various years revealed little change in public attitudes with respect to federal support for environmental, health, education, welfare, and urban aid programs (see Table 22.3). The average percentage favoring cuts in these five programs in 1980 was 21, the same figure reported by polls taken in 1976, 1977, and 1978. A much larger proportion, 42 percent in 1980 (and, it should be noted, in 1977 and 1978 as well) wanted the government to spend more. Added together, those who endorsed more or the same level of spending constituted 72 percent in 1980, 73 percent in 1978, 72 percent in 1977, and 74 percent in 1976. Clearly, these surveys do not reveal a shift toward less spending for specific domestic social programs in the years preceding Ronald Reagan's election.

These basic attitudes—(1) support for cutting taxes, spending, and regulations to improve the economy and (2) opposition to reducing specific controls and to spending for particular programs designed to help the underprivileged—appeared in many surveys taken after the inauguration of Ronald Reagan. An ABC News/*Washington Post* nationwide poll, for example, conducted just after President Reagan's February 1981 address to Congress outlining his economic program

Table 22.3

Support for Domestic Spending 1976–1983
(percentages)

"We are faced with many problems in this country, none of which can be solved easily or inexpensively. I'm going to name some of these problems, and for each one I'd like you to tell me whether we're spending too much money on it, too little money, or about the right amount" (environment, health, education, welfare, urban aid, asked separately for each). (NORC general social surveys)

	Level of Spending[a]			
	Too little	About right	Too much	Don't know
1976	44	30	21	5
1977	41	31	21	7
1978	42	31	21	6
1980	42	30	21	6
1982	45	30	19	7
1983	47	31	16	7

[a]The percentages are the average of the responses for five items: environment, health, education, welfare, and urban aid.

found overwhelming approval (71 to 21 percent) for "the spending cuts Reagan proposed." By 64 percent to 28 percent, the respondents felt that Reagan's economic program would help end inflation. Yet the same people, when asked whether spending should be increased, decreased, or kept the same for the four general areas of education, the poor, health, and crime fighting, were much more likely to support increases than decreases.

The NBC News/Associated Press poll also reported large majorities (62 to 28 percent in February 1981 and 58 to 16 percent in April) approving the president's budget program when it was described to them in the following terms: "Reagan has proposed cutting federal spending by $49 billion in the next year, reducing many programs." But by a margin of 56 to 34 percent the February sample answered no to the question: "Given the nation's current economic condition, do you think that federal benefits for poor people have to be cut, whatever the impact of such cuts?" The April respondents reacted similarly, agreeing by 71 to 23 percent with the statement: "The federal government has the responsibility to provide certain kinds of services—such as medical care and legal advice—to those who cannot afford to pay for them."

Later in 1981, the president found it necessary to propose further budget cuts as the recession was beginning. When Harris inquired in September whether people favored various specific cuts or "*not* balancing the federal budget," majorities rejected cutting "federal aid to the elderly, poor, and handicapped," "federal health programs," and "federal aid to education."

As the recession deepened and the rate of unemployment increased, the proportion critical of domestic cuts gradually grew. When the NBC News poll asked whether Reagan was "going too far in attempting to cut back or eliminate government social programs," those saying the cuts were too great climbed from 37 percent in April 1981 to 45 percent in October 1981 to 49 percent in March 1982 and to 52 percent in January 1983. In spite of the improvement in the economy during 1983, the ABC News/*Washington Post* survey reported overwhelming disapproval (59–35 percent) in early August with the way Reagan was "handling cuts in social programs," and a *Los Angeles Times* poll taken in September found agreement by 56 to 36 percent with the statement, Reagan "is cutting back on worthwhile government programs."

Increased unemployment brought greater support for spending on domestic programs. When NORC surveyed attitudes toward domestic spending in 1982 and 1983 (see Table 22.3), the average percentage favoring more spending was 45 in 1982 and 47 in 1983, up from 42 percent in 1980. Those endorsing less spending fell from 21 percent in 1980 to 19 in 1982 to 16 in 1983. Surveys conducted for the Chicago Council on Foreign Relations in 1978 and again in October/November 1982 found that the difference between those who said "expand" and "cut back" various federal government programs increased by 26 percentage points with respect to "welfare and relief programs," generally the most unpopular government aid activity since many people identify such programs with welfare chiselers.[28]

These changes in public attitudes clearly reflect the impact of economic malaise and a high unemployment rate. Respondents increasingly stated in all polls that unemployment was the number one problem facing the country.

The improvement in the economy in 1983 reduced the level of concern with unemployment, but it remained the dominant economic issue. Penn and Schoen found that the number of respondents citing unemployment as "the most important issue," while still the largest group, gradually dropped from 60 percent in December 1982 to 58 percent in February 1983, 54 percent in April, 49 percent in June, 46 percent in August, and 38 percent in October. The Gallup Poll, which had reported in October 1982 that 62 percent felt unemployment was "the most important problem facing this country," found that the proportion citing unemployment as their prime concern had declined to 54 percent in mid-April 1983 and to 32 percent in late November. Inflation was the main worry of small minorities in both surveys.[29]

Wishful thinking has led some administration spokespersons to believe that unemployment is more acceptable politically than inflation since high prices hit everyone, while unemployment affects only a small minority directly. In line with this view, most Americans felt, according to a June 1983 Harris poll, that they and their families were more likely to be seriously affected by "rising prices" than by "high unemployment" (by 70 to 25 percent). But the same survey found that when asked which was more serious "for the country," respondents said, by 66 to 27 percent, that high rates of unemployment were worse than rising prices, and by 60 to 33 percent that "in order to keep the rate of inflation down to 5% or 6%," they would *not* "be willing to accept a rate of unemployment as high as 10%." Six months earlier in January, the Roper Survey reported similar reactions when it gave respondents the following choice: "As you probably know, in 1982 inflation came down to 5% and unemployment went up to 10%. If you had a choice, would you favor 5% inflation and 10% unemployment, or the other way around—10% inflation and 5% unemployment?" The response was decisive: 65 percent favored a high inflation rate and a lower unemployment rate, while 21 percent opted for lower prices and more unemployment. Seemingly the disaster inherent in unemployment, even for others, is regarded as a worse calamity for the nation than higher prices for all, which hurt but do not destroy livelihoods.[30]

Given such feelings, it is not surprising that sizable majorities favored a federal jobs program for the unemployed. By a three-to-one margin, 76 to 24 percent, those interviewed by the NBC News poll in November 1982 supported such a "program to help reduce unemployment." And a CBS News/*New York Times* poll found in January 1983 that 74 percent of a national cross-section responded yes to the question, "Even if it means increasing the size of the federal budget deficit, do you think it is necessary at this time for the federal government to create jobs for the people who are out of work?" Less than a quarter, 23 percent, said no.

Egalitarianism and Fairness

The reluctance of a majority of Americans to approve of spending cuts in most programs designed to benefit the underprivileged stems in large part from their continued commitment to egalitarianism.[31] In February 1981, shortly after Ronald Reagan took office, an ABC News/*Washington Post* poll found that 64 percent of a national sample agreed with the statement: "The government should work to substantially reduce the income gap between rich and poor." Only 31 percent disagreed. When this same poll asked who would be hurt the most by Reagan's spending cuts, 42 percent replied poor and lower-income people; 22 percent said middle-income people.

The ABC News/*Washington Post* poll tracked changes in popular perceptions of the class bias of the president by repeatedly inquiring from the start of his administration to June 1983: "Would you say Reagan cares more about serving low-income people, middle-income people, or upper-income people, or does he care equally about serving all the people?" The proportion replying that he cares more about the well-to-do increased from 23 percent in February 1981 to 58 percent in June 1983 (see Table 22.4).

The perception that the administration's policies harmed the poor and benefited the wealthy was also reported in various surveys taken by the Harris and Gallup organizations, as well as in those taken by Reagan's pollster, Richard Wirthlin. In February 1983, for example, when the Gallup Poll inquired whether various groups were being "treated fairly or unfairly" by the Reagan administration, a large majority (90 to 3 percent) responded that wealthy people and business executives were treated fairly, while the preponderant opinion with respect to other less privileged groups was that they were receiving unfair treatment (the poor, by 62 to 30 percent). Perhaps the most negative finding for the political position of the president was that more respondents believed that "people like you" (51 to 42 percent), "middle-income people" (49 to 41 percent), and "the average citizen" (50 to 40 percent) were more likely to be treated unfairly than fairly.

The upswing in the political standing of the president during 1983 was not associated with a change in the perception of his attitudes toward the less privileged. In August, Gallup found that 23 percent felt that Reagan "sides with the average citizen," while only 21 percent said he is "sympathetic to the poor." Similarly, in mid-September, the *Los Angeles Times* reported 67 percent agreeing and 29 percent disagreeing with the statement, "Reagan has no idea what it's like to be poor nowadays."

Table 22.4

Reagan's Concerns for Different Income Groups
(percentages)

Reagan's primary concern is:	February 1981	April 1981	September 1981	January 1982	August 1982	June 1983
Low-income people	3	1	2	1	2	1
Middle-income people	6	6	6	7	8	1
Upper-income people	23	29	43	52	56	58
All groups equally	64	58	45	39	29	32

The view that the Reagan administration has been biased in favor of the well-to-do, and unfair to others, especially the underprivileged, has seriously contributed to its political weakness. According to political journalist Elizabeth Drew, a study for the White House analyzing the reasons for the sharp losses suffered by the Republicans in the popular vote for state and congressional offices in 1982 concluded that "the fairness issue" hurt the GOP more than any other.[32] More recently, in reporting the results of a survey taken at the end of April 1983, the president's pollster, Richard Wirthlin, noted that "while he is in much better political shape . . . than a few months ago, Americans are still concerned that he favors the rich over the poor."[33]

Defense Policy

The volatility of public opinion is most evident in the response of Americans to defense issues since the 1960s. Beginning with the negative reactions to the Vietnam war, the public increasingly voiced its judgment that the United States should cut back on military expenditures. But as the effect of Vietnam ended and the Soviets continued to expand their armaments, the proportion favoring an increase in U.S. military spending began to grow. Three different national surveys, the Gallup Poll, NORC, and the Harris Survey, that inquired about the issues in different ways reported similar results.

The Gallup Poll found that the belief the government spent too much on defense declined from 50 percent in 1971 to 36 percent in 1976 to only 15 percent in 1981. Those saying it spent too little rose from 11 percent in 1971 to 22 percent in 1976 to 51 percent in 1981. However, the percentage believing defense spending was too high more than doubled to 36 in March 1982 and rose to 45 by January 1983, while the number of those believing it was "too little" fell to 19 percent in March 1982 and to 14 percent in January 1983. NORC reported that those favoring less defense spending declined from 38 percent in 1973 to 11 percent in 1980, but rose to 32 percent by 1983. Support for greater military expenditures dropped from 56 to 24 percent between 1980 and 1983. Harris found that the percentage in favor of "increasing . . . the present defense budget" moved up from 10 in 1971 to 71 in February 1980, but fell to 14 by March 1983. The ABC News/*Washington Post* poll indicated that the proportion who felt that "Reagan's plans to increase military spending . . . [are] going too far" increased from 28 percent in April 1981 to 51 percent in August 1983.

The survey organizations reported that only a tenth of those interviewed favored an increase in defense spending in the early 1970s. By 1980–1981 this view had become the majority response, although by 1982, Americans were once again in favor of cutting the military budget. This latter trend continued into 1983, to the point where the distribution of attitudes resembled those of the early 1970s.

Since Congress in 1981 and 1982 had approved the president's requests for sharp increases in defense spending, some of the change in sentiment may have reflected "satisfaction with administration policy on the part of some former advocates of greater defense spending."[34] They had had their way and could see no need for further increases, even though the president still advocated them. But the fact that the most frequent and by 1983 the majority response in many polls had become "reduce military expenditures" indicated that the public no longer placed a high priority on this item.

It is difficult to account for the drastic reversal in public opinion. Some of it may reflect acceptance of the charges of the peace movement that the administration is too hawkish, that it is exaggerating the Soviet threat. In line with this interpretation are the results of Roper, CBS News/*New York Times*, and Harris polls. Roper found that the proportion responding that the United States should "be stronger than the Russians in nuclear arms capability" fell from 58 percent in September–October 1980 to 51 percent in October 1981 to 41 percent by December 1982. Those responding that the United States did not need to be as strong as the Russians increased from 8 percent in the 1980 polls to 15 percent at the end of 1982. (The remainder of those interviewed replied the United States should be just as strong.) The CBS News/*New York Times* surveys reported a general falloff in the proportion who believed that the United States was "not as strong as the Soviet Union" from 44 percent in January 1982 to 32 percent in January 1983. Harris polls also found a decline in the percentage who felt that "the military defense system of the U.S. is . . . weaker . . . [than] the Russian military defense system" from 41 percent in January 1980 to 35 percent in October 1982 to 27 percent in April 1983. As William Schneider commented in a review of changing attitudes toward military spending: "In part, this shift represents an increased sense of military security under Reagan . . . The irony is that the public saw the country as getting stronger while the President was justifying his call for higher military budgets by arguing that the United States was still in a position of inferiority."[35] Clearly the president's efforts to convince Americans that it was necessary to respond to the Soviets with a tough foreign policy had either not succeeded or had run their course.

By stressing the need to meet Soviet power with increased U.S. weaponry and favoring increased involvement by the United States in Central American conflicts, Ronald Reagan "also reawakened fears that he might get the country into a war."[36] The CBS News/*New York Times*, Gallup, and Harris polls found expressions of such concerns increased during 1983. The former reported that the percentages who felt Reagan "might get us into a war" rose from 34 to 41 percent between January and April, and Harris noted that agreement with the statement "While it's good to have someone as President who is firm with the Russians, I worry that Reagan may get us into another war," which stood at 45 percent in February, was 53 percent in August. These sentiments led to a reduction in support for the president's conduct of foreign policy. In April 1981, those who approved of his role in this area outnumbered disapprovers by 54 to 22 percent in the CBS News/*New York Times* poll. By late September 1983, the critics were in the lead by 47 to 38 percent.

The pacific or "dovish" statements of the American public also affected responses to direct military intervention in Central America and Lebanon. In July 1983, Harris found that 62 percent expressed negative judgments about Reagan's "handling of the situation in El Salvador" compared with 25 percent who expressed positive views. Gallup noted that the number of those who thought it was likely "that the U.S. involvement in El Salvador could turn into a situation like Vietnam" reached 72 percent in July, up from 68 percent in March. When Penn and Schoen put the issue in extreme terms in August by asking,

"If a Communist takeover in El Salvador were imminent and President Reagan responded by sending American troops to that country, would that make you more likely to vote to re-elect him or less likely to vote for him" 45 percent replied "less likely," 29 percent said "more likely," while the remainder were uncertain. As of the end of August, Gallup reported that the death of U.S. Marines in Lebanon had produced a "solid majority," 54 to 41 percent, in opposition to "President Reagan's decision to send U.S. Marines to Beirut to help keep the peace," a reversal from the 52 to 40 percent approval a year earlier. When the *Los Angeles Times* asked a national cross-section in mid-September, "what we should do in Lebanon," it found 48 percent responding, "pull out our troops," 23 percent saying "keep present strength" and 17 percent answering "beef up forces." And a Harris poll taken about the same time indicated a negative reaction, 61 to 35 percent, to Reagan's handling of the situation in Lebanon. Harris went on to note that public opinion was almost as negative with respect to the president's "efforts to work for peace in the Middle East and his handling of nuclear arms negotiations."[37] Similar reactions were reported in surveys taken in late September by the ABC News/*Washington Post* and the CBS News/*New York Times* polls.

The president's response to the Soviet destruction of a Korean airliner at the end of August 1983, however, produced majority approval in the September Harris and *Los Angeles Times* surveys. The *Los Angeles Times* found in mid-September that 51 percent said the president's reaction to the affair was "about right," 37 percent felt that it "wasn't tough enough," while only 2 percent replied that he had been "too tough." But as Louis Harris commented he was "being praised more for what he did *not* do than for the actions he actually took." His tempered response—outrage and condemnation of the action, but restraint with respect to sanctions against the Soviets and refusal to break off arms-reduction negotiations with them—gained the approval of most Americans.[38]

Fear that the president is too bellicose may explain a large part of the "gender gap," the greater opposition to him by women. In May, the Harris Survey found a difference of 16 percentage points between men and women. The Gallup Poll, which reported a dramatic decline in the president's approval rating in a late July survey taken immediately after he had escalated U.S. military involvement in Central America, noted that the change largely reflected a sharp increase in disapproval by women. The difference between the sexes was 17 percentage points. Commenting on these results, George Gallup noted

Table 22.5

Preferences for Cuts in Defense Versus Social Programs (percentages)

"If you had to choose, would you prefer to see cuts in federal spending on [read each item] or would you prefer cuts in defense spending?" (Harris Survey)

Programs	Cut social programs	Cut defense
Federal aid to cities		
September 1981	52	41
February 1982	42	52
November 1982	36	57
Unemployment compensation		
September 1981	46	46
February 1982	31	62
November 1982	24	70
Federal aid to education		
September 1981	34	60
February 1982	29	65
November 1982	22	71
Federal health programs		
September 1981	35	58
February 1982	27	66
November 1982	21	73

that "in past surveys women have been particularly sensitive to what they perceive as threats to world peace."[39]

The "waning of sentiment for more defense spending [was also linked to] . . . much greater domestic unemployment and significantly growing budget deficits."[40] Since, as we have seen, Americans responded to the recession by approving increased expenditures to help the unemployed and the poor and were also uneasy about the growing budget deficit, the only ways to meet these concerns were higher taxes, which they opposed, or reductions in allocations for military or social programs. Faced with a choice between spending for domestic purposes or defense, the majority chose the latter.

The Harris Survey, which pitted support for defense programs against various social programs, found a steady increase since Reagan took office in the proportion favoring cuts in defense rather than in various social programs (see Table 22.5).

Similar results were obtained by the ABC News/*Washington Post* poll in response to questions dealing with different categories of federal government expenditures. Support for increased spending for domestic programs moved up steadily between February 1981 and August 1983, from 49 to 67 percent for the poor, from 43 to 75 percent for education, and from 49 to 66 percent for health. But the percentages favoring increased military expenditures fell from 72 to 33.

Seemingly, after more than two and a half years of exposure to Reaganite ideology and Reaganomics, most Americans took the traditional liberal position—regulate to reduce various social problems, help the poor, tax the wealthy more, spend more on entitlements (programs for the underprivileged), and cut back on military and defense spending. At the same time, however, they continued to voice approval for reductions in the level of government activity generally.

Speaking in terms reminiscent of Richard Wirthlin's analysis of the 1980 elections, that Ronald Reagan won in spite of the fact that his views were out-of-step with those of most Americans, Senator Paul Laxalt, the chairperson of the Republican National Committee, noted in September 1983 "the strange phenomenon" that most Americans expressed approval of the president although they disliked his policies. As he pointed out: "People have deep differences with his policies. But they still have trust in him and they look beyond the issues to style and character, not his policies. And Ron will run next year on his record of honesty and consistency, of conducting office with style and no real embarrassment." But given the negative reaction of the public to many of the president's policies, Laxalt emphasized that he disagreed with those "on both sides [who] say he is a shoo-in for re-election."[41]

Conclusion

The findings of the myriad surveys of American public opinion, as well as the results of the 1982 mid-term elections, are in line with the conclusions of studies on the correlates of election outcomes—that democratic electorates are more responsive to the state of the economy than to any other factor. Worsening conditions after late 1981 led Americans to become increasingly critical of their president, to grow more supportive of government intervention and aid to the underprivileged and to those hurt by the recession, and to become more opposed to defense spending.

More significantly, the public also became more depressed about the performance of institutions, both governmental and private. Survey responses had indicated a sharp decline in confidence in all major institutions and a growth in social and political alienation during the Vietnam period. Confidence continued to move down in a gradual, although irregular, slope during the 1970s. Polls measuring confidence during the Reagan period produced contradictory results, although they all agree that it remained low. Harris and NORC surveys reported a continuing decline, Gallup indicated no change, but one taken by the Center for Political Studies (CPS) of the University of Michigan, which dealt only with government, suggested an upswing. After analyzing responses to five questions designed to measure alienation from the society and polity, Harris reported as of February 1983 that "a record high 62 percent of Americans have expressed sad and bitter alienation toward those running the society and feel powerless to do anything about it."[42] Similarly, confidence in the leadership of ten major institutions, both public and private, surveyed by Harris since 1966 and by NORC since 1973 using the same format, reached all-time lows in surveys taken by Harris in October and November 1982 and by NORC in February to April 1983. The average level dropped by 2 percentage points in Harris polls between the fall of 1981 and 1982, and by the same percentage in NORC polls between the spring of 1982 and 1983.[43]

Confidence in the three branches of the federal government fell even faster during the Reagan years. Harris found that confidence in the executive branch was down 8 percentage points; the leaders of Congress, 3 points; and the Supreme Court, 4 points between 1982 and 1983. NORC's results for 1982 and 1983 revealed drops of 6, 3, and 4 points for the same institutions. Gallup has inquired about confidence in the same six institutions, rather than their leaders, since 1973. Comparing his August 1983 results with those for previous years indicates that they continued to drop in the most recent poll, although only marginally, one half of a percentage point, below those for 1981. The U.S. Supreme Court fell off by two percentage points, while Congress dropped by one. In both cases these were the lowest ever reported by this survey.[44]

These results were countered, however, by a poll taken by CPS in November 1982. In response to four questions designed to measure trust in government, the Michigan pollsters found an increase, which, with the exception of blacks, "occurred equally across most demographic groups."[45] The variations in the findings between Harris, NORC, Gallup, and CPS, however, reflected the greater influence of partisanship and ideology in the questions asked by CPS than in those asked by Harris, Gallup, and NORC. Since the Reagan administration is the first antigovernment one since Herbert Hoover's, it is not surprising that the CPS data revealed that trust in government rose among people who are normally distrustful of government. But those expressing a lack of faith in government continued to far outnumber those voicing trust, by 33 percentage points in 1982. And confidence continued to decline in response to more ideologically neutral questions concerning evaluations of leadership in our political, social, and economic institutions posed by Harris, NORC, and Gallup. Other surveys on related questions by Roper and Gallup taken in 1983 also did not reveal any rebound of public confidence in government or other institutions.[46]

What will it take to restore confidence? One clue may be found in the analyses by William Schneider and myself of all the Harris and NORC polls dealing with confidence in institutions that revealed, as might be expected, significant negative correlations with the unemployment (-.68) and inflation rates (-.36). As we noted in *The Confidence Gap*:

> Overall the results indicate that much of the decline in institutional confidence can be attributed to adverse economic conditions. Unemployment alone accounts for 48 percent of the variance; inflation adds another 10 percent. Every one percent increase in unemployment, with no change in inflation, tends to lower the general confidence level by 2.8 percent. Every one percent increase in inflation, with no change in unemployment, tends to lower the confidence level by 0.6 percent. Each factor—unemployment and inflation—has an effect independent of the other.[47]

Given these findings, subsequent surveys of confidence taken after an improvement in the economy should reveal an upswing in the public mood. Such changes occurred in the mid-1970s, only to be reversed by economic downturns. Hence, as long as there is good news about the economy and no countervailing bad news from other sectors, such as Central America, it is possible that public confidence in major institutions will move up. But as of mid-1983, no evidence of such a reversal in trends had occurred.

The instability of the economy has produced an electorate that is not only increasingly cynical, but also gives out contradictory signals to its political leaders. The felt failings of government in the United States have strengthened support for conservative antistatist ideologies, but the egalitarian belief system of most Americans fosters their commitment to specific liberal programs, particularly in the context of high unemployment. Hence, they favor curtailing the role of government, while supporting increases in social spending and the continuation or expansion of regulation. The stress on conservative or liberal policies varies with the state of the economy.

The political process itself has become a source of economic instability and derivatively of political malaise. If newly elected officeholders change economic policies and thereby upset capital markets and business expectations, the economy worsens and public opinion shifts in favor of the opposition. And the entire cycle of approval and disapproval based on the economy begins anew.

The public's concern with international affairs also affects reactions to political leaders. In early May 1983, Richard Wirthlin noted that the president's political position is threatened by "the fear that he might get the country into an unnecessary war."[48] And his former campaign manager, John Sears, also emphasized that the president "must convince voters that he is genuinely seeking peace; Republicans . . . win the first time with pledges of getting tough with the Commies, but are reelected when seen as peacemakers."[49]

The findings reported here have obvious implications for the immediate future of politics in the United States. Reactions to foreign policy may intervene, as noted earlier, to change the broad picture; a Central American or Lebanon effect could help elect or defeat Ronald Reagan in 1984. But foreign affairs aside, whether Ronald Reagan, or any other Republican, is elected in 1984 still appears to rest on the unemployment and inflation rates. With the improvement in the economy during 1983, the president made a strong comeback in the polls, both with respect to his general approval ratings and in trial heats against prospective Democratic opponents. In a trip to Washington, D.C., in the spring of 1983, I found both Republicans and Democrats uneasy about their prospects. The Democrats were worried that the decline in the unemployment rate would result in Reagan's re-election. The Republicans expressed concern that the economy was peaking too soon, that an end to the recession would produce a new wave of inflation in 1984, which could defeat them. Meanwhile, most Americans still exhibit a serious lack of confidence in the behavior of their institutions and leaders, as well as cynicism about their ability to affect their future through the electoral process. These developments, rather than the public's reaction to specific policies and candidates, should concern us.

Postscript: The Fall Upsurge

The shifts in public opinion during the fall of 1983 emphasize the ways in which unexpected developments can upset any effort to anticipate the future of electoral politics. The KLG effect (the shooting down of the Korean airliner, the terrorist attack on U.S. Marines in Lebanon, and the short triumphal war in Grenada) produced higher approval ratings for the Reagan administration generally, a major improvement in the president's standing in trial heats against prospective Democratic opponents, a gain in support for increases in military spending, and a general toughening of attitudes toward the Soviet Union.

The upswing in sentiment for the administration was also related to the concurrent good news from the economy. Unemployment dropped to 8.4 percent in November, 2.4 percentage points below the recession's highest level in December 1982. The annual inflation rate was around 3 percent for 1983, down over 10 percent in 1981. The University of Michigan's Survey Research Center reported that its Index of Consumer Sentiment was 91.6 for the third quarter of 1983, 25 points above a year earlier and the highest quarterly reading since the third quarter of 1972.

The effect on public morale of the changes in the economic indicators may also be seen in an increase in the average level of confidence in the leadership of the ten major institutions reported on regularly by Harris and NORC. As indicated earlier, confidence had continued to decline during the Reagan years in both polls. But as anticipated by Schneider's and my analysis of the relationship between unemployment and inflation rates and variations in confidence ratings, the latter moved up from an average of 21 points in a fall 1982 Harris poll to 25 points in early October 1983. Still it must be noted that this improvement only brought the level back to the average of the last three Carter years, 1978–1980, and considerably below those of 1977, or during the Ford and Nixon administrations.[50]

As noted, public reaction following President Reagan's tempered response to the Soviet destruction of the Korean airliner on September 1 was favorable. His job rating in the Harris Survey moved up from 46 percent positive in July to 56 percent in early September. This was the first time since January 1982 that Reagan was over 50 percent in this poll. The Gallup Poll reported as of mid-September that "President Ronald Reagan's job performance rating is now at its highest level in 21 months." The Yankelovich *Time* and CBS News/*New York Times* surveys in late September also found sizable increases in the Reagan approval rate.

Reactions to the killing of over 235 Marines in Lebanon were more ambivalent since, as indicated earlier, most Americans had been unhappy about the decision to send and keep troops there. The CBS News/*New York Times* survey of September 24–28 and the Gallup Poll of October 7–10 reported almost identical results with respect to approval or disapproval of the decision to ship Marines to Lebanon. The ratio in favor of disapproval was 53–36 percent in the first and 51–37 percent in the second.

The rapid-fire succession of the attack on the Marines in Beirut on October 23 and the invasion of Grenada on October 25 did not allow an independent estimate of public reaction to each event. Backing for U.S. troops' remaining in Lebanon moved up dramatically from earlier surveys. The ABC News/*Washington Post*, Gallup, and CBS News/*New York Times* polls all reported, as of the end of October, greater support for a continued U.S. military presence in Lebanon than for evacuation. The dominant view seemed to be that a withdrawal after the attack on the Marines would be seen as capitulation to terrorism. Still, most Americans were not convinced that the American presence in Lebanon was worthwhile. Those interviewed in an ABC News/*Washington Post* survey taken on October 28 disagreed by 56 to 34 percent with President Reagan's opinion that the Marine mission there had been successful, and 59 to 35 percent thought the situation in Lebanon was not important enough for the United States to risk going to war there.

The quick, successful invasion of Grenada gained a substantially higher vote of approval from the American public. The ratio of positive to negative expressions, in polls taken shortly after the landing of American troops, was 53 to 34 percent in the Gallup Poll, 55 to 31 percent in the CBS News/*New York Times* poll, and 68 to 21 percent in the Harris Survey. The ABC News/*Washington Post* poll found a striking and steady increase in support in three surveys taken on October 26 and 27 and at the end of the first week in November; from 52–37 percent approval to 67–27 percent and then to 71–22 percent. The last figure was close to that found a week later by the *Los Angeles Times*, 69–23 percent in support "of the invasion of Grenada by U.S. troops." Seemingly, a quick and triumphant military engagement and a decline in opposition in Congress and by the press resulted in increased public support. Americans were glad to have a clear-cut victory.

The responses to other questions dealing with foreign and military policy posed from September to early November also showed an increase in generally hawkish sentiments. Gallup reported that the proportion believing that the United States was spending "too little" on defense had risen from 14 percent in August to 21 percent in mid-September. The ABC News/*Washington Post* poll found an increase in the percentage who thought "Reagan's plans to increase military spending" were not going far enough, from 23 percent at the beginning of August to 28 percent in late September. Those who felt that "the United States should spend whatever is necessary to achieve military superiority over the Soviet Union" rose from 22 percent to 32 percent over the same time period.

The autumn polls also indicated a growth in hostility toward the Soviet Union and a concomitant decline in the concern that President Reagan had been too aggressive in his dealings with the dominant communist power. Gallup noted that as of mid-September, feelings toward the Soviet Union were more negative than at any time since 1956. Anti-Soviet sentiment increased greatly in the fall 1983 ABC News/*Washington Post* polls. A late September CBS News/*New York Times* survey found that 63 percent (up from 57 percent in April) believed that "the military threat from the Soviet Union is constantly growing and presents a real, immediate danger to the United States," while the percentage who felt there was no immediate danger fell from 37 to 28 percent in the same period. The ratio of approvals to disapprovals "of the way Reagan is handling relations with the Soviet Union" changed from 44-49 percent in late September to 53-41 percent at the end of October.

President Reagan's general approval rating moved up in the national surveys over the same period. The CBS News/*New York Times* poll reported a gain from an approval to disapproval ratio of 46-41 percent in late September to 48-38 percent on October 27. The ABC News/*Washington Post* survey indicated an even greater upsurge, from 52-42 percent in late September to 63-35 percent as of October 28. A few days later, in a poll taken between November 3 and 7, the latter organization found the president's support ratio had improved again, to 63-31 percent.

President Reagan had been behind both Mondale and Glenn in trial heats conducted by the ABC News/*Washington Post* poll in late September (see Table 22.1). But he moved to a lead over both in early November, just one year before the 1984 election: 50 percent to Mondale's 44 percent and 48 percent to Glenn's 45 percent. The *Los Angeles Times* survey reported similar shifts between mid-September and mid-November.

Will there be a long-term KLG effect in favor of Ronald Reagan similar to the Falklands effect for Margaret Thatcher? November 1983, when this chapter went to press, was obviously too early to reach any definite conclusion. Students of public reaction to foreign policy crises have noted that such events almost invariably have a positive effect on presidential popularity.[51] But upsurges in support for the incumbent president, such as those following the invasion of Korea in 1950, the U.S. Marines landing in Lebanon in 1958, the Bay of Pigs affair in 1961, the invasion of the Dominican Republic in 1965, and the Iranian seizure of the American Embassy in 1979, typically did not last more than a few months.[52] The fluctuations in Reagan's job ratings in the Harris Survey illustrate the instability of public reactions to international crises. As noted earlier, his positive evaluation moved from 46 percent in July to 56 percent following the Korean airliner incident in September. By early October, Reagan's approval rating had dropped back to 47 percent, only to rise again to 56 percent following the invasion of Grenada, and then down to 52 in mid-November.

Although Americans rallied around Ronald Reagan in response to the Korean, Lebanese, and Grenadian events, the results of the fall 1983 opinion surveys indicated that while clearly in good shape for the 1984 election, he was still not a "shoo-in." His margin in presidential trial heats was below his job performance approval ratings in late October and early November polls. Americans remained dubious about the wisdom of his policies in Lebanon, overwhelmingly opposed to those in Central America, and fearful that American intervention in both areas could lead to an unnecessary war.

According to the post-Grenada CBS News/*New York Times* poll, the public still *rejected* by 58 to 23 percent the administration's efforts to "help people in Nicaragua who are trying to overthrow the pro-Soviet government there." A Harris survey taken soon after the Grenadian victory found a substantial vote, 54 to 37 percent, in *opposition* to "the U.S. continuing the same policy we followed in Grenada of sending in troops to overthrow other unfriendly governments" in other parts of the Americas. Two weeks later, in mid-November, the *Los Angeles Times* found Americans opposed to "landing troops in Nicaragua to help overthrow the leftist Sandinista government there" by 58 to 26 percent and to "landing troops in El Salvador to help the government defeat leftist rebels who are supported by Cuba and Russia" by 53 to 32 percent.

Continued distrust of the administration surfaced in replies to the CBS News/*New York Times* poll, which found the public saying by 52 to 31 percent that the Reagan administration is "too quick to get American military forces involved" in its dealings with foreign countries, that it does not try "hard enough to reach diplomatic solutions." And when Harris, in a post-Grenada survey, repeated the question dealing with "worry that Reagan might get us into a war," he found Americans expressing such concerns by a 54 to 39 percent margin, up three points from August.

President Reagan was still vulnerable on the domestic front as the 1984 election season approached. He not only faced a continuing gender gap, but as William Schneider demonstrated, a growing class gap as well. He had lost considerable support among the less-privileged, traditionally Democratic groups—blue-collar workers, trade-unionists, and ethnics—who in 1980 gave him a higher vote than Republicans normally obtain among them.[53] The experience of the recession and the "fairness" issue returned many defectors to the Democratic fold. And the majority of the electorate remained committed to economic liberalism, federal government programs aiding the underprivileged, caring for the sick and aged, improving the educational system, and regulating various aspects of the economy. As noted, the KLG effect increased public support for spending for national defense. But although the mid-November *Los Angeles Times* poll found that 48 percent favored spending more money for national defense while 41 percent favored spending less, backing for increased domestic programs was much stronger. In the same survey, 60 percent replied that the federal government should spend more for domestic programs; only 30 percent answered less.

There are clearly many imponderables that could affect the outcome of the 1984 election: the Democratic nominee, how well John Anderson does, and whether Jessie Jackson's campaign for the Democratic nomination increases black registration and voting participation. But in the last analysis, given the volatility of the electorate—as exhibited in 1983 opinion polls—events, the state of the domestic economy, and foreign relations will be the determining factors.

Notes

1. As D. Roderick Kiewiet notes: "Although the explanatory power of different economic indicators varies considerably from study to study, the finding of a positive relationship between economic performance and electoral outcomes

is quite robust, present in several different time series employing many different statistical models. Furthermore, strong evidence of this link has been found for presidential as well as congressional elections, as well as for many other countries." (*Macro-economics and Micro-politics: The Effects of Economic Issues* [Chicago: University of Chicago Press, 1983], p. 154, *n*8. This footnote and others contain references to various American studies.) For other countries, see the articles in Douglas A. Hibbs and Heinz Fassbender, eds., *Contemporary Political Economy* (Amsterdam: North-Holland Publishing Co., 1981); and Paul Whiteley, ed., *Models of Political Economy* (Beverly Hills, Calif.: Sage Publications, 1980).

2. James A. Davis, "Conservative Weather in a Liberalizing Climate: Changes in Selected NORC General Social Survey Items, 1972–1978," *Social Forces* 58 (1980): 1129–56; Benjamin Page and Robert Y. Shapiro, "Changes in Americans' Policy Preferences, 1935–1979," *Public Opinion Quarterly* 46 (Spring 1982):30; S. M. Lipset and William Schneider, *The Confidence Gap: Business, Labor, and Government in the Public Mind* (New York: Free Press, 1983), pp. 221–56, 342–46; and Janet S. Chafetz and Helen R. F. Ebaugh, "Growing Conservatism in the United States?" *Sociological Perspectives* 26 (1983):293–95. Chafetz and Ebaugh report, however, that "on most issues concerning civil liberties and personal morality, Americans became, if anything, slightly less conservative during . . . [1972–1980], continuing a trend established prior to this time," p. 295.

3. Hadley Cantril and Lloyd A. Free, *The Political Beliefs of Americans* (New Brunswick, N.J.: Rutgers University Press, 1967), pp. 36–38, 53–57; and Raymond Wolfinger, Martin Shapiro, and Fred Greenstein, *Dynamics of American Politics* (Englewood Cliffs, N.J.: Prentice-Hall, 1980), pp. 130–32.

4. Everett Carll Ladd, Jr., and Seymour Martin Lipset, "Public Opinion and Public Policy," in Peter Duignan and Alvin Rabushka, eds., *The United States in the 1980s* (Stanford: Hoover Institution Press, 1980), pp. 63–64, 67–71.

5. Richard B. Wirthlin, "The Republican Strategy and Its Electoral Consequences," in S. M. Lipset, ed., *Party Coalitions in the 1980s* (San Francisco: Institute for Contemporary Studies, 1981), p. 239.

6. Ibid.

7. Richard Wirthlin, "Seven Conditions of Victory," campaign memo reproduced in Elizabeth Drew, *Portrait of an Election: The 1980 Presidential Campaign* (New York: Simon and Schuster, 1981), p. 386.

8. S. M. Lipset, "No Room for the Ins: Elections Around the World," *Public Opinion* 5 (October/November 1982):41–43.

9. Although I have combined the inflation and unemployment rates in the misery index, the two factors have different effects, as noted below. They are disaggregated in two articles by Douglas A. Hibbs, Jr., "Political Parties and Macroeconomic Policy," *American Political Science Review* 71 (1977):1467–87; and "The Mass Public and Macroeconomic Policy: The

Dynamics of Public Opinion Toward Unemployment and Inflation," *American Journal of Political Science* 2 (1979):705–31.

10. S. M. Lipset, "France's Warning to the Reagan Administration," *Journal of Contemporary Studies* 4 (Fall 1981):35–38.

11. For a detailed report on the ratings over time, see "Reagan, Thatcher and Mitterrand," *Public Opinion* 6 (February/March 1983):38–39. As of May 1983 "opinion polls showed the Socialist President with lower personal approval after two years in office than any of his Fifth Republic predecessors." ("Tide of Bitterness for Mitterrand," *New York Times*, May 8, 1983, p. 2E.) Only 33 percent of those interviewed by the French Institute of Public Opinion expressed satisfaction with Mitterrand in May, down from 38 percent in April ("L'Indice de popularité," *Le Monde*, May 24, 1983, p. 5).

12. John E. Mueller, *War, Presidents, and Public Opinion* (New York: John Wiley, 1973); Lee Sigelman and Pamela J. Conover, "The Dynamics of Presidential Support During International Conflict Situations: The Iranian Hostage Crisis," *Political Behavior* 3 (1981):303–18; Jong R. Lee, "Rallying Around the Flag: Foreign Policy Events and Presidential Popularity," *Presidential Studies Quarterly* 7 (1977):252–56; and Kenneth Waltz, "Electoral Punishment and Foreign Policy Crises," in James N. Rosenau, ed., *Domestic Sources of Foreign Policy* (New York: Free Press, 1967), pp. 263–93.

13. *London Sunday Times*, "For a British Electoral Reform," reprinted in *Christian Science Monitor*, June 17, 1983, p. 24.

14. Andrew Neil, "Next Thatcher Moves," *New York Times*, June 12, 1983, p. EY21.

15. "The Thatcher Style: The Trials and Triumphs of a Party Ideologue," *Economist* 287 (May 21, 1983):25–28.

16. All the voting and poll statistics in this section, including those quoted from the *Economist*, are from the reports of Marketing and Opinion Research International (MORI).

17. Richard A. Brody, "That Special Moment: The Public Response to International Crises" (paper delivered at the 1983 Annual Meeting of the Western Political Science Association, Seattle, Washington, March 24, 1983), pp. 10–11.

18. Neil, "Next Thatcher Moves," p. EY21. For detailed analyses, see Ivor Crewe, "Why Labour Lost the British Elections," *Public Opinion* 6 (June/July 1983):7–9, 56–60; and William Schneider, "When the Opposition Party's Competence Becomes the Issue, It's in Trouble," *National Journal* 15 (1983):1360–61.

19. Jack Nelson, "Poll Finds Reagan Support High, but Public Fears War," *International Herald-Tribune*, May 25, 1983, p. 3.

20. George Gallup, "Reagan Job Performance Rating at Highest Level in 16 Months," *Gallup Poll*, July 24, 1983, p. 1. Richard Wirthlin also reported: "Last January, polling showed 50 percent of Americans disapproved of the

way Mr. Reagan handled his job and 44 percent approved; by the end of April the figures were reversed with 50 percent approving and 44 percent disapproving" (Nelson, "Poll Finds Reagan Support High," p. 3).

21. Personal communication from Stephen Cole, July 8, 1983.
22. George Gallup, "Reagan Gets Lower Grade," *San Francisco Chronicle*, August 11, 1983, p. 17.
23. *Washington Post*, "New Poll on Reagan's Policies," *San Francisco Chronicle*, August 8, 1983, p. 5.
24. The question asked by both polls is "Which political party do you think can do a better job of handling the problem you have just mentioned—the Republican Party or the Democratic Party?"
25. Martin Plissner, "Reagan's First Year and the Outlook for 1982," CBS News/*New York Times* poll, release, January 18, 1982, p. 4.
26. Louis Harris, "Country Becoming Less Conservative, More Moderate," *Harris Survey* no. 45 (June 6, 1983), p. 1. These figures are the averages for polls taken between January and the second week in May of each year.
27. For a review of attitudes toward regulation, see Lipset and Schneider, *The Confidence Gap*, pp. 221–56.
28. John E. Rielly, ed., *American Public Opinion and Foreign Policy, 1983* (Chicago: Chicago Council on Foreign Relations, 1983), p. 10.
29. For a chart of the way the public's concerns shifted between inflation and unemployment from 1977 to 1983, see "Opinion Outlook," *National Journal* 15 (1983):822.
30. Analyzing the effects of unemployment and inflation on the evaluation of presidents, Richard Brody found that the public is more sensitive to changes in rates of unemployment than to variations in levels of inflation (Richard A. Brody, "Public Evaluations and Expectations and the Future of the Presidency," in James S. Young, ed., *Problems and Prospects of Presidential Leadership in the Nineteen-Eighties* [Washington, D.C.: University Press of America, 1982], p. 44). Similarly, analysis of the correlates of shifts in confidence in various major institutions, including the presidency, indicated that unemployment rates are a more powerful determinant than inflation (Lipset and Schneider, *The Confidence Gap*, pp. 62–64).
31. For an analysis of the meaning of egalitarianism in America, see S. M. Lipset, *The First New Nation: The United States in Historical and Comparative Perspective* (New York: W. W. Norton & Co., 1979).
32. Elizabeth Drew, "A Political Journal," *New Yorker*, May 9, 1983, p. 48.
33. Nelson, "Poll Finds Reagan Support High," p. 3.
34. Rielly, *American Public Opinion*, p. 28.
35. William Schneider, "Military Spending: The Public Seems to Say, 'We've Gone Far Enough,'" *National Journal* 15 (1983):867.
36. Ibid.

37. Louis Harris, "Reagan's Gains on Economy Offset by Foreign Policy Criticism," *Harris Survey*, August 22, 1983, pp. 1-2.
38. For data on this point, see Louis Harris, "Americans Support Reagan's Actions Re Downed Korean Plane," *Harris Survey*, September 19, 1983, pp. 1-3.
39. Gallup, "Reagan Gets Lower Grade," p. 17.
40. Rielly, *American Public Opinion*, p. 28.
41. Jack Nelson, "Despite High Popularity, Reagan Faces Tough Race," *Los Angeles Times*, September 25, 1983, p.1.
42. Louis Harris, "Alienation Rises to Record Highs," *Harris Survey*, March 17, 1983, p. 1. For the text of the Harris questions and a discussion of earlier results, see Lipset and Schneider, *The Confidence Gap*, pp. 110-11.
43. For a review and analysis of the studies of confidence conducted by Harris and other pollsters, see Lipset and Schneider, *The Confidence Gap*, pp. 13-96; see also Louis Harris, "Public Confidence in Institutions Is Down," *Harris Survey*, November 25, 1982, pp. 1-3.
44. George Gallup, "Confidence in Key Institutions No Higher Than in Watergate Era," *Gallup Poll*, September 11, 1983, pp. 1-2.
45. Arthur Miller, "Is Confidence Rebounding?" *Public Opinion* 6 (June/July 1983):17. Earlier findings of CPS are discussed in Lipset and Schneider, *The Confidence Gap*, pp. 16-19.
46. For an analysis of the more recent surveys, see S. M. Lipset and William Schneider, "Confidence in Confidence Measures," *Public Opinion* 6 (August/September 1983):42-44. This discussion is elaborated in that article.
47. Lipset and Schneider, *The Confidence Gap*, pp. 62-64.
48. Nelson, "Poll Finds Reagan Support High," p. 3.
49. Albert H. Hunt, "Out of the Picture, John Sears Is Still in Focus," *Wall Street Journal*, May 24, 1983, p. 24.
50. Lipset and Schneider, *The Confidence Gap*, pp. 48-49.
51. Nelson Polsby, *Congress and the Presidency* (Englewood Cliffs, N.J.: Prentice-Hall, 1964), p. 25; and Brody, "That Special Moment," p. 6. Brody notes that the incumbent president picked up support in 30 out of 40 situations.
52. Lee, "Rallying Around the Flag," pp. 254-55.
53. William Schneider, "The Divided Electorate," *National Journal* 15 (1983):2207, 2210.